Technocracy and the Epistemology of Human Behavior

In *Power Without Knowledge: A Critique of Technocracy* (2019), Jeffrey Friedman presented a sweeping reinterpretation of modern politics and government as technocratic, even in many of its democratic dimensions. Building on a new definition of technocracy as governance aimed at solving social and economic problems, Friedman showed that the epistemic demands that such governance places on political elites and ordinary people alike may be overwhelming if technocrats fail to attend to the ideational heterogeneity of the human beings whose control is the object of technocratic power. Yet a recognition of ideational heterogeneity considerably complicates the task of predicting behavior, which is essential to technocratic control—as Friedman demonstrated with pathbreaking critiques of the homogenizing strategies of neoclassical economics, positivist social science, behavioral economics, and populist democratic politics.

In *Technocracy and the Epistemology of Human Behavior,* thirteen political theorists, including Friedman himself, debate the implications of *Power Without Knowledge* for social science, modern governance, the politics of expertise, post-structuralism, anarchism, and democratic theory; Friedman responds to his critics with an expansive defense of his vision of contemporary politics and his political epistemology of ideationally diverse human beings.

This book was originally published as a special issue of the *Critical Review.*

Paul Gunn is Lecturer in Political Economy and Public Policy in the Department of Politics and International Relations at Goldsmiths, University of London, UK, and Associate Editor of the *Critical Review.*

Technocracy and the Epistemology of Human Behavior

The Debate over *Power Without Knowledge*

Edited by
Paul Gunn

Routledge
Taylor & Francis Group
LONDON AND NEW YORK

First published 2023
by Routledge
4 Park Square, Milton Park, Abingdon, Oxon, OX14 4RN

and by Routledge
605 Third Avenue, New York, NY 10158

Routledge is an imprint of the Taylor & Francis Group, an informa business

ISBN13: 978-1-032-35753-9 (hbk)
ISBN13: 978-1-032-35754-6 (pbk)
ISBN13: 978-1-003-32838-4 (ebk)

DOI: 10.4324/9781003328384

Typeset in Times New Roman
by codeMantra

Publisher's Note
The publisher accepts responsibility for any inconsistencies that may have arisen during the conversion of this book from journal articles to book chapters, namely the inclusion of journal terminology.

Contents

Citation Information

The chapters in this book were originally published in the journal *Critical Review*, volume 32, issue 1–3 (2021). When citing this material, please use the original page numbering for each article, as follows:

Introduction
Political Epistemology Beyond Democratic Theory
Paul Gunn
Critical Review, volume 32, issue 1–3 (2021) pp. 1–31

Chapter 1
Exit, Voice and Technocracy
Jonathan Benson
Critical Review, volume 32, issue 1–3 (2021) pp. 32–61

Chapter 2
Disagreement, Epistemic Paralysis, and the Legitimacy of Technocracy
Étienne Brown and Zoe Phillips Williams
Critical Review, volume 32, issue 1–3 (2021) pp. 62–84

Chapter 3
A Family Affair: Populism, Technocracy, and Political Epistemology
Kevin J. Elliott
Critical Review, volume 32, issue 1–3 (2021) pp. 85–102

Chapter 4
Technocracy, Governmentality, and Post-Structuralism
Oscar L. Larsson
Critical Review, volume 32, issue 1–3 (2021) pp. 103–123

Chapter 5

Social Science and the Problem of Interpretation: A Pragmatic Dual(ist) Approach
Adam B. Lerner
Critical Review, volume 32, issue 1–3 (2021) pp. 124–144

Chapter 6

The Spiral of Responsibility and the Pressure to Conflict
Eric MacGilvray
Critical Review, volume 32, issue 1–3 (2021) pp. 145–163

Chapter 7

Architects and Engineers: Two Types of Technocrat and Their Relation to Democracy
Alfred Moore
Critical Review, volume 32, issue 1–3 (2021) pp. 164–181

Chapter 8

What Follows from the Problem of Ignorance?
Zeynep Pamuk
Critical Review, volume 32, issue 1–3 (2021) pp. 182–191

Chapter 9

Power, Knowledge, and Anarchism
Robert Reamer
Critical Review, volume 32, issue 1–3 (2021) pp. 192–217

Chapter 10

Why Do Experts Disagree?
Julian Reiss
Critical Review, volume 32, issue 1–3 (2021) pp. 218–241

Chapter 11

Political Epistemology, Technocracy, and Political Anthropology: Reply to a Symposium on Power Without Knowledge
Jeffrey Friedman
Critical Review, volume 32, issue 1–3 (2021) pp. 242–367

Notes on Contributors

Jonathan Benson, Ethics Institute, Utrecht University, Netherlands.

Étienne Brown, Department of Philosophy, San José State University, USA.

Kevin J. Elliott, Department of Political Science and Sociology, Murray State University, USA.

Jeffrey Friedman, Committee on Degrees in Social Studies, Harvard University, USA.

Paul Gunn, Department of Politics and International Relations, Goldsmiths, University of London, UK.

Oscar L. Larsson, Military Studies, Swedish Defence University, Stockholm, Sweden.

Adam B. Lerner, Politics and International Relations, Royal Holloway, University of London, UK.

Eric MacGilvray, Department of Political Science, Ohio State University, USA.

Alfred Moore, Department of Politics, University of York, UK.

Zeynep Pamuk, Department of Political Science, University of California, San Diego, USA.

Zoe Phillips Williams, Associate, Economic Law and Policy Program, and Managing Editor, *Investment Treaty News*, The International Institute for Sustainable Development, Geneva, Switzerland.

Robert Reamer, Department of Politics, Oberlin College, USA.

Julian Reiss, Institute for Philosophy and Scientific Method, JKU Linz, Austria.

Paul Gunn

INTRODUCTION: POLITICAL EPISTEMOLOGY BEYOND DEMOCRATIC THEORY

ABSTRACT: *Jeffrey Friedman's* Power Without Knowledge *builds a critical epistemology of technocracy, rather than a democratic argument against it. For its democratic critics, technocracy is illegitimate because it amounts to the rule of cognitive elites, violating principles of mutual respect and collective self-determination. For its proponents, technocracy's legitimacy depends on its ability to use reliable knowledge to solve social and economic problems. But Friedman demonstrates that to meet the proponents' "internal," epistemic standard of legitimacy, technocrats would have to reckon with the heterogeneity of people's ideas, which he presents as one of two aspects of a political anthropology of ideational beings. The other aspect is ideational determinism: the shaping of our conscious actions by our interpretations, and of our interpretations by "ideational exposures" (which are, to some extent, heterogeneous). For the most part, our symposiasts agree with this anthropology or leave it uncontested, but they fall back on democratic theory to point toward alternatives to technocracy. This raises the question, which Friedman does not ask, of whether his political anthropology undermines a certain brand of democratic theory: the liberal brand that attaches respect to people's opinions as products of "free reflection," i.e., as underdetermined.*

Until now, the primary critique of technocracy has been supplied by democratic theorists, who have equated technocracy with epistocracy. As an inherently undemocratic project, they argue, rule by epistemic elites is illegitimate on its face—regardless of whether it accomplishes its objectives. Jeffrey Friedman's *Power Without Knowledge: A Critique of Technocracy* (Oxford University Press, 2019) poses an entirely different challenge to technocracy. Friedman asks if technocracy may be illegitimate even on its own, negative-utilitarian terms, regardless of its democratic illegitimacy, because it is ineffective at achieving its goal: the relief of human suffering.

The aim of this symposium is to confront some of the many implications of Friedman's subtle and nuanced critique of technocracy. However, a key aspect of Friedman's argument, which passes largely without comment in the symposium, is that it is not intended as a contribution to democratic theory so much as an attempt to extend political theory beyond democracy. This may have been missed because, as a critique of technocracy, *Power Without Knowledge* can be leveraged to support what many theorists take to be their *raison d'être*: defending the people's democratic authority against impingement by technocratic experts, among others. Yet Friedman's critique of technocracy is not grounded in a principle of democratic authority, but in a political epistemology that suggests the possible unreliability of technocratic knowledge claims. This epistemology, in turn, is built on a political anthropology grounded in our status as ideational creatures: creatures who, unlike other biological entities, consciously interpret the world before acting in it. This is an anthropology that may (it seems to me) have disturbing ramifications for regime types other than technocracy, including democracy (in certain conceptions of it), although it is *particularly* troubling for technocracy.

Because of the sweep and intricacy of the book's progression from anthropology to epistemology to technocratic critique, my first order of business will be to provide a blow-by-blow account of how the argument proceeds. Section II will then introduce the symposium's ten responses to the book, followed in section III by brief questions about its implications for democracy and democratic theory.

I. A PRÉCIS OF *POWER WITHOUT KNOWLEDGE*

The book's Introduction addresses what Friedman sees as confusion created by the standard view of technocracy as rule by "experts." By assuming, rather than demonstrating, the validity of experts' knowledge claims, theorists such as Isaiah Berlin and Jürgen Habermas long ago elided the question of whether technocrats do in fact possess the knowledge they require: knowledge of how to efficiently manipulate individual behavior for utilitarian ends. Following their example, political theorists have persistently bracketed this question.

In Friedman's view, the standard equation of technocracy with epistocracy contributes to this bracketing of whether technocratic knowledge claims are unreliable, as it simply stipulates the adequacy of the knowledge of technocratic social scientists or other "cognitive elites." The Introduction additionally points out that the type of knowledge claimed by epistocrats is also claimed, in less sophisticated form, by many ordinary citizens in contemporary democracies. Friedman maintains that in the United States (and, I would add, in Europe), utilitarian knowledge claims are the bread and butter of *mass* politics. If we understand technocracy as a polity's attempt to "solve, mitigate, or prevent social and economic problems among its people," using broadly utilitarian criteria of what is socially and economically problematic, we will be led to acknowledge that ordinary citizens often think that they can engage in this project and, indeed, that they might be right (5; parenthetical page references without citations, here and throughout the volume, refer to *Power Without Knowledge*.)

Thus, Friedman redefines technocracy as a polity dedicated to solving, mitigating, and preventing utilitarian social and economic problems, *regardless* of whether these efforts are made by epistocrats or by ordinary citizens ("citizen-technocrats"). This definition suggests that rather than being an inherently elitist project, technocracy is an inherently epistemic one. This is because the technocratic project requires answers to epistemic questions—how widespread are social and economic problems, what are their causes, and how can they be solved?—that are asked, and answered, by elites and masses alike. Thus, an *empirical* political epistemology of technocracy would examine the actual basis on which both citizen-technocrats and epistocrats make their knowledge claims in any given time and place. Friedman makes a wide-ranging start in this direction in Part II (Chapters 4-6). A *normative* political epistemology of technocracy would try to determine the likely adequacy of these knowledge claims. This is the goal of Part I (Chapters 1-3).

Chapter 1: Naïve Technocratic Realism

Chapter 1 attempts to pre-empt an objection to both normative and empirical epistemology derived from an epistemic disposition that

Friedman, adapting psychologists' usage, labels "naïve technocratic realism." The naïve realist holds that some aspect of reality is self-evident, such that our ideas about (for example) how to solve a social or economic problem are not, in fact, "ideas" so much as theoretically unmediated and accurate reflections, or intuitions, of a transparent reality. If this were true of technocratic realities, an empirical political epistemology of technocracy would collapse into the political epistemologist's own unerring perceptions about how to solve social problems, which would then be projected into the heads of technocrats in the real world (whether epistocrats or citizen-technocrats), who would be seen as perceiving these realities as unproblematically as the theorist does. And normative political epistemology would have no point, as all political actors' knowledge would be just as reliable as the political epistemologist's own knowledge, and would require no critical evaluation.

The most obvious objection to naïve technocratic realism is what Friedman calls "the fact of technocratic disagreement." Insofar as technocrats disagree about what Friedman delineates as the four types of technocratic knowledge—knowledge of (1) the scope of social and economic problems and (2) their causes, and knowledge of (3) the efficacy of solutions to them and (4) the solutions' costs—then technocratic knowledge cannot be self-evident: disagreement entails the non-transparency of the realities being perceived. The naïve realist, however, might respond to the fact of technocratic disagreement by challenging whether it is really a fact or whether it is, instead, a ruse created by special interests, or class interests, to mask the self-evident truth. Friedman responds to this challenge by pointing out that in actual technocratic debate, it is often argued that technocratic policies cause *counterintuitive, unintended* consequences. If such consequences are possible, he argues, honest technocratic disagreement *would* be warranted, since an unintended consequence is, by definition, not self-evident, and thus might legitimately be disagreed about.

Friedman is not, at this early point in the book, in a position to argue that counterintuitive unintended consequences are real. But since plausible mechanisms are routinely proposed that would explain why such consequences *might* be real, he contends, we can conclude that technocratic debate *might* always be warranted, as the intuitions that naïve realists treat as reflections of self-evident truth may actually be misleading. Thus, we cannot avoid the need to investigate whether technocratic knowledge claims are, in fact, reliable, nor should we avoid asking how, empirically, people's technocratic knowledge claims are created—since they are apparently not caused by technocratic realities in themselves. If they were, then there would be no fact of technocratic disagreement.

Chapter 2: The Lippmann-Dewey Debate

In Chapter 1, Friedman did not argue that technocracy is hobbled by irresolvable disagreement, nor that it is plagued by unintended consequences. This is because, as he emphasizes in his reply to the symposium, in Chapter 1 he was merely noting, in effect, that all human action, being the action of fallible beings, is imperfect, such that it *might* be the subject of legitimate disagreement. This almost truistic fallibilism grounds the need for political epistemology in general, in opposition to the infallibilism of the naïve realist. But no critique of a specific form of human action, such as technocracy, can be built on such a broad foundation. In Chapter 2, then, Friedman begins to produce a deeper foundation by reconstructing Walter Lippmann's political epistemology, and the responses to it that John Dewey published in the 1920s and beyond.

Friedman portrays Lippmann as not just a fallibilist but an interpretivist, according to whom our ideas about society and government are "stereotypes" based on partial and possibly unrepresentative information samples. Lippmann held that society presents us with too much information for anyone to process. To make this blooming, buzzing confusion intelligible, we must impose interpretations on it that screen out most of it, and screen in only information that our interpretations process, by virtue of inferences about society as a whole, as plausible. In the Lippmann-Dewey debate, Friedman contends, Dewey never recognized this interpretive dimension of Lippmann's argument. Thus, he treated journalists and social scientists as able to give ordinary citizens the technocratic knowledge they need, but without any explanation of what would ensure that the interpretations that screen in journalists' and social scientists' "information samples" will tend accurately to represent the whole of the societies whose social and economic problems they are trying to solve.

Chapter 3: Interpretation, Ideational Determination, and Heterogeneity

In Chapter 3, which is the theoretical heart of the book, Friedman contends that the particular interpretive problem facing technocrats is a function of a further complicating factor, beyond the problem of too much information and, thus, the need for interpretation. This is the problem of ideational heterogeneity.

Friedman brings this factor into view by noting that the problem of interpretation afflicts not only those whom Lippmann studied, namely the subjects of technocratic policy making—citizen-technocrats and epistocrats—but also the objects of their decisions, the agents whose behavior they seek to shape through their policy interventions. Even in areas of technocracy that border on the hard sciences, such as epidemiology or climate policy, technocratic initiatives are legal decrees that are intended to change the behavior of human beings. This entails predicting how human beings' actions will be affected by a given law or regulation. Thus, technocratic subjects must produce subjective predictive interpretations of the actions of other people, actions that are, in turn, based on those people's subjective interpretations of how they should respond to a given technocratic policy.

Friedman judges this double hermeneutic problematic in light of his political anthropology. Interpretations stem from the organization of our beliefs into structured webs. The nodes of these webs are, in culturally and experientially variegated modern societies, likely to be somewhat heterogeneous across individuals. Thus, the interpretations that guide the conscious actions of those whom the technocrat would predict and control may vary among the population to be predicted and controlled. However, this variability is not statistical noise that, as such, could be predicted by means of probability theory. It is strictly determined, Friedman holds, by nonrandom processes of individual belief formation and of the interpersonal communication of ideas. In addition, interpretations may differ between the subjects and the objects of technocratic prediction and control. The subject may impute to the objects (agents) a certain interpretation of the social environment, but the objects' interpretations of the social environment may differ from those of the subject (the technocrat). Both of these forms of ideational heterogeneity—within a population and between the population's members and the technocrat—may cause the technocrat to make predictive errors, leading, in turn, to unintended consequences.

However, Friedman also points out the limits of this cause for concern about technocracy. If everyone's ideas were *completely* heterogeneous, there would be no hope for technocratic knowledge; technocrats would be completely at sea. But our ideas are only presumptively and defeasibly heterogeneous, and only to some extent. A defeasible presumption of heterogeneity is grounded in the fact that there is no "unitary human idea generator" (147), but mass media and educational systems are *partly* unitary idea generators (171). Thus, it would seem, the same cultural forces that give rise to a degree of heterogeneity also give rise to a degree of homogeneity, leading to shared behavioral norms and shared interpretations of the social environment (169).

Part I closes, then, by suggesting that social scientists should, case by case, "judiciously" research the empirical balance between ideational heterogeneity and homogenizing counterforces in the particular populations whose behavior technocrats would attempt to predict and control. Friedman proposes, as the model for this kind of social science, intellectual history, which tackles the webs of belief of the individuals who are its objects of inquiry in all their idiosyncracy, yet does not foreclose ideational homogeneities between interpreter and interpreted that may allow the interpretation to be accurate. A judicious technocracy would embrace the intellectual historian's defeasible presumption of ideational heterogeneity and would apply it forwards to those who are the object of technocratic prediction and control (not just "intellectuals"), with the aim of identifying whether the targets of specific future interventions will likely be subject to particular ideational homogeneities on the basis of which reliable policy forecasts can be made. This approach requires, above all, the intellectual charity necessary to understand others on their own terms.

In effect, Part II (Chapters 4-6) will take this approach to understanding contemporary technocrats, asking whether the ideational homogeneities they display are likely to allow them to recognize ideational heterogeneity in others. Friedman's answer is a resounding no, because a lack of intellectual charity is the *sine qua non* of contemporary social science and popular politics alike. But Friedman leaves no doubt that this could change—if social scientists' and ordinary citizens' ideas changed. Part II, then, is both an empirical description of contemporary modes of technocratic thinking and an attempt to trigger, through this description, a "cultural revolution" (342) against these uncharitable patterns of thought. This normative thrust against technocratic culture emerges from Friedman's claim that contemporary modes of thought are so pathologically uncharitable that it is as if both epistocrats and citizen-technocrats are under a malign pressure to make behavioral predictions for their own sake, regardless of their accuracy. Part II makes this argument over the course of two chapters (Chapters 4–5) that deal with contemporary social scientists and one (Chapter 6) that deals with contemporary citizen-technocrats.

Chapter 4: Economic Theory, Positivism, and Uncharitability

Friedman observes that social scientists tend to hook their claims to predictive knowledge of individual behavior on various *objective* variables, such as the incentives treated as causal by neoclassical economists, the internal (putatively psychological) mechanisms treated as causal by behavioral economists, and the vast array of other causes, from the trivial to the grandiose, for which positivist empiricists seek correlative observational or experimental evidence. In each case, the price of the social scientist's claim to predictive knowledge is to foreclose the possibility that those being predicted have idiosyncratic beliefs (or, in many cases, any beliefs at all), since beliefs are subjective.

Thus, neoclassical economic theorists insist, a priori, that "incentives matter," meaning that people mechanically, and therefore predictably, respond to objective incentives, sans interpretation. This allows the economist-technocrat to assume that she can manipulate people so as to solve social and economic problems by changing the objective incentives they face. Behavioral economists, such as Daniel Kahneman and Amos Tversky, tweak this assumption by adding an ever-growing list of "irrational" (psychological) exceptions to the rule of "rational" (incentives-based) behavior. These exceptions are established through experimentation that treats artificially induced laboratory behavior as the mechanical expression of psychological heuristics and biases, not the ideational product of subjects' interpretations of the laboratory situation and the tasks given to them during the experiment. More generally, both laboratory and field experiments are predicated on the assumption of human uniformity, which is the only thing that could ground the external validity of their findings across all humankind.

However, Friedman contends that all of these bad ideas are only figuratively a function of a perverse technocratic system intent on prediction at the cost of accuracy. The bad ideas are not caused by an "injudicious" technocracy; *they* cause *it*. Thus, for example, the lack of intellectual charity that we see among social scientists whose findings have technocratic relevance is equally hegemonic in the branch of social psychology dedicated to studying the authoritarian personality, an area of research that has few technocratic applications or ambitions—indicating that there is a broader culture of intellectual uncharitability that sometimes happens to lead to "injudicious," ideationally insensitive forms of technocratic social science. In the authoritarian-personality literature, even arch-enemies of a certain conception of positivism, such as Theodor Adorno (in *The Authoritarian Personality*), show themselves to be masters of uncharitability, mangling and ignoring evidence of ideational determination and ideational heterogeneity to maintain that what might otherwise seem to be hideous misinterpretations of the social world (such as anti-Semitism) are the products of noninterpretive unconscious psychosocial determinants. Adorno's complaint about positivism, of course, is that it universalizes for all time the particularities of our present, oppressive era (Adorno [1969] 1976). Friedman would undoubtedly agree, but he goes farther and denies that, even within our era, human beings can be reduced to noninterpretive products of their psychic (rather than ideational) or social (structural) environments.[1]

Chapter 5: The Spiral of Conviction

Friedman maintains that an important obstacle to a cultural revolution against positivism and other technocratically pathological patterns of thinking is a tendency toward dogmatism among experts. Here again he builds upon Lippmann, who contended that interpretations confer intelligibility on the world in a manner that encourages partiality. An interpretation judges incoming information with a bias toward confirming what the interpretation illuminates. Only this information is intelligible, plausible, and interesting—in light of the interpretation; the overabundance of other information is screened out as misinformation, or irrelevant information, or craziness. Thus, the more information an interpretation screens in, the more the interpretation will seem to be confirmed, even though it is possible that what is really happening is that a false picture of the world is being unfairly reinforced through the selective perception and retention of information.

This produces a tendency towards interpretive dogmatism among those who have assimilated a great deal of information, a tendency Friedman labels the "spiral of conviction." Spirals would seem likelier to occur among those whose interpretations have screened in a large amount of confirmatory information, which builds confidence in the interpretation, and Friedman argues that this is what may really be indicated by studies that show "motivated reasoning" to be more intense and widespread among the relatively well informed than the relatively uninformed. Friedman illustrates the operation of spirals of conviction by delving into several technocratic economists' analyses of what caused the financial crisis of 2008. These highly credentialed, politically influential social scientists were, Friedman contends, aware of information that undermined their mainstream neoclassical view of the crisis, but they were able to dismiss this information as utterly implausible—although doing so required intellectual somersaults that are classic markers of dogmatism.

Chapter 6: Public Ignorance, the Intentions Heuristics, and Populism

The asymmetrical tendency of the well informed to spiral into dogmatism suggests, to Friedman, that epistocrats may be at a cognitive disadvantage relative to uninformed citizen-technocrats.

In his discussion of the Lippmann-Dewey debate, he pointed out that if one accepts (as Dewey did) that social-scientific knowledge is reliable, one starts down a slippery slope toward epistocracy—so long as one also accepts that solving social problems is the overriding goal of the polity. If the goal is to solve social problems, and if social scientists are likelier to know how to do it than ordinary citizens, why should the latter be involved in crafting the solutions? Even if the people are involved in *defining* the problems, i.e., determining the ends to be pursued, "the fundamental dilemma of democratic technocracy" is, in Friedman's view, that if technocratic truths are not self-evident, and if we grant that social scientists are likelier than everyone else to gain access to them, the people have no legitimate role in determining the policy means for meeting those ends (108-13). However, if social science, being injudicious, does *not* provide reliable predictive knowledge, as Chapter 4 suggests may be true, then we have no reason to start down the slippery slope. And while citizen-technocrats, being non-expert by definition, lack social-scientific "knowledge," their ignorance should also leave them relatively free of the spirals of conviction that would follow from having too much of this type of knowledge, as suggested by Chapter 5. In Chapter 6, then, having delineated the epistemic pathologies of epistocrats, Friedman turns hopefully to citizen-technocrats. Unfortunately, he finds that, at present, they seem to be as injudicious as epistocrats tend to be.

Friedman begins with an exacting demolition of the manner in which political scientists have analyzed survey research on the political ignorance of ordinary citizens. According to these writers, whose analysis reproduces that of the economist Anthony Downs (1957), it is only to be expected that the public will be politically ignorant, as each individual voter has but a minuscule chance of affecting the outcome of a mass election. Voters, *knowing* these odds, correctly estimate that it is not worth their time to "study up" on politics and government, as it is highly unlikely that their votes will affect public policy or the conduct of government. This is a classic "incentives matter" story that, as usual with neoclassical economics, imputes to agents accurate subjective knowledge of the objective incentives they face.

Friedman contends, however, that in fact there is no evidence that voters are aware of the odds against their individual votes mattering, and that there is much evidence against it. There is, he points out, survey evidence indicating that they think their votes do matter; there is the massive fact that they continue to vote, by the hundreds of millions, every year; and there is the fact that when they vote, they do not cast random ballots. Friedman exploits this last fact to argue that voters *must* think that their vote choices are adequately informed: if they did not, they would be unable to decide whom they should vote for, and would have no way of proceeding other than by flipping a coin. The real question, then, is not why they vote despite the odds, but why they think themselves capable of rendering sound political judgments on the slender informational foundation that survey research shows that they often have.

To answer this question, Friedman assembles survey and focus-group data suggesting that in the United States in recent decades, voters have often tended to treat the solutions to social and economic problems as so straightforward that they do not require very much knowledge or even very much thought. Rather, they seem to think, social and economic problem solving requires leadership that is forceful enough to overcome the resistance of special interests to doing what "obviously" needs to be done. In short, Friedman suggests, American voters have been naïve technocratic realists. Accordingly, they have viewed politics as a contest that pits "strong" politicians with good intentions against either "weak" but good politicians or evil ones—those with bad intentions, who have been bought out by the dark powers of the establishment. Such voters, Friedman infers, will tend to assume that all they need to know about politics is which politicians are well intentioned and strong.

In this analysis, naïve technocratic realism takes shape as a real empirical phenomenon (and a volatile, populist, Manichean one)—not merely, as in Chapter 1, a theoretical position that would militate against political epistemology. However, the connection between naïve realism in Chapters 1 and 6 is more than merely fortuitous. A naïvely realistic electorate, fixated on the question of politicians' intentions, will be as bereft of an awareness of *un*intended consequences as the naïvely realistic theorist constructed in Chapter 1. Thus, the true concern, for a normative political epistemologist of technocracy, is not the fact that voters may be ignorant of the often-trivial political information tested for by survey researchers, but that they will be ignorant of the very possibility that public policy may backfire. Moreover, such voters will tend to reject the possibility of genuine technocratic disagreement, like the cynical naïve realist of Chapter 1, for they will be unaware of any epistemic difficulties that might justify such disagreement—such as the difficulty we face, as technocrats, in putting ourselves into the shoes, or rather the heads, of those whose behavior we intend to manipulate.

The first thing to note about the argument of this chapter is that it is intellectually charitable to ordinary citizens in their technocratic capacity—despite Friedman's contention that they are populists in the making, ready to follow their tribune as he tramples institutional and normative constraints in the fight against special interests. It might be useful to contrast this intellectual charity to the stance taken by epistocratic critics of democracy, such as Bryan Caplan (2007) and Jason Brennan (2016). These writers follow Downs in crediting voters with knowing the crucial fact that their (individual) votes do not really matter—a flattering concession to public knowledge, given that no theorist of democracy recognized this mathematical truth until Anthony Downs did in 1957. Yet intellectual charity is not a matter of projecting flattering thoughts into the minds of others; this is what analytic philosophers do under the guise of "interpretive charity." Rather, *intellectual* charity is a matter of trying to grasp what is actually in the real minds of real people, and Friedman contends that there is no reason to think that very many contemporary voters have the knowledge that Downs, Caplan, and Brennan ascribe to them.

Moreover, when such theorists use voters' "recognition" that their votes don't matter to explain both public ignorance and the policy views of ordinary citizens, their conclusion is that while citizens are rational in deciding to be ignorant, this decision licenses—in their minds—*irrational* opinions, since voters "know" that these opinions will not be translated into law. However, as Friedman argued in a long review essay on Caplan's *Myth of the Rational Voter* (Bennett and Friedman 2008), the assertion that voters' opinions are "rationally irrational" tells us nothing about the specific opinions voters hold. The theory of rational irrationality licenses voters to believe anything they might fancy, but cannot tell us why voters fancy the particular ideas they hold except by saying, tautologically, that they must "prefer" these "irrational" opinions over others or they would not hold them. By contrast, Friedman's approach is to ask what it would be *rational* for voters to believe if they were raised in a culture that, like ours, is hospitable to democratic technocracy. In a culture in which it is endlessly reiterated that voters' individual votes *do* matter and, moreover, that this is a good thing, a citizen might be expected to infer that each voter's opinions are valuable *regardless of how well-informed* the voter is: we do not, after all, impose knowledge requirements on voters of the sort that epistocratic theorists favor. Thus, they might conclude, the issues about which they have opinions are readily deciphered; anyone can do it, and everyone is encouraged to do it in the voting booth.

This line of reasoning, in the mind of a citizen-technocrat interpreted with intellectual charity, produces what Friedman calls the ontology of a simple society, in which social and economic problems are easily solved —since, epistemically, the solutions are readily deciphered. On this foundation, Friedman builds up the ideal type of a "naïve technocratic worldview" that seems to fit actual public opinion and actual voter behavior, while creating a compelling picture of the inner life of the citizen-technocrat in cultures like ours (283-303). One key feature of this picture is the voter's equation of good intentions with good policy outcomes and bad intentions with the creation or perpetuation of social and economic problems. Friedman points to a great deal of evidence suggesting that voters bypass any consideration of unintended policy consequences, such that good or bad intentions are all that matter. This collapse of consequences into intentions would make sense, given the simple-society ontology.

Another useful contrast here might be with defenses of voter knowledgeability produced by democratic theorists such as Habermas (2006) and Robert Goodin and Kai Spiekermann (2018), according to which underinformed citizens can get by with knowledge proxies such as cues and heuristics. Logically, such proxies work only if voters are sufficiently knowledgeable to be able to assess their accuracy—in which case, Friedman points out, knowledge proxies would not be needed. Moreover, it seems likely that voters who fit the profile Friedman develops would be uninterested in deliberately choosing knowledge proxies to begin with, as they would not think they need to know much beyond the intentions of candidates (and parties, and bills). In effect, theorists such as Habermas attribute to voters the same awareness of their need for more than intuitive knowledge that neoclassical economists such as Caplan ascribe to them, producing a deliberate search for heuristics. By contrast, Friedman sees the use of intentions as "heuristics" as an *as-if* process: citizen-technocrats act as if intentions are valid proxies for knowledge of technocratic consequences, but they actually believe that good intentions ontically *cause* good consequences and bad intentions cause bad consequences. This is intellectually charitable to citizen-technocrats because, given the premise of a simple society, it is quite reasonable for them to assume that intentions will not face complications on the road to outcomes.

Part III: Third-Order Uncertainty about Second-Order Heterogeneity

Chapter 6 concludes Part II on a doubly tentative note. First, Friedman maintains, it is not clear whether it is better to be ruled by relatively open-minded citizen-technocrats who are, however, innocent of the very possibility of unintended consequences; or by relatively well-informed epistocrats (well-informed, at any rate, about the possibility of unintended consequences, if not about the heterogeneous ideas that may cause them) who are, however, as experts, likely to be relatively dogmatic. Friedman calls this the Hobson's choice of technocracy. More importantly, though, from the perspective of a theorist of technocracy rather than a theorist of democracy, Parts I and II do not establish the *magnitude* of the errors that might be committed by injudicious technocrats or even by judicious ones. This uncertainty is expressed in a three-page section (317-19) that leads off Part III.

Given our inevitable ignorance of future history, Friedman points out, we cannot know if the unintended consequences of the mistakes made either by judicious technocrats or by clueless citizen-technocrats, doctrinaire neoclassical economists, or positivist empirical researchers will outweigh the social and economic problems their efforts might solve. Yet if we are to be truly internal critics of technocracy, our most natural standard of legitimacy will be the utilitarian standard of doing more good than harm, overall. Since we (theorists) cannot, however, know the magnitude of the mistakes that judicious technocrats or injudicious technocrats will make in the face of ideational heterogeneity, this internal standard of legitimacy does not allow us to render normative judgment on either form of technocracy—judicious (ideationally sensitive) or injudicious—because we cannot know if the unintended consequences of the mistakes outweigh the social and economic problems that particular technocrats will mitigate in the unknowable future.

In his reply to the symposium, Friedman emphasizes that this type of uncertainty is distinct from the problem of ignorance facing injudicious technocrats with which we are left at the end of Part I: ignorance of the ideas of the agents manipulated by technocratic policies. The problem with which we are left at the end of Part II is theorists' *third-order* ignorance about the performance *of technocrats*, who in turn will encounter second-order ignorance of the ideas of the human objects of their efforts at prediction and control when they (technocrats) come up with first-order policy analyses and recommendations. Any political theorist (not just a theorist of technocracy) who wants to render a normative judgment about a political system that will produce emprical tendencies, but not certainties, will face third-order ignorance. No political theorist can divine the future, so no political theorist can forecast the magnitude of effects produced by any political system—unless by means of a philosophy of history like Marx's.

Lacking such a philosophy of history (which I suspect Friedman would accuse of insensitivity to the contingencies of people's ideas), Friedman suggests that all we can do is make logical comparisons among alternatives that allow judgments of their relative, not absolute, consequences. Just as it is logical that a judicious (ideationally sensitive) technocracy is preferable to a technocracy that, like our own, ignores the ideational determination of conscious human action, Friedman proposes that to evaluate the legitimacy of a judicious technocracy, we need some other point of comparison. He finds this in exitocracy, which he sketches in Chapter 7.

Chapter 7: Capitalism, Socialism, and Exitocracy

Exitocracy is the ideal type of a technocracy that takes advantage of a more reliable epistemic device than even judicious technocrats' attempts to understand and predict the ideas of the objects of their actions. This device is what Albert O. Hirschman (1970) called "exit," in contrast to "voice." In applying this dichotomy to technocracy, Friedman includes the ratiocinations of epistocrats as well as those of citizen-technocrats under "voice."

Friedman argues that exit enables people, to some extent, to take advantage of their knowledge of their own unhappiness in a given situation versus their satisfaction after they leave this situation behind. Even as he details how inaccurate this type of personal knowledge can be, he maintains that, for all its imperfections, it is more reliable than the four types of technocratic knowledge, because the latter require even judicious technocrats to grasp the conditions of society as a whole and the presumptively heterogeneous ideas of the millions of anonymous agents within it. Recurring to Dewey's famous metaphor, Friedman writes that it is easier to judge whether one's own shoes pinch than to decide which shoes will avoid pinching the feet of everyone in a mass society (321). Both injudicious and judicious technocrats must "judge the significance of social problems for anonymous others . . . speculate about their causes, and . . . speculate about the efficacy of various solutions and the side effects they may cause. . . . Inasmuch as it is inherently difficult for anyone to have such knowledge—even those who are judiciously attentive to ideational heterogeneity—the exitocratic alternative would appear to be the better one," epistemically speaking (330).

Friedman constructs exitocracy as a society somewhat like our own, in principle. It has a capitalist element, in that competition among owners of the means of production can provide workers and consumers choices of employment, goods, and services from which they may exit if they are dissatisfied. There is also a robust private sphere in which non-economic exit and personal voice play a significant role. However, economic exit is a dead letter without the economic means to take advantage of it, so Friedman sketches a neo-Rawlsian Difference Principle with "entry goods" replacing "primary goods," grounding a potentially radical wealth redistribution (335).

Plainly, both the capitalist and socialist elements of this ideal type require technocratic judgments. Thus, exitocracy is a type of technocracy, not an alternative to it. It is an "extraordinary" type of technocracy, though, in that it aims, wherever possible, to devolve decision-making authority to exit users, rather than using the authority of voice to block exit (322).

As a form of technocracy, exitocracy faces the same second-order epistemic problem—ideational heterogeneity—that faces "ordinary" judicious and injudicious technocracy. As Friedman puts it,

> The administration of an exitocratic Difference Principle would require the administrators to make behavioral predictions that nobody—no matter how judiciously attentive to ideational heterogeneity—is well positioned to make. . . . A judicious technocrat attempting to decide which level of taxation is "excessively" high . . . would have to answer the empirical question of how the ideationally heterogeneous capitalists of her time and place will respond to various possible rates of taxation. This question is no less difficult to answer than the question of how they might respond to various levels of a minimum wage or to other "ordinary" technocratic initiatives. Thus, the epistemological critique of technocracy presented in Part I would apply to redistribution in the service of enhancing people's entry opportunities. The same critique would apply, as well, to the provision of other public goods, including the good of legally establishing and defending the private sphere. All of these exitocratic activities would entail highly fallible, speculative behavioral predictions about anonymous, presumptively heterogeneous others. (340-41)

Nevertheless, the fact that exitocracy is a type of technocracy is, in Friedman's view, a feature, not a bug. The technocratic status of exitocracy is what allows it to serve the comparative function that is the rationale for Part III. It is true that the "ordinary" technocratic aspects of an exitocracy are epistemically problematic, but just as a judicious technocracy would address this problem by attempting to charitably understand the ideas of the populations whose behavior is being predicted, an exitocracy would address the problem by devolving decision making authority, wherever possible, from collective voice users to individual exit users. This would reduce the scope of ordinary technocratic decision making, producing a comparative advantage over judicious technocracy, but without completely eliminating ordinary technocracy, which is impossible. Thus, we have a "hierarchy of technocratic legitimacy" (343), with exitocracy (or rather, as Friedman clarifies in his reply, judicious exitocracy) at the top, followed by judicious ordinary technocracy, followed by injudicious ordinary technocracy.

Of these three options, injudicious ordinary technocracy is the least equipped to deal with the problem of ideational heterogeneity. But since there is nothing below injudicious technocracy in the hierarchy, we have nothing *worse* to compare it to. Therefore, Friedman holds, we cannot pass judgment on its stand-alone or absolute legitimacy. We know that it is *relatively* illegitimate compared to either a judicious exitocracy or a judicious ordinary technocracy, but if pressed to say whether our own technocracies, which are primarily injudicious, are illegitimate in the abstract, Friedman maintains that we must be silent. However, this does not entail silence about the cultural status quo. In noticing the pathological epistemic consequences of contemporary ideas, we are enlisting comparisons "upward" in the hierarchy, contrasting the injudicious (ideationally insensitive) status quo against a culture in which we came to grips with our ideational determination and heterogeneity.

Cultural critique of this sort is what Friedman envisions as the future of the political epistemology of technocracy. This would entail a shift of theorists' attention from institutions and policies to ideas. Just as Friedman did in Part II, future theorists would attempt to critically assess (and, unlike Friedman, historically contextualize) the culture that generates injudicious technocracy—not just the culture of positivism and neoclassical economics, but of intellectual uncharitability, "of moralizing, and opinionating, and arguing; the culture of the inhuman humanism that effaces our ideational nature" (345). Thus, we return to political anthropology.

The political anthropology of ideational *heterogeneity* explains our disagreements without recourse to dehumanizing psychological or structural explanations (or, as I think Friedman would say, pseudo-explanations). And the political anthropology of ideational *determinism* entails a culture of tolerance, for nobody deliberately chooses to hold bad ideas: therefore, they cannot be blamed for holding them. Our task, then, as political actors and theorists alike, is to understand and resist bad ideas, not demonize as willfully evil those who hold them. This includes understanding and resisting the dehumanizing methods that currently blind us to their existence *as* ideas, and which occlude the interpretive and thus fallible nature of *our own* ideas. Thus, cultural critique includes an auto-critique of the antihumanist ideas that have invaded our own webs of belief. *Power Without Knowledge,* then, is ultimately a book that is less about technocracy than false consciousness.

Afterword: Technocracy and the Left

In a brief afterword, Friedman follows Foucault in comparing technocracy to early modern Cameralism, about which he makes two points. First, Cameralism was, as Foucault saw, a project with a potentially infinite remit. Its goal was to increase state revenue by tending to the welfare of the society that generated it, and this opened absolutely everything to state control. Friedman (349) quotes the historian of Cameralism, Keith Tribe (1988, 75): "'The range of matters that eventually became the object of regulation . . . is quite bewildering in its variety,' in that anything and everything, including not just the processes of industry and agriculture but the conduct of what we would call personal life, might bear on the people's well-being and therefore be a fit object of *gute Polizei.* (*Polizei*—usually translated as 'police,' sometimes as 'policy'—was derived from *polis.*)" Second, Cameralist writers recognized that this very wide remit entailed great epistemic demands, but they had a quite naïve view of how to meet these demands: namely, by writing ever-more-massive encyclopedias to advise Cameralist bureaucrats about "everything from silver mining, viticulture, fruit growing, vegetable gardening, and animal husbandry to medicinal herbs, flowers, 'brewing, bleaching, advice on how to get spots off clothes, how to get rid of headaches'" (350, quoting Tribe 1988, 25-26). The needed knowledge was vast but readily available. A recognition that knowledge of something so difficult to understand as people's ideas might be required was very far from the Cameralists' imagination, as they were naïvely ignorant of ideational complexities that might cause unintended consequences.

Following historians such as Daniel T. Rodgers (1998), Friedman then speculates that this naïveté was passed down to the contemporary left by Progressives, who were frequently educated by such students of Cameralism as Gustav von Schmoller and Adolf Wagner. Unlike the Cameralists, however, the Progressives were democrats. Thus, their epistemic naïveté concerned the knowledge of the people, not the bureaucrats. (Newspapers, not encyclopedias, were to be the transparent medium of "the facts.") We inherit, then, two left traditions: the democratic, reformist, technocratic-utilitarian, Progressive, post-Cameralist tradition and the democratic, revolutionary, non-utilitarian, non-technocratic, emancipatory Marxist tradition.

In the former tradition, the naïve and simplistic Cameralist approach remains unchallenged, awareness of unintended consequences remains untheorized at best, and ideational humanism remains unimaginable. This tradition should also be hostile to the message of *Power Without Knowledge* on the grounds that, in challenging technocratic legitimacy, it challenges the legitimacy of *democracy*—conceived, narrowly, as democratic technocracy. (I will return to this point in section III.) At the same time, the capitalist element of exitocracy should prompt hostility from those in the Marxist tradition, despite the fact that the redistributive element would enable people to exit from social problems more effectively (arguably) than would even judicious popular attempts to centrally plan solutions to them. Anticipating these hostile responses to the book, Friedman suggests that both traditions have backed themselves into an embrace of technocracy not because they, any more than the Cameralists, have come up with an epistemic justification for technocracy; but because both traditions, like Cameralism, have simply failed to think about the political epistemology of technocracy.

II. CRITICAL RESPONSES TO *POWER WITHOUT KNOWLEDGE*

I would like to thank Jonathan Benson, Étienne Brown and Zoe Phillips Williams, Kevin Elliott, Oscar Larsson, Adam Lerner, Eric MacGilvray, Alfred Moore, Zeynep Pamuk, Robert Reamer, and Julian Reiss for their thought-provoking contributions to the symposium. Each of their papers is preceded by an abstract that summarizes their arguments in some detail, so in this section I will restrict myself to saying a few words about conceptual relationships among them. I will delay until section III any mention of Friedman's extensive responses to each of these contributions. Friedman's reply is a major work in its own right that puts each of the symposium papers, which fasten on one or at most two chapters of the book, into the context of the book's argument as a whole.

For example, Reamer's paper, and especially Benson's, focus on the "ordinary" technocratic features of an exitocracy (Chapter 7). Contrary to Friedman, they consider these features to be flaws that undermine the legitimacy of exitocracy, given (for the sake of argument) that ideational heterogeneity poses a serious problem for behavioral prediction. Insofar as ordinary injudicious technocrats are unable to make reliable predictions of the behavioral effects of their policy proposals, Reamer and Benson argue, exitocrats should likewise be unable to predict the effects of the various institutions, such as property rights and redistributive regimes, that they might implement. Therefore, Reamer turns to anarchism as an alternative to exitocracy, while Benson alludes to an alternative regime of "pure procedural legitimacy."

Benson's paper consists of a detailed list of the ordinary technocratic projects in which an exitocracy would have to engage, and the unintended consequences that might flow from them. In addition to providing an abbreviated list of the same kind, however, Reamer's paper minimizes the magnitude of ideational heterogeneity, on the Wittgensteinian grounds that language homogenizes the ideas of the native speakers of a given language. Reamer goes so far as to suggest that technocrats in our day capitalize on this homogeneity, allowing them to make accurate inferences from the behavior of population subsamples (so long as the larger population speaks the same language as the subsample). Thus, Reamer is defending the judiciousness of ordinary technocracy while also proposing anarchism as an even more extraordinary type of alternative to it than exitocracy is, as anarchism would more comprehensively institutionalize the exit mechanism by doing away with the state's monopoly legal system. Anarchism is intended, however, to supplant exitocracy as a superior form of technocracy, while Benson's pure procedural legitimacy would abandon technocracy altogether—assuming (for the sake of argument) that ideational heterogeneity is so troublesome that it undermines all forms of technocracy.

Larsson, like Reamer, attempts to minimize ideational heterogeneity, but he does so by attributing homogenizing effects not to language, but social structures. He then proposes that to some extent, some technocracies already seize on this homogeneity in order to predict human behavior reliably (just as Reamer contends that technocrats already seize on linguistic homogeneity to predict behavior reliably). The fact that these technocracies are injudiciously inattentive to ideational heterogeneity does not matter to Larsson, because he, like Reamer, minimizes the impact of that problem. That Larsson does so by citing Foucault on the predictability of human behavior—but in order to endorse technocracy, rather than condemn it—makes his contribution particularly fascinating. He attempts to square this apparent circle by appealing to the *democratic* use of structural homogeneities, whereby stakeholders "attend to public problems, often with a technocratic outlook, in an effort to resolve social and political problems through the pragmatic utilization of existing knowledge" of the homogeneities. Larsson thus merges a version of Foucault with a version of Habermas.

Lerner takes a different path than Larsson's and Reamer's. He thinks that Friedman *underestimates* heterogeneity because he notices only heterogeneous ideas, not heterogeneous mental qualia. Even though accounting for diverse qualia would put even more pressure on judicious technocrats, Lerner proposes no alternative forms of technocracy or alternatives to technocracy, as he is interested in ideational heterogeneity as a pure researcher, not as an institutional reformer. However, in his field of research—international relations—he finds grounds for bracketing the individualist ontology that Friedman connects to ideational determinism. Friedman locates the site of both heterogeneous and homogeneous ideas in the webs of belief characteristic of individual minds, while Lerner wants to allow for the possible existence of collective ideational entities, such as states.

Larsson's and Lerner's contributions engage with Friedman's political anthropology more directly than do any of the other papers. Brown and Williams, for example, defend the appropriateness of naïve technocratic realism, at least in some cases, which has the effect of bypassing the question of ideational heterogeneity. As I said in summarizing Chapter 1, a rejection of naïve realism, while a necessary precondition for a critical epistemology of technocratic knowledge claims (or any others), is insufficient as a critique of any *particular* type of knowledge claim (such as technocratic knowledge claims). Such a critique requires something specific, such as the presumption of ideational heterogeneity, that would raise doubts about whether this particular type of knowledge claim is more dubious than human knowledge in general—which is fallible, yes, but not necessarily so fallible as to be unreliable. By focusing on naïve realism to the exclusion of ideational heterogeneity, then, Brown and Williams are foregoing a critique of Friedman's critique of technocracy. This may be linked to concerns, expressed at the end of their paper, about the *democratic* legitimacy of technocracy. If technocratic truths are self-evident, as suggested by a defense of naïve realism, then surely they can be put to work by ordinary citizen-technocrats, securing democratic legitimacy for technocracy but ignoring the challenge to technocracy—ideational heterogeneity—that stems from Friedman's political anthropology. The same approach seems to undergird Brown and Williams's suggestion that, at least *in extremis,* we should take "epistemic gambles"—even in the absence of judicious ideational knowledge. Without the need for such knowledge, ordinary citizen-technocrats can govern by intuiting that, at least in otherwise-hopeless situations, some technocratic policy would be worth a shot in the dark, once again taking advantage of a type of self-evident truth.

MacGilvray, I think, might be said to make a similar end run around the problem of ideational heterogeneity. Drawing on the classical tradition and on Weber, he defends the possibility of an open-minded technocracy that is judicious—but only in the colloquial sense of the term. For MacGilvray, exposure to conflicting perspectives can attune citizen-technocrats to the complexity of political issues, as Aristotle and Polybius maintained. And responsible leaders, of the sort envisioned by Weber, can sort through the claims of dueling, doctrinaire epistocrats. MacGilvray's focus, then, is on the "complexity" of policy consequences in a general sense, and on the spiral of conviction, but not on the predictive problem posed by ideational heterogeneity.

Pamuk and Reiss, in contrast, do grapple with ideational heterogeneity, but indirectly. Both authors attend exclusively to Friedman's critique of positivist epistocracy. While neither is persuaded that positivist social science is unable to cope adequately with ideational heterogeneity, both are open to that possibility. Pamuk, however, would like to see evidence of the magnitude of the difficulties caused for positivist technocracy by ideational heterogeneity, while Reiss, who endorses the claim that "pernicious" ideational heterogeneity is a serious problem, nonetheless believes that there can be positivist progress toward an understanding of the laws of human behavior.

Another similarity between these two papers is that insofar as technocracy *cannot* cope adequately with pernicious heterogeneity, both papers depict *non-technocratic* democracy as the obvious normative alternative. Pamuk sees popular sovereignty as an alternative to technocracy simply because, as a form of sovereignty that is not grounded in epistemic claims, its legitimacy is immune from epistemic doubts. Reiss conceptualizes technocracy in the standard way, as epistocracy, such that "technocracy" becomes a foreign entity inside the democratic body politic. He therefore sees ideational heterogeneity and other forms of pernicious heterogeneity—among many problems for positivist social science that he beautifully schematizes—as plaguing experts, not ordinary citizens. In this view, what Friedman calls the "fact of epistocratic disagreement" (69) becomes the central problem for technocratic legitimacy, because all of the problems discussed by Reiss are bound to cause experts to disagree about how to solve social and economic problems; yet the demos is, by definition, unqualified to adjudicate these disagreements. Therefore, technocracy (epistocracy encased in democracy) is, for Reiss, "a bad idea"—which seems to leave a democracy purged of technocracy as the alternative.

Like Benson, then (if we take democracy to be a pure procedure of the sort he has in mind), Pamuk and Reiss think of democracy as *beyond technocracy*: a form of decision making that need not confront the epistemic quandaries explored in *Power Without Knowledge*. None of these authors, however, explain why *democracy* should serve this role. To use Pamuk's example, Hobbes viewed absolute sovereignty as an alternative to epistemic uncertainty and conflict; yet Hobbes's sovereign was hardly democratic. An absolute democracy would remove us from the epistemic vagaries of technocracy, but so would an absolute monarchy or any other regime in which power is vested unconditionally in some individual or group, regardless of the consequences of their actions. Of course, democratic theory abounds in reasons for preferring democracy to other regime types, but from Friedman's deliberately adopted internal normative perspective, technocratic legitimacy stands or falls on its consequences—its ability to deliver the (negative-utilitarian) goods—not on whether it allows for popular participation or consent. In this sense, technocracy is *beyond democracy,* even when the former is conceptualized as including a democratic element, democratic technocracy.

Elliott's and Moore's contributions, unlike most of the others, touch on the legitimacy of *democratic technocracy*. In line with Friedman's remarks about populism, Elliott contends that democratic technocracy has supplanted democracy simpliciter in the minds of a significant body of citizens, who have unwittingly picked up Progressive normative assumptions. These assumptions undermine democracy not in the fashion of Friedman's "fundamental dilemma of democratic technocracy" (the slippery slope from democratic technocracy to epistocracy, given certain epistemic assumptions), but because if technocracy does *not* deliver the goods, post-Progressive citizen-technocrats are perfectly willing to endorse nondemocratic alternatives. Elliott, then, can be read as envisioning non-technocratic democracy as an alternative to democratic technocracy, just as Pamuk and Reiss, and possibly Benson, envision non-technocratic democracy as an alternative to epistocracy.

In a sense, the same is true of Moore. He objects to Friedman's redefinition of technocracy to include the category of democratic technocracy, for while this definition illuminates the lawless tendencies of technocratic populists, who want social and economic problems solved at any cost, it obscures non-technocratic aspects of modern democracy, such as the pluralism that Moore sees as being opposed by both populists and epistocrats. If we follow Friedman too far, according to Moore, "the critique of technocracy becomes an undifferentiated critique of more or less the whole of modern democratic politics," such that even pluralism is subsumed by technocracy: "parties compete to offer solutions to social problems, epistocrats claim to be able to solve social problems without input from voters, and populists claim to know how to solve social problems if only they could win the acclaim of the majority and execute their program without obstruction or compromise." This picture of modern politics is precisely what Elliott finds illuminating about Friedman's redefinition of technocracy: it allows us to see how far modern democracy has strayed into technocratic problem solving. I should note that Friedman does not actually claim that democratic technocracy has *completely* subsumed democracy. In the book's Preface, he recognizes the rise of a decidedly non-technocratic emancipatory politics alongside democratic technocracy (ix), and in its Afterword, he alludes to Marxism as the historical source of this type of politics (351). But Elliott and Moore are referring to Chapter 6, where Friedman paints such a compelling picture of the ideal-typical dynamics of naïve democratic technocracy that one comes away seeing it *almost* everywhere one looks in contemporary mass politics.

I hope to have suggested that all the papers but two (Lerner's and MacGilvray's) attempt to escape the problems identified in *Power Without Knowledge* by turning to democracy (although this is far from the only thing the papers attempt to do). Brown and Williams, like Larsson, attempt to defend democratic technocracy by pushing back against Friedman's critique of naïve technocratic realism—which Friedman depicts as the backbone of democratic technocracy as currently practiced. Pamuk, Reiss, and perhaps Benson turn to non-technocratic democracy as an alternative to epistocracy. Elliott turns, by implication, to non-technocratic democracy as an alternative to the populist tendencies of democratic technocracy. Finally, Moore is concerned to defend non-technocratic democracy against both populist antipluralism and what he sees as the antidemocratic implications of exitocracy. Thus, he worries about the prospect that the "architects" of exitocratic policies and institutions would want to shield their creations from popular interference. Of course, from the internal perspective of technocracy, that is irrelevant. Legitimacy stems from getting the job done, regardless of who does it; this is why either citizen-technocrats or epistocrats, or both, might be the architects, depending on who is thought to know what they are doing. Like each of the other appeals to democratic legitimacy, then, except Larsson's and Brown and Williams's defenses of naïve technocratic realism, Moore's paper reaches beyond technocracy to democracy.

But it is not really a critique of *Power Without Knowledge*, which is, after all, not defending technocracy in *any* of its forms (including exitocracy) so much as exploring the ramifications of technocracy from within, bracketing the legitimacy of its utilitarian orientation. I read the book to be saying that *if* one attaches normative significance to solving, mitigating, or preventing social and economic problems, *then* one must face up to the attendant epistemic demands, which should drive one up the hierarchy of legitimacy, from injudicious technocracy to judicious ordinary technocracy to judicious exitocracy. If one does not want to follow this logic, however, as appears to be true of many of the contributors, one needs either to deny the epistemic demands by defending naïve realism or challenging the importance of ideational heterogeneity; or else to renounce, or at least subordinate, the goal of social and economic problem solving. Only then can democratic legitimacy be allowed to prevail over a putative technocratic legitimacy that may be, but often is not, democratic.

III. POLITICAL EPISTEMOLOGY BEYOND TECHNOCRACY

In assessing the symposium, then, I think we must begin by reiterating that *Power Without Knowledge* is not intended as a contribution to democratic theory. As Friedman says in the book's Introduction, only one relatively minor strand of democratic theory, the Utilitarian-Progressive strand—which finds few (if any) defenders among contemporary theorists—equates political legitimacy with technocratic problem solving (18–19). This is why *Power Without Knowledge* is best seen as an attempt to expand political epistemology beyond democracy. Nonetheless, I wonder if Friedman's political anthropology does not pose a challenge to at least one mainstream justification of democracy—not democratic technocracy, but democracy as a form of egalitarianism predicated on mutual respect, or what Niko Kolodny (2014b) describes as "social equality."[2] This type of justification may stand behind some contributors' desire to return from technocracy to democracy.

As we have seen, Friedman's political anthropology consists of two elements, ideational heterogeneity and ideational determinism. The first of these does most of the heavy lifting in his critique of technocracy. Thus, his response to the symposium, which discusses the anthropology even more extensively than does the book itself (where the term *political anthropology* does not appear), fixes attention on the positivist leanings of the majority of his interlocutors (Benson, Larsson, Lerner, MacGilvray, Pamuk, Reamer, and Reiss) precisely because positivism, in Friedman's view, has no anthropology—officially. The positivist is willing to consider any independent variable as a possible determinant of human behavior, such that nothing is ruled out as constitutive of the human. Yet unofficially, Friedman argues, all independent variables are required, by the positivist, to be capable of imposing themselves on all human beings, grounding external validity and thus the aspiration to produce lawlike generalizations. Thus, positivist anthropological openness, or nullity, is shadowed by a refusal to contemplate causes of human behavior that might be perniciously heterogeneous, including human ideas. For this reason, Friedman argues, the commitment to universalism that makes positivism an ideal device for generating empirically grounded technocratic behavioral predictions also guarantees that these predictions will be insensitive to the empirical diversity of human ideas, making positivism unscientific and eroding the reliability of its predictions.

Ideational heterogeneity, then, receives the lion's share of Friedman's attention, both in his reply and in his book. It is true that ideational *determinism* links ideational heterogeneity with pernicious *behavioral* heterogeneity: one aspect of ideational determinism is the determination of conscious behavior by subjective interpretations. This is the aspect that is most salient to the critique of technocracy, as the epistemic goal of the technocrat is behavioral prediction. But the other aspect of ideational determinism is the mental dimension: the creation of interpretations from beliefs and of beliefs from mental operations performed on ideational inputs that are, for the most part, communicated to each of us (somewhat heterogeneously) from other people. The inputs that are communicated to us determine our webs of belief, and these webs determine our conscious actions (including communicative actions). To be sure, at each step we may consciously work on the materials given to us, but Friedman assumes that this work, the work of thinking, is nomological, determined by neurological architecture that is not itself under our control (137). Thus, the whole process is determined. The communicative starting point of the process distinguishes Friedman's view from atomistic individualism, as he notes in his reply to Lerner, but it also raises the prospect that we are robots programmed by ideational inputs, each marching to the slightly discordant beat of the ideas to which we happen to have been exposed over the course of our lives. Thus, the opinions that, according to an important strand of democratic theory, deserve respect, and entitle us each to an equal share of political power, would seem to have no value in themselves, as they are in fact (in Friedman's view) the strictly determined products of whatever newspaper articles, blog posts, Twitter screeds, movies, novels, and courses in political theory we happen to have read or watched. This is particularly true for our political opinions, as we know (or think we know) very little about politics, government, or society that is not communicated to us from others.

What may be problematic here, for democratic theory, is not the heterogeneity or homogeneity of these ideational exposures, nor their fallibility, but the fact that there is no escaping them: we cannot resist our beliefs, which are coercive over us or, perhaps better put, constitutive of us. Friedman contends that in this sense, free will is a myth. To believe in it "is to believe in uncaused causes: determinants of action that come from nowhere to close the putative gap between reasons and actions." Friedman denies that there is such a gap: "an agent whose action stemmed from her free (underdetermined) will would lack sufficient reasons for action: that is to say, ideational determinants. Human minds, however, are saturated with reasons for action, and we know that these are sufficient to determine their actions because otherwise (lacking sufficient reasons for an action) a human being would be unable to act. Like Buridan's Ass, she would be unable to 'choose'" (142).

Setting aside the age-old philosophical questions, this is a compelling picture of what political ideas—not just technocratic ideas—look like. What predictability we do find in them stems from the cultural streams (journalism, high culture, mass culture, pedagogy) to which we and our fellow citizens are exposed; both the heterogeneities and the homogeneities across individuals are traceable to each individual's ideational exposures. Seen in this light, one must wonder why we are each entitled to equal respect for our political beliefs rather than, say, equal concern for our welfare—the starting point of technocracy. Pursuing the deterministic side of Friedman's ideational anthropology, then, widens the object of political epistemology to encompass all the political thoughts, and conscious actions, of human beings; but having left technocracy behind, it may also return us to technocracy because, arguably, it makes more sense to care for one another as sensual, suffering creatures than to respect one another as transcendent minds.

The last section of Friedman's reply reiterates a theme taken up in his chapters on Lippmann and on democratic technocracy: the scandal that neither political scientists nor political theorists pay much attention to journalism, despite the fact that virtually all knowledge of political issues must flow to us through journalistic hands. But the same scandal attends political scientists' and theorists' tendency to neglect cultural influences more widely, beyond mere journalism. Does it not matter that our ideas about justice, equality, emancipation (and democracy itself)—not merely our ideas about the scope, causes of, and solutions to social and economic problems—are mediated to us by human interpreters who are themselves ideationally determined?

Our mutual determination by the streams of self-confirming ideas we communicate to one another would seem to defeat any case for respecting our beliefs as independent or free, even as it dictates that we must treat one another with intellectual charity if we want to understand the idiosyncracies that separate us from one another. Intellectual charity acknowledges the empirical reality of ideational determination even as it undermines the notion that any idea deserves respect apart from its objective truth value. Democratic theorists should find much to think about in Friedman's warning (in his reply) that *any of us*—the people at large, technocratic elites or masses, journalists, or political theorists—can get caught in spirals of conviction even more insidious than the shadows on the wall of the cave.

NOTES

1. An important part of Chapter 3 is likewise a critique of Charles Taylor's social holism, which, like Freudianism and Marxism, effaces ideational determination. Although Taylor, as a *cultural* theorist, does not deny people's determination by ideas, he does (Friedman argues) portray the ideas expressed in cultural wholes as functional responses to self-evident social truths, not contingent products of autonomous streams of ideas (autonomous from both human will and objective realities).
2. Kolodny's epic examination of the justification of democracy argues that it amounts to "equal opportunity not only for informed influence, but also for

autonomous influence: influence knowingly in accord with judgments that are themselves reached by *free reflection* on what one takes to be relevant reasons" (Kolodny 2014a, 310, emph. added). Though Kolodny leaves the resemblance unremarked, this principle is similar to Rawls's "criterion of reciprocity," according to which contributors to public reasoning over the form of social institutions must "think it at least reasonable for others to accept them, as free and equal citizens. . . . Citizens will of course differ as to which conceptions of political justice they think the most reasonable, but they will agree that all are reasonable, even if barely so" (Rawls 2005 [1997], 446). Similarly, Amy Gutmann and Dennis Thompson maintain that democracy is "a conception of government that accords equal respect to the moral claims of each citizen, and is therefore morally justifiable from the perspective of each citizen" (1996, 26).

REFERENCES

Adorno, Theodor W. [1969] 1976. "Introduction" to Theodor Adorno, Hans Albert, Ralf Dahrendorf, Jürgen Habermas, Harald Pilot, and Karl R. Popper, *The Positivist Dispute in German Sociology*, trans. Glyn Adey and David Frisby. London: Heinemann.

Bennett, Stephen E., and Jeffrey Friedman. 2008. "The Irrelevance of Economic Theory to Understanding Economic Ignorance." *Critical Review* 20(3): 195-258.

Benson, Jonathan. 2020. "Exit, Voice and Technocracy." *Critical Review* 32(1-3).

Brennan, Jason. 2016. *Against Democracy*. Princeton: Princeton University Press.

Brown, Étienne, and Zoe Phillips Williams. 2020. "Disagreement, Epistemic Paralysis, and the Legitimacy of Technocracy." *Critical Review* 32(1-3).

Caplan, Bryan. 2007. *The Myth of the Rational Voter: Why Democracies Choose Bad Policies*. Princeton: Princeton University Press.

Downs, Anthony. 1957. *An Economic Theory of Democracy*. New York: Harper & Row.

Elliott, Kevin. 2020. "A Family Affair: Populism, Technocracy, and Political Epistemology." *Critical Review* 32(1-3).

Friedman, Jeffrey. 2019a. "Populists as Technocrats." *Critical Review* 31(3-4): 315-76.

Friedman, Jeffrey. 2019b. *Power Without Knowledge: A Critique of Technocracy*. New York: Oxford University Press.

Friedman, Jeffrey. 2020. "Political Epistemology, Technocracy, and Political Anthropology: Reply to a Symposium on *Power Without Knowledge*." *Critical Review* 32(1-3).

Goodin, Robert E., and Kai Spiekermann. 2018. *An Epistemic Theory of Democracy*. New York: Oxford University Press.

Gutmann, Amy, and Dennis Thompson. 1996. *Democracy and Disagreement*. Cambridge, Mass.: Belknap Press of Harvard University Press.

Habermas, Jürgen. 2006. "Political Communication in Media Society: Does Democracy Still Enjoy an Epistemic Dimension? The Impact of Normative Theory on Empirical Research." *Communication Theory* 16(4): 411-426.

Hirschman, Albert O. 1970. *Exit, Voice, and Loyalty: Responses to Decline in Firms, Organizations, and States*. Cambridge, Mass.: Harvard University Press.

Kolodny, Niko. 2014a. "Rule Over None I: What Justifies Democracy?" *Philosophy and Public Affairs* 42(3): 195-229.

Kolodny, Niko. 2014b. "Rule Over None II: Social Equality and the Justification of Democracy." *Philosophy and Public Affairs* 42(4): 287-336.

Larsson, Oscar L. "Technocracy, Governmentality, and Post-Structuralism." *Critical Review* 32(1-3).

Lerner, Adam B. 2020. "Social Science and the Problem of Interpretation: A Pragmatic Dual(ist) Approach." *Critical Review* 32(1-3).

MacGilvray, Eric. 2020. "The Spiral of Responsibility and the Pressure to Conflict." *Critical Review* 32(1-3).

Moore, Alfred. 2020. "Architects and Engineers: Two Types of Technocrat and Their Relation to Democracy." *Critical Review* 32(1-3).

Pamuk, Zeynep. 2020. "What Follows from the Problem of Ignorance?" *Critical Review* 32(1-3).

Rawls, John. [1997] 2005. "The Idea of Public Reason Revisited." In idem, *Political Liberalism: Expanded Edition*. New York: Columbia University Press.

Reamer, Robert. 2020. "Power, Knowledge, and Anarchism." *Critical Review* 32(1-3).

Reiss, Julian. 2020. "Why Do Experts Disagree?" *Critical Review* 32(1-3).

Rodgers, Daniel T. 1998. *Atlantic Crossings: Social Politics in a Progressive Age*. Cambridge, Mass.: Belknap Press of Harvard University Press.

Tribe, Keith. 1988. *Governing Economy: The Reformation of German Economic Discourse, 1750-1840*. Cambridge: Cambridge University Press.

Jonathan Benson

EXIT, VOICE AND TECHNOCRACY

ABSTRACT: *In* Power Without Knowledge, *Jeffrey Friedman develops a critique of technocracy and in doing so makes an epistemic case for exit over voice. He argues that a technocracy that fails to take people's ideational heterogeneity into account is unlikely to possess the knowledge required to solve social problems, and that the alternative of "exitocracy" may, in some cases, overcome these limits. By creating the conditions under which individuals can exit from undesirable social situations, an exitocracy may allow people to escape their social ills without knowing their society-wide causes or solutions. As Friedman recognizes, however, an exitocracy still requires technocratic knowledge, and this paper explores these requirements in further detail. First, it investigates the limits of exit as a solution to social problems, and the extent to which technocratic policies can be substituted for exit. Second, it considers the need for technocratic knowledge in the promotion of exit opportunities, and how this undermines Friedman's defense of exitocracy.*

In *Power Without Knowledge* (Oxford University Press, 2019), Jeffrey Friedman develops a powerful critique of technocratic politics. Unlike previous critics, such as Habermas, who aimed to steer the power of technocracy towards democratically determined ends, Friedman argues that technocracy may lack the very knowledge it requires for its legitimacy: reliable knowledge of how to solve social problems and improve the human condition. Given the epistemic complexity of social problems, there is no assurance that a technocratic state would pass the very test it sets for itself: that of creating more benefits than costs.

As the book's preface notes, the arrival of a detailed and sustained critique of technocracy may seem untimely. The current political situation in the United States (the focus of the book) and elsewhere seems to feature a greater threat of populism than of technocracy. Friedman's argument, however, is very far from irrelevant or outdated. It cuts to the core of a widely held belief that is common on all sides of the political spectrum, even among those who would not think of themselves as sympathetic to technocracy. This is the belief that the solutions to social problems are readily apparent. For Friedman, this belief is at the center of technocracy but also underlies much of our political discourse. Public-policy debates involve high levels of disagreement, but all sides share the assumption that they already know or can easily discover which policies will best address our social ills.

A similar assumption is also found in recent debates within political and democratic theory, which pit epistemic democrats (e.g., Landemore 2013 and 2014) against defenders of epistocracy (e.g., Caplan 2007 and Brennan 2016). While differing greatly in the form of political rule they favor, both sides in this debate share the belief that someone—whether ordinary citizens or social-scientific elites—can unproblematically know how to solve, alleviate, or prevent social ills. Friedman's critique of this assumption has wide-ranging implications, then, for the contemporary theory of politics as well as its practice. The argument developed in *Power Without Knowledge* makes important contributions to both political theory and political science, and will surely come to be seen as a key work in the burgeoning field of political epistemology.

Power Without Knowledge proceeds in three parts. The first analyzes the complexity of social problems, the likelihood of unintended consequences in public policy, and therefore the underappreciated burden facing those who claim to know which policy intervention is likely to be most effective. The second investigates whether technocrats are likely to possess such knowledge, and argues that the prospects currently appear to be bleak for both epistocrats, such as trained social scientists, and "citizen-technocrats"—ordinary citizens who hold opinions about technocratic policy issues. The third part then considers "exitocracy" as a partial solution to these problems. By promoting the ability of individuals to exit from social arrangements, exitocracy allows them to escape their problems instead of waiting for a society-wide technocratic fix. Friedman argues that such a system, in some cases, can enable people to improve their condition even in the absence of judicious technocratic knowledge.

I will focus on the last of these three parts. Its claim that we can produce better outcomes by prioritizing exit in the private sphere over voice in the public sphere is not new, but such claims have previously tended to come from classical-liberal theorists (e.g., Hayek 1945 and 1960; Kirzner 1985; Pennington 2011; Tebble 2016), while being a target for critique (including epistemic critique) from those on the political left (e.g., Bennett 2016; Benson 2019a and 2019b; Gamble 1996; Greenwood 2007 and 2010; O'Neill 2012). Friedman, however, bucks this trend by advocating an egalitarian form of exitocracy that would facilitate exit by means of the redistributive state. Friedman's proposal therefore has as much of a claim to being socialist as capitalist.

Sections I and II will give a brief overview of the epistemic challenges that Friedman sees as facing technocracy, will outline his idea of exitocracy, and make some general comments along the way. The remaining sections follow Friedman in considering the ways an exitocracy must itself rely on technocratic forms of knowledge. Section III looks at the need for such knowledge at the margins of exitocracy, where the possibility of effective exit is limited or non-existent. These limits reduce the ability of exitocracy to serve as an alternative to technocracy, as Friedman acknowledges. I explore these problems in further detail and introduce some additional limits that have implications for our ability to replace voice with exit. Recognizing these issues, however, does not challenge the general case for exit when and where it can be effectively exercised.

Sections IV and V then consider the more problematic need for technocratic knowledge at the heart of exitocracy. An exitocratic state must make technocratic judgments in order to fulfill its role of promoting and sustaining the ability of individuals to exit. While Friedman acknowledges this dilemma and admits that it limits the policy conclusions of his critique, he argues that we can still endorse a normative hierarchy that places exitocracy above ordinary technocracy. I, however, argue that this dilemma may create deeper problems for his view. Once we recognise that technocratic knowledge is needed to understand which actions increase or decrease exit opportunities, we cannot be sure whether an exitocratic state will actually create any of the benefits Friedman associates with exit. If Freidman's critique of technocratic knowledge is correct, then, it is inconclusive whether we should prefer exitocracy to technocracy.

I. THE CRITIQUE OF TECHNOCRACY AND TECHNOCRATIC KNOWLEDGE

Friedman defines technocracy as a "polity that aims to solve, alleviate, or prevent its people's social and economic problems" (5). On this account, technocracy is distinguished from other forms of politics not by the structure of its institutions but by its problem-solving mission. Typically, or as Friedman says "ordinarily" (Part III), technocracy attempts to accomplish its mission by implementing government policies to deal with discrete social problems, such as poverty, the need for education, and the need for health care. Technocracy's social programs and regulations do not aim at achieving any broad conception of social justice, but rather at the consequentialist and specifically "negative utilitarian" goal of producing "the least amount of avoidable suffering for all" (Popper 2013, 602).

Given that it is defined in terms of its mission, Friedman offers a view of technocracy that differs greatly from the scholarly and popular image of it as rule by technical experts. If a technocracy is a polity that aims to solve social problems so as to minimize human suffering, then it is only once we determine who can best do this that we can say whether technocracy should involve rule by the many or the few (21).[1] Yes, technocracy may involve the elite rule of experts ("epistocrats"), but it may also take the form of direct rule by the people if it turns out they can better solve our social problems. Technocracy is, then, a "fundamentally epistemic project" (ibid.) that may take oligarchic, democratic, or mixed forms.

Negative utilitarianism, like its positive cousins, requires a calculation of the costs and benefits of any action. A negative-utilitarian technocrat is, therefore, someone who claims (explicitly or implicitly) to know the costs and benefits of public policies, and to know the scope and causes of the problems that public policies aim to solve. Without such knowledge, technocracy cannot be relied on to do more good than harm. To be more precise, technocrats need to have the following four types of technocratic knowledge, according to Friedman (46-47):

1. Knowledge of which social problems are not only real but significant, in the sense that they affect large numbers of people—or small numbers intensely.
2. Knowledge of what is causing the significant problems, and (preferably) knowledge of what might cause significant new problems in the future.
3. Knowledge of which technocratic actions can efficaciously solve, mitigate, or prevent the significant problems.
4. Knowledge of the costs of efficacious solutions, including not only anticipated costs but those that are not intended, and thus are not anticipated.

Friedman labels his critique of technocracy "internal" because it questions whether technocrats are likely to possess these four types of knowledge, which is to say, whether they are likely to have the knowledge necessary for technocracy to be legitimate according to its own negative-utilitarian standards. While citizen-technocrats or epistocrats may possess the needed knowledge in any given case, all technocrats, according to Friedman, face epistemic problems that call the adequacy or reliability of their knowledge into question. His argument is therefore distinct from external critiques of technocracy, such as those put forward by the early Habermas (1970 and 1976), which object to technocracies' lack of democratic credentials but do not question the likelihood of attaining reliable technocratic knowledge itself.

The Problem of Unintended Consequences

Why is it that Friedman believes that technocratic politics, whether at the elite or mass level, is inherently problematic? The main force of his argument relates to the difficulty of predicting unintended consequences, and thus the tenuousness of technocratic knowledge of the fourth type.

Friedman points out that determining the actual consequences of any technocratic policy requires making predictions of human behavior. Thus, knowing whether an increase in the minimum wage will have beneficial consequences, all in all, requires making a prediction about the likely behavioral response of employers when the policy increases their labor costs. Will they, for instance, respond by reducing their demand for labor, as neoclassical economists might argue, and if so, by how much? Without such a prediction, a technocrat would not know whether the higher wages that the policy will direct toward the lowest-paid workers is beneficial overall or is outweighed by increases in unemployment.

In general, technocracy is only able to achieve its ends to the extent to which human behavior can be reliably predicted by technocrats. Friedman, however, wonders if human behavior can be accurately predicted by anyone, at least when it comes to the "anonymous others" who are usually the objects of technocratic policy making (30 and passim).

Ideational Heterogeneity and the Problem of Prediction

At the core of Friedman's challenge to the reliability of predictions in the social world is an ideational account of human behavior that he develops from the work of Walter Lippmann ([1922] 1997) and W.V.O. Quine (Quine and Ullian 1978). Simplifying for the purpose of brevity, Friedman's account focuses on the importance of interpretation in the behavior of social actors, and particularly the role of heterogeneous ideas in these actors' interpretations of how they should behave in a given case.[2]

Individual decisions about how to act, according to Friedman, do not involve the objective registry of the objective facts of one's environment, but are rather based on subjective interpretations produced by individuals' webs of belief. The ideas that constitute a given web include perceptions, beliefs, interpretations, hypotheses, theories, inspirations, and assumptions (140). Friedman's view that individual behavior is ideationally determined does not by itself lead him to question the reliability of behavioral predictions. Rather, a problem arises because the ideas in various individuals' webs of belief are heterogeneous and inaccessible to observation. None of us knows the content of the ideational inputs into others' webs, but we have reason to think that, to some extent, they vary from person to person (144-48). Therefore, to some extent, we do not know how people will respond to their situations as they interpret them. To some extent, then, public policies designed to manipulate their actions so as to solve social problems may have behavioral consequences that we do not anticipate.

Friedman points out that every person's web of beliefs is formed by tens of thousands if not millions of different inputs over the course of their lives, from their upbringing and social class, to the books they read and the films they watch. These will differ, across a given population, in somewhat unknowable ways. A degree of ideational heterogeneity among social actors means that they will interpret their environments differently to that degree (ceteris paribus) and, as a result, behave differently. In reaction to an increase in the minimum wage, for instance, one firm's managers may interpret the situation as requiring that they reduce the number of their employees, another may find savings in other areas of production, while another may not change their behavior at all (204). The presence of ideational heterogeneity, then, makes prediction in the social sciences a much more difficult task than in the natural sciences, as it requires that the social scientist understand the subjective beliefs of those whose behavior is being predicted. One cannot simply assume an individual's motivation (e.g., self-interest) and from this derive their objective rational action (e.g., decrease demand for labor when its price increases). Instead, one must, like an intellectual historian, come to an understanding of the particular webs of belief of the actors (160-63). Although we may be able to do this with those people we are close with, or (to an extent) with "anonymous others" who have already acted, doing so prospectively for a large number of anonymous others is another matter.[3] It is the latter task, however, that confronts any would-be technocrat, who must predict the behavior of "unseen men" (Lippmann [1922] 1997, 165).

The Possibility of a Judicious Technocracy

There may, however, be homogenizing forces in society that push back against ideational heterogeneity (169-77). Uniform social norms, for instance, can cause regularity and predictability in the behavior of otherwise heterogeneous individuals. The task of the "judicious" technocrat is, therefore, to determine in any given case where these regularities in behavior lie, and to distinguish them from otherwise unpredictable actions. With this challenge in hand by the end of Part I of *Power Without Knowledge*, Part II goes on to investigate whether real-world technocrats, be they epistocrats or average citizens, can rise to meet the challenge of judiciousness. Here Friedman asks how judicious real-world technocrats are; why they might not be very judicious, at a systemic level; and, therefore, what the prospects are for change.

There is not space here to survey the three chapters of Part II in detail, but suffice it to say that Friedman paints a pessimistic but not entirely hopeless picture. He argues that modern social scientists tend to ignore ideational heterogeneity due to a cultural "pressure to predict" (Chapter 4), and that this produces both the apriorism of neoclassical economics and the positivism of empiricist correctives to apriorism, such as the use of randomized controlled trials. In addition, he argues, the process by which one becomes an expert, and thus an epistocrat, tends to produce dogmatism, the result of which is that the most informed are also the least open minded (Chapter 5). Citizen-technocrats, on the other hand, are less dogmatic than experts, but have little technocratic knowledge and therefore tend to focus on the intentions of politicians rather than the consequences of their policies (Chapter 6).

None of this, however, rules out the possibility that a judicious technocracy may come into being. It is possible that there could be a "cultural revolution" (314) against the ideationally insensitive culture of epistocrats and citizen-technocrats. Such a revolution could lead technocrats to be interpretively charitable to those they want to predict, empirically scrupulous, open-minded, and familiar enough with their subjects to locate areas of homogenization on which to base policy interventions (although they would need to make sure these interventions did not themselves disrupt such homogenization; 172). However, Friedman argues that it is unlikely that we will achieve such a judicious technocracy in the foreseeable future, pending such a cultural revolution. On his view, as I understand it, the possibility of a judicious technocracy means that we cannot conclusively reject the legitimacy of technocracy, but pending such a revolution, the difficulty of predicting human behavior means that we should be skeptical that any would-be technocrat has gotten hold of reliable technocratic knowledge.

II. THE EPISTEMIC ADVANTAGES OF EXIT OVER VOICE

As Friedman points out at the beginning of Part III, however, it would beg the question for him to claim that technocracy has, a matter of empirical fact, done more harm than good (or vice versa). All that Part I did is establish a presumption in favor of ideational heterogeneity, and argue that it is the task of technocracy to judiciously investigate the possibility of homogenizing forces. While Part II suggests that this is not being done very much at present, it still might be done in the future if there is a cultural revolution against the injudicious neglect of ideational heterogeneity. We are left, then, with the theoretical possibility that, in empirical reality, there is a significant amount of unpredicted behavior, and thus of unintended consequences flowing from technocratic action; but it is also possible that the unintended technocratic consequences are not of sufficient magnitude to render technocracy internally illegitimate.

To resolve this uncertainty, Part III presents an ideal type of "exitocracy" as an alternative to "ordinary" technocracy. Ordinary technocracies address social and economic problems by attempting to gain the four types of technocratic knowledge for each problem that is to be solved —knowledge that is voiced and acted upon through some sort of deliberation. This deliberation is aimed at crafting the best policy response to social problems, case by case. Exitocracy serves as a point of comparison against ordinary technocracy—whether it be democratic, epistocratic, judicious, or injudicious—allowing Friedman to avoid the uncertainties created by Parts I and II. The ability of ordinary technocracy to do more good than harm depends on such factors as the degree to which ideational heterogeneity will be neutralized by ideational homogeneities in particular cases, and the degree to which judicious technocrats will become aware of this, which Friedman does not feel capable of predicting (317-319). This leaves unresolved the question of whether ordinary technocracies are legitimate, according to their own negative-utilitarian standards. Answering this question would require Friedman to make assertions about the magnitude of the unintended consequences caused by technocratic action, presupposing his access to the very type of technocratic knowledge whose reliability was undermined in Part I. By comparing technocracy to exitocracy, however, Friedman can make relative claims that do not require him to possess such knowledge.

Exitocracy as an "Extraordinary" Form of Technocracy

In contrast to ordinary technocracy, Friedman defines exitocracy as an extraordinary form of technocracy that seeks to alleviate the presumptive unreliability of technocratic knowledge, or more accurately avoid it, by prioritizing exit over voice. In Albert Hirschman's (1970) original formulation of the exit/voice dichotomy, individuals have two options when they are dissatisfied with the goods or services of a provider. Either they can express their concerns by voicing their dissatisfaction, or they can exit from the service. Someone dissatisfied with a train service, for instance, can either complain directly to the train company or exit from it and experiment with the services of a rival company. While Hirschman was concerned that exit might undermine the potential to improve public services through voice—his example was of a government-run train service that has a monopoly of provision, such that the only alternatives to it are buses or taxis—Friedman (330) is interested in the epistemic advantages of exit in allowing people to escape from their social problems, and thus from their need to know how to solve them at a society-wide level.

The principal benefit of exit, then, is, according to Friedman, that it reduces the need for reliable technocratic knowledge in the alleviation of social problems. Compare, for instance, an individual voicing a complaint to a technocratic state with the same individual utilizing exit in a private market. In the first case, the individual expresses dissatisfaction with a social problem based on personal, experiential knowledge of the problem. For the problem to then be solved, however, the individual's relatively reliable experiential knowledge must be coupled with relatively unreliable technocratic knowledge. The voiced complaint highlights a problem, but before it can be fixed, knowledge is also required about whether this problem is widely experienced, what its causes are, and which changes would address the problem without causing too many unintended consequences. In the second case, the individual uses experiential knowledge of the problem as the basis for exiting from it—for example, to another private firm—in search of relief. If this experiment works, then the individual will have escaped the problem without needing unreliable technocratic knowledge of the scope, causes of, or solutions to the problem not only for her but for everyone else in the society. As long as one can recognize the effects of one's exit on one's own well-being, one can exit without needing to be aware of the scale, the cause, or the society-wide solution to the problem. Individuals can, for instance, switch from one private provider of transportation to a better one without requiring any knowledge about *why* this alternative performs better.

Private firms are, of course, attempting to offer goods or services and, in doing so, are required to make technocratic judgments (in the sense of predictions about customers', employees', suppliers', and investors' behavior). Friedman believes that private firms are just as prone to error in making these judgments as are ordinary technocrats. The difference, however, is that in a private market multiple firms are attempting to provide goods and services as opposed to a single technocratic state. The presence of ideational heterogeneity among the providers of private goods and services, therefore, becomes an epistemic advantage, as it may lead firms to offer a diversity of solutions to people's problems. An exitocracy allows for exit between these alternatives, so that people can escape their problems without needing to know how many others are experiencing the problems or even how the better experience that they might discover was brought into existence. Thus, Friedman maintains, exit-based action in the private sphere, while imperfect, should be better able to solve social problems, in some cases (and thus overall), than voice-based technocratic action in the public sphere. Exit allows people to escape (some of) their problems "without understanding the society-wide significance or cause of the problem, without knowing the efficacy of a society-wide solution, and without weighing the costs and benefits of such a solution" (333).

The contrast Friedman draws here between mechanisms of voice in the public sphere and those of exit in the private sphere may be overly stark. Although he recognizes opportunities for voice in the private sphere (331–32), he does not explore the opportunity for exit in the public sphere (and therefore in ordinary technocracy). Exit, however, comes in many more forms than Friedman, and for that matter Hirschman, seem to recognize (Dowding and John 2012). Individuals can exit from one private service to another but also from a private service to a public one (and vice versa), from a public or private service to no service at all (and vice versa), or from one public service to another public service. The latter could involve moving from a publicly provided service in one geographical location to another (such as from a public hospital in Manchester to one in Liverpool) or from different public service within the same location (such as taking the public bus service to and from work in London rather than the public underground train).[4] The public sphere can, therefore, involve forms of exit by offering multiple kinds of services/solutions to social problems. The voice/exit distinction does not as neatly map onto the public/private distinction as Friedman sometimes seems to suggest when he runs the two distinctions together.[5] That being said, the market and the private sphere do seem to provide a greater opportunity for exit than does the public sphere, given the number of private firms that can compete at any one time (at least subject to the level of market concentration). The private sphere may thus provide greater scope for exit-based action.

Exitocracy and Redistribution

Unlike an ordinary technocratic state, which aims to find direct solutions to society's many discrete social problems, the exitocratic state's "cardinal" and "distinctive" goal would be to provide a framework within which individuals (as consumers and employees) would be able to use exit to avoid the problems that afflict them (322, 341). It would provide public goods that are vital to the private sphere in order to create an environment "in which individuals using exit can flourish" (322). An exitocracy, then, is technocratic in seeking to address social problems and, as we shall see, it is technocratic in requiring an array of technocratic knowledge. But wherever possible, it aims to solve social problems indirectly, by promoting individuals' ability to exit in the private sphere rather than by deliberate efforts in the public sphere. As a result, an exitocracy reduces our reliance on relatively untrustworthy technocratic knowledge while still helping people to improve their lot, in a negative-utilitarian sense.

An appeal to the private sphere as an epistemically superior alternative to voice and politics is not completely new. Classical-liberal theorists, particularly in the tradition of Friedrich A. Hayek (1948 and 1960), have long pointed to the epistemic advantages of markets and the private sphere more broadly (e.g., Kirzner 1985; Pennington 2011; Tebble 2016). As Friedman rightly points out, however, there are important distinctions between these arguments and those he develops in his book. His argument differs, for instance, from that of the early Hayek's (1945) focus on the information-aggregating function of the price system. Friedman (335-36) argues that Hayek ideologically assumed that the fallible opinions of entrepreneurs constitute reliable "knowledge," even while denying that central planners have reliable knowledge rather than fallible opinions. Hayek also placed emphasis on the dispersed, fragmented, and tacit nature of social knowledge, while Friedman's account does not rely on knowledge taking any such form.[6] There are also some interesting similarities, however, between Friedman's defense of exitocracy and Hayek's epistemic justification of a market society. In *The Constitution of Liberty* (1960, 377), for instance, Hayek argues that a key problem with granting a monopoly to the state to solve social problems is that it will "prevent the emergence of more effective alternatives" and deprive "individuals of any choice in the matter."[7] The ability of private firms to offer different solutions and to allow individuals to choose between them was important to Hayek's epistemology of the market as well as Friedman's. Others who have analyzed the epistemic properties of markets have also pointed to the role that market competition plays in decreasing the need for scientific knowledge, as it allows individuals to make simultaneous comparisons of alternatives (DeCanio 2014).[8]

Friedman's account of exitocracy, however, has as much of a claim to being socialist as capitalist, and is therefore far from being classically liberal. In addition to the divergence between his and Hayek's justifications of the private sphere, their views differ greatly over the role of the state in terms of redistribution. Friedman's exitocratic state would engage in very significant forms of redistribution as part of its core function of providing exit opportunities to as many people as possible. Exit is not costless, and it also requires opportunities to enter alternatives. Friedman (335), therefore, suggests that the negative-utilitarian goals of technocracy require the implementation of a version of the Rawlsian Difference Principle—one not aimed at maximizing the "primary goods" of the least advantaged, in line with the demands of justice, but rather their "entry goods," in line with the goal of helping them solve their problems. An exitocratic state, then, would aim to "maximize, for as many people as possible, the opportunity to use exit to solve problems affecting them personally," by affording them the means "to enter into as many alternatives as possible, consistent not only with others' roughly equal opportunity to do the same, but with the expansion of such opportunities for all" (ibid.). Friedman's Afterword therefore provides an explicitly egalitarian defense of exit and the private sphere, which he believes could form the basis of a new left that would be both non-technocratic and non-Marxist.

It is therefore useful to distinguish what I will call *classically liberal exitocracy* from *egalitarian exitocracy*.[9] While the former involves redistribution in order to provide a minimum level of income, the latter involves a much greater level of redistribution in line with a version of the Rawlsian Difference Principle. We will briefly return to the distinction between these two forms of exitocracy later. For now, the distinction highlights an interesting aspect of Friedman's epistemic endorsement of exit. Unlike others on the political left who have tended to critique the emphasis classical liberals put on the private sphere (Bennett, 2016; Benson, 2019a, 2019b; Greenwood, 2007, 2010; O'Neill, 2012), Friedman offers an egalitarian defense of exit.[10] This egalitarian exitocracy is said to reduce our reliance on problematic technocratic knowledge by promoting and sustaining the ability of individuals to exit, and therefore to escape their social problems rather than waiting for a technocratic fix.

III. TECHNOCRATIC KNOWLEDGE AT THE MARGINS OF EXITOCRACY

The extent to which an egalitarian exitocracy can alleviate the problems of technocracy will depend on the extent to which it reduces the need for technocratic knowledge. As Friedman recognizes, however, there is, in fact, a large need for such knowledge in an exitocracy. It is this need for technocratic knowledge on which I will focus in the rest of this paper. Sections IV and V will consider the technocratic knowledge required to promote and sustain exit opportunities, and I will argue that this requirement challenges Friedman's view that we should prefer exitocracy to technocracy. This section will look at the need for such knowledge at the margins of exitocracy. That is, it will look at the limits facing the ability of individuals to exit from their problems, such that reliance on technocratic knowledge and voice-based solutions cannot be avoided. Some of these limitations are recognized by Friedman (332–34), and they do not negate the benefits of exitocracy when and where exit can be effectively exercised. Friedman calls exitocracy an extraordinary form *of technocracy* precisely because, while prioritizing exit over voice, it will often have no recourse but to "ordinary" technocratic solutions. These limits to exit do not, therefore, challenge the legitimacy of exitocracy. My aim in this section is to explore these limits further and add some additional considerations that bear on the extent to which exit can be substituted for voice.

We can see the restricted potential for replacing technocratic policies with exit when we consider the origins of ordinary technocracy. As understood by Habermas (1970, 102) and Friedman (351–52), technocracy developed to address the "dysfunctions" of free exchange and capitalist markets. Many of these dysfunctions, however, occur precisely because private exit is not an option. This is not true of all of the problems of markets; there are social ills from which people could exit if not for lack of resources, and these problems may be dealt with by the redistributive function of Friedman's exitocracy (although as we will see in the next section, this solution does not come without its own problems). The issue, however, is that there are a host of common and pervasive problems that affect markets precisely because exit from them is not possible, and in such cases, exitocracy will offer no alternative to voice and technocratic knowledge.

The first set of these dysfunctions goes under the rubric of public goods (and, conversely, public bads), in the technical sense of goods or services that are non-excludable and non-rivalrous. The problems facing private markets when it comes to the provision of such goods and services are well known. The important point for our purposes is that they cannot always be effectively escaped by means of exit. If people experience public bads such as low air quality, there is not necessarily an exit option which allows them to escape. This is because the very publicness that makes such goods difficult to provide in private markets also restricts people's ability to exit from their occurrence.[11] This is also true of some kinds of externalities. Although the costs of externalities are not necessarily public, as they can, for example, be locally confined—as in the case of effluents that run from a stream onto private land—they can also be difficult to exit from when they are of significant scope.

As has been argued, particularly by green political theorists and economists, public goods and externalities present pervasive limits to market institutions (e.g., Jacobs 1991, Daly 1992, Barry 1999, Benson 2018, and Eckersley 2004). If such problems were uncommon and isolated, then they would not present a significant limit to the substitution of exit for voice. However, in fossil-fuel economies, problems of environmental public goods and externalities are connected to almost all forms of production and market exchange, and their possible costs for human and non-human well-being range from significantly damaging to catastrophic. The profit motive can also exacerbate these problems by incentivizing individual firms to externalize costs wherever possible. These problems are not simply confined to anthropogenic climate change but involve a host of related environmental issues, from biodiversity loss to water/ocean acidification, ozone depletion, and acid rain. Problems of public goods and externalities may represent, therefore, not exceptions to efficient markets but the rule. They are a pervasive dysfunction of markets from which exit is not possible—a dysfunction that technocratic knowledge is essential to solve.

In some cases, Friedman (341) argues that public goods can be fitted with "exit-like" options that would, like exit itself, reduce the need for technocratic knowledge. While "no exit is available from the provision of any public good," the exit mechanism "can be mimicked in some cases. Thus, an exitocracy might address global warming through something like a carbon tax rather than through something like the Green New Deal, as a carbon tax would not require technocratic knowledge of how to get people to reduce their carbon emissions: the discovery of how to do so would be left to individual agents seeking to reduce the tax they pay" (ibid.). However, as he recognizes, policy tools of this type still require significant forms of technocratic knowledge: "the size of the carbon tax, and many other details, would have to be set through ordinary technocratic deliberation about the human behavioral consequences to be expected from different policy designs" (342). Such policies therefore require technocratic knowledge to be successful. Friedman (ibid.) also acknowledges a class of public goods where exit-like policies are not even possible. While he defines "secondary" public goods as those that allow for exit-like mechanisms, "tertiary" public goods are resistant to exit options.[12] Military defense and foreign policy, for instance, do not offer any scope for exit and their provision must be wholly voice-based.

Even when exit-like policies are possible, however, they may in some cases require more problematic behavioral predictions than standard technocratic policies do. Determining which level of taxation will reduce natural gas fracking to the desired level, for instance, may be more difficult than directly limiting fracking production to that level through regulation. While the latter mandates a certain behavior to achieve a desired target, the former requires the policy maker to predict the individual's responses to different increases in costs. Of course, calculating the desired target requires technocratic knowledge, and there may be unintended consequences, but this is true for both the exit-like policy and the more traditional technocratic policy. Similarly, if we want manufacturers to stop using environmentally damaging or inefficient technologies, and replace them with better alternatives, then simply banning the undesirable technologies may involve less significant technocratic judgments than predicting at which level of taxation manufacturers will change their behavior.[13] It is not always clear, then, that introducing more exit options into the provision of public goods will reduce our reliance on technocratic knowledge, and it may even increase it. Public goods and externalities thus exemplify a pervasive dysfunction of markets that does not allow for exit, and for which exitocracy will be dependent on voice and technocratic knowledge as much as will an ordinary technocracy.

Another set of exit-resistant problems, which Friedman does not directly consider, stems from the inability of individuals to choose effectively among exit options (Akerlof 1970; Benson 2019a; Stiglitz 1991 and 1994). The ability to exit requires not just entry options but knowledge of which of these options are better for one's well-being. However, there is a whole range of areas in which individuals do not possess, or are unlikely to possess, the knowledge required to make effective exit decisions. Take, for instance, decisions relating to one's health.[14] There can be significant health effects associated with the use and manufacture of various products and services, but of which consumers and workers will not always be aware. A product might, for example, affect the background risk of someone contracting a health condition and therefore be unnoticeable to the consumer or worker, or alternatively it may only be one among many possible and hard-to-distinguish causes of an illness. This lack of feedback means that the impact of different options on one's well-being may not be apparent, and individuals will require a large amount of additional information in order to make effective exit decisions (Benson 2019a).[15] They would, for instance, need to know about the different chemicals used in all the different goods and services they may use and the potential effect of these on their health. Obtaining this amount of often technical information creates a significant cognitive and epistemic burden (particularly given the many other demands on our time and energy) that we will be unlikely to overcome.

Similar limits on the ability of individuals to make effective exit decisions can be found in other areas. When it comes to financial products, for instance, the long-terms effects of alternatives are not always easily observable, and individuals often require technical information that they cannot always be expected to have. Failure to possess such information, however, can result in making decisions that are detrimental to one's long-term well-being. Thus, even an exitocracy would have to rely on voice and technocratic knowledge to solve such dysfunctions. Of course, the epistemic limits facing individuals may also point to an additional role of the exitocratic state in helping to promote exit. The state may provide consumer information to citizens through public information campaigns or mandated forms of product labeling. However, there are significant limits to these methods of communicating information, which is often complex and difficult to understand (Benson 2019a; O'Neill 2012). Such problems can affect such a large number of goods that they place excessive burdens on individuals, who often make a number of market transactions in any one day.

One may argue that while individuals often lack information in certain areas and are therefore prone to making mistakes, these mistakes on the individual level will likely be less serious than the mistakes associated with technocratic intervention and policies. It is not clear, however, that this is necessarily the case. While it is true that any one individual mistake may be less serious than a political mistake, the aggregate effect of large numbers of individual mistakes may be just as serious if not more so. In those areas where individuals significantly lack information, exit may not be the best option when compared to technocratic intervention

Whether in the form of public goods, externalities, or the epistemic constraints facing individuals, then, there are many limitations to using exit to solve the social problems that ordinary technocracy aims to address. Given that technocracy developed to address the dysfunctions of markets and free exchange, this should not come as any great surprise. Many of these dysfunctions directly result from the inability of individuals to make effective use of exit, and it is therefore the failure of exit that often motives technocratic programs in the first place. For many of the problems that ordinary technocracy is interested in solving, exitocracy will simply not offer a viable alternative solution. This fact does not undermine the value of exit-based action when and where it is possible, but it does point to the limitations of exit as a solution to social problems and as a mechanism for avoiding a reliance of technocratic knowledge.

IV. TECHNOCRATIC KNOWLEDGE AT THE HEART OF EXITOCRACY

The previous section highlighted the need for technocratic knowledge in those cases where the ability to exit, or to make effective epistemic use of exit, is limited. It did not, however, challenge the epistemic benefits that exitocracy may have in cases where exit can be effectively exercised. This section therefore turns to the need for technocratic knowledge in achieving exitocracy's distinctive mission of promoting and sustaining exit. The promotion of exit requires the provision of certain "primary" public goods, such as redistribution and a system of property rights, which itself require very significant predictions about the behavior of ideationally heterogeneous individuals. Indeed, "the administration of an exitocratic Difference Principle would require the administrators to make behavioral predictions that nobody—no matter how judiciously attentive to ideational heterogeneity—is well positioned to make" (340), and the same is true of "legally establishing and defending the private sphere."

This requirement for technocratic knowledge at the very heart of exitocracy introduces a dilemma. If Friedman's critique of technocracy is correct, then "we must accept . . . that the unintended costs of providing public goods, including those created by these essential exitocratic activities, may exceed their benefits, because technocratic reasoning will have to be deployed in the course of these activities" (341). For Friedman, however, this dilemma does not undermine the superiority of exitocracy over technocracy, or the justifiability of providing exit supporting public goods. He argues that while "technocratic reasoning will have to be deployed in providing exitocratic public goods . . .the inevitable errors that result will be offset, to some (putatively significant) extent, by the fact that these public goods will enable people to solve social problems in the private sphere" (ibid.). Thus, Friedman continues, we are still "entitled to say that the mix of benefits and costs should be more favorable in an exitocracy, despite the errors that will undoubtedly plague both exitocrats and ordinary technocrats" (ibid.).

Thus, the dilemma presented by the need for technocratic knowledge in providing exit-supporting goods does not, according to Friedman, undermine a normative hierarchy in which exitocracy is preferable to ordinary technocracy, just as a judicious technocracy is preferable to an injudicious one (319, 343). In this and the following section, however, I aim to argue that the dilemma does, in fact, undermine the primacy of exitocracy in this hierarchy. If we accept Friedman's critique of technocracy, then we have no reason to believe that attempts to provide primary public goods will increase people's ability to exit rather than decrease it, and therefore no reason to believe that an exitocratic state will produce any more of the benefits Friedman associates with exit. To see this, however, we first need to spell out exactly why reliable technocratic knowledge is required to determine which actions will increases the ability of individuals to exit. The next section will draw out the consequences of this for Friedman's defense of exitocracy.

Consider first the redistributive role of an exitocratic state in the promotion of exit. Friedman is certainly right that for many individuals, limited resources and opportunities reduce and may remove their ability to escape their social problems. Knowing if redistribution will improve their ability to exit, however, and knowing which levels of redistribution to enact, requires technocratic forms of knowledge (340). Friedman thinks that redistribution by the exitocratic state should aim to "maximize, for as many people as possible, the opportunity to use exit to solve problems affecting them personally" by allowing them to enter into "as many alternatives as possible" (335), but there are many ways that redistribution at different levels could lead to no improvement or a decline in people's exit opportunities. Consider, for instance, the following possible scenarios.

1. The exitocratic state increases the level of taxation on wealthy individuals and/or businesses in order to redistribute to those with relatively few exit options. This, however, leads many existing employers to cut back on their demand for labor while others struggle to produce profits and go out of business altogether. Would-be entrepreneurs are also deterred from setting up new businesses, which removes the employment opportunities that would have been created, as well as the potential of these new companies to solve people's social problems through the services and goods they would have provided. The number of exit and entry opportunities open to individuals is, therefore, reduced.

2. The exitocratic state increases the level of taxation on wealthy individuals and/or businesses in order to redistribute to those without exit options. In seeing these taxes as a threat to their profits, however, businesses react not by reducing demand for labor but by increasing their prices and pushing any additional costs onto consumers. The extra money in the pockets of the worst off is then offset by inflation. Their position in terms of resources for exit is, therefore, left the same as it was before.

3. The exitocratic state decides to redistribute a certain amount of wealth to the worst off in order to significantly improve their ability to exit from undesirable jobs. This increase in income, however, leads many of the worst off to exit the employment market altogether and live off these publicly provided resources. This results in decreases to both economic growth and overall tax revenues, which together reduce the resources available for the exitocratic state to improve exit opportunities in the future.

4. As in the previous scenario, the exitocratic state decides to redistribute a certain amount of wealth to the worst off in order to significantly improve their exit options in terms of employment. However, given the costs of the alternative exit options they face, the worst off find that this increase in their income is insufficient to improve their exit opportunities.

In each of these scenarios, a redistributive intervention by an exitocratic state either fails to improve people's exit opportunities or it reduces them, overall. I do not claim that any of these four scenarios would result from a state engaging in redistribution; they may well not. However, it is not self-evident that none of these scenarios would result from a particular level of redistribution. Discovering if they would requires technocratic knowledge about how individuals are likely to react to the specific changes in their social environment effected by various types and levels of redistribution. Will employers cut their demand for labor or increase their prices when confronted with high tax burdens? Will would-be entrepreneurs be deterred from creating new companies, jobs, and products by increasing taxation? What are the costs of exit for different groups? Are people likely to leave the job market altogether if they receive a certain level of redistributed wealth? The exitocratic state will need to have answers to such questions if it is to promote the ability of individuals to exit, but discovering such answers requires that one can understand and predict how a large number of ideationally heterogeneous individuals will react to different rates of taxation and social provision.

These questions about the effect of redistribution on exit opportunities take a very similar form to questions about the costs and benefits of technocratic policies aimed directly at solving social problems. Understanding the likelihood of scenarios 1 and 2, for instance, requires predictions about the reactions of employers to higher costs very similar to those required for understanding the effects of taxes and wage regulations. As Friedman puts it, such questions are "no less difficult to answer than the question of how [employers] might respond to various levels of a minimum wage or to other 'ordinary' technocratic initiatives" (340). Understanding the likelihood of scenarios 3 and 4, alternatively, requires making predictions about the effects of increased resources/incomes in similar ways to those required to understand the effects of an introduction of, or change to, a social welfare or benefit program. Determining how to promote and not diminish exit opportunities through redistribution requires knowledge about how ideationally heterogeneous individuals will change their behavior in response to a government intervention.

If Friedman's critique of technocratic knowledge is correct, then, it is unclear whether he should support his egalitarian exitocracy over a classical liberal exitocracy, by the standards of negative utilitarianism.[16] Friedman (322) writes that an egalitarian exitocracy "would undertake wealth redistribution far more ambitious than a universal basic income —redistribution along the lines of Rawls's Difference Principle—to make the exit mechanism accessible to all." However, determining whether a basic income or a more ambitious level of redistribution is best for people's exit opportunities would require exitocrats to make predictions about the reactions of an ideationally heterogeneous population to different levels of taxation and resources.[17] Perhaps an exitocracy with limited redistribution would guarantee everyone a minimal ability to exit while allowing the greatest possible scope for free markets to create new opportunities for entry. Alternatively, perhaps the market is less reactive to state interventions, and therefore more redistribution can significantly improve the exit options of the worst off without reducing the potential of the market to create more options. Determining which of these scenarios is likely, and therefore which form of exitocracy is preferable, requires significant technocratic judgments.[18]

Another exit-supporting good is the provision and enforcement of a system of property rights. As with redistribution, Friedman recognizes that the provision of such goods requires technocratic forms of knowledge (340-41). To see the problems this produces for his defense of exitocracy, it is important to understand the role of technocratic knowledge in determining whether a system of property rights will actually promote exit and its associated benefits. Alternative property systems can have varying effects on the ability of people to exit, and these effects can be negative as well as positive (Greenwood 2007). Consider, for instance, the following possible scenarios.

5. The exitocratic state provides a system of property rights that includes rights to intellectual property. Although the exitocrats predict that this will provide incentives for technological innovation, the unintended result is the creation of large monopolies in certain industries (such as those that suffer from network effects), which reduce competition and therefore the exit options of individuals within them.

6. The exitocratic state provides a system of property rights that recognizes extensive common-property regimes. Although the exitocrats predict that this will provide many people with access to property, the unintended result is to increase the cost of exit, as property rights become less flexible.

7. The exitocratic state develops a system of property rights that does not grant the state significant powers of eminent domain. Although the exitocrats predict that this will give individuals the greatest scope to use their resources to improve their condition, the unintended result is

to make the provision of secondary and tertiary public goods more difficult, resulting in greater costs from which individuals cannot escape.

Again, I do not wish to claim that any of these scenarios would actually result from these alternative property systems; they may not. However, determining whether or not these problems will come about, and which rules of property will produce them, requires technocratic forms of knowledge on the part of the exitocratic state. Factors such as the balance of private and common property, the status of intellectual property, and the extent of (or need for) eminent domain can have very different effects on the efficiency of a property-rights system, and thus on the ability of individuals to exit from problematic arrangements. Determining which bundles of rights and duties will promote or decrease the ability of individuals to exit from their social problems, like judging the consequences of redistribution, requires making predictions about the behavior of heterogeneous individuals.

Different property systems can, for instance, produce different levels of market concentration and different risks of monopoly, as can be seen in scenario 5. These factors directly affect the number of exit and entry options consumers and employees face. Even if property rights are evenly distributed to begin with, in order to avoid concentration, markets can lead to large levels of inequality over time, which can threaten the ability of the worst off to exit. An exitocratic state would, therefore, need to make long-term predictions about the behavior of individuals in order to compare alternative property systems in terms of their results for exit. Of course, an exitocratic state may instead rely on competition policies (e.g., antitrust law) in the event of the unexpected development of an oligopoly or monopoly. However, the use of such policies would leave the exitocratic state in a very similar position to a technocratic state in needing to judge the consequences of policy interventions in the market economy. It would need to know how a given intervention would affect the behavior of a large number of ideationally diverse individuals, and the resulting effect of this on overall exit opportunities.

One might reply that although the choice between competing legal systems would require technocratic knowledge, we know that the exitocratic state must provide *some* system of private property rights in order to create an environment in which individuals can utilize exit. It does not matter which system the exitocratic state chooses to provide, as any system of property rights would promote the ability of individuals to exit in comparison to having no system at all. However, the claim that any one state-provided private property system is better for people's exit opportunities than no state-provided system is itself a claim that requires technocratic knowledge to justify. There are examples of many ineffective state-provided legal systems, as well as examples of effective anarchist systems that manage the use of resources outside of the authority of any state, whether exitocratic or otherwise (Scott 1998 and 2009). It is possible, then, that there are some circumstances in which the best thing an exitocratic state can do to promote exit opportunities is not to define or enforce any system of private property rights at all. Knowing whether the provision of a particular property-rights system actually increases the ability of individuals to exit therefore requires significant amounts of technocratic knowledge on the part of the exitocratic state, just as does knowing how to redistribute property.

V. THE DILEMMA OF TECHNOCRATIC KNOWLEDGE

The dilemma facing exitocracy is that its distinctive mission of promoting and sustaining exit itself requires the prediction of human behavior and therefore technocratic knowledge. For Friedman, however, this dilemma should not stop us from preferring exitocracy to ordinary technocracy. He argues that although ordinary technocratic judgments are required in the provision of exit-supporting goods, "the inevitable errors that result will be offset, to some (putatively significant) extent, by the fact that these public goods will enable people to solve social problems in the private sphere," and thus "the mix of benefits and costs should be more favorable in an exitocracy" compared to a technocracy (341). So although it is not possible to know *how much better* an exitocracy could be, we can know that it is likely to be *somewhat better*, overall. The normative hierarchy in which we should "prefer exitocracy to ordinary technocracy and judicious to injudicious technocracy" therefore remains intact (343).

The discussion of the previous sections, however, gives reason to question this claim.

If technocratic knowledge is required to understand whether the actions of an exitocracy will actually promote or undermine exit, and if we accept Friedman's critique of such knowledge, then we can have no confidence that an exitocracy will provide any of the benefits associated with exit. In other words, we can have no confidence that the errors of an exitocracy will be offset by the resulting ability of people to exit, as Friedman claims.

Exitocracy is an extraordinary form of technocracy, which means that while it is similar to an ordinary technocracy, it is distinctive in the fact that it intervenes to increase exit opportunities whenever possible. Without reliable technocratic knowledge, however, it is not at all clear that these attempts at exit promotion will in any one case, and therefore overall, increase the ability of individuals to exit. These interventions may, in fact, lead to fewer exit opportunities overall than there would have been otherwise, as shown in scenarios 1-7 above. Thus, just as we can have no confidence that an ordinary technocracy can improve the human condition in the absence of reliable technocratic knowledge, we can have no confidence that an exitocracy can improve the ability of individuals to exit, and therefore enable these individuals to improve their own condition.

We are not therefore only ignorant of *how much better* an exitocracy would be, but also ignorant of whether it will be *better or worse overall*. In the absence of reliable technocratic knowledge, an extraordinary technocracy that attempts to promote exit may not result in a society where exit opportunities are more readily available compared to a society with an ordinary technocracy. Whether it is a change to the level of redistribution or an alteration to the property system, we cannot be sure that any exitocratic interventions will lead to more exit opportunities than there would be otherwise. We therefore have no reason to think that the errors of an exitocracy will be offset by the resulting benefits of exit, or that the mix of costs and benefits will be more favorable in an exitocracy compared to an ordinary technocracy. Without some reliable technocratic knowledge then, it is simply unclear which system is preferable. In other words, it is unclear whether the state should provide primary public goods, if the critique of technocratic knowledge given in Parts I-II of *Power Without Knowledge* is correct.

It could be claimed that an exitocracy would at least be preferable to ordinary technocracy *when it is successful*. A successful exitocracy would increase exit opportunities and therefore supplement its less reliable technocratic knowledge with the more reliable experimental knowledge of individuals in the private sphere. For exitocracy to be successful, though, it would need to have access to technocratic knowledge of some level of reliability (as established in the previous section). It would need to be able to make accurate predictions about how a population of ideationally heterogeneous individuals respond to its attempts to provide exit-supporting goods. If this level of technocratic knowledge existed, however, then it might also enable an ordinary technocracy to directly solve certain social problems. If predictions of human behavior can be made with sufficient reliability that an exitocracy can successfully promote exit options, then a technocracy may also be able to design successful technocratic policies.

A successful exitocracy may then allow more opportunities for individuals to exit and make use of their experimental knowledge. The problem is that these uses of experimental knowledge are parasitic on a prior use of reliable technocratic knowledge in the supply of exit-supporting goods. If technocratic knowledge can be used reliably in this way, then technocratic solutions may also be effective, and it is unclear whether it is best to use voice or exit in any given case. In other words, it would be unclear whether a successful exitocracy is better than a successful ordinary technocracy, given that the success of either presupposes access to reliable technocratic knowledge.

If Friedman's critique in Parts I-II of *Power Without Knowledge* turns out to be correct, then, I see no reason to rank exitocracy above ordinary technocracy in the normative hierarchy. Whether we are talking about institutional practice or ideal types, or whether we have access to reliable technocratic knowledge or are ignorant of it, it is not clear that an exitocracy will produce better outcomes than an ordinary technocracy. To make any claim about the relative superiority of technocracy and exitocracy, or about which combination of exit and voice is preferable, we would need to know more about the kinds of technocratic knowledge we can access, the conditions under which we can possess it, and the kinds of social interventions such knowledge makes possible. Whether through voice or exit, some form of technocratic knowledge will be required to deal with our persistent and significant social problems, and we therefore need to further investigate when and where such knowledge can be obtained, and what it allows us to do.

One can, of course, follow Friedman in making an "Adornoesque" cultural critique (344-45). *Power Without Knowledge* calls out the epistemi cally naïve attitudes, interpretively uncharitable theorizing, blindly positivistic research, and simplistic heuristics with which technocrats "injudiciously" approach politics and public policy, and indeterminacy over whether exitocracy can help alleviate the problems of ordinary technocracy may place additional emphasis on the need for a cultural revolution in the direction of a more judicious technocratic politics. The extent to which one supports such a revolution will depend on how convincing one finds Friedman's critique of currently exiting technocracy, and I have simply assumed this critique for the purpose of this paper. What I have argued is that if this critique turns out to be correct, then it will be inconclusive whether we should prefer exitocracy to ordinary technocracy. By elaborating on the epistemic quandaries of public good provision, this paper has questioned whether the problems that Friedman sees as facing ordinary technocracy can be reduced by having the state prioritize exit over voice. Determining the relative role of exit and voice will require further investigation into which kinds of reliable technocratic knowledge can be obtained and which kinds social interventions can be made of the basis of such knowledge.

It is possible that such an investigation will find that no form of reliable technocratic knowledge can be achieved either now or in the foreseeable future. However, an appropriate response to this ignorance would not be exitocracy, which itself requires such knowledge, but perhaps an alternative such as some form of pure procedural legitimacy. If we cannot possess any kind of technocratic knowledge, then we may have to give up hope of solving our social problems through the political or economic system, and the only remaining basis for a just politics would be its procedural fairness. Alternatively, however, if we can possess some technocratic knowledge, then we need to know what form this knowledge takes before we can rule in favor of ordinary technocracy, exitocracy, or any combination of the two.

NOTES

1. Friedman (108-9) does argue that technocracy has a tendency to move in the direction of elite rule or epistocracy if people determine that specialized knowledge, not available to the general public, is required to address social problems. As a matter of definition, however, technocracy, on his view, is compatible with a diversity of different forms of rule.
2. The main focus of the essay is the extent to which an exitocracy can avoid reliance on technocratic forms of knowledge, rather than Friedman's direct critique of the likelihood of such knowledge. A brief account of this critique will, therefore, suffice for our purposes, and I will simply take the critique as given for the rest of the paper.
3. People's ideas are also open to change over time, which adds another layer of difficulty to the prediction of an individual's behavior. Even if you know someone's

ideas at time T1, this does not mean you can necessarily predict their behavior at time T2, as her web of beliefs may have changed (143).

4. The first of these, which Dowding and John 2012 refers to as "geographical exit," can be more costly, as it requires moving locations. DeCanio 2014 argues that this is also a less epistemically valuable form of exit, as it involves making comparisons of services across different jurisdictions, and therefore different conditions, rather than within one jurisdiction.
5. Throughout Chapter 7 Friedman (330-31, 322-23) tends to conflate the distinction between exit and voice with the distinction between the private and public spheres.
6. For a direct critique of these Hayekian arguments for markets, including those that focus on dispersed and tacit knowledge, see Benson 2019a and 2019b.
7. Hayek also appeals to the ability of firms to learn from and imitate each other's successes. For many classical liberals the ability of firms to emulate each other's successes and avoid their failures is an important part of the market's epistemic value, as it allows good ideas to spread throughout society. Given Friedman's pessimism about our ability to uncover the causes of and solutions to social problems, I suspect that he would question how effective any process of imitation or emulation could be. Even if some firms are more successful than others, it may be difficult, on Friedman's view, for other firms to work out how they are successful and copy their methods.
8. For a critical comment on these claims see Benson 2019a.
9. These terms are my own and are not used by Friedman to describe his preferred system or any other.
10. It is important to note that these epistemic critiques of classical liberalism do not reject markets and their epistemic benefits outright. Rather they tend to point to their limits and the need for a greater role for the public sphere.
11. Goods are often not simply public or private but rather fall somewhere between the two. The argument of this section covers goods that tend to exhibit significant publicness characteristics.
12. The labels "secondary" and "tertiary" do not therefore speak to the importance of these goods, but to the extent to which they can utilize exit.
13. See Jacobs 1991 for examples of the problems facing these kinds of policies.
14. Friedman (333-334) does discuss medicine and pharmaceuticals, but only in relation to the problem of irreversibility or repeatability, and not in relation to the feedback problem I discuss here. In these passages Freidman rightly points out that certain products have possible fatal effects from which individuals could not possibly exit.
15. I have elsewhere referred to goods which exhibit this lack of feedback as *low feedback goods* Benson 2019a.
16. We may also judge these systems in terms of other normative criteria, such as standards of justice.
17. The very same problem faces classical liberals who wish to resist significant levels of redistribution.
18. Friedman's book opens the possibility of further research comparing different kinds of exitocracy, including varieties beyond the egalitarian and the classical liberal. There could, for instance, be a *libertarian exitocracy* which involved no redistribution at all, or a *radical egalitarian exitocracy* which involved redistributions along the lines of strike equality (Carens 1981; Cohen 2009).

REFERENCES

Akerlof, George. 1970. "The Market for 'Lemons': Quality Uncertainty and the Market Mechanism." *Quarterly Journal of Economics* 84(3): 488–500.

Barry, John, 1999. *Rethinking Green Politics*. London: SAGE.

Bennett, Michael. 2016. "Experiments in Distributive Justice and Their Limits." *Critical Review* 28(3-4): 461-83.

Benson, Jonathan. 2018. "Environmental Law and the Limits of Markets. *Cambridge Journal of Economics* 42(10): 215-30.

Benson, Jonathan. 2019a. "Knowledge and Communication in Democratic Politics: Markets, Forums and Systems." *Political Studies* 67(2): 422-39.

Benson, Jonathan. 2019b. "Deliberative Democracy and the Problem of Tacit Knowledge." *Politics, Philosophy & Economics* 18(1): 76-97.

Brennan, Jason. 2016. *Against Democracy*. Princeton: Princeton University Press.

Caplan, Bryan. 2007. *The Myth of the Rational Voter: Why Democracies Choose Bad Policies*. Princeton: Princeton University Press.

Carens, Joseph. 1981. *Equality, Moral Incentives, and the Market*. Chicago: University of: Chicago Press.

Cohen, G. A. 2009. *Why Not Socialism?* Princeton: Princeton University Press.

Cordato, Roy E. 1997. "Market-Based Environmentalism and the Free Market: They Are Not the Same. *The Independent Review* 1(3): 1086-1653.

Daly, Herman E. 1992. *Steady-State Economics*. London: Earthscan.

DeCanio, Samuel. 2014. "Democracy, the Market, and the Logic of Social Choice." *American Journal of Political Science* 58 (3): 637–52.

Dowding, Keith, and Peter John. 2012. *Exits, Voices, and Social Investment*. Cambridge: Cambridge University Press.

Eckersley, Robyn. 2004. *The Green State*. Cambridge, Mass.: MIT Press.

Friedman, Jeffrey. 2019. *Power Without Knowledge*. New York: Oxford University Press.

Gamble, Andrew. 1996. *Hayek: The Iron Cage of Liberty*. Cambridge: Polity Press.

Greenwood, Dan. 2007 "The Halfway House: Democracy, Complexity, and the Limits to Markets in Green Political Economy." *Environmental Politics* 16(1): 73–91.

Greenwood, Dan. 2010. "Facing Complexity: Democracy, Expertise and the Discovery Process." *Political Studies* 58: 769-88.

Habermas, Jürgen. 1970. *Toward a Rational Society: Student Protest, Science, and Politics*, trans. Jeremy J. Shapiro. Boston: Beacon

Habermas Jürgen. 1976. *Legitimation Crisis*, trans. Thomas McCarthy. Cambridge: Polity Press

Hayek, F. A. 1948. "The Use of Knowledge in Society." In idem, *Individualism and Economic Order*. Chicago: University of Chicago Press.

Hayek, F. A. 1960. *The Constitution of Liberty*. London: Routledge.

Hayek, F. A. 2014. "The Facts of the Social Sciences." In idem, *The Market and Other Orders*, ed. Bruce Caldwell. Chicago: University of Chicago Press.

Hirschman, Albert O. 1970. *Exit, Voice and Loyalty*. Cambridge, Mass.: Harvard University Press.

Jacobs, Michael. 1991. *The Green Economy*. London: Pluto.

Kirzner, Israel M. 1985. *Discovery and the Capitalist Process*. Chicago: University of Chicago Press.

Landemore, Hélène. 2013. *Democratic Reason*. Princeton: Princeton University Press.

Landemore, Hélène. 2014. "Yes, We Can (Make It Up on Volume): Answers to Critics." *Critical Review* 26(1-2): 170-83.

Lippmann, Walter. [1922] 1997. *Public Opinion*. New York: Free Press.

O'Neill, John. 2012. "Austrian Economics and the Limits of Markets." *Cambridge Journal of Economics* 36: 1073–1090.

Pennington, Mark. 2011. *Robust Political Economy*. Cheltenham: Edward Elgar.

Popper, Karl. 2013. *The Open Society and Its Enemies*. Princeton: Princeton University Press.

Quine, W.V.O., and J. S. Ullian. 1978. *The Web of Belief*, 2nd ed. New York: Random House.

Scott, James C. 1998. *Seeing Like a State*. New Haven: Yale University Press.

Scott, James C. 2009. *The Art of Not Being Governed*. New Haven: Yale University Press.

Spash, Clive. 2005. *Greenhouse Economics*. London: Routledge.

Stiglitz, Joseph. 1991. *The Invisible Hand and Modern Welfare Economics*. NBER Working Paper w3641.

Stiglitz, Joseph. 1994. *Whither Socialism?* Cambridge, Mass.: MIT Press.

Tebble, Adam J. 2015. *Epistemic Liberalism*. London: Routledge.

Étienne Brown and Zoe Phillips Williams

DISAGREEMENT, EPISTEMIC PARALYSIS, AND THE LEGITIMACY OF TECHNOCRACY

ABSTRACT: *Jeffrey Friedman convincingly argues that technocrats may often lack the knowledge required to enact public policies that will effectively promote their consequentialist goals. Friedman's argument is strong enough to produce technocratic paralysis, in many cases, but "epistemic gambles" may present a way out of this problem. His discussion of exitocracy also raises the question of how to square his internal form of technocratic critique with the question of democratic legitimacy.*

Contrary to what its preface suggests, Jeffrey Friedman's *Power Without Knowledge: A Critique of Technocracy* (Oxford University Press, 2019) is a timely contribution to political epistemology in the so-called post-truth era. In a polarized age, it is all too easy for citizens to explain away political conflicts by assuming that those who disagree with them do so because they lack interest in the truth or are solely interested in ideological dominance. By way of contrast, Friedman argues that policy disagreements may occur not because citizens and epistocrats have bad intentions or poor epistemic standards, but rather because they apprehend facts through unavoidably incompatible and self-reinforcing interpretations of social reality. Such individuals may have good intentions and sincerely hope to minimize widespread suffering in society through their preferred course of political action, yet may seem to their political opponents to be malign. Before discussing Friedman's critique of technocracy at length, it is therefore worth noting that *Power Without Knowledge* has the potential to be a conciliatory force in a deeply divided society, as it incites us to envision our political rivals as individuals who think they see a different aspect of reality instead of malevolent lunatics against whom we have no choice but to engage in a fight to the death.

Power Without Knowledge is also a provocative book for the left. Friedman points out that technocratic egalitarians are epistemically complicit in assuming that we can easily predict how individuals who hold heterogenous ideas will react to the incentives embedded in social policy. In his view, attentiveness to differences among individuals' ideas, a commitment to a private sphere in which people can use the exit mechanism to maneuver their way around the problems they encounter, and substantial redistributive policies that give people maneuvering resources might better serve left-wing goals than does the traditional technocratic state, as the knowledge needed to replace individual maneuvering with technocratic manipulation may elude us. Whether or not one ultimately endorses Friedman's defense of a judicious "exitocracy," his epistemic argument, according to which state actions motivated by negative-utilitarian purposes might ultimately be counterproductive to human well-being, is bound to stimulate novel conversations in left-wing circles.

In what follows, we set aside the book's manifest strengths to make three points about different parts of its argument. First, despite concurring with Friedman's tolerationist attitude toward political disagreement, we contend that badly intentioned political actors do exist and do manipulate technocratic policy debate. Second, we suggest that while Friedman admits that his argument produces theoretical perplexity when it comes to institutional recommendations beyond the use of exit, there may be ways of reducing this perplexity. Finally, we wonder what happens when the political theorist draws back from the purely internal inquiry in which Friedman engages, according to which technocracy is judged according to its own utilitarian standards rather than external standards such as democratic legitimacy.

As we conceive of them, our discussions of these issues do not fundamentally challenge Friedman's central argument. Instead, we hope that that they will spark a discussion about some central themes of Friedman's book: his conception of interest-driven and value-driven policy disagreements, the nature of his critique of technocracy, and the question of the political legitimacy of technocracy.

I. THE ROOTS OF POLICY DISAGREEMENT

For a variety of reasons, Friedman defines "technocracy" not as rule by epistemic elites—epistocracy—but as rule by anyone, elite or not, who claims to know how to solve a social or economic problem besetting a given polity. This broad definition points to the "inherently epistemic" nature of the technocratic project (10), because one cannot solve a problem without knowing its causes and the effect that one's remedy is likely to have. The broad definition also suggests that even the democratic parts of our polity can be seen as technocratic, to some extent.

Friedman takes two dives into public-opinion research: a brief one in the Introduction and a very long one in Chapter 6. In these discussions, he argues (inter alia) that at least in the United States, members of the general public often have policy opinions that presuppose tacit knowledge claims about social and economic problems. For example, he points out that (at least until recently) there has been a widespread consensus among American citizens around "ends that can be pursued technocratically" (7). Most U.S. citizens long seem to have believed, for example, that full employment, a high standard of living, and peace are legitimate public goals (8). These goals lend themselves to technocratic policy making because they are consequentialist goals. As such, they require policy makers—whether epistocrats, who claim to have esoteric social-science knowledge, or "citizen-technocrats," who do not—to know, reliably if not perfectly, what the consequences of various policy options are likely to be: that is, their empirical costs and benefits. If disagreements amongst epistocrats or citizen-technocrats cannot be explained by conflicting views about the ends they ought to pursue, an alternative possibility is that disagreement emerges as a result of the difficulties they have in identifying which policies would most effectively help them achieve their shared consequentialist values.

The Fact of Technocratic Disagreement

Friedman's argument about these difficulties begins with a ground-clearing exercise in Chapter 1: a critique of what he calls "naïve technocratic realism," or the assumption that technocratic truths are self-evident. If this assumption held true, then there would be no possibility of criticizing technocratic knowledge claims, which is the purpose of the book. Therefore, naïve realism must be dispelled before Friedman can begin to argue that technocratic realities are not merely un-self-evident, but difficult to discern (Chapters 2-3). As he puts it in the book's Introduction,

> Some readers may find it odd to ask, as I will, whether we have sufficient knowledge of how to solve social and economic problems. These readers may come to think it clear that at least in some cases, technocratic questions have fairly obvious answers: namely, the answers that they themselves would give if they were asked such questions. A critical epistemology of technocracy may therefore fall on deaf ears. If it is to gain a hearing, the reader must be willing to interrogate her own technocratic opinions, asking of them: *How do I know?* "Naïve technocratic realism" stems from the failure to ask this question. It is the view that . . . technocratic questions have self-evident answers. Chapter 1 confronts naïve technocratic realism. . . . It does so, in part, by analyzing examples of unintended policy consequences that have been alleged in real-world policy debates. If, as is alleged, technocratic policies produce *unintended* effects, then the truth about the policies' effects must not have been self-evident to the technocrats who designed the policies.
>
> However, to argue that technocratic actions *may* cause unintended consequences, as I will do in Chapter 1, is not equivalent to arguing that these consequences will in fact occur. . . . Such an argument would amount to a critique of the reliability of technocratic knowledge, to which the rest of Part I and Part II will be devoted. Chapter 1 merely sets the stage by introducing the thought that there is something about modern social problems, or modern society, that *might* make it difficult to acquire the knowledge necessary to quell technocratic disagreement. (25-26)

Friedman's initial rebuttal to naïve technocratic realism invokes what he calls "the fact of technocratic disagreement" (39-46). If technocrats disagree, then whatever they disagree about cannot be self-evidently true. Thus, the "fact of technocratic disagreement is fatal to the naïve technocratic realist's assumption that her opinions about social problems are self-evidently true" (42). This is only the case, however, when disagreements are caused not by value conflicts, or by the pursuit of clashing private interests, but by a sincere "sociotropic" or public-spirited difference of opinion over the nature of a given social problem, or about which policy measures would solve, alleviate, or prevent it. Thus, one might defend naïve technocratic realism on the grounds that technocratic debate does not, in fact, concern empirical matters, rather than values, a point to which we will return; or on the grounds that what may seem to be sincere disagreement about how to solve social problems for society in general is actually a cover for a clash of private interests, some or all of whom are lying about the empirical effects of the policies they advocate so as to hoodwink decision makers into doing the wrong thing.

The latter possibility may be asserted as an empirical claim about the bad motives of particular participants in a given policy debate, as we will show below. But it may also be asserted as a self-evident truth by the naïve technocratic realist, in an attempt to rebut the fact of technocratic disagreement. Friedman calls this move "the naïvely cynical rejoinder to the fact of technocratic disagreement" (43). According to the naïvely cynical rejoinder, the claims made in technocratic debate by those who disagree with the naïve technocratic realist—who assumes that her own technocratic views are self-evidently true—must, *of necessity*, be dishonest, such that the fact of technocratic disagreement is really the fact that there is a sham debate going on under the cover of an honest one. The naïvely cynical rejoinder, in short, is an a priori denial that there *could* be honest technocratic disagreement among reasonable people, which Friedman calls "ideal policy debate" (44). Insofar as the truth is self-evident, no honest disagreement about it could ever occur.

In reply to the naïvely cynical rejoinder, Friedman does not maintain that in empirical reality, ideal policy debate is what we witness whenever we read a newspaper or turn on cable news. He does not deny "that some (or conceivably all) real-world policy debate is insincere" (ibid.). Rather, he contends that there are two reasons to think that ideal policy debate, or honest technocratic disagreement, is always warranted, *regardless* of whether it actually occurs.

First, ideal technocrats would need four types of technocratic knowledge that may be difficult to acquire: knowledge of which social problems are widespread (amounting to knowledge of the benefits of solving them), knowledge of their causes, knowledge of which technocratic actions can efficaciously solve them, and knowledge of the costs of these efficacious solutions. The difficulty of acquiring these types of knowledge (for example, statistical knowledge) entails that they cannot be self-evident; therefore, disagreement about them may be warranted

(46-49). Second, some of the costs of a policy may be unintended, and an unintended cost clearly cannot have been self-evident (to those who failed to intend it). In this sense, unintended consequences may be *counterintuitive*. In Chapter 1, Friedman does not argue that unintended consequences actually occur, such that counterintuitive claims in real-world policy debate (as opposed to ideal policy debate) are actually true. But he does try to establish that unintended consequences might conceivably occur, warranting counterintuitive claims in ideal policy debate.

He tries to establish that by discussing some examples of the counterintuitive mechanisms adduced by participants in real-world policy debate (49-57). Friedman maintains that regardless of whether such mechanisms actually come into play a given case or in any real case, so long as their existence is *plausible,* then honest policy debate over them would be warranted, because their counterintuitiveness would demand that we go beyond our perceptions of self-evident truth: when we do that, we *may* end up disagreeing with one another, contra the naïve technocratic realist. By reflecting on the nature of counterintuitive mechanisms, then, Friedman argues that it is *always* possible that one can construct honest counterintuitive technocratic arguments, such that honest technocratic disagreement among ideal technocrats might always be warranted, however often this fails to occur in practice (57).

Beyond Ideal Technocratic Debate

Without denying that political theorists (ibid., Introduction) and real-world technocrats alike (ibid., Part II) often underplay the possibility of honest disagreement about policies viewed as technocratic means to consensual, consequentialist ends, it is worth reflecting upon the extent to which real-world policy disagreements may nevertheless be underpinned by conflicts about ends or by dishonesty about facts. In this section we will discuss both possibilities. First we turn to value conflicts. For a technocratic policy consensus to obtain, it must be the case that citizens and epistocrats agree both about which ends are legitimate *and* about how they should be ranked. For example, there is widespread disagreement in the United States about the desirability of implementing a single-payer health-care system. But what are epistocrats and citizen-technocrats actually disagreeing about when they differ over this policy? Friedman's framework invites us to envision the disagreement as technocratic in character. Perhaps, for instance, people disagree about the likelihood that a single-payer system will lead to a general increase in the American population's health. A second possibility, however, is that they agree about the likely consequences of single payer, but disagree about whether an increase in health is worth sacrificing economic freedom through higher taxation. If this is so, then their putative agreement on ends will be superficial: all can agree that *both* economic freedom and health are important democratic goals while disagreeing that the latter should systematically trump the former, or vice versa.[1] As Gerald Gaus (2003) argues, people might disagree about a specific policy not because it appeals to an end that they do not share, but because they appeal to a ranking of ends that they do not share. Yet disagreements about the ranking of ends still count as value conflicts. It also seems reasonable to assume that citizen-technocrats or epistocrats may disagree among themselves because they are primarily interested in advancing their own private interests, those of a specific interest group, or those of a restricted part of the population. The idea that interest groups work to influence policy makers and outcomes is not controversial (Milner 1997). The billions of dollars spent annually on lobbying, campaign finance, Super PACs and other avenues for so-called "dark money" suggests that, at the very least, members of special-interest groups themselves believe that they have the capacity to influence policy making to be favorable to their private ends.[2]

A contemporary example is illustrative of what we take to be the effect of bad intentions in shaping policy decision-making in the United States: efforts by fossil-fuel corporations to conceal scientific evidence of climate change from the public, spread misinformation about its causes, and "capture" political actors in order to further their policy preferences. Of course, selecting the best set of policies with which to tackle climate change is an area rife with legitimate technocratic disagreement. However, we are here focusing on the outright denial of the existence of anthropogenic climate change and efforts to spread disinformation about this reality, efforts that seem intended to prevent honest technocratic discussion of the issue altogether.

Chapter 6 of *Power Without Knowledge*, which concerns public opinion, provides a sweeping reinterpretation of research on the subject since the Columbia and Michigan schools of the mid-twentieth century. Friedman suggests that the researchers' discovery of high levels of "public ignorance" may not indicate, as is so often asserted (e.g., Caplan 2007, Somin 2013, and Brennan 2016), that voters recognize the insignificance of their individual votes, and thus the pointlessness of adequately informing themselves. Instead, it may indicate that voters assume that technocratic issues are so easy to resolve, epistemically, that what the voters require is not technocratic information (such as the four types of technocratic knowledge), but information about whether politicians actually *intend* to solve social and economic problems. Voters seem to assume that if elected officials have good intentions, it will be child's play for them to solve the people's social and economic problems, but if they have bad intentions, the problems will never be solved. Thus, it is as if voters are using their impressions about politicians' good or bad intentions as "heuristics" for whether or not politicians will accomplish technocratic goals. In Friedman's view this is overly simplistic, because even a well-meaning politician may lack reliable technocratic knowledge. Friedman might therefore reply to what we have said about climate-change skepticism by contending that those who deny the existence of anthropogenic climate change might be motivated by sincere belief, and that while Exxon Mobil and other fossil fuel companies might be bad *actors* for engaging in a decades-long cover-up of evidence linking fossil fuels to global warming, we should not attribute bad *intentions* to politicians or citizens who fell for the ruse.

While this type of skepticism may be warranted in some cases, for several reasons we doubt that it can be the primary explanation for why climate-change denial continues to be spouted by important political actors. First, in response to Exxon's own admission that it engaged in this coverup and the purposive spread of misinformation (Dunlap and McWright 2011), there has not been a widespread, publicly announced commitment by formerly climate change-denying politicians to take a second look at the scientific evidence. Second, it is worth noting that climate skepticism is not popular amongst the electorate. According to recent poll data, a plurality of both Democrats and Republicans think the government should do more to tackle climate change (Funk and Heffernan 2019). Thus, it is not plausible that rather than having bad intentions, climate-denying politicians are merely reflecting the priorities of their constituents.

In summary, while the bad-intentions heuristic is undeniably a heuristic, it may not always be a bad one—something that Friedman himself suggests when he abstains from assessing whether citizens' suspicion that Congress is too heavily influenced by interest groups is warranted (296). This is not to say, however, that Friedman is wrong to claim that political theorists or technocrats who deny that policy conflicts result from honest disagreement about means may, in a given case, be epistemically naïve. In our view, demonstrating that social reality is much harder to apprehend than what such political theorists or technocrats seem willing to admit is, in fact, the central achievement of *Power Without Knowledge*.

From Non-Self-Evident to Unreliable Knowledge

As we have seen, Friedman's critique of naïve technocratic realism, and thus of the assumption that technocratic realities are self-evident, occurs as a ground-clearing exercise in Chapter 1 of *Power Without Knowledge*. This critique is designed to block a pre-emptive dismissal of the book's question—*Is technocratic knowledge likely to be reliable?*—on the grounds that technocratic knowledge is not only reliable but infallible, because technocratic realities are self-evident (25). Having appealed to the fact of technocratic disagreement as prima facie evidence for the non-obviousness of technocratic truths—there could be no honest debate about them if they were self-evident—Friedman has "set the stage" for the rest of the book by establishing the inherent *fallibility* of technocratic knowledge claims (26). Chapters 2 and 3 then offer an argument for the possibility that technocratic knowledge claims are, on the whole, *unreliable*. This new argument is predicated not on the fact of technocratic disagreement, but on two propositions for which Friedman offers suggestive evidence that we find plausible: (i) that people's conscious behavior is governed by their ideas about how to respond to their situations, as they themselves interpret these situations; and (ii) that these interpretations are likely to differ, to some extent, because of interpersonal heterogeneity in the webs of belief on which each person's interpretations draw (134-46). These propositions, concerning our nature as ideational beings, are relevant to technocracy for the following reason. Technocratic initiatives almost invariably aim to manipulate people's behavior so as to solve a social or economic problem, and successfully doing this entails predicting how people will act in response to the manipulations. Yet technocrats are people too, so their webs of belief may differ, to some extent, from those whose behavior they are attempting to manipulate, and this may cause the manipulations to produce unintended behavioral consequences. In short, they may believe that people will respond to a given policy by behaving in a manner that solves a social problem, but this belief will be grounded in an interpretation of how people in a given situation will interpret that situation, and this interpretation may differ from the one that emanates from the webs of belief of those people themselves. This may make technocratic knowledge not only fallible (Chapter 1), but unreliable (Chapters 2-3). While the naïve technocratic realist believes in the infallibility of her knowledge of a particular social problem and its solution, a view that is defeated by the fact of technocratic disagreement (and by Friedman's rebuttal to the naïvely cynical rejoinder to this fact), this defeat does not say anything about the *likelihood,* rather than the mere possibility, that any given technocratic claim is true.

By the time Part I of the book (Chapters 1-3) has concluded, however, Friedman has provided a theoretical argument for only the *possibility* of unreliable (as opposed to merely fallible) technocratic knowledge. To be sure, if ideational heterogeneity were the only thing affecting people's behavior, then there might be reason to believe that technocratic predictions about their behavior will be unreliable. However, ideational heterogeneity may be offset, to a greater or lesser extent, by homogenizing ideational forces such as shared social norms (169-71). Thus, Friedman does not claim that ideational heterogeneity decisively renders technocracy illegitimate by invalidating all technocratic knowledge claims or even by invalidating any such claims at all, because the possibility of unpredictable *behavioral* (as opposed to ideational) heterogeneity may be counteracted in any given case or, potentially, in every single case (ibid.). Therefore, Friedman maintains, the upshot of Part I is that any technocracy should "judiciously" try to investigate both heterogenizing and homogenizing ideational forces in attempting to craft policy responses to social and economic problems (171-77). Part II (Chapters 4-6), therefore, will explore whether this type of judiciousness is the norm in contemporary technocracies, and if not, why not.

Injudiciousness and Dissensus

Part II argues that at present, technocrats seem to be anything but judicious. Chapter 4 contends that neoclassical economists, our leading technocrats, try to predict people's behavior from their objective circumstances, skipping over agents' subjective interpretations of these circumstances entirely; this means that, of necessity, neoclassical economists are ignoring the possible heterogeneity of those interpretations (183-96). This a priori effacement of ideational heterogeneity has recently been challenged by various forms of positivism, such as the vogue for natural and controlled experimentation in economics, but here what tends to happen is that an otherwise-admirable empiricism is undercut by the positivists' default assumption that people are homogeneous, with exceptions made only for heterogeneous but easily measured and non-subjective "factors," such that findings in one experimental setting tend to be seen as applicable everywhere and always (196-228). This approach, then, like the apriorism of neoclassical economists, rules out any appreciation for the possibility of unpredictable ideational heterogeneity.

In addition, Chapter 5 argues that epistocrats, being relatively knowledgeable, are prone to dogmatically reaffirm their interpretations of empirical evidence, falling victim to a process Friedman calls the "spiral of conviction"—an interpretivist take on confirmation bias and motivated reasoning. Only with a given interpretation, Friedman argues, can one begin to make sense of the welter of technocratic information, as an interpretation highlights some of this information as plausible while dismissing the rest of it as either implausible or incomprehensible. One becomes an epistocrat, then, by using interpretations to screen in a great deal of information that confirms the interpretations that make *this* information seem plausible—while unfairly screening out incongruent information as untrustworthy. The spiral of conviction leads epistocrats to accumulate a mass of self-confirming evidence, to which their *rational* response is to dogmatically reaffirm the initial interpretation.

On the other hand, according to Chapter 6, citizen-technocrats, being relatively uninformed (compared to epistocrats) by definition, are relatively open minded. Yet they may well lack the four types of technocratic knowledge. At present, they compensate for this ignorance by using simplistic shortcuts such as the intentions heuristics. These particular heuristics are encouraged by naïve technocratic realism, but Friedman's point here is not to criticize citizen-technocrats for treating the truth as self-evident but to observe that in doing so, they overlook the possibility of ideational heterogeneity. The upshot is not so much an unreasonably high level of certainty as the likelihood that citizen-technocrats will reach unjustifiable conclusions about which policies, politicians, and parties to support.

One might draw from Part II an explanation for why there may be disagreement among ideal (honest) technocrats that goes beyond the mere fact that technocratic truths are not self-evident to them. Technocrats' own ideational heterogeneity might lead them to adopt myriad theoretical and interpretative frames (including frames that make the truth *seem* self-evident to some of them, such as naïvely realistic citizen-technocrats). This possibility comes out with particular clarity in Chapter 4, when Friedman discusses the vagaries in epistocratic positivists' interpretations of various natural experiments with minimum wages (203-5); and in Chapter 6, when he discusses the intolerance that is likely to stem from citizen-technocrats' divergent conclusions about which political actors have bad intentions (301-14). Given ideational heterogeneity, then, sincere technocrats may genuinely disagree with one another about which policy is most likely to solve a given social problem not merely because the truth is not self-evident, but because they differ over how to interpret the non-self-evident truth.

Conversely, however, technocrats may *agree* with one another not because they have gotten hold of reliable knowledge of the non-self-evident truth, but merely because they share relatively homogeneous interpretive frameworks. Thus, a consensus in favor of a technocratic policy recommendation, even on the part of honest technocrats, does not itself warrant the conclusion that we should implement it. This is because even concurring technocrats might be unable to reliably predict the consequences such policies will produce, given the heterogeneity that might occur between their ideas and the ideas of the actors whose behavior they need to predict. An honest technocratic consensus may therefore converge around an incorrect prediction.

Thus, the role of dissensus (and consensus) undergoes a significant shift between Chapter 1 and the rest of the book. In Chapter 1, the a posteriori fact of technocratic dissensus initially falsifies naïve technocratic realism. Then, in response to the naïvely cynical, a priori rejoinder to the fact of technocratic disagreement, which holds that technocratic disagreement *must be* fake (since the truth is self-evident), Friedman contends that there is an a priori warrant for dissensus among honest technocrats: the fact that unintended consequences *might* occur. This should put an end to the *absolute* self-confidence of the naïve technocratic realist. The rest of Part I is dedicated to showing, theoretically, that there may be a posteriori grounds for further reducing technocratic confidence: namely, a neglect of ideational heterogeneity may, in a given case, spoil technocrats' predictions, *even if* these are both honest and consensual. Thus, we may be entitled to discount real-world technocratic consensus, even when it is honest, because real-world technocrats, at present, tend to ignore the ideational nature of human beings and therefore homogenize their conception of how people behave.

II. EPISTEMIC PARALYSIS AND EPISTEMIC GAMBLES

As we have seen, Chapter 1 of *Power Without Knowledge* is intended to establish that technocratic truths may not be self-evident. But this may mean nothing more than that technocrats need to do some kind of non-intuitive research (such as statistical research) in order to discover technocratic truths (50). Thus, Chapter 1 contends only that "gaps in technocratic knowledge *might* lead to policies that produce unintended consequences" (60, author's emphasis), producing enough uncertainty among technocrats to justify their honest disagreement about these policies—but not justifying a critique of the likelihood that they will, on the whole, enact counterproductive policies. The need for a bit of empirical research (reading a newspaper might count) says nothing about the likelihood that the research will be unsuccessful.

Thus, the fact that Chapter 1 contends that technocrats should display some level of certainty lower than the absolute certainty of naïve technocratic realists (who treat their technocratic opinions as self-evidently true) does not entail that we should be *so* uncertain that we doubt our ability to produce beneficial technocratic policies. It only entails that we should do some kind of research to confirm or deny our self-evident technocratic intuitions. Similarly, while Chapters 2 and 3 address the unreliability of technocratic knowledge, as opposed to its mere non-self-evidence, they do not establish its unreliability definitively or even presumptively. Rather, Friedman holds in these chapters that ideational heterogeneity *may* lead to unpredictable behavior (if it is not sufficiently counterbalanced by homogenizing ideas), such that predictive technocratic knowledge *may* be unreliable and technocratic initiatives *may* backfire—if and only if technocrats fail to judiciously and accurately gauge the clash of heterogeneous and homogeneous ideas from case to case. In turn, while Part II paints an empirical picture of the injudiciousness of contemporary technocracy, Friedman's analysis indicates that this may merely be a temporary problem that is itself a product of the cultural hegemony, among both epistocrats and citizen-technocrats, of unsound (anti-ideational) ideas—such as neoclassical economic beliefs, positivist assumptions about human uniformity, and the simplistic presuppositions that underlie the intentions heuristics. Like Part I, then, Part II offers no conclusive answers to the question of technocratic legitimacy.

Exitocracy as a Solution to Epistemic Quandaries

In light of all this theoretical uncertainty, Friedman opens Part III with a short section outlining three "quandaries" produced, for the theorist of technocracy, by Parts I and II. First, "it may be impossible to determine whether a technocracy transformed by the hoped-for, ideationally sensitive approach to public policy could reasonably be expected to pass the test of doing more good than harm." This uncertainty leads to the following question: "Even were they judiciously attentive to ideational heterogeneity, would technocrats, on the whole, be able to overcome the problems identified in Part I sufficiently to reduce the magnitude of their errors to an acceptable level?" (317). Second, neither Part I nor Part II establishes "the magnitude of the unintended consequences we can expect from an *in*judicious technocracy," because an a priori argument about the nature of human ideas cannot specify the degree of the empirical consequences to be expected from it. On the other hand, Friedman maintains that it would beg the question of the reliability of his own technocratic knowledge for him to try to assemble a posteriori evidence for or against the proposition that technocratic action tends to, or rather has tended to, backfire in the real world (317-18). Third and finally, "even if we were to conclude that either injudicious technocratic action or technocratic action of all kinds is illegitimate on internal grounds, technocratic *inaction* is not necessarily a logical alternative," as "'doing nothing,' that is, leaving the status quo as it is, holds no inherent epistemic advantages over 'doing something' unless the status quo has some inherently beneficial epistemic property in comparison to epistemic action" (319).

In short, Parts I and II of the book merely establish, at best, that unintended consequences produced by unpredictable behavior contingent on ideational heterogeneity is a *potential* source of technocratic illegitimacy, but they do not establish that this potential has been or is likely to be actualized. Friedman proposes, in Part III, to deal with this uncertainty, and the three quandaries to which it leads, by abjuring any claims about the absolute "magnitude" of the undesirable consequences that might or might not be produced by either injudicious or judicious technocracy. Instead, the one chapter in Part III (Chapter 7) will restrict itself to making relative comparisons among types of technocracy.

Speaking comparatively, for example, it seems clear (if one accepts the argument of Part I) that we should prefer a judicious technocracy to an injudicious one, even though we do not know either the magnitude of the unintended problems that might be caused by the latter, or the relief from these possible problems that we can expect from the former. For similarly comparativist reasons, Chapter 7 constructs an ideal type of an exitocracy to serve as a point of contrast against both judicious and injudicious technocracy, which might resolve the quandaries.

An exitocracy is an "extraordinary" type of technocracy that supplements the "ordinary" technocratic attempts to gather the four types of technocratic knowledge that are discussed in Parts I and II—whether these attempts are conducted judiciously or injudiciously—by making use of the knowledge that is sometimes available to people when they contemplate their own personal situations. This knowledge can be put to use if people have the power to exit from situations they find problematic and, crucially, if they have the power (such as financial resources) necessary to enter into other situations that may be more satisfactory.

Friedman's claim here is that one's knowledge of one's own degree of dissatisfaction with various situations is relatively unmediated by fallible interpretation, since dissatisfaction is a psychological state that is directly accessible to oneself (although this relative immediacy is not absolute, i.e., self-evident). An exitocracy would allow people to make use of this personal, experiential knowledge, wherever possible, by letting them experiment with alternatives to the problematic situations they personally experience—as when they exit from an inefficient rail service to more reliable buses or trains, to use Alfred O. Hirschman's classic example (Hirschman 1970). To the extent that people can engage in such experimentation, Friedman argues, they may be able, on the whole, to improve their condition more effectively than when they are required, as technocratic decision makers, to reliably know, and "voice," accurate interpretations of social problems.

In using the voice mechanism, "the technocratic decision-maker must reach far beyond experiential knowledge so as to judge the significance of social problems for anonymous others, to speculate about their causes, and to speculate about the efficacy of various solutions and the side effects they may cause" (319). Putting together the comparison between personal and impersonal knowledge and judicious and injudicious technocracy, Friedman continues, we can decide that an exitocracy would have epistemic advantages over an ordinary technocracy, whether or not it is judicious, "even as we keep in mind that judicious technocracy is preferable to the injudicious kind" (323). And we can reach this conclusion "without having to know the magnitude of the adverse unintended consequences of judicious or injudicious technocratic actions, or, on the other hand, the degree to which these actions achieve their intended objectives. Thus, we may be able to say that, in light of the interpretive difficulties that would face even judicious technocrats, ordinary technocracy is, comparatively speaking, illegitimate"(ibid.).

These two comparisons, however, do not add up to a blanket endorsement of the exit mechanism, and thus of exitocracy, over voice and ordinary technocracy in every case, for two reasons. First, there are imperfections of people's personal knowledge (332-34), which may sometimes make the exit mechanism ineffective, epistemically. Second, the institutional creation and defense of the exit mechanism will itself require ordinary technocratic knowledge (343-44). For example, Friedman holds that private property rights coupled with private property redistribution can, to some extent, give everyone the opportunity to use the exit mechanism to experiment with various options. Therefore, he characterizes an exitocracy as both capitalistic and socialistic (323 and Afterword). But both capitalist property rights and socialist redistribution can be organized in many different ways, and choosing among these will depend on our predictions about how people will respond to alternative institutional setups—technocratic predictions (340-41).

Public Goods and the Nature of Epistemic Critique

Friedman treats that problem as an opportunity for one final comparison by distinguishing among types of technocratic state functions. This comparison, however, leads him to an important impasse to which we may have something of an answer. Friedman divides technocratic functions into the provision of three types of public good, corresponding not to their normative importance but their contrasting roles in an ordinary technocracy and in an exitocracy.

First there are the public goods that directly enable people's ability to exit, such as a system of private property and redistribution. These he labels the "primary" goods of an exitocracy, because their provision would be the distinctive feature of an exitocratic state in contrast to an ordinary technocracy. "Secondary" public goods operate in a gray zone: there is no exit from them, strictly speaking, making them somewhat "ordinary." Yet ordinary technocratic reasoning can sometimes be used to create "exit-like devices," such as a carbon tax, that mimic exit by allowing individuals to experiment with heterogeneous behavior that may contribute to a solution to a public problem. In contrast to a carbon tax, a Green New Deal would count as an ambitious example of ordinary technocracy, insofar as it commands people to reduce carbon emissions in a host of particular, universally enforced ways, such as by installing solar panels. A carbon tax would mimic exit by allowing individuals to find their own way to solutions to the collective problem of climate change. Finally, there are "tertiary" public goods that can be provided only through ordinary technocratic reasoning, with no admixture of the exit mechanism. On epistemic grounds, Friedman argues, just as it is preferable for a technocracy to proceed judiciously rather than injudiciously, it is preferable for it to provide primary goods where possible, then secondary goods, followed by tertiary goods. This amounts to "a normative hierarchy of technocratic legitimacy" that, like the superiority of judicious to injudicious technocracy and the overall superiority of exitocracy to ordinary technocracy, enables us to "avoid the magnitude question" to some extent (343).

However, these comparative rankings must eventually stop—with tertiary public goods. Thus, even if it is preferable to provide people with exit opportunities or exit-like devices on epistemic grounds, there will be cases in which this is impossible, "such as territorial military defense, foreign policy, and many, many others" (342). In these cases it would, of course, be preferable for technocrats to be judicious, meaning ideationally sensitive. But this leaves us with the question of whether to provide tertiary public goods when there is no exitocratic or judicious alternative—given the mere possibility of unintended consequences that was established in Part I. Does this mere possibility justify hesitation in providing tertiary public goods?

Friedman cannot say. "While we have reason to prefer exitocracy to ordinary technocracy and judicious to injudicious technocracy," he writes, "it is not clear, at least to me, that the epistemological critique [of technocracy] tells us anything about whether to provide tertiary public goods, or any particular tertiary public goods, let alone how to do so" (343). As he recognizes, this is quite a serious problem if *Power Without Knowledge* is viewed as an *institutional* critique of technocratic knowledge, i.e., one that issues in recommendations for institutional design. For the tertiary public goods may well be the most important ones, from a negative-utilitarian point of view; a comprehensive list of the many tertiary public goods would be very long indeed. If *Power Without Knowledge* were intended to be an internal institutional critique of technocracy, then, its inability to say anything about tertiary public goods provision would leave the book silent about most of the things technocracies do and, from an internal perspective, should do in principle—barring epistemic problems of *high* magnitude.

Precisely because Friedman does not feel able to say anything about magnitudes that is not comparative in nature, he is left with a huge question mark when it comes to tertiary public goods. Friedman concludes that *Power Without Knowledge* should not be seen as being addressed primarily to questions of institutional design. "Political theory need not necessarily answer such questions," he writes. "It can simply be a spur to reflection on present realities." In that light, *Power Without Knowledge* "might be seen as a form of Adornoesque critical theory that cannot necessarily guide political action; or as a form of cultural action, not political action" (ibid.). Although Chapter 7 does produce the institutional recommendation that primary and secondary public goods be provided when possible, then, some of the most important passages of the book as a whole turn out to be allusions, at the end of each chapter in Part II, to what Friedman calls the "cultural revolution" that would be required in order to bring about a judicious technocracy (342; see also 228-29, 261-62, and 314-16). Friedman portrays this as a revolution against "the forms of false consciousness that seem to go with technocracy," among which are the "moralization" of political disagreement, which is predicated on seeing the truth as self-evident and one's political opponents, therefore, as deliberate propagators of evil (344).

Escaping the Trap of Theoretical Uncertainty

While we endorse this call for civility, we wonder if the question of tertiary public goods provision can be answered more definitively than Friedman thinks. We begin by concurring with Friedman about the last of the three quandaries he is trying to address. We agree that "doing nothing" has no epistemic advantage over doing something. But we would like to go a step further by suggesting that while there is no inherent epistemic advantage to doing nothing over doing something, doing something is often more rational than doing nothing.

If I find myself lying in a hospital bed dying of cancer, for instance, I might rationally choose to undergo a new experimental treatment even though I am told that medical researchers disagree about its risks and the nature of its potential benefits.[3] This is because the status quo, in this case, has very little value; if I don't do *something*, then my chances of recovery are practically nonexistent. Generalizing from this example, our suggestion is that the value of the status quo depends on the amount of suffering that it imposes on citizens. When the latter find the status quo unbearable, then a bias in favor of technocratic action—i.e., the belief that we ought to try *something* to solve a specific social problem—might be warranted. This something might be an exit option (as in the cancer example), and it might be an exit-like option (such as a carbon tax); it might also be a judicious ordinary technocratic action; and it might even, we think, be an injudicious technocratic action: one that does not gauge the balance between ideational heterogeneity and homogeneity.

Let us illustrate this point with a thought experiment. Imagine that you are witnessing the inhabitants of your village being violently assaulted by pillagers. Arguably, this is enough evidence for you to believe that the status quo is negatively affecting the well-being of your peers and that you ought to attempt to prevent the assault from continuing. Imagine also that you are aware of the following fact: when a similar raid happened in a nearby village, one inhabitant successfully convinced the pillagers to stop the attack by offering them all the luxury goods she possessed. This gives you a reason to believe that if you offered your own luxury goods to the pillagers, then the assault on your peers might stop. Of course, you do not *know* that this strategy will work, because of the possibility of ideational heterogeneity. The pillagers assaulting your peers might not be as interested in luxury goods as the ones who raided the nearby village. In your current situation, however, the status quo is so bad that it may be justified to try to stop the assault by offering luxury goods to the pillagers, even if you fall short of possessing judicious technocratic knowledge that this will work. This would not necessarily be the case if the status quo had more value than we are positing: if the pillagers were not attacking your peers, but merely tickling them, you might decide that offering them your luxury goods is not worth it. After all, luxury goods are not that easy to come by.

Of course, this thought experiment stipulates that you can evaluate both the significance and the causes of the problem facing the village through direct observation, something that technocrats who attempt to solve complex social problems may be unable to do. You also have evidence that the strategy you are contemplating worked elsewhere, and a clear estimate of this strategy's cost. Thus, you have the four types of technocratic knowledge, but it may not be reliable knowledge because you cannot investigate the question of whether your pillagers are dissimilar to the previous pillagers. Still, the status quo may have so little value that an episetmic gamble—i.e., an attempt to solve a social problem through technocratic action, despite the lack of reliable knowledge—might be worthwhile.

Let us consider, then, a situation in which a given country's health-care system causes distress as citizens struggle to afford drugs and necessary care.[4] If we have evidence that a health-care policy implemented in a neighboring country—e.g., regulating the price of brand-name and generic medications—proved effective at reducing the costs of medicines, then we may judge that it is worth adopting a similar policy even though it may have unintended consequences. Here again, the utilitarian value of the status quo is low enough for technocrats to escape epistemic paralysis about the provision of a tertiary public good, choosing action over inaction.

III. DEMOCRACY AND EXITOCRACY

We now turn to the implications of Friedman's critique of technocracy for the philosophical debate on the legitimacy of democracy. As Friedman points out (17), the conventional defenses of democracy are usually not technocratic in character. For instance, democracy is often portrayed as the regime that can most effectively promote non-utilitarian goods such as the moral autonomy of citizens, intellectual self-development, and non-domination. Scholars and citizens who conceive of the legitimacy of democracy in such terms are justifiably unmoved by contemporary defenders of epistocracy, such as Bryan Caplan (2007) and Jason Brennan (2016), according to whom we should remove political power from the hands of citizen-technocrats who are too ignorant or irrational to determine which public policies can best achieve negative-utilitarian goals. Against the likes of Caplan and Brennan, it is usually assumed that democracy is legitimate even if other political regimes reduce human suffering to a larger extent.

Caplan and Brennan are, in effect, conducting *external* critiques of democracy on the basis of a utilitarian criterion that is compatible with technocracy. In their hands, therefore, technocracy turns into epistocracy, because they assume that epistocrats, such as economists, somehow have access to reliable technocratic knowledge and that they use this knowledge rationally. Friedman, by contrast, is conducting a clearly specified "internal" critique of both citizen-technocracy and epistocracy, stipulating the negative-utilitarian norms of both types of technocracy as the criterion of legitimacy rather than attempting, as theorists such as Habermas have done, to evaluate technocracy externally, according to democratic criteria (21).

Friedman defends his approach on the grounds that previous critics of technocracy have taken for granted the ability of technocracy to meet its own goals. The young Habermas, for example, attributed to epistocrats almost magical epistemic powers but without explaining whence these powers derive (3-4). Since his criterion for evaluating technocracy, the criterion of democratic legitimacy, was an external one, he judged technocracy (which he, too, equated with epistocracy) as illegitimate no matter how well it performs. Indeed (Friedman argues), by positing epistocratic efficacy, Habermas was able to describe a dire situation in which epistocrats' successes at solving the populace's problems buy political legitimacy at the cost of stifling democratic discussion of the ends to be collectively pursued (3-4). Friedman brackets external criteria of legitimacy, such as democratic legitimacy, so he can begin an investigation of technocratic efficacy. In effect, this is what Caplan and Brennan also do, but they investigate only the internal legitimacy of citizen-technocracy, not that of epistocracy.

If we use Friedman's approach, however, practical questions would arise if we attempted actually to implement exitocratic reforms. What should happen, for example, if democratic citizens prefer ordinary technocratic solutions to exitocratic ones? What if they preferred public parks to private property in the same places, foregoing primary public goods in favor of tertiary ones? What if they preferred to confer in-kind benefits such as public housing on the poor rather than redistributing Rawlsian-Friedmanite primary goods, such as cash, to them—at least prior to such time as socialist redistribution is politically feasible? Or what if they preferred to provide public housing rather than giving housing vouchers to the poor, which exemplify secondary public goods? Those who defend democracy on non-utilitarian grounds are likely to argue that we must respect the will of the people in such cases even if we grant that bypassing it would lead to welfare gains.

In line with that view, one might argue that the practical prospects of exitocracy will depend on the majority of citizens' appreciation of its efficacy, which, as Friedman's chapter on public opinion suggests, will not necessarily be forthcoming. In this chapter, Friedman envisions a scenario in which some citizens attempt to explain the need for technocratic restraint (which we might think of as either the need for judiciousness or the need for primary or secondary public goods in preference to tertiary ones, where possible). In response, other citizens, using the bad-intentions heuristic, accuse those who favor restraint of wanting to aggravate social problems rather than solving them more effectively than can be expected from an unrestrained, ordinary technocracy (312–14). In response to the poor reception the members of the first group receive from their compatriots, it seems to us, they might be tempted to disregard the will of the people or to argue in favor of restrictions on voting, as Brennan has done—not on his grounds, that only those who possess a high quantity of an amorphous substance called "political knowledge" should rule, but on the more specific grounds that only those who understand exitocracy should be able to decide whether to use it.

None of these questions undermine the force of Friedman's critique of technocratic knowledge. In the end, these questions show that Friedman's arguments are sophisticated enough for readers to interpret them in more than one way. Does the book offer a powerful argument against the traditional welfare state, or does it remind us that welfare gains will elude us so long as material inequalities between citizens remain acute? Does it corroborate the epistocratic argument, going back to Plato, according to which we should remove political power from the hands of the ignorant masses, or does it subvert that argument by underlining that the legitimacy of democracy does not solely depend on its ability to reduce suffering? In the end, *Power Without Knowledge* does all of these things, which is a sure sign that it is as provocative as political epistemology can be.

NOTES

1. Alternatively, we can picture a citizen-technocrat or epistocrat who rejects health-care system x even though she agrees with others that it would optimally promote health in the American population, for instance because she believes that an alternative system y would provide individuals with fairer access to health care.

In this case, fairness would be conceived by some (but not by all) technocrats as a deontic constraint on the pursuit of welfare. We thank Joseph Stenberg for suggesting this example.

2. For example, it is estimated that the pharmaceutical industry spent over $280 million in government lobbying in the United States in 2018.
3. We thank Anand J. Vaidya for suggesting this example.
4. According to a recent Gallup poll (Witters 2019), 13.4 percent of Americans have reported that there has been a time in the last five years when a friend or family member passed away after not receiving treatment for their condition due to their inability to pay for it. In addition, 22.9 percent reported that there has been a time in the last 12 months when their household has been unable to pay for medicine or drugs that a doctor had prescribed for them because they didn't have enough money to pay for them.

REFERENCES

Berelson, Bernard R. 1952. "Democratic Theory and Public Opinion." *Public Opinion Quarterly* 16(3): 313–30.

Brennan, Jason. 2016. *Against Democracy*. Princeton: Princeton University Press.

Caplan, Bryan. 2007. *The Myth of the Rational Voter: Why Democracies Choose Bad Policies*. Princeton: Princeton University Press.

Dunlap, Riley E., and Aaron McWright. 2011. "Organized Climate Change Denial." In *The Oxford Handbook on Climate Change and Society*, ed. John S. Dryzek, Richard B. Norgaard, and David Schlosberg. Oxford: Oxford University Press.

Friedman, Jeffrey. 2019. *Power Without Knowledge. A Critique of Technocracy*. New York: Oxford University Press.

Funk, Cary, and Meg Heffernan. 2019. "U.S. Public Views on Climate and Energy." *Pew Research Center*, November 25..

Gaus, Gerald. 2003. "Liberal Neutrality: A Compelling and Radical Principle." In *Perfection and Neutrality*, ed. Steven Wall and George Klosko. Lanham, Md.: Rowman and Littlefield.

Hirschman, Albert O. 1970. *Exit, Voice, and Loyalty: Responses to Decline in Firms, Organizations, and States*. Cambridge, Mass.: Harvard University Press.

Milner, Helen. 1997. *Interests, Institutions and Information*. Princeton: Princeton University Press.

Open Secrets. 2020. "Coal Mining."

Somin, Ilya. 2013. *Democracy and Political Ignorance*. Stanford: Stanford University Press.

Witters, Dan. 2019. "Millions in U.S. Lost Someone Who Couldn't Afford Treatment." *Gallup*, November 12 2019.

Kevin J. Elliott

A FAMILY AFFAIR: POPULISM, TECHNOCRACY, AND POLITICAL EPISTEMOLOGY

ABSTRACT: *Jeffrey Friedman's* Power Without Knowledge *provides not only a critique of technocracy but a compelling story about the intimate relationship between three of today's most important political phenomena: populism, technocracy, and democracy. In contrast to many recent accounts that treat populism as a backlash against technocracy, Friedman's theory suggests that populism is a lineal descendent of technocracy, with which it shares substantial intellectual DNA. Friedman's implicit theory of populism helps to explain many of its core features, including its political stances, emotionality, and hostility to mediating institutions, in interpretively charitable ways. Central to Friedman's analysis is the importance of political epistemology, which supplies key connective tissue between the three phenomena. The relations between technocracy, democracy, and populism revealed by Friedman's theory generate both enlightening and disturbing implications for democratic theory.*

Perhaps the greatest irony of Jeffrey Friedman's book, *Power Without Knowledge* (Oxford University Press, 2019), is that it provides a powerful lens for understanding contemporary politics in the United States, and elsewhere, despite one of its central claims being that the social world is too complex for any individual to comprehend well. In modern conditions, Friedman argues, we are left to interpret the great buzzing confusion of the world as best we can within our necessarily incomplete (and thus partly obfuscatory) webs of belief. Nonetheless, if we combine Friedman's discussions of (1) technocracy as a political ideology, (2) naïve technocratic realism, and (3) the bad-intentions heuristic, we have something approximating a working model of populism that makes sense of some major elements of contemporary politics. This model has challenging implications for democratic theory, as it suggests that technocracy is a lineal descendent of—and, perhaps, a de facto successor to—democracy.

Understanding Populism Through Political Epistemology

Friedman has written perhaps the most insightful book on populism that I have yet seen, despite not setting out to do so. Populism is explicitly discussed across only seven pages (in the Introduction), yet it can be found between the lines in almost every chapter, with clusters around some of the most important topics of the book. Technocracy, as Friedman portrays it, leads to populism as a natural result of, *not* as a backlash against, the politics that technocratic legitimacy generates—because technocracy interacts with naïve technocratic realism and the resulting bad-intentions heuristic. Naïve realism and the bad-intentions heuristic, in turn, are simplistic ways of dealing with the technocratic responsibilities that devolve to citizens in what Friedman calls a democratic technocracy. Together, naïve realism and the bad-intentions heuristic constitute a primitive technocratic "political epistemology"—not, of course, in the sense of the scholarly study or theory of political knowledge, but in the sense of a set of interlocking assumptions about the availability to citizens and politicians of the knowledge required for them to fulfill their roles in a technocratic regime.

This understanding of populism goes beyond the usual accounts because it elucidates the specific hermeneutical or, in Friedman's terms, "ideational" mechanisms underlying populist politics. It does this by delving beneath the superficial features of populism, such as democratic erosion, exclusionary rhetoric, and the inhumane treatment of disfavored groups, which understandably occupy popular and scholarly attention. This political-epistemological approach also differs from other ideational approaches that seek to capture the essence of populism in a definition, or taxonomically, by means of a set of necessary and sufficient conditions (Mudde 2017). Instead, it illuminates the interpretations of the world and the normative presuppositions that drive populist politics from inside populist citizens' heads.

This last notion, that *ideas* drive populist politics, requires some brief unpacking that will help introduce three of Friedman's key methodological assumptions or commitments: ideational determinism, ideational heterogeneity, and interpretive charity.

Friedman assumes that human actions, like all empirical phenomena, are determined and thus are, *in principle*, predictable, even though in practice, such prediction is difficult, to say the least. For Friedman, it is not class or group identity as such that determines our behavior so much as it is our ideas. Understanding why Napoleon invaded Russia requires not just looking at the objective situation he faced in 1812, but also, and primarily, looking at his own *interpretation* of his situation. This is ideational determinism. Thus, Friedman posits intellectual history in a very broad sense—encompassing genealogies of ordinary people's interpretations of their situations, not just the interpretations of "intellectuals"—as the key to understanding their actions.

However, for Friedman, the trouble that historians have in identifying the ideas that led to the actions of a Napoleon is multiplied enormously when attempting to identify the ideas behind the actions of millions. One of Friedman's key insights is to insist on a truth universally acknowledged but rarely remembered: that people have widely varying and idiosyncratic understandings of the world around them. This is the assumption of ideational heterogeneity. Neglect of this important truth explains, according to him, the inscrutability of so many of the actions of others.

If we are to begin to grasp why someone acted a particular way, then, we must engage in an act of profound and thoroughgoing interpretive charity. We must take up, as best we can, their perspective, as alien as it may often be to us, and seek an explanation of their action that makes good sense in terms of their ideas, and not necessarily our own. Thus, to claim that ideas drive populism, as Friedman's analysis allows us to do, is not to assert an untenable idealism but rather to acknowledge the decisive empirical role that people's ideas about the world play in determining their behavior—in particular, in the case of politics, their interpretations of how society works and how it *should* work.

The normative side of *Power Without Knowledge* consists of an attempt to work through, in interpretively charitable ways, the implications of ideational determinism and ideational heterogeneity for the legitimacy of the technocratic enterprise. In brief, the question is how likely we are to achieve an intellectually charitable understanding of others in the mass societies governed by technocracy. This fundamental problem is set forth in Part I. Part II asks how the experts and "citizen-technocrats" of our day deal with this problem. In the final chapter of Part II, turning from experts to citizen-technocrats, Friedman sets out the simplistic technocratic presuppositions that lead to populism.

Populism and Technocracy, a Familial Relation

Technocracy is generally defined as rule by "experts"—those with special knowledge, such as scientists. Though the idea of rule by those who know is very old, technocracy as we know it—and, I would argue, technocracy as a *political* force and ideology today—are not. The contemporary notion of technocracy is the product of the politics of the early twentieth century, during which reform (or, rather, Reform) swept the emerging mass democracies of North America and Europe. As a political force in the United States, technocracy emerged in opposition to, and as a solvent for, the corruption of clientelistic systems of mass politics, especially urban machines, but also that of political parties and party government in general (Buenker 1988). This history matters because technocracy was once a fighting creed, and this creedal history has left indelible impressions that continue to shape politics today. Friedman's analysis reveals the *politics* that technocracy has made and continues to make in the United States. And I contend that part of the politics that technocracy has made is, in fact, contemporary populism (at least in the United States).

Thus, I suspect that Friedman's analysis reveals the true origin of populism, but not in the sense that previous analyses have suggested. Other analysts have juxtaposed populism and technocracy, often in almost Manichean terms. Jan-Werner Müller (2016) conceives them as "mirror images of each other," where technocracy sees there only being one correct policy and populism as there being only one authentic popular will. Likewise, Vivien Schmidt (2006) spots a tension between technocracy as "policy without politics" and populism as "politics without policy." Such neat formulations fail to account for the complex ways populism and technocracy are intertwined, both in real politics—observe Ecuador's Rafael Correa being called a "technocratic populist"—and conceptually, as I outline below. These accounts of their relationship may therefore obscure more than they enlighten.

Perhaps the most common understanding of the relationship between populism and technocracy is as a kind of *backlash*. In this view, excessive technocratic manipulation has triggered an outpouring of demotic energy opposed to experts and elites of all stripes. Friedman's theory suggests that this understanding is almost precisely backward. Rather than populism being a reaction to technocracy, it is instead an *outgrowth* of it: a working out, in politics, of the logic of technocratic legitimacy in the presence of naïve technocratic realism and the bad-intentions heuristic. Thus, while backlash theorists are probably right to say that dissatisfaction with incumbent democratic elites and institutions is fueled by their failure to fulfill expectations, Friedman's theory invites us to consider where those expectations come from. I suggest they are essentially technocratic expectations, shaped by the understandings of the proper role of government bequeathed to us from the era of Progressive reform.

The key theoretical move that unlocks this insight is the definition of technocracy not as government by experts but rather as a *political ideology* that legitimates power on the basis of solving social problems. Friedman's switch from defining technocracy in terms of who rules to the aims of the regime illuminates technocracy as an ideology with an identifiable lineage in the history of political thought.

Thinking of technocracy as a political ideology reveals that in contemporary politics, citizens often judge the legitimacy of their government by the standard of whether it solves problems. The essential point is that populists interpret the persistence of social problems as a manifestation of the failure of government to discharge its most fundamental duty. So when serious problems are not solved, citizens are not just disappointed—their belief in the legitimacy of their regime is shaken. This is why populism leads to democratic erosion. Populism draws on wells of dissatisfaction with democracy *as a regime,* not because of a rejection of democratic values like equality and popular rule, but because democratic ideology, for a vast swath of citizens, has developed into a technocratic ideology that has little to do with such values as equality and popular rule. Democracy's aim of "doing the people's will" has become "solving the people's problems": that has become the central and proper task of government. This transformation is the product of the politics of Progressive reform, which reimagined the purpose of the state in an activist mold. Once we conceive of the state as a problem solver, what could be more natural than to conceive of the will of the people in terms of an ever-present directive to solve their problems?

However, technocracy as an ideology does not, on its own, explain the phenomenon of populism. We might, after all, believe in technocratic legitimacy while also recognizing that the persistence of social problems is due to a variety of factors, such as the difficulty of the problems. This brings us to the role of naïve realism and the bad-intentions heuristic as key elements of populism.

What Friedman calls "naïve technocratic realism" is the view that the solutions to social problems are self-evident (25). This is a variant of the more general epistemological phenomenon of naïve realism, which consists in assuming that one's opinions are direct reflections of reality (37-38). The implication is that one sees things as they truly are, as if they have been revealed by pure common sense. Naïvely realistic technocratic citizens come to believe that either their own views about how to solve problems are self-evidently true (first-person naïve realism) or that someone else's views—such as a leader's—are self-evidently true (third-person naïve realism).

Naïve technocratic realism functions as less of a necessary condition for populist leanings than as a source of susceptibility to them. Insofar as citizens see public problems as admitting of simple, straightforward solutions, they will tend to struggle to understand why social problems persist. If a simple fix is all that is needed, why isn't it administered? The most natural answer to this question brings us to the bad-intentions heuristic: "Given a simple society, the persistence, and perhaps even the existence, of social problems is most easily explained by the resistance to change of political actors with bad intentions, who must be overcome by uniting good intentions with a strong will" (292). Problems fester because powerful actors, animated by nefarious motives, resist solving them. This simple heuristic seems to explain why populists are likely to blame the persistence of problems on the incumbent class of elites. Once we've neglected the possibility that the world in its complexity and stubbornness might throw up formidable and sometimes insuperable barriers to solving problems, or that some solutions create new problems as unintended consequences, where else would blame for persistent problems lie but with those with their hands on the levers of power?

Alternative Theories of Populism and Technocracy

This rough theory of populism clarifies numerous elements of the phenomenon observed by other scholars. Christopher Bickerton and Carlo Invernizzi Accetti (2017), for instance, argue for a purely conceptual connection between technocracy and populism based on a shared opposition to party democracy. This theory misses the fact that in much actual political contestation, the jousting between parties concerns precisely their ability to solve problems and their alternative approaches to doing so. Friedman's definition of technocracy, according to which popular politics can itself be technocratic, draws our attention to this kind of contestation. At the same time, real-world populists do not seem to have any problem working with or through political parties so long as they are controlled by populists—rather than by the "elites" who, it is thought, fail to solve, or may even cause, the people's problems. Moreover, parties generally try to define their coalitions as virtuous and deserving of power and respect, sharing a core populist claim to represent the "real" people, those deserving of political power because they are not tainted by malign intentions.

If party democracy were truly at odds with populism (and with technocracy), these important continuities would be hard to explain. If, instead, we recognize a lineal relationship between technocracy and populism, much becomes clear. Their shared disdain for party democracy makes sense in almost the mode of a family tradition: they both oppose it —under certain circumstances—but for rather different reasons. Both dislike the untidiness of reasonable disagreement inherent in the *plurality* of parties, but technocrats do so because it unsettles confidence in their policy solutions, while populists think it signals that those in the other party—or even in all the parties—are working to obstruct the solving of the people's problems.

Nadia Urbinati (2019) articulates a broader version of Bickerton and Accetti's view. As she sees it, populist movements oppose not only political parties but other mediating institutions as well, such as the news media and civil society groups, on the grounds that these institutions interfere with the direct, plebiscitarian connection between the populist leader and the people. The technocratic theory of populism suggests a different analysis. Rather than opposing intermediary institutions in order to embody a quasi-spiritual connection with the leader, populists might do so on pragmatic grounds if these institutions are seen as obstructing the solving of problems. When a populist leader inveighs against the media or another party, it is invariably on the grounds that journalists or opposition politicians are trying to block the leader's agenda, which (at least ostensibly) aims to solve the people's problems. The sin of mediating institutions is thus not interfering with the mystical communion between the leader and the people but instead preventing the leader from smoothly cleaving the Gordian knot of the country's problems.

The difference here is subtle but important, since many commentators have puzzled over the intensity of support for populist leaders who often lack any semblance of charisma (Pappas 2016, 381–83). When "social problems" are seen as the focal point of the relationship between the leader and the people, their connection is solidified by means of a narrative of shared journey toward a polity that works for ordinary people, not nefarious elites. The frequent speciousness of this rhetoric should not lead us to dismiss the ideational importance of opposition to intermediary institutions for pragmatic (technocratic) reasons rather than outright plebiscitarian ones.

Non-Technocratic Accounts of Populism

One of the most common theories of the origin of populism is the economic anxiety account, which explains the endorsement of populism as a natural if regrettable reaction to objective social conditions, such as the decline of middle-class economic mobility and the rise of social and economic inequality. The problem with this approach has been that it fails to connect the social conditions that it supposes to be the ultimate roots of populism with the actual conscious endorsement of populist leaders (Hawkins, Read, and Pauwels 2017). It thereby neglects the ideas that drive populist supporters, substituting an interpretively uncharitable understanding of them as an economically traumatized mass whose members are stripped, as individuals, of agency. Theories that point to economic anxiety without working out in detail the connection between economic conditions and anxiety and, in turn, between anxiety and support for populism threaten to open up (or widen) a gulf of incomprehensibility between those attracted to populism and those repelled by it.

In the model I am ascribing to Friedman, by contrast, populism is a logical outcome of technocratic ideology in the presence—in the minds of citizens—of a particular type of political epistemology. Thus, one cannot understand populism, at least not in the minds of those who are susceptible to it, without an understanding of the epistemology they bring to politics. Friedman's central methodological claim is that when we attempt to understand the behavior of masses of social and economic actors in response to technocratic governance, but without respectful attention to the ideas that motivate their actions, we are bound to go wrong (to some extent). Thus, we need to be explicit political epistemologists, and sometimes—as when discussing a fundamentally epistemic project, such as technocratic governance—the object of our analysis will be others' tacit political epistemologies. In contrast, analyses of populism that reduce it to anxiety and other emotions, such as anger and resentment, fail to explain why such intense emotions might follow from citizens' political ideas. Even when commentators identify real social problems experienced by those who support populist movements, they do not explain (with interpretive charity) the reasonableness of the emotions the problems trigger by exploring the ideas about the causes of these problems that give rise to these emotions. Instead, analysts have tended to psychologize populists, seeing their emotions as essentially knee-jerk reactions rather than reasonable responses to the world as they see it. Friedman methodologically impels us to look for the latter type of explanation, and his idea-focused political epistemology provides us a framework and toolbox for understanding the actions of others in these terms.

Thus, Friedman's analysis helps illuminate one of the most difficult-to-understand features of populism: the depth, thoroughgoingness, and, in particular, the anger of its rejection of the status quo and its constitutional and legal niceties. It is often thought that the mere persistence of problems just doesn't justify such anger and rejection. Perhaps those expressing this thought are more aware than populists are of the difficulties of all policy making, especially in the veto-laden American context, and so can think of many reasons for problems to continue other than political elites' malevolence. This is why Friedman's insights about naïve realism and the bad-intentions heuristic are so useful; they explain the anger of populists in an interpretively charitable way, making sense of it in light of their fundamental interpretations of the world. If we can think of no other explanation for festering problems that afflict the lives of one's fellow citizens and community but the bad intentions of those with political power, anger seems like an apt response.

The similarity between doing the people's will and solving their problems can help us understand another form of confusion sparked by populism. When some observers of populism look at the world around them, they see challenges but not an insuperable "swamp" that sinks every effort to meet them. For this group, there is little reason for burning it all down. Yet it is this perspective, which does not even see a systemic problem, that is itself the problem, in a way. It indicates the vast interpretive gulf between populist and non-populist technocrats, a gulf that makes the behavior and beliefs of those on the other side incomprehensible. One group thinks the system works only if it solves problems, but sees a host of problems persisting, and the other thinks that the system *is* solving problems, even some of the most pressing problems in the world, and is democratically legitimate to boot. But where many analyses in the U.S. context chalk this gulf up to polarization, Friedman suggests that it runs deeper than raw partisanship. It goes to the fundamental technocratic ideology of a considerable share of citizens, as well as differences in political epistemology among them. This is one of the core lessons of *Power Without Knowledge*: that mutual incomprehension is often a function of the heterogeneous ideas, including the varying political epistemologies, of citizens, which require independent attention as a topic of analysis. Psychologizing citizens as mindlessly tribal leaves in place gulfs of incomprehension.

The nature of mutual misunderstanding, in this case, may turn out to be a family squabble within the technocratic paradigm about *whose* problems matter, and thus about whether existing elites and institutions are solving them. Those who generally see things getting better often take a global perspective and see the relative peace and reduction of intense poverty in the past few decades as the product of a fundamentally successful international order, including especially the national-level elites and institutions that work to perpetuate that order (e.g., Pinker 2018). For these individuals, we should properly recognize the alleviation of extreme poverty as success in addressing an extremely significant global problem, and so credit, in the form of technocratic legitimacy, ought to redound to everyone involved, particularly incumbent elites. Moreover, we might think that problems like extreme poverty, even if they are found in other parts of the world, have a moral priority over the "first-world problems" of those who live in developed societies.

Interpreted this way, "establishment" institutions take on substantial technocratic legitimacy.

Thus, neither side in the debates about whether the resurgence of nationalism is worrisome are being irrational in the context of their own beliefs and epistemologies. Friedman (24) offers good reasons to expect local leaders to have special concern for local people and their problems (although he does not approve of this tendency), just as there are good reasons to prioritize particularly acute suffering even if its victims live far away. Thus, populists care—not unreasonably, given their upbringing in nationalist cultures—about solving "our" problems, while more globally oriented technocrats care about solving *the biggest* problems in the world, even if they don't afflict the techocrats' own conationals.

Together, then, the assumption that solving social and economic problems is the test of political legitimacy, and the assumption that the persistence of problems means that those in charge are malevolent, constitute the ideological building blocks of populism. When these two assumptions are combined, we have the ideational building blocks for the core stances, emotionality, and opposition to mediating institutions associated with populism. Moreover, this interpretation of populism provides a lens for understanding populist politics in an interpretively charitable way rather than rejecting it, as many critics do, as the unthinking reflex of an irrational mob.

A Lens for Contemporary Politics

Friedman's approach in *Power Without Knowledge* makes interpretively charitable sense not only of populist anger and resentment, but also of many fixtures of political rhetoric, strategy, and reaction that are not usually seen as being particularly populist (Friedman 2019b).

If we live in a technocracy rather than a democracy, it would explain why even non-populist politicians and ordinary citizens emphasize the importance of elected officials "getting things done," which constitutes one of the most pervasive tropes in modern campaign rhetoric. The simple boast of a candidate that she can get things done is, on reflection, a bit silly, since it does not specify whether the things to be done are negative or positive—policy disasters or policy coups. Yet it makes sense for those imbued with naïve technocratic realism. For them, "getting things done" is positive because—so long as the politician has good intentions—

what gets done is bound be positive, as it is likely to solve problems. If candidates can convey their good intentions by seeming to be "regular guys" with whom one would like to "have a beer," the rhetoric of accomplishment can establish the other necessary condition of problem solving, in the minds of naïve technocratic realists: the strength to battle against those with bad intentions (291). Someone who got things done must have been persistent, hard-working, and willing to sacrifice for the public. This form of rhetoric makes perfect sense when we take into account how naïve technocratic epistemology shapes the way citizens think about politics.

Friedman's theory also makes sense of ordinary citizens' perennial complaints that politicians "do nothing," are useless, and are corrupt (290; cf. Huey-Burns 2016 and Plutzer and Berkman 2018). Each of these grievances makes sense in light of the technocratic theory of populism. If problems persist but are easily solvable, then by definition politicians aren't doing what they were elected to do. They are doing nothing, then, in the sense that they're not doing what they ought to be doing. Since they manifestly aren't solving problems, they are, moreover, useless. Finally, if they aren't spending their time solving problems, they must be corrupt, since neglecting their duty as elected representatives is a kind of corruption of their office—to say nothing of their other activities, which likely include the apparently corrupt practice of soliciting campaign donations (296).

The theory also makes sense of the anger ordinary citizens voice when they consider that nothing in their lives has changed after politicians promised improvement. Recurrent complaints that politicians always break their promises—despite convincing empirical evidence that they strive to keep them and succeed in the majority of cases (Hill 2016)—make good sense if the implicit, overarching promise against which politicians are being judged is the technocratic vow to solve the people's problems. When serious problems persist, politicians have ipso facto broken that vow.

The rhetoric of accomplishment, disappointment, and anger might seem so obvious and commonsensical as to not require explanation. Yet there is nothing inevitable about any political language. Why, for instance, would we expect our politicians to do anything to solve our problems in the first place? In earlier ages, citizens did not expect governments to solve problems, if only because governments usually lacked the bureaucratic capacity to do so. This did not change for centuries, even after the advent of strong states in the early modern period, since early states concerned themselves almost exclusively with war fighting, colonization, and dynastic advancement. It took huge transformations in people's *ideas* about the proper scope of states and the obligations of government to give birth to the quotidian language of expectations met and unmet that we use today.

My argument is that technocracy played an essential role in the transition from the democratic ideologies and mass politics of the nineteenth century to the populist politics of the twenty-first: it served as a practical interpretation of what democracy in the real world actually means. Today, we can recognize the indelible marks of technocracy on our politics in these perennial features of our political discourse and cognition. Democratic ideology thus seems to have developed, among many citizens, into a basically technocratic ideology.

Populism, Technocracy, and Democratic Theory

What are the implications of such a transformation for democratic theory, reform, and practice?

Friedman does not present technocracy as a development of democratic ideology, as I suggest, but rather as a freestanding ideology with utilitarian roots that ultimately extend back to the sixteenth century and the rise of what Foucault called "the art of government" (349). For Foucault and Friedman, the art of government denotes a commitment to regulating the activities of the populace, for its own good—which, according to the Cameralist theorists of the early modern Holy Roman Empire, would have the side effect of increasing the wealth of the principality and thus the resources available to the state treasury (the *Kammer*). In institutional terms, the art of government dovetailed with the increasing professionalization of administration that went along with the rapid growth of state capacity in the early modern period. But what makes technocracy as an ideology in the Progressive Era so interesting is that it arises at the collision point between this paternalistic, elitist development and mass democracy, which began to spread in the late nineteenth century at the same time that state-building entered a new period of massive growth. Technocracy, I would say, is the art of government pressed into service of democracy.

Since a technocratic bureaucracy must operate with clear, written goals, the theoretical will of the people had to be hypostatized into a concrete list of problems that the bureaucracy could tackle. This was a transformation of democracy, even a deviation from it, but it was done in such a way as to be virtually unobjectionable on democratic grounds. This is because technocracy developed as a concrete interpretation of what the will of the people *is* at any given time. Unless we maintain that the people would prefer their government not to address the problems that beset them, or that the people would prefer to address them individually, without the aid of coordination, organization, or political power, democrats willy-nilly become technocrats.

In this light, recent work advocating epistocracy and meritocracy as viable rivals to democracy make a certain kind of sense that is internal to technocracy (just as Friedman's critique of epistocracy is internal), even if their malignity is not dispelled. When Daniel A. Bell (2015), Jason Brennan (2016), and Bryan Caplan (2007) argue for exclusionary political systems on the grounds that they can better solve the people's problems, they are appealing to technocratic standards of legitimacy against democracy; they are not attempting to resurrect the Platonic philosopher-king but rather enthrone the social-scientific bureaucrat. But a key reason their arguments have any normative plausibility is that technocracy developed its theory of legitimacy as an interpretation of what the people want, and not unreasonably. Because of this, those who resist creeping epistocratic practices and attitudes struggle to articulate a normative response that does not presuppose a sharp dichotomy between democracy and technocracy, as with some of the theories of populism I have criticized. Meanwhile, internal responses to epistocracy have, like the epistocratic theories themselves, tended to take an epistemological approach, outlining why experts are unlikely to make the good, problem-solving decisions promised by expert rule. I suspect that this explains why the burgeoning epistemic democracy literature has been so concerned with epistemological mechanisms by which mass publics can make better decisions than small groups of cognitive elites (Estlund 1994; Waldron 1995; Page 2007; Estlund 2008; Landemore 2013; Elliott 2020). This response implicitly concedes that solving problems generates legitimacy, but contends that experts do not inherently outperform democracy in doing so.

It may come as a shock to many readers that Friedman thinks there is a "technocratic value consensus" in the United States, and perhaps elsewhere (15). If Friedman is right about this value consensus, it can be interpreted in a number of ways. One is to see it as a predictable symptom of a privatizing liberalism (or, perhaps, neoliberalism) that privileges private life over the politically active life of the citizen. Such an orientation, when combined with the problem-solving orientation of technocracy, suggests that many citizens just want their problems solved for them, and do not necessarily care to take an active part in public life—in line with the thesis of John Hibbing and Elizabeth Theiss-Morse's *Stealth Democracy* (2002), on which Friedman relies (289-90). Many democratic theorists respond to disengaged citizens like these as if they are in need of enlightenment, and as if, once adequately educated, they will change their minds and affirm the value of active citizenship. They point to the fact that civic attitudes are often endogenous to social conditions, meaning that when people are made to take an active part in civic life, such as by serving on a jury, it can spark deeper patterns of political engagement and participation (Gastil et al. 2010). This is no doubt correct—the evidence is persuasive—yet none can deny that the power of education and experience to inspire political engagement is far from perfect. Jury service increases the likelihood of voting, for instance, by several percentage points, but does not move every single individual. Thus, I want to suggest, for the sake of argument, something rather uncomfortable for many democratic theorists: that no amount of experience or education will convince *everyone* that political participation is an intrinsically worthwhile pastime. Instead, we should consider the possibility that modern polities are durably divided into groups with different evaluations of the worth of democratic engagement.

Recognizing technocracy as a lineal descendant of democracy helps to clarify this possibility, and makes it plausible. It might be that the polity is divided into a democratic group of citizens actively and enthusiastically performing the classic rituals of democratic participation and a technocratic group of policy consumers who are looking for government to solve their problems and who view participation mainly as a chore. I want to insist that we consider such a division permanent, such that there is an enduring multiplicity in the citizen-types populating modern polities (Elliott 2017).

There are two things to note about this possibility. First, the supposition is not that the technocratic citizens are politically apathetic or passive in the sense of giving politics no mind. Rather, they find no reason to see politics as intrinsically valuable. They are thus willing to participate, at least if it is not too taxing, but not for its own sake. Second, their difference with conventionally democratic citizens transcends ordinary political disagreements, as it concerns the type of regime and the obligations and expectations that go with it. Although we might all *verbally* agree that the regime is a democracy, technocratic citizens bring a different set of expectations than democratic citizens for both themselves and their representatives. In line with the thesis of *Stealth Democracy*, the technocratic group wants to minimize its participatory input but maximize the performance of its representatives in solving social and economic problems.

A durably divided polity consisting of conventional democrats and citizen-technocrats puts democratic reformers in a serious bind. On the one hand, they want to expand the openness of democratic institutions and create new ways to bring ordinary citizens into the halls of power (Landemore 2017). Usually, too, they wish to revise the modes of democratic participation to encourage the wider use of deliberation. On the other hand, if there is a sizable group of citizens who will not, of their own volition, pursue new institutions and forms of participation because they are relatively costly and demanding, the new institutions may become dominated by the democratic group. If you build it, they will not *all* come; democrats will come disproportionately. If the democrats are the main group using these institutions, and if the institutions are truly politically empowering—as all reformers would insist—the result will be a substantial power imbalance between the democrats and the technocrats, constituting a sizable new source of political inequality.

This is the dilemma generated by the coexistence of democrats and citizen-technocrats. If reformers pursue democratic innovations that involve costly and demanding forms of participation, they stand to actually move their polity farther from their own democratic ideals by generating new patterns of political inequality, ones that track preferences for political engagement as an end in itself.

Power Without Knowledge has, ironically, made me more concerned about this likelihood than ever before. By emphasizing the diversity of people's webs of belief and the gulfs of inscrutability that will inevitably beset them, Friedman has convinced me that the technocratic outlook that includes no love for democratic participation is not going anywhere. There will always be citizens who do not love democracy, even if they will begrudgingly fulfill a civic duty that is not too onerous. Nowadays, we may call these citizens populists.

In that case, it seems to me that democratic reformers face a dilemma. They can either persist in pressing for reforms that they know will reliably exclude those who would rather spend their time doing other things, perhaps telling themselves some version of the excuse that as long as people have the opportunity to participate—even if we know for a fact that they won't—political equality is secured. This approach seems untenable to me, but my anecdotal experience suggests that some democratic theorists would be willing to embrace this horn of the dilemma. The other option is to rethink the predominant menu of reforms and develop alternatives that will truly empower all citizens, even if this requires retreating from deeper modes of participation and institutionalizations of them. I suspect that this direction is likely to prove more fruitful, though I cannot properly defend this intuition here. In either case, it remains, I believe, a genuinely difficult choice.

If the best kind of reading is that which makes one think discomfiting thoughts, then *Power Without Knowledge* would very much qualify for myself, and likely for most democratic theorists, in spades.

REFERENCES

Bell, Daniel A. 2015. *The China Model: Political Meritocracy and the Limits of Democracy*. Princeton: Princeton University Press.

Bickerton, Christopher, and Carlo Invernizzi Accetti. 2017. "Populism and Technocracy." In *The Oxford Handbook of Populism*, ed. Cristóbal Rovira Kaltwasser, Paul Taggart, Paulina Ochoa Espejo, and Pierre Ostiguy. New York: Oxford University Press.

Brennan, Jason. 2016. *Against Democracy*. Princeton: Princeton University Press.

Buenker, John D. 1988. "Sovereign Individuals and Organic Networks: Political Cultures in Conflict During the Progressive Era." *American Quarterly* 40 (2):187-204.

Caplan, Bryan. 2007. *The Myth of the Rational Voter: Why Democracies Choose Bad Policies*. Princeton: Princeton University Press.

Elliott, Kevin J. 2017. "Against Democracy." *Contemporary Political Theory* 17: 94-97.

Elliott, Kevin J. 2020. "Democracy's Pin Factory: Issue Specialization, the Division of Cognitive Labor, and Epistemic Performance." *American Journal of Political Science* 64(2): 385-97.

Estlund, David M. 1994. "Opinion Leaders, Independence, and Condorcet's Jury Theorem." *Theory and Decision* 36(2): 131-62.

Estlund, David M. 2008. *Democratic Authority: A Philosophical Framework*. Princeton: Princeton University Press.

Friedman, Jeffrey. 2019a. "Populists as Technocrats." *Critical Review* 31(3-4): 315-76.

Friedman, Jeffrey. 2019b. *Power Without Knowledge: A Critique of Technocracy*. New York: Oxford University Press.

Gastil, John, E. Pierre Deess, Philip J. Weiser, and Cindy Simmons. 2010. *The Jury and Democracy: How Jury Deliberation Promotes Civic Engagement and Political Participation*. New York: Oxford University Press.

Hawkins, Kirk A., Madeleine Read, and Teun Pauwels. 2017. "Populism and Its Causes." In *The Oxford Handbook of Populism*, ed. Cristóbal Rovira Kaltwasser, Paul Taggart, Paulina Ochoa Espejo, and Pierre Ostiguy. New York: Oxford University Press.

Hibbing, John R., and Elizabeth Theiss-Morse. 2002. *Stealth Democracy: Americans' Beliefs about How Government Should Work*. New York: Cambridge University Press.

Hill, Timothy. 2016. "Trust Us: Politicians Keep Most of Their Promises." FiveThirtyEight, 21 April.

Huey-Burns, Caitlin. 2016. "Angry Voters: They're 'Sick of Politics'." RealClear Politics, 11 January.

Landemore, Hélène. 2013. *Democratic Reason: Politics, Collective Intelligence, and the Rule of the Many*. Princeton: Princeton University Press.

Landemore, Hélène. 2017. "Deliberative Democracy as Open, Not (Just) Representative Democracy." *Daedalus* 146(3): 51-63.

Mudde, Cas. 2017. "Populism: An Ideational Approach." In *The Oxford Handbook of Populism*, ed. Cristóbal Rovira Kaltwasser, Paul Taggart, Paulina Ochoa Espejo, and Pierre Ostiguy. New York: Oxford University Press.

Müller, Jan-Werner. 2016. *What Is Populism?* Philadelphia: University of Pennsylvania Press.

Page, Scott E. 2007. *The Difference: How the Power of Diversity Creates Better Groups, Firms, Schools, and Societies*. Princeton: Princeton University Press.

Pappas, Takis S. 2016. "Are Populist Leaders 'Charismatic'? The Evidence from Europe." *Constellations* 23(3): 378-90.

Plutzer, Eric, and Michael Berkman. 2018. "New Poll: Voters Are Just as Angry as in 2016." *Washington Post*, 11 October.

Schmidt, Vivien A. 2006. *Democracy in Europe: The EU and National Polities*. New York: Oxford University Press.

Urbinati, Nadia. 2019. *Me the People: How Populism Transforms Democracy*. Cambridge, Mass.: Harvard University Press.

Waldron, Jeremy. 1995. "The Wisdom of the Multitude: Some Reflections on Book 3, Chapter 11 of Aristotle's Politics." *Political Theory* 23(4): 563-84.

Oscar L. Larsson

TECHNOCRACY, GOVERNMENTALITY, AND POST-STRUCTURALISM

ABSTRACT: *The technocratic dimension of government—its reliance upon knowledge claims, usually in scientific guise—is of great importance if we wish to understand modern power and governance. In* Power Without Knowledge: A Critique of Technocracy, *Jeffrey Friedman investigates the often-overlooked question of the relationship between technocratic knowledge/power and ideas. Friedman's contribution to our understanding of technocracy can therefore be read as a contribution to governmentality studies, one that introduces the possibility of adding normative solutions to this critical tradition.*

In *Power Without Knowledge: A Critique of Technocracy* (Oxford University Press, 2019), Jeffrey Friedman investigates the important but often overlooked question of technocracy in democratic systems. He notes that while political theorists have been preoccupied with the ends of politics—the fair, the just, and the desirable—they have directed little attention to the issue of how to realize the political goals that are established by popular rule. Thus, the chief concerns of political theorists have become alienated from political reality, because most areas of public policy are in fact technocratic by nature, and technocracy focuses on means, not ends.

Friedman's definition of a technocracy is "a polity that aims to solve, mitigate, or prevent social and economic problems among its people" (5). This recalls the role ascribed to policy experts and political analysts during the 1980s, namely, that of "speaking truth to power" (Wildavsky 2017)—articulating the truth about the causes of the people's problems, so that the powerful can solve, prevent, or mitigate them—along with the importance of evaluating public policy and programs, which is an agenda that has been advanced by Evert Vedung (1997). In this, its epistemic aspect, technocracy lends itself naturally to governance by elite scientific advisers to politicians. The involvement of knowledge in policy processes, public programs, and politics have been topics of major interest for public administration and policy scholars for quite some time, comprising an ongoing research agenda that includes such issues as how to implement evidence-based policies and how to resolve wicked and complex problems (Clarence 2002). A researcher working in this tradition might inquire, for example, when and why politicians and policy makers are prepared to take into consideration existing knowledge in the effort to resolve social and political problems (Head 2013; Lundin and Öberg 2014). Insofar as such research appears to regard knowledge as consisting of objective and neutral facts, it accords with the tenor of Wildavsky's discussion. Friedman's agenda is quite different, though. He seeks to problematize the notion that technocratic knowledge is something readily available to politicians and experts that makes it possible for them to craft programs and reforms that can mend social ills.

Alternative Views of Technocratic Knowledge Problems

The foundation of Friedman's position is the view that human beings are individuals who possess complex sets of ideas and beliefs, so it is difficult to create incentive structures that will shape their behavior in predictable ways—which effective public policy must do. In this conception, the expertise of experts may not suffice to produce good policy advice. On the other hand, Friedman emphasizes that the involvement of politicians at all, even as the recipients of expert advice, indicates the participation of the politicians' constituents in the technocratic project. Thus, "epistocracy" is not the only form of technocracy; there is also "democratic technocracy," which includes members of the general public as "citizen-technocrats" when they share the goal of solving social problems, and when they make knowledge claims about how best to do so. Thus, working immanently, from within the means-end logic of technocrats themselves, Friedman arrives at a broad definition of technocracy as a regime in which either experts or ordinary citizens (or both) claim to know how to solve the people's social and economic problems, even when the people's knowledge claim amounts merely to the conviction that a certain politician has the people's interests at heart and can therefore be trusted to solve their problems. A technocracy is thus defined by its problem-solving end, and our theoretical focus can be on whether it is likely to have the epistemic means of achieving that end.

This broad definition of technocracy points to a promising approach that can supplement current discussions concerning the analytical and ideological shift from government to governance (Rhodes 1997; Larsson 2013; Larsson 2019b). Along with other scholars, Friedman notes that ever more aspects of modern societies and democratic systems are controlled, or at least influenced, by the technocratic dimension of social and political issues. However, this has led to an impoverished public debate, marked by the claim that there are "no alternatives" to technocracy—i.e., epistocracy—such that ordinary citizens are sidelined by experts (Torfing and Triantafillou 2013; Larsson 2019a). Theorists who follow in the footsteps of Jürgen Habermas, for example, and criticize the undemocratic nature of epistocratic technocracy, are, in Friedman's view, too external to the instrumentalist logic of technocracy to be able to interrogate epistocratic knowledge claims (20). Because Habermas was primarily concerned with the illegitimacy of undemocratically chosen ends, he failed to question the efficacy of technocratic means to those ends.

However, it is worth noting that in contemporary circumstances, technocratic politics may favor the means over the ends in a different respect than the one problematized by Friedman. Although political leaders and bureaucrats may know what is required to address a specific social and political problem, they may deem it to be either too costly or unrealistic to address it, given a lack of public support. Since the means available for solving, mitigating, or preventing economic and social problems are limited in times of austerity, tax cuts, and budget deficits, we are a long way from the satisfactory solution of certain problems, even when we possess substantial knowledge of how to solve them.

However, an *unwillingness* to address such problems constitutes a non-epistemological issue, in contrast to the issues treated by Friedman.

Power Without Knowledge is welcome in that epistemological questions are highly political, as has long been pointed out by scholars devoted to social constructivism (Larsson 2018). Consequently, I will seek to connect the book more closely to this line of scholarship, including the ongoing debate concerning knowledge, power, policy, and the post-truth society (Fuller 2108). For instance, Deborah Stone (2002) has argued, like Friedman (291), that perceived facts derive from social and political theories rather than direct observation. This places great importance upon the social dimensions of knowledge, since there would be no foundation for these perceptions without reference to theoretical premises. Knowledge claims, for the most part, follow an infinite regress through previous, theoretically mediated claims. We are also substantially influenced by a person's race, appearance, social manners, reputation, and credentials as we assess any information or facts they provide. While a skeptical approach regarding factual claims is generally advocated in the media and educational institutions, fact resistance comprises an acute problem today insofar as the truth and facts are politicized (Stone 2002, 320–23).

Steve Fuller (2018) argues, similarly, that we are living in the era of post-truth, in which the facts presented by policy makers are not always based on trustworthy sources, having been gathered to fit pre-selected policy solutions regardless of whether or not they reflect public opinion and sentiment. The choice of facts and knowledge claims are thus elements of social and political processes, and they do not reflect honest and rational procedures for attaining truth. Frank Fischer et al. (2015) note that such questionable facts and claims undercut the previous—and flawed—ideal of speaking truth to power. The new task facing social scientists who explore politics and policy making is rather to problematize and make explicit the entanglement of ontology, epistemology, and the manner in which knowledge follows from certain perspectives and premises that not everyone shares.

Post-truth society does not pose a fundamental problem for post-structuralists and constructivists, but rather for those who believe in neutral facts and objective knowledge. The critical tradition of policy scholars has already accepted the social and political construction of "reality" on the basis of knowledge and constitutive causality (Larsson 2018; Fischer 1998; Yanow 2000; Fischer et al 2015; Morcol 2002).

Instead of fighting against multiple perspectives, we thus need to accept and embrace the co-existence of multiple and contradicting facts, which can provide us with more comprehensive approaches to understanding social and political problems. The conclusion to be drawn from these insights is not that we should forego deliberation in the face of inadequate knowledge, but that deliberation is now more important than ever insofar as knowledge and facts are contested, with technocracy having become a key element of our political existence.

However, Friedman's primary message does not concern deliberation, or voice, but rather the importance of creating voluntary exit options for individuals. What is the motivation for this position, and is the latter a viable and desirable alternative? In order to fully understand Friedman's conclusion, we must first recapture the reasoning underlying his arguments.

Methodological Individualism, Subjectivism, and Collective Institutions

Any investigation of society should identify the ontological premises that support it. Friedman is very clear concerning the ontological premises of his own analysis, explicitly stating that he builds his theoretical position upon "the individualistic ontology of ideas" that he has "drawn from [Walter] Lippmann" (149). He develops this position, in part, through a critique of Charles Taylor's methodologically collectivist version of hermeneutics, as expressed in his influential essay on "Interpretation and the Sciences of Man" (Taylor 1985). Friedman's critique of Taylor paves the way for his own view, "epistemological individualism," which "unites four elements: methodological individualism, the fallibility and potential ignorance of individuals, communication among individuals, and the possibility that their ideas will be heterogeneous" (149). This methodological posture determines and conditions much of the argumentation in *Power Without Knowledge.*

For instance, a holistic view of society would maintain that institutions and discourses subsume the players. If individuals either act or resist in accordance with what is socially expected of them, at least in respect to their social capacities, desires, and beliefs, then we may analyze society from the top down and produce systemic theories of society (Hollis 1994, 18). In contrast, a fully individualistic approach would proceed in the reverse direction. If meanings, ideas, and knowledge are primarily subjective, becoming intersubjective only through mutual effort and agreement, then institutions and social systems arise as a result of individuals' actions and interactions (ibid., 19). The fact that Friedman also wishes to "complexify" human behavior and beliefs renders it even more difficult to analyze, predict, and plan for human interactions, although this does not per se rule out the ideal of deliberation and intersubjective meaning-making.

Friedman argues that "ideas," including perceptions, beliefs, and interpretations, "along with hypotheses, theories, strokes of inspiration, and assumptions, implicit or explicit," are individual and subjective, although they may be intersubjectively communicated (140). The connection to technocracy is that the reception of communicated ideas is likely to be somewhat heterogeneous even in a mass society, producing heterogeneous webs of belief across the population whose actions technocrats are trying to control in the interest of solving social and economic problems. Insofar as any of the ideas in given agents' webs of belief or ideas may contribute to the agents' interpretation of their own circumstances and, consequently, their reactions to these circumstances, technocrats attempting to predict the agents' actions may have different webs of belief than those they are trying to predict, leading to erroneous predictions. Thus, Friedman writes, there is bound to be some degree of "unpredictable interpretive heterogeneity among the agents whose actions technocrats are trying to predict, and, even more crucially, between these agents and the technocrats themselves—all of whom are human and thus subject to heterogeneous ideational inputs" (ibid.). Thus, epistemological individualism is compatible with enough ideational heterogeneity that technocrats' predictions may go awry. If we do not know the actor's subjective perceptions and interpretations (which Friedman groups under the rubric of ideas), we may be unable to predict the resulting actions.

Although I agree that individuals are complex, and that their sets of ideas have multiple sources that result in a unique composition at the individual level (an issue referred to as intersectionality in identity studies), I see a danger in overemphasizing the importance of subjective ideas and knowledge claims. As a post-structuralist, I am more inclined to take into consideration the linkages that exist between institutions, discourses, and collective entities, including how intersubjective and shared understandings influence individuals, rather than what separates them. In a previous publication in these pages, I have argued that ideational scholars such as Colin Hay (2017) and Vivien Schmidt (2017) overly emphasize the ability of individual actors to navigate, oppose, and even change societal institutions, particularly if we regard institutions as intersubjective and collective in nature (Larsson 2015). Although *Power Without Knowledge* does not discuss institutions and institutional change, its analysis of what guides human behavior and how individual actions generate stable patterns that form informal institutions, such as societal norms, are relevant to this debate.

The danger is that placing too great an emphasis upon individual perceptions and an individual's ability to change social and political institutions could be said to fall prey to voluntarism. Friedman suggests that it is at least possible that each individual has such a unique set of ideas, beliefs, and interpretations that it is basically impossible to govern and predict their behavior in any meaningful way, although he denies that we can know if the "magnitude" of ideational heterogeneity (being dependent on variable and contingent processes of belief communication and assimilation) is likely to be as great as that (171). As we cannot know in detail the composition of each individual's web of beliefs, we arrive at a conundrum, of uncertain magnitude, for technocracy. I believe that this way of reasoning too quickly turns methodological individualism away from general patterns of behavior, overstating individualism while downplaying holistic and societal institutions that may generate patterned behavior (Larsson 2018).

Think of the following situation. You have decided to go for a Black Friday sale at the hardware store to get a bargain deal on a set of tools. Due to poor planning and bad luck, you arrive only shortly before the store opens and there is a long queue of other bargain hunters. I think it is safe to assume that despite stinging disappointment you are likely to take the last place in the queue in order to play by the informal rules of queueing. However, if you arrive at the store and there is no queue but rather a tight gathering in front of the doors, you may go so far as to push your way through the crowd to make sure you get your hands on the tools you wish to buy. Behavior is situational, and this makes it quite easy to manipulate if technocrats know the situation.

Government agencies may invent an app through which to sign up for benefits. You may not wish to register, but in order for you to get your child care you simply have to register, and you do. In the Swedish municipality in which I live, the school board decided to buy a managerial system called "Unikum" for all communications between the schools, the pupils, and the parents. Despite my fierce desire to resist starting an account on this inferior and low-tech website, in the end, I had to cave in because of the inconvenience of the alternative. I believe that there are many such examples of how individual complexity and heterogeneity in the composition of ideas and beliefs matters little in how technocratic and, more broadly, societal developments change human behavior. Thus, while complexifying human agency is important, this endeavor must not overlook the linkages between, on the one hand, the collective and intersubjective elements of society, such as institutions and norms, that may enable technocracy to efficaciously regulate individual behavior despite heterogeneous ideational resistance. A social science as such should thus investigate the shared meanings, collective elements, and institutions that shape and regulate human behavior.

Friedman recognizes this need, and in fact devotes Part II of *Power Without Knowledge* to an exploration of whether technocrats can "judiciously" discover, case by case, the balance between the unpredictable force of individuals' ideas and "homogenizing behavioral counterforces to the heterogeneity of people's ideas." These counterforces, such as shared norms that override people's unruly ideas, may cause "slippage" between heterogeneous ideas and the behavior people actually display (169). Thus, even if people do not share "homogeneous beliefs in general," they may share

> specific normative tenets (norms) that they view as obligatory in their situations, as they interpret them—despite the fact that, apart from this shared interpretation of their situations, their webs of belief may be wildly heterogeneous. Shared norms can act as a counterweight to the heterogeneous behavior that would otherwise be expected to issue from such webs of belief. The intercession of shared norms, then, may create a gap between the (presumptively great) frequency of anonymous others' unpredictable ideas and the frequency of their unpredictable behavior. (Ibid.)

However, this does not necessarily mean that technocracy is back on track. Given the existence of ideational heterogeneity across individuals, one cannot deny that technocrats may produce unintended consequences by mispredicting people's behavior. Thus,

> If theorists of technocracy could demonstrate on second-order grounds that, for example, technocrats should be reliably able to determine the

> effects of various superordinate norms (or other homogeneous or behavior-homogenizing ideas), as well as being reliably able to discern the limits of their knowledge of the predictability conferred by such homogenizing factors, then we could expect that technocrats might be reliably able to predict people's behavior in those cases, despite the presumptive heterogeneity of human ideas. This might reduce the magnitude of the unintended consequences caused by ideational heterogeneity, rescuing technocratic legitimacy. Otherwise, we would have established, I think, that technocrats cannot justifiably claim to know that the benefits of their actions will outweigh the costs. (171)

However, I am not convinced by this conclusion. I doubt that any technocrat ever believed that they were able to fully control human behavior. Governance is never total in that sense.

Neoclassical and Behavioral Economics

Three specific questions emerge from the way in which Friedman presents the epistemological problems of technocracy, and potential solutions: why not nudge, why not deliberate, and why not Foucault?

The first question arises because Friedman devotes substantial space to a critique of neoclassical economic theory and the impact it has had—and continues to have—on the social sciences, particularly policy sciences. Friedman maintains that policy designed on the basis of economic theory is quickly turned into a rational-choice exercise that seeks to predict what people will do through an analysis of what they would do if they were rational, with rationality equated with what a given economist thinks would be optimal (28). Neoclassical economists, according to Friedman, efface possible heterogeneities between economic agents and the economists interpreting them by treating both as responding to objective realities rather than to their subjective interpretations of them. This critique is reminiscent of the tradition of behavioral economics, which seeks to theorize and understand "actual human economic behavior." Richard Thaler (2015, 4) argues that a significant weakness in traditional economic models and neoclassical economic theory is that they replace human beings with a "fictional character called homo economicus," which he terms an "econ." In contrast to econs, humans engage in a great deal of irrational behavior that little resembles the economic and rational behavior that is described and postulated by neoclassical economic theory. Yet Friedman dismisses this tradition. His main argument for why we should not rely upon behavioral economics for answers is that it, too, suffers from the pathology of homogenizing human behavior (conceptually) in order to predict it. Thus, while behavioral economists recognize that neoclassical economics is unrealistic, behavioral economists themselves treat actual people's deviations from neoclassical predictions as resulting from "homogeneous cognitive defects rather than unpredictably idiosyncratic ignorance" (197). While "behavioral economics complicates the simple model of predictable behavior used by economists such as [Nobel laureate James M.] Buchanan," it "does not complexify it in the epistemic sense (ibid.).

Of particular note is that behavioral economics has laid the foundation for "nudging," a theory and concept popularized by Thaler and Cass Sunstein. This position presumes that we can know what individuals would choose if they were fully rational, such as to eat healthy foods, save for retirement, and so forth. Once we have identified these ends and the types of human behavior that would serve them, technocrats should be able to establish a choice architecture that can assist them in making the right choices even when they are not fully rational:

> A nudge, as we will use the term, is any aspect of the choice architecture that alters people's behavior in a predictable way without forbidding any options or significantly changing their economic incentives. To count as a mere nudge, the intervention must be easy and cheap to avoid. Nudges are not mandates. Putting fruit at eye level counts as a nudge. Banning junk food does not. (Thaler and Sunstein 2009, 6)

In general, the examples that Thaler and Sunstein provide entail that individuals have to make an active choice to opt out rather than opt in, which involves making the "best" choices readily available to individuals rather than waiting for them to identify and actively seek them out. For example, it has been shown that informing given households that they have the highest electrical consumption in the neighborhood is a better way to encourage behavioral change than raising the price of electricity (ibid., 129).

Nudging is a way of governing that takes into consideration the actual behavior of humans, not econs. It preserves the right of individuals to make poor choices, and it does not imply that all individuals will make the same decision even though it is based upon behavioral economic theory. Nudging simply suggests that deliberate choice architecture will help certain people to make better decisions. As such, it is an instrument of technocracy that relies upon "knowledge of how to control human action effectively" (4).

The nudging literature suggests that society is not completely ungovernable. More important, it suggests that it is possible to employ a technocratic instrument of governance that is normatively justifiable insofar as it permits individuals to freely opt out of preselected schemas and does not seek to ban undesired behavior. Choice architecture causes no harm, and its intent is to provide assistance to actors rather than dominate human behavior. It would be informative to know, then, why Friedman does not take nudges or choice architecture into consideration as potential resolutions of at least some of the problems that mark a defective technocracy.

My own doubts regarding nudging are that it appears blind to competing normative concerns and outcomes and seems to assume that all actors involved in a given area would be equally happy to support the choices that are promoted. In this regard, we need to take into consideration the fact that a broad set of actors make very substantial profits today from individuals' poor economic choices. This is very likely an important reason why, for example, we see junk food at eye level, with fruit near the back wall of the store or next to our feet. We thus cannot assume that all actors involved in complex governing systems are equally inclined to choose desirable political ends, and we likely need to complement the discussion of nudging with critical theories that address the issue of conflict among various groups and actors.

In democratic and capitalist societies, we have to take into consideration the fact that private actors may have a much greater influence than the state upon the lives of citizens. For instance, many scientific studies have shown that obesity rates and a variety of other health problems are on the rise among the poor, who are being pushed toward unhealthy diets because healthy choices are much more expensive. Technocratic solutions to such structural and systemic problems could well involve addressing how they are sustained by the economic interests of private companies instead of seeking to alter individual behavior. Such issues provide examples of the many social ills about which we possess substantial knowledge in respect to both problems and desirable normative solutions, but lack the political will or resources needed to act.

Back to Habermas

Friedman notes on the very first page of *Power Without Knowledge* that Isaiah Berlin and the young Jürgen Habermas displayed scant interest in the means of technocratic politics. Berlin even suggested that questions of means are "unworthy" of political theorists insofar as they are "not political," regarding them as technical matters "capable of being settled by experts or machines" (Berlin 1958, 118). Habermas remarked, half a century ago, that the scientific knowledge that technocrats possess enables them to craft efficacious policy means towards given political ends, exemplifying rationality in an instrumental sense. He thus favored a version of technocracy in which "scientific experts advise the decision-makers and politicians consult scientists in accordance with practical needs" (Habermas 1970, 66–67) so long as these needs, as Friedman says, are "democratically determined" (2). However, Habermas may have been overly strict in dichotomizing technocratic means and ends. Collaborative governance arrangements, for example, are co-managed and influenced by public and private stakeholders who jointly, through either consensus or conflict, seek to influence both political means and political ends through pragmatic bargaining. Such new governance arrangements move political disputes from the public arena into more concealed and intimate locations where stakeholders attend to public problems, often with a technocratic outlook, in an effort to resolve social and political problems through the pragmatic utilization of existing knowledge (Erikson and Larsson 2019; Larsson 2019b).

Although most political action, including the crafting of the ends of politics, now takes place during the implementation phase of public policy, in what may be framed as the technocratic sphere of the state, this may have a negative effect upon the realization of a given policy, restricting the possibility of holding politicians accountable for outcomes (Weale 2011). Thus, collaborative governance may serve not only the purpose of democratizing the selection of ends but making the selection of means more effective. Collaborative governance arrangements possess the potential to increase the participation of ordinary citizens, give rise to deliberation regarding multiple perspectives on difficult or wicked problems, make possible further critical scrutiny of public rule and public elites, and mitigate the problematic aspects of liberal/elite democracy. Such concerns associate the technocratic aspects of the polity with the normative ideal of political participation in order to identify common solutions to common problems in a way that merely being left alone, to exit the voice option, does not. As Archon Fung and Erik Olin Wright (2003, 3) put it,

> As the tasks of the state have become more complex and the size of the polities larger and more heterogeneous, the institutional forms of liberal democracy developed in the nineteenth century—representative democracy plus techno-bureaucratic administration—seem increasingly ill-suited to the novel problems we face in the twenty-first century. Democracy as a way of organizing the state has come to be narrowly identified with territorially based competitive elections of political leadership for legislative and executive offices. Yet increasingly, this mechanism of political representation seems ineffective in accomplishing the central ideas of democratic politics: facilitating active involvement of the citizenry forging political consensus through dialogue, devising and implementing public policies that ground a productive economy and healthy society, and, in more radical egalitarian versions of the democratic ideal, ensure that all citizens benefit from the nation's wealth.

In this vein, many scholars have now advanced various forms of collaborative governance on the basis of a wide range of similar concepts, such as co-governance, associative governance, participatory governance, polycentric governance, mosaic governance, and collaborative governance. What unites these variants is the concern that the institutions of liberal democracy have become inadequate and thus need to be supplemented by governance reforms that make possible the participation of a greater number of actors, voices, citizens, and stakeholders. The aim is to attain pluralism in terms of both input and output regarding political reforms by means of expanded deliberation among the various actors on the basis of thoughtful and sensitive discussion that takes into consideration the perspectives, interests, and arguments advanced by the actors involved. This normative concern for increased political participation and the construction of intersubjective knowledge stands in stark contrast to "the relatively genuine (albeit very imperfect) expertise that we each have regarding our own lives," which is Friedman's reason for preferring exit to voice whenever possible (331).

This raises the question of whether solutions to problems associated with contemporary technocracy run counter to the ideal of deliberative democracy. Joshua Cohen (1997, 67) defines deliberative democracy as "an association whose affairs are governed by the public deliberation of its members … that treats democracy itself as a fundamental ideal and not simply a derivative ideal that can be explained in terms of the values of fairness or equality of respect." The normative concerns that have produced governance reforms aimed at encouraging increased pluralism and deliberation have frequently been based upon the mature Habermas's theories of communicative action, rational argumentation, and deliberation as providing means for arriving at an enlightened consensus (Phelps and Tewdwr-Jones 2000; Lenoble and Maesschalck 2003; Beaumont and Nicholls 2008). This may provide a foundation for reforming technocracy, governance, and societal planning insofar as communicative rationality comprises a means for mediating among strongly divergent interests. As John Pløger (2001, 223) puts it, technocratic governance can in this way become

> an arena for conversation among "equals" in a normative sense building upon, at the very least, equal argumentative rights or opportunities. In order to secure this equality, planners and other experts, on the one hand, need to work on producing power-reducing procedures and, on the other, they constantly have to be critical of their own dialogical practice and its institutional form. … Habermas in fact introduces the discourse ethic as a precondition to develop intersubjective commonly accepted rules and ways of judgment based on moral principles on "how to communicate democratically." This power-equalising communicative practice is ensured by having a procedure where all claims are evaluated through commonly accepted principles of judgments, which, according to Habermas, should be the comprehensibility, integrity, legitimacy, and truth of statements.

Thus, I wonder if it is correct to say that "political theorists' chief concerns have become detached from most areas of contemporary politics and government: those that are technocratic" (9).

Policy and governance research, too, is concerned, to a great extent, with finding the right balance between realism and normative ideals in designing and evaluating governance systems, including their democratic viability. Even if the researchers involved may not term themselves political theorists, they are nonetheless interested in normative questions related to technocratic solutions and how governance could and should be re-designed. They have also brought Habermas along with them on this crusade.

Technocracy and Governmentality

Another giant who comes to mind when discussing power and knowledge is Michel Foucault, who appears only at the very end of *Power Without Knowledge*, in the Afterword, in a discussion of the rise of technocracy—labeled by Foucault the rise of "the art of government"—in sixteenth-century Europe. The underlying principles of this art concerned the welfare of the population, including ameliorating social conditions, increasing wealth, and improving health, suggesting an ever-expanding technocratic agenda (348).

One of Foucault's main points was that technocracy and the governance of society are explicitly tied to knowledge claims. The fact that he regarded knowledge and power as inseparable serves to illustrate the novelty of his way of theorizing power beyond the formal model of sovereign power. Friedman appears to follow the spirit of Foucault's concern for how scientific knowledge both makes possible and informs the ways in which governance and technocracy are conducted. Greater engagement with Foucault and the Foucauldian tradition of analysis that has emerged since the 1980s, which sharply contrasts with the Enlightenment conception of knowledge as promoting the ideal of emancipation, could have been fruitful for the overall argumentation in *Power Without Knowledge*.

Foucault maintains that the knowledge of human beings, as social and biological creatures, refines and intensifies the exercise of power. It fosters the disciplinary effects of self-governance and self-control instead of providing a corrective for the repressive mechanisms of power and control that are present in, for example, hospitals, schools, military facilities, airports, and workplaces. The techniques of governance do not stand in opposition to technocratic knowledge claims, but are rather based upon them: knowledge makes possible a granular control of human actions and interactions in the governance of things, places, populations, and target groups (Bacchi and Goodwin 2016). Knowledge thereby promotes the exercise power in a more refined, "concentrated," and "formalized" manner (Foucault 1980, 226).

Foucault regards power and knowledge not only as mutually reinforcing, but as inextricably bound to each other. Rather than speaking of power and knowledge as independent concepts, the notion of "power–knowledge–discourse" more accurately reflects the intrinsic connection between them. One of the key aspects of how Foucault approached and developed the connection between power/knowledge and governance involves identifying programs and practices that are focused on directing or correcting the behavior of specific subjects. In particular, the principal strengths and contributions of this discourse follow from an emphasis upon political rationalities and technologies of rule, which forms the analytical framework and unfolding tradition of governmentality studies (Burchell et al. 1991; Dean 2010).

Foucault provided two similar and informative definitions of governmentality: as "the ensemble formed by the institutions, procedures, analyses and reflections, calculations, and tactics that allow the exercise of this very specific, albeit very complex, power that has the population as its target, political economy as its major form of knowledge, and apparatuses of security as its essential technical instrument" (Foucault 2007, 108), and as "the way in which one conducts the conduct of men" (Foucault 2008, 186). Noteworthy here is the emphasis upon the technocratic aspects of society, namely, how knowledge, at times incorrect or incomplete, informs the programs by which technocrats and experts seek to "conduct the conduct of men." Friedman argues in a similar vein that a given technocracy presupposes reliable knowledge of human behavior if it is to be successful, and he appears to be equally interested in the conduct of conduct, which is what technocracies attempt to achieve by creating systems of penalties for bad behavior that are designed to internalize the norms of good behavior.

It is important to add that the focus regarding how to resolve problems of a social, economic, or political nature has recently been shifted from social and economic structures to individuals, which may be termed responsibilization (Rådestad and Larsson 2018; Erikson and Larsson 2019). Against this background, it is unfortunate that Foucault is discussed only at the end of *Power without Knowledge*, for I believe that Friedman should be read as a contributor to the tradition of governmentality studies.

Exitocracy: Liberal or Socialist?

The inescapability of power can be highlighted by taking into consideration the relational understanding of power that Foucault advanced. The most extensive account of his view of power/freedom is presented in *The*

History of Sexuality: The Will to Knowledge, originally published in French in 1976, where he states that

> Power must be understood in the first instance as the multiplicity of force relations immanent in the sphere in which they operate and which constitute their own organization: as the process which, through ceaseless struggle and confrontation, transforms, strengthens, or even reverses them; as the support which these force relations find in one another, thus forming a chain or a system, or on the contrary, the disjunctions and contradictions which isolate them from one another; and lastly, as the strategies in which they take effect, whose general design or institutionalized crystallization is embodied in the state apparatus, in the formulation of the law, in the various social hegemonies. (Foucault 1990, 92-93)

Friedman argues that the creation of an exitocracy, understood as a technocracy with extensive exit options, constitutes a means for resolving some of the difficulties associated with technocratic solutions that suffer from an imperfect knowledge of human behavior and imperfect knowledge of responses to incentives. He presents this solution in the last chapter of *Power Without Knowledge*, and although it initially seems attractive, it raises several questions that require further discussion.

The first of these is whether it is indeed possible and normatively justifiable to exit from various aspects of social and political life, insofar as this type of alternative appears to rely upon a liberal misconception of a space or life outside power relations—contrary to Foucault—along with a notion of the individual as socially and politically primary.

A second issue is that, as Friedman points out (322, 340-41), exitocracy would require a substantial political and societal organization and, paradoxically, technocratic knowledge and judgment. If we find the idea of an exitocracy morally justifiable, and at least to some extent organizationally plausible, we would thus immediately run into significant problems concerning precisely how it can be organized.

Similarly, Friedman briefly discusses the fact that an exitocracy would require an "egalitarian socialism" insofar as

> exit opportunities will more often than not require economic resources. Only economic resources can allow one to enter into alternatives to the situation from which one would like to exit. Thus, if the experimentation promised by the exit option is to be possible for more than the rich, economic redistribution is called for. (335)

How could an economic redistribution that appears more ambitious than the most generous forms of the welfare state be put in place? How could we tax the rich in order to create exit possibilities for the poor? Would there be the risk of capital flight made possible by globalization, or a free-rider problem among the recipients of exit options? As Friedman argues, "The administration of an exitocratic Difference Principle would require the administrators to make behavioral predictions that nobody—no matter how judiciously attentive to ideational heterogeneity—is well positioned to make" (340).

Friedman maintains that

> An exitocracy is a regime in which the policies of government are, wherever possible, power conferring–or, more conventionally put, where the policies are conducive to roughly equal positive freedom … but where the rationale for these policies is not a liberal goal, such as the maximization of freedom or equality as an end in itself, but the technocratic goal of minimizing human distress. By conferring equal power on people to solve their problems in the private sphere, an exitocracy would live up to the egalitarian premise of all forms of utilitarianism and of socialism, too. (324)

I am eager to see how such a collective system can follow from the methodological individualism and subjective understanding of knowledge that were discussed above. Also valuable would be a further discussion of how collective knowledge could make possible a generous project of welfare distribution that sustains exitocracy without generating distrust among citizens.

* * *

There is much of value in *Power Without Knowledge*, not least in that it highlights the importance of technocracy within the democratic system. Friedman pointedly reminds us that we need to direct greater attention to the means of politics, not merely the ends. Perhaps most importantly, Friedman calls us to engage in a discussion of how questions of ontology and epistemology underlie and shape our political imagination concerning the types of polity that we can regard as in fact possible to construct.

REFERENCES

Bacchi, Carol, and Susan Goodwin. 2016. *Poststructural Policy Analysis: A Guide to Practice*. New York: Springer Nature.

Beaumont, Justin, and Walter Nicholls. 2008. "Plural Governance, Participation and Democracy in Cities." *International Journal of Urban and Regional Research* 32(1): 87-94.

Berlin, Isaiah. 1958. *Two Concepts of Liberty*. Oxford: Clarendon.

Burchell, Graham, Colin Gordon, and Peter Miller. 1991. *The Foucault Effect: Studies in Governmentality*. Chicago: University of Chicago Press.

Clarence, E. 2002. "Technocracy Reinvented: The New Evidence Based Policy Movement." *Public Policy and Administration* 17(3): 1-11.

Cohen, Joshua. 1997. "Deliberation and Democratic Legitimacy." In *Deliberative Democracy: Essays on Reason and Politics*, edited by James Bohman and William Rehg. Cambridge, Mass.: MIT Press.

Dean, Mitchell. 2010. *Governmentality: Power and Rule in Modern Society*, 2nd ed. London: SAGE.

Erikson, Josefina, and Oscar L. Larsson. 2019. "Beyond Client Criminalization: Analyzing Collaborative Governance Arrangements for Combatting Prostitution and Trafficking in Sweden." *Regulation and Governance*. DOI: 10.1111/rego.12259.

Fischer, Frank. 1998. "Beyond Empiricism: Policy Inquiry in a Post-Positivist Perspective." *Policy Studies Journal* 26(1): 129-46.

Fischer, Frank, Douglas Torgerson, Anna Durnova and Michael Orsini. 2015. "Introduction to Critical Policy Studies." In *Handbook of Critical Policy Studies*, ed. Frank Fischer, Douglas Torgerson, Anna Durnova, and Michael Orsini. Cheltenham: Edward Elgar.

Foucault, Michel. 1980. *Power/Knowledge: Selected Interviews and Other Writings* 1972-1977. Ed. Colin Gordon, trans. Colin Gordon and others. New York: Pantheon.

Foucault, Michel. 1990. *The History of Sexuality: An Introduction*, vol. 1. Trans. Robert Hurley. New York: Vintage.

Foucault, Michel. 2007. *Security, Territory, Population: Lectures at the Collège de France, 1977-78*. Basingstoke: Palgrave Macmillan.

Foucault, Michel. 2008. *The Birth of Biopolitics: Lectures at the Collége de France, 1978-* 1979. Basingstoke: Palgrave Macmillan.

Friedman, Jeffrey. 2019. *Power Without Knowledge: A Critique of Technocracy*. New York: Oxford University Press.

Fuller, Steve. 2018 *Post-Truth: Knowledge as a Power Game*, vol. 1. London: Anthem.

Fung, Archon, and Erik Olin Wright. 2003. 4 *Deepening Democracy: Institutional Innovations in Empowered Participatory Governance*. The Real Utopias Project, Vol. 4. London and New York: Verso.

Habermas, Jürgen. 1970. "The Scientization of Politics and Public Opinion." In *Toward a Rational Society: Student Protest, Science and Politics*. Boston: Beacon.

Hay, Colin. 2017. "The Interdependence of Intra- and Inter-Subjectivity in Constructivist Institutionalism." *Critical Review* 29(2): 235- 47.

Head, Brian W. 2013. "Evidence-Based Policymaking: Speaking Truth to Power?" *Australian Journal of Public Administration* 72(4): 397-403.

Hollis, Martin. 1994. *The Philosophy of Social Science: An Introduction*. Cambridge: Cambridge University Press.

Larsson, Oscar L. 2013. "Sovereign Power Beyond the State: A Critical Reappraisal of Governance by Networks." *Critical Policy Studies* 7(2): 99-114.

Larsson, Oscar L. 2015. "Using Post-Structuralism to Explore the Full Impact of Ideas on Politics." *Critical Review* 27(2): 174-97.

Larsson, Oscar L. 2018. "Advancing Post-Structural Institutionalism: Discourses, Subjects, Power Asymmetries, and Institutional Change." *Critical Review* 30 (3-4): 325-46.

Larsson, Oscar L. 2019a. "The Governmentality of Network Governance: Collaboration as a New Facet of the Liberal Art of Governing." *Constellations* 27(1): 111-126.

Larsson, Oscar L. 2019b. "A Theoretical Framework for Analyzing Institutionalized Domination in Network Governance Arrangements." *Critical Policy Studies* 13 (1): 81-100.

Lenoble, Jacques, and Marc Maesschalck. 2003. *Toward a Theory of Governance: The Action of Norms*. London: Kluwer.

Lundin, Martin, and PerOla Öberg. 2014. "Expert Knowledge Use and Deliberation in Local Policy Making." *Policy Sciences* 47(1): 25-49.

Morcol, Goktug. 2002. *A New Mind for Policy Analysis: Toward A Post-Newtonian and Post-Positivist Epistemology and Methodology*. Westport, Conn.: Praeger.

Phelps, Nicholas A., and Mark Tewdwr-Jones. 2000. "Scratching the Surface of Collaborative and Associative Governance: Identifying the Diversity of Social Action in Institutional Capacity Building." *Environment and Planning A* 32(1): 111-130.

Pløger, J. 2001. "Public Participation and the Art of Governance." *Environment and Planning B: Planning and Design* 28(2): 219-41.

Rhodes, R.A.W. 1997. *Understanding Governance: Policy Networks, Governance, Reflexivity and Accountability*. London: Open University Press.

Rådestad, Carl, and Oscar L. Larsson. 2018. "Responsibilization in Contemporary Swedish Crisis Management: Expanding 'Bare Life' Biopolitics through Exceptionalism and Neoliberal Governmentality." *Critical Policy Studies* 14(1): 86-105.

Schmidt, Vivien A. 2017. "Theorizing Ideas and Discourse in Political Science: Intersubjectivity, Neo-Institutionalisms, and the Power of Ideas." *Critical Review* 29(2): 248-63.

Stone, Deborah. 2002. *Policy Paradox: The Art of Political Decision Making*, rev. ed. New York: W. W. Norton.

Taylor, Charles. 1985. "Interpretation and the Sciences of Man." In idem, *Philosophical Papers*, vol. 2, *Philosophy and the Human Sciences*. Cambridge: Cambridge University Press.

Thaler, Richard H. 2015. *Misbehaving: The Making of Behavioral Economics*. New York: W. W. Norton.

Thaler, Richard H., and Cass R. Sunstein. 2009. *Nudge: Improving Decisions about Health, Wealth, and Happiness*. London: Penguin.

Torfing, Jacob, and Peter Triantafillou. 2013. "What's in a Name? Grasping New Public Governance as a Political-Administrative System." *International Review of Public Administration* 18(2): 9-25.

Vedung, E. 1997. *Public Policy and Program Evaluation*. New York: Transaction Publishers.
Weale, Albert. 2011. "New Modes of Governance, Political Accountability and Public Reason." *Government and Opposition* 46(1): 58-80.
Wildavsky, Aaron. 2017. *Speaking Truth to Power: Art and Craft of Policy Analysis*. London: Routledge.
Yanow, Dvorah. 2000. *Conducting Interpretive Policy Analysis*. Thousand Oaks, Calif.: SAGE.

Adam B. Lerner

SOCIAL SCIENCE AND THE PROBLEM OF INTERPRETATION: A PRAGMATIC DUAL(IST) APPROACH

ABSTRACT: *In* Power Without Knowledge, *Jeffrey Friedman contends that ideational complexity can stymie social-scientific understanding and prevent the reliable predictive knowledge required of a well-functioning technocracy. However, even this somewhat pessimistic outlook may understate the problem. Ideational complexity has both cognitive and phenomenal dimensions, each of which poses unique dilemmas. Further, due to its methodological individualism, Friedman's vision may neglect emergent layers of knowledge produced through social interaction, creating yet another source of unknowns. Given these two factors, social science should embrace a pluralism regarding levels of analysis. This would recognize the multifaceted limitations on social-science knowledge production, furthering epistemic humility about the potential role of social science in technocratic policymaking.*

Why don't social scientists know what they don't know?

Though related to the basic epistemological question of how researchers know what they know, the condition of not knowing can involve distinct issues related to the complexity of the systems under investigation

(Friedman 2012; Jervis 1998; Lerner 2020b). To address these issues, it is helpful to begin with Charles Manski's (2013, 11) simplification of the scientific process of knowledge attainment:

$$\textit{assumptions} + \textit{data} \rightarrow \textit{conclusions}$$

In periods of "normal" science (Kuhn 2009)—for instance, physics operating entirely within longstanding Newtonian or Einsteinian paradigms—researchers hold the "assumptions" variable constant, such that variations in conclusions stem entirely from variations in data. During such research periods, discoveries are taken to be either "findings" or spurs to collect data that will generate new findings. Accordingly, not-knowing stems entirely from insufficient data. Of course, in Kuhn's model scientific revolutions augur paradigm shifts that can undermine or complicate previously well-established "knowledge." But such revolutions are rare, and the majority of research in the natural sciences is grounded in shared, unquestioned assumptions.

Despite considerable efforts to "normalize" the social sciences, their paradigmatic background assumptions remain considerably more contested and contestable than those in the natural sciences. For this reason, not-knowing in the social sciences is a commensurately more complex condition. Not-knowing in the social sciences can stem not only from inadequacies in data collection, but also from contestation over human actors' background assumptions and, perhaps most importantly, from the oftentimes problematic system effects produced by inaccurate provisional assumptions and the data collected in their shadow.

Background assumptions vary considerably, depending not only on researchers' and their subjects' philosophical wagers (see Jackson 2011), but also on the historical and cultural milieu within which concepts and theories are formulated and applied. As social scientists conduct research, their assumptions often infect their research subjects and pervert data through experimenter effects and related biases. Further, the social systems they study are often complex adaptive systems, with parameters and frameworks shifting over time in unexpected ways (Bousquet and Curtis 2011; Kavalski 2007). Taken together, these complications can hinder the progressive accumulation of universalistic knowledge in social sciences. While some research communities come to intersubjective agreement about baseline assumptions, a birds'-eye view of the social sciences reveals irreconcilable, foundational debates that inhibit widespread consensus on baseline facts, let alone policy solutions.

This added complexity implicit in social sciences' unknowns, and the conundrums it creates for policy makers, is at the heart of Jeffrey Friedman's lucid new book *Power Without Knowledge* (Oxford University Press, 2019). Friedman argues that a particular type of complexity—ideational complexity—may make social scientists unable to comprehend the behaviour of those whom they study, let alone predict this behavior, as they must do when they act as technocrats. Unknowns stemming from the complexity of the ideational world may leave technocrats unable to design policies that both decisively address social ills and account for the seemingly endless universe of possible unintended consequences that stem from governing individual behavior.

Although in his preface, Friedman questions his book's suitability to the current political moment, *Power Without Knowledge* sheds enormous insight on one potent source of frustration with elites that may have fueled the rise of Donald Trump. In this view, complexity and the not-knowing it produces are not simply byproducts of science's slow and oftentimes uneven accumulation of knowledge. Rather, not-knowing can be seen as inherent, to some degree, in social life. The intractability of not-knowing in social science can have enormous policy consequences. If the social world is defined by its partial unknowability—and if, as Friedman contends, it is in the nature of this unknowability that its contours are irregular and thus cannot easily be predicted—citizens have good reason to lose faith in elites who profess an uncanny (yet oftentimes opaque) ability to predict and control behavior.[1]

In this brief essay, I delve deeper into what Friedman identifies as the roots of this complexity—ideational heterogeneity. Drawing on insights from philosophy of mind, I argue that Friedman's discussion of complexity runs together two types of unknowns—the cognitive and the phenomenal—each of which presents distinct problems for social scientists. Although these two variants collapse into one larger realm under certain materialist ontologies of consciousness, their division proves useful not only given the limitations of current science, but also in elucidating new contours of the challenges Friedman identifies. In the final section, I build on this more complete vision of complexity to problematize Friedman's epistemological individualism. Although Friedman favors privileging individuals as the loci of ideational heterogeneity and, thus, as the source of the complexity that hinders social science analysis, this individualism may neglect further variants of complexity and resultant unknowns found in system-level emergent properties. Much of this problematization is suggestive and does not undermine the potency of Friedman's critique. Nevertheless, it does reveal the depth of the complexity problem Friedman identifies, as well as new avenues for its analysis.

I. IDEATIONAL HETEROGENEITY

The first chapter of *Power Without Knowledge* clears the ground for Friedman's analysis by pointing out that the truth about the scope and severity of public problems, and about the efficacy and costs of solutions, is not self-evident. The question of technocratic knowing or not-knowing, then, must be answered through some sort of empirical attempt to test our initial impressions. In Chapter 2, Friedman draws on Walter Lippmann's writings from the 1920s to suggest that these empirical attempts will constitute *interpretations*, and in Chapter 3 he argues that they are interpretations of the interpretations produced by the human agents who cause social and economic problems. *Heterogeneity* between the technocrats' interpretations of how agents are likely to behave in response to a technocratic initiative and the agents' own interpretations of how they should behave can cause technocrats' behavioral predictions to go awry. This is because, under modern conditions, no two people are likely to have identical webs of belief. Thus, technocrats' webs of belief may differ from agents' webs of belief significantly enough that the former incorrectly predict the responses of the latter.

Despite frequent assumptions to the contrary, Friedman argues that ideational heterogeneity is not random, so we have little reason to believe that it will average out as sample sizes increase. People's interpretations of how to behave stem from "non-random but opaquely determined" webs of belief that are logical but built upon unobservable, and, to some extent, heterogeneous inputs. These inputs stem from interpersonal communication from a variety of sources, taking place over the course of people's lives (144). While on a local scale, among friends and colleagues, or for diligent intellectual historians analyzing research subjects, ideas can be somewhat reliably understood and anticipated,[2] on a macro level ideational heterogeneity leads to complexities that may be insuperable. This is because the modeler, or the technocrat, is attempting to predict the behavior, and thus the ideas, of masses of people whose webs of belief are somewhat opaque; unlike friends and colleagues, after all, the modeler/technocrat has never even met the people whose behavior is being modeled/predicted. Friedman does not claim, however, to know *how much* of a problem this will pose, as this will vary from case to case (317-19).

Most positivist social scientists would agree that some realms of human behavior—falling in love, enjoying a work of art—involve such a complex web of prior beliefs and preferences that they are opaque to the non-intrusive methods available to most researchers. Nevertheless, they would argue that such factors as "homogenizing norms" (147), incentives, and biases lead to behavioral patterns that are significant and reliable enough to guide large-scale policymaking. Friedman agrees, in principle, and he grants, too, that the psychological processing behind ideational heterogeneity may be nomological, but he suggests that the ideational inputs into nomological processes may be so diverse that the resulting interpretations are too complex for social scientists to reasonably model in a given case (139). In a long section on the failures of neoclassical economics, he elucidates the fact that ideational heterogeneity can undermine predictions even in an arena—the marketplace—where many social scientists fallaciously assume that the single, unidimensional goal of wealth accumulation ensures individuals' predictability. Friedman argues that the requirement that individuals interpret their circumstances before acting may render even this rational realm too complex for reliable, durable predictions (183-95).

This conclusion does not, however, entirely preclude effective policymaking. Friedman maintains that there may be homogenizing factors that suppress ideational heterogeneity, or that preserve it but suppress the idiosyncratic behavior to which it would otherwise lead. This leaves room for a "judicious technocracy" that crafts public policy by investigating the balance of heterogenizing ideas and homogenizing forces, case by case (171-73). Thus, he does not deny the possibility of reliably predicting mass human behavior, and in fact he calls more than once for a "cultural revolution" against such anti-ideational assumptions as those found in positivist social science and neoclassical economics (314, 342, 352)—such that future technocrats would produce more accurate, judicious predictions. The larger message of *Power Without Knowledge,* then, is that we should recognize our ideational differences, leading to humility, tolerance, and a more humane society (343-45). Its narrower point about technocracy is that behavioral predictions could be improved if technocrats did not tend to ignore heterogeneous ideas.

However, along with Friedman's own epistemic humility goes an inability to predict *how much* a judicious social science would improve technocratic prediction, and thus how much of a problem would remain—or, for that matter, how much of a problem idiosyncratic ideas can be expected to pose in the first place (317-19). Friedman rejects not only neoclassical apriorism, but social-scientific positivism, on the grounds that it attributes lawfulness to human behavior to the neglect of the possibility that future individuals, with different webs of belief from past individuals, will behave differently too (196-228). This, however, puts serious limits on his own predictive capacities: he does not think it makes sense to assume that even if he could adduce data about the degree to which technocratic predictions have backfired in the past—which he does not think he can do —these data would allow him to predict the future. In the future, different technocrats than those in the past will be trying to predict different populations' different behaviors (ibid.).

The Limits of Judiciousness

That said, Friedman may still be too optimistic about a judicious technocracy. Identifying reliable pockets of homogeneity in a sea of ideational heterogeneity would involve deciphering a level of complexity that seems likely to remain beyond the purview of social scientists. How can technocrats who are unable to access the opaque webs of belief in others' minds reliably predict which of the behavioral patterns they identify are stable and suitable for long-term policy making (with minimal unintended consequences) and which ones are simply spurious correlations liable to change over time? If these questions cannot be answered, then a judicious technocracy may be a mirage.

In his final chapter, Friedman attempts to avoid such questions by constructing an ideal type of a technocratic regime founded on the principle of voluntary exit (an "exitocracy"). Such a regime would take advantage of the fact that people's knowledge of their own dissatisfaction with a given set of circumstances is likely to be relatively reliable. This is especially the case when compared to the knowledge anyone is likely to have of the webs of belief of the millions of "anonymous others" who are the targets of technocratic behavior-modification programs. Insofar as personal, experiential knowledge is more reliable than predictive knowledge of anonymous others, Friedman argues, exit is epistemically preferable to "ordinary" technocracy, although exit mechanisms are themselves technocratic, such that an exitocracy counts as an "extraordinary" type of technocracy (322). An exitocracy, then, is a technocracy that engages in limited, targeted, and preferably judicious technocratic policymaking to ensure that individuals have the means and ability to exit, but refrains from the injudicious technocratic ambitions that, according to Friedman, characterize much of contemporary politics and government. Exit would relieve some of the problems that might be caused by the attempt to predict and then voice theories about others' anonymous behavior, even though Friedman does not pretend to know how bad those problems might be or how much relief an exitocracy could offer. And even though there would be many areas of policy making left over where exit is not possible, this approach would leave the judicious "ordinary" provision of public goods as a path to relief (343)—if that is not itself impossible.

II. BEYOND COGNITIVE COMPLEXITY

Friedman's critique of social scientists' lofty ambitions, as well as his rejection of behaviorism in favor of a focus on ideas and (to whatever extent possible) a massified version of intellectual history, in which the ideas of the people whose behavior technocrats try to control become the topic of social science, will be a balm for post-positivists frustrated by the encroachment of scientism and technologically driven methods into their fields. Such methods oftentimes downplay agency and dehumanize policymaking processes, with various negative results. Further, his call for epistemic humility in the face of the social world's complexity proves vital, especially considering the so-called digital humanities' assault on the funding and prestige of traditional humanistic work (Da 2019).

Nevertheless, the opacity he identifies in our webs of belief is (ironically) a more complex phenomenon than Friedman outlines. Complexity à la Friedman (140) stems from the heterogeneity of ideas, a category in which he includes "'perceptions,' 'beliefs,' and 'interpretations,' along with hypotheses, theories, strokes of inspiration, and assumptions, implicit and explicit." This is perhaps an overly broad concept, covering multiple types of mental processes (including the psychological and phenomenal) that, in many ways, present distinct epistemological challenges.

In this section, I draw on the distinction David Chalmers (1995) makes between the easy problems of consciousness—those that can be explained functionally via cognitive models—and the hard problem of consciousness relating to phenomenal experience, in order to distinguish between the potentially irreconcilable cognitive and phenomenal roots of complexity. Cognitive aspects of consciousness relate to functionalist variants of mental processing that can be modeled "objectively," as if the brain were purely an electrochemical computer. This maps loosely onto the cognitive products discussed by Friedman (137), for the most part, when he refers to "ideas": these are the "inputs" into our webs of belief that are received from the variable streams of communication to which we are all exposed, which can combine to produce interpretive outputs. By contrast, phenomenal consciousness relates to the qualia of purely subjective experience: the fact that there is something that it is *like* to be a phenomenally conscious being (Chalmers 1997; Nagel 1974). "Qualia" refer to the phenomenal aspect of human experience —what it is like to see the color red, feel sandpaper, or confront the frustrations of bureaucracy at the Department of Motor Vehicles. Though the ontological status of qualia is hotly contested in philosophy of mind (Tye 2018), they are intuitively distinguishable from cognitive knowledge[3] or "thoughts," and their unapproachability via traditional social science methods poses an epistemological conundrum for researchers (Lerner 2020c). For this reason, even as scientists and philosophers debate whether qualia are illusions potentially explicable in conventional physical terms or whether explaining qualia requires the discovery of a new property or substance (Bennett 2005; Wendt 2015), a recognition of the division between thoughts and qualia can prove potent in epistemological critiques of conventional approaches to agency. Understanding how and why the DMV bureaucracy produces long, boring waits is substantively different from *experiencing* these waits oneself, and social scientists must recognize how these two forms of knowledge can differentially affect webs of belief and contribute to differing behaviors.

Although many philosophers and neuroscientists believe that these two aspects of consciousness, thoughts and qualia, are indistinct and that phenomenal experience is ultimately an illusion created by material forces (see Frankish 2017), current science has no means of linking the two, nor any widely accepted theory of how they could possibly be linked. For this reason, maintaining the dualism, without committing to it metaphysically, can prove pragmatic for scholars in the social sciences seeking to mobilize philosophy of mind's insights for their analysis (Lerner 2020c). Instead of the catchall term *ideas* that Friedman employs to describe the units of both cognitive processing and phenomenal consciousness, then, I will refer to the simplest possible units of the former as "thoughts" and of the latter as "qualia." This division reveals two deeply intertwined yet distinguishable aspects of complexity that hinder technocratic understanding.

Cognitive Complexity Due to Thoughts

Although Friedman refers at times to "experience" in ways that implicate qualia (145), the diversity of agents' cognitive thoughts—representations of the outside world that combine to form thoughts about how an agent should *act* in a given situation—is the chief source of epistemic complexity with which Friedman is concerned. Thus, different individuals are likely to receive somewhat heterogeneous inputs into their webs of belief, rendering their thoughts about the circumstances in which they must act somewhat opaque to those, such as social scientists and technocrats, who are trying to understand their ideas sufficiently to predict their behavior (144-46). This does seem to pose quite a problem, although Friedman is careful to point out that the very nature of the problem prevents him from predicting precisely how significant it is likely to be (146). That is, the degree of heterogeneity across various individuals' webs, based on the specific differences in the ideational inputs into those webs, is unobservable and thus, as a pragmatic matter, unpredictable for technocrats and political theorists alike. Granting this caveat about the magnitude of the resulting problem for technocracy, Friedman may nevertheless be too optimistic about its susceptibility to a "judicious" solution—not only, as previously indicated, because of the difficulty of the judicious technocrat's position vis-à-vis thoughts, but because of the added need to take account of qualia.

To predict people's behavior, judicious social scientists must not simply understand the component parts of their webs of belief, but also how these component parts interact depending on timing, emphasis, emotional regulation, and a host of other factors. Moreover, focusing solely on the complexity inherent in the construction of individuals' webs of belief can neglect how responding and reacting to these webs may beget further layers of complexity—a point especially relevant to policy making. Even social and economic policy initiatives that judiciously recognize the ideational roots of behavior are liable to create second- and third-order complications as individuals react to their incentive structures. Policy makers, in response, face incentives to respond to individuals' reactions, potentially creating cycles shaped by unintended consequences (see Hoffmann and Riley 2002). This dynamic describes, for example, why policy initiatives designed to crack down on the flow of drugs across borders tend to fail. As policy-makers respond to smugglers' tactics, smugglers interpret policy makers' methods and adjust, leading to a seemingly endless game of cat-and-mouse (Nixon 2017). These cycles of policymaking and response create second- and third-order complications distinct from the second-order complexity that Friedman thinks will face a judicious technocracy. And even acknowledging all of these different layers of complexity, social scientists must further consider how they may interact with various contexts—another source of complexity.

Given this situation, it should be no surprise that many social scientists have come to view webs to belief and qualia alike as red herrings. In this sense, behaviorism—focusing on individuals' actions rather than their ideas—is a natural approach for pragmatists wary that policies that account for slippery thoughts and feelings will only lead to adaptations beyond their control, as well as for defeatists resigned to finding broad historical trends, at best, rather than accurately predicting future changes. Nevertheless, despite the rabbit holes to which both thoughts and qualia may lead, Friedman is right to point out that ideas are vital to policy making and cannot simply be ignored. In key cases, for example, buried in them may be the reasons why an individual either chooses to reject violence, offer sympathy to violent actors online, join an extremist group, or even organize a violent attack. For a society concerned about predicting such future events rather than simply recognizing broad historical trends liable to change alongside shifting cultural mores, behaviorism will prove utterly insufficient.

Phenomenal Complexity Due to Qualia

The addition of qualia to thoughts, however, reveals that such local comprehensibility can be a mirage, belied by an added layer of potentially incomprehensible policy-relevant *phenomenal* complexity.

In making this argument, I recognize that introducing phenomenal consciousness into debates about policy making might inspire skepticism. Indeed, some who accept an intuitive division between thoughts and qualia might still object that qualia do not constitute *policy-relevant* knowledge. Qualia, after all, must be translated into thoughts before they can affect the physical world by motivating actions. According to this line of thinking, while qualia constitute a form of knowledge, they are not policy-relevant knowledge until they are intellectualized in some way and transformed into a cognitive disposition or thought. In other words, what it is like to be thirsty is not relevant to policy making; it is only relevant if this becomes a thought that could potentially shape language or action.

However, such a quick dismissal of the role of qualia in policy making can be problematic. Indeed, this rejection of the subjective realm is, in many ways, an extension of the anti-agentic behaviorism that Friedman criticizes for neglecting individuals' mostly inaccessible, sometimes mystifying, yet behaviorally determinative webs of belief. No matter one's ontological disposition regarding consciousness, all philosophers of mind would agree that qualia (even if they are, ultimately, a sophisticated illusion) are deeply linked to the material world. These links are multifaceted and opaque, yet they allow the physical world to shape experience and experience to shape thoughts and behavior. Many intellectualized thoughts woven into an individual's web of beliefs can remain either silent or salient in memory due to their experiential corollaries (qualia), and oftentimes qualia lead to instinctual behaviors that are only intellectualized as thoughts after they are performed. For example, as anyone would attest, the abstract thought that hot things burn the skin is made all the more memorable when learning it is accompanied by the qualia of excruciating pain. Without reference to the qualia of pain, researchers lose a crucial insight into what makes the abstract thought meaningful for individuals and what behaviors become more or less likely to arise if they do not heed this meaning.

Thus, the thought that hot things burn the skin is likely to be present in a great number of individuals' webs of belief. A recognition of this simple fact contributes to numerous policy decisions, including regulations surrounding infrastructure and even the permissibility of such activities as public barbeques. Oftentimes policymakers assume—perhaps because of their past experiences—that people will know not to perform difficult, vigorous dance numbers adjacent to active barbeques, and thus they fail to legislate against such activity, choosing only to intervene in less obvious scenarios. But the abstract thought must contend with an array of others in any given web of belief, such that people do occasionally burn themselves on barbeques during lapses of judgment. Once in a while, a relaxing Sunday in the park can lead to a hospital visit.

In this sort of situation, qualia can play a vital role in determining the topography of individuals' webs of belief, as different thoughts become more or less prominent due to past experiences. Because having felt the qualia of burning oneself is likely to make the thought that "hot things burn the skin" far more salient in an individual's web of belief, policy-makers cannot neglect the potential role of the traces of this experience in determining how people will behave and, ultimately, the policy responses necessary to govern this behavior. Were someone to lack all experience of being burned, it is likely that the dangers of hot things would be less prominent in her web of belief than had she been burned —even though the same thought might be in this person's mind as well as the mind of one who had been burned. Thus, qualia can make otherwise banal factual knowledge (thoughts) come alive for individuals, shaping the topography of ideas in their webs of belief even in cases where the cognitive thought content does not change. Given the limitations of science in understanding the roots and shape of qualia, however, as well as the enormous difficulty scientists have in gaining access to the subjective residue of experience, epistemologists should, pragmatically speaking, consider qualia both a form of knowledge and yet another inaccessible locus of complexity and unknowability (Lerner 2019b and 2020b). To the extent that this source of complexity shapes the topography of webs of belief, which, in turn, shape behavior, it too should be incorporated into policy analysis.

Unfortunately, those inclined to recognize the importance of qualia to people's policy-relevant webs of belief cannot cordon them off as a single variable that can be controlled for in the usual ways. Rather, qualia must be understood as producing a further layer of phenomenal complexity, complete with its own system effects as it integrates into heterogeneous webs of belief. This layer stems from the complex and opaque linkages between qualia and objective material facts. Qualia do not predictably and evenly align with various physical realities, but rather heterogeneously associate with them. For example, while most people would find burning themselves painful, they would likely do so to different degrees that do not correlate linearly with the severity of the burn's material damage. Some people will feel the same burn and find the pain mild, while others will find it excruciating. Indeed, some masochists may even endure the exact same physical experience and material damage to skin, but associate the burn instead with the qualia of pleasure. The non-random, adaptive, and opaquely determined connections between qualia and the objective facts that determine them multiply the already complex picture painted by cognitive complexity, creating further inaccessible policy-relevant complications.

While the example of burn-related pain may seem risibly simplistic and distant from social scientific inquiry, qualia-induced complexity has been at the heart of the recent debate over "trigger warnings" on college campuses, as well as the relevant policy making that should govern them at the university, state and federal levels (Manne 2015; Robbins 2016). The premise of a trigger warning is that some content produces unpleasant, sometimes horrific qualia in certain people, despite no presence of *physical* danger. Oftentimes, these qualia stem from associations between content and past traumatic experience, but such connections are rarely systematic or, for that matter, easily discernible (Lerner 2020a). Some trauma sufferers do not desire trigger warnings, some do, and some may request them at certain points but not others. Other people who have not themselves experienced trauma may nonetheless desire trigger warnings as the content brings up unpleasant feelings due to vicarious learning or associations. In this sense, just as with the interpretive diversity highlighted by Friedman, the qualia produced by certain academic material is not reducible to its intellectual, explicit cognitive thought content—it is interwoven in webs that include both thoughts *and* qualia.

III. THE PROBLEM WITH EPISTEMOLOGICAL INDIVIDUALISM

The distinction between qualia and thoughts outlined in the previous section helps elucidate just how complex ideational complexity really is. It poses a variety of epistemological challenges, including the opaque interactions of thoughts and qualia in individuals' webs of belief, the problematic accessibility of thoughts and qualia to the methods of current science, and the multiplicity of possible interactions of individuals in social settings that will shape decision-making. In addition, the complex interactions of thoughts, qualia and the external world that produces webs of belief *within* individuals also suggests that Friedman's epistemological individualism may neglect yet further layers of complexity created *between* individuals. Indeed, the complex interactions of individuals' webs of belief can produce emergent logics and knowledge that are irreducible to individuals.

Adding these emergent properties into the analysis problematizes Friedman's decision to regard individuals as the sole "creators and loci" of ideational complexity (149) and suggests the need for pluralism regarding levels of analysis. In this section, I outline how this emergent knowledge can problematize Friedman's parsimonious epistemological individualism. I further outline how pluralism regarding levels of analysis might prove pragmatic, as it shelves thorny ontological questions in favor of more tractable epistemological ones.

Friedman's argument for epistemological individualism stems from his belief that individuals are the sole source of novel, fallible ideas that are communicated from person to person in social life. This belief implies that attributing behavioral patterns to the logic of groups of individuals, rather than of the individuals themselves, ignores the need for such logics to be interpreted by individuals if they are to result in actions. When groups of individuals "are treated as unitary actors infallibly following the logic of their situations, as if the situations did not have to be interpreted by someone," Friedman argues, scholarship overlooks the fact that "only individuals can produce such interpretations (or any other interpretations)." Ultimately, Friedman argues that we need to attend to individuals' interpretations because "individuals are the biological loci of the webs of belief that give rise to interpretation." Though interactions within groups can homogenize interpretations, individuals also produce the ideational heterogeneity that frustrates social science's predictive capacity. Thus, according to Friedman, the move from individual-level to group-level analysis effaces the possibility of erroneous homogenized interpretations of the environment (e.g., conveyed to the masses by the news media) and heterogeneous interpretations among individuals, in both cases leading to behavior we would not predict from the environment alone.

This line of thinking benefits from Friedman's critique of Charles Taylor's assertion, in "Interpretation and the Sciences of Man," that "intersubjective social reality" has an ontological status independent of its individual members (Taylor 1971, 29). Taylor's approach, Friedman argues, reifies collective metaphors such as "culture," "society," and "the state." According to Friedman, this approach neglects the fact that social, cultural, and political realities are entirely reducible to actions taken by individuals, because of ideas developed and interpersonally communicated by individuals (149). Taylor's view, in contrast, lends itself to an uncritical functionalism whereby individuals' ideas are homogeneous reactions to societal realities (159). Therefore, Friedman contends, an ideationally sensitive (that is, "judicious") social science would reject such holistic analysis as providing false comfort to technocrats seeking to simplify large numbers of research subjects' heterogeneity. A judicious approach would necessarily model itself not after sociology or economics, which so often ignore or explain away ideas at, respectively, the societal and individual levels. Rather, it would veer towards intellectual history, broadly conceived to include analyses of public opinion, so as to interrogate the ideational sources, differences, tacit assumptions, inconsistencies, and errors in people's webs of belief —which shape the social world through the actions to which they lead (160-64).

While I am sympathetic to Friedman's ontological critique of Taylor's holism, as political epistemology it may prove equally problematic for two main reasons. The first is simply practical, regarding the impossibility of meaningfully reducing certain forms of social knowledge, such as language or culture, to the actions of individuals. Friedman rejects Taylor's assertion of the reality of intersubjective realms on the basis that all presumably shared understandings between individuals can be traced back to individuals' interpretations and communicative actions. Borrowing Alasdair MacIntyre's example of the sport of hockey, which rests on "collective expectations" about rules and strategy, Friedman argues that uncritically reifying these expectations neglects the role of individuals in hockey's intellectual history. "If we could investigate with perfect hindsight the history of hockey, we would surely find that the game was originated by individuals, either deliberately or through the evolution of forms of play over time brought about by individual innovations, deliberate or accidental" (153).

Yet, even in the case of a single sport, played primarily by Westerners in the nineteenth and twentieth centuries, such a complete intellectual history may not be possible. In the case of more complex forms of collective knowledge, such as language and culture, with more opaque historical origins, this is almost surely impossible. If the goal of political epistemology is to produce knowledge of political life, then surely an approach that favors unravelling every thread of every social sweater is counterproductive. For this reason, accepting social knowledge as a methodological tool may be vital to the sort of intellectual history Friedman favors, so long as it does not entail uncritically reifying such social knowledge ontologically. Indeed, this is exactly the move that Friedman favors regarding "the individual," which he regards as a useful "methodological construct" due to the brain's role in editing and housing webs of belief, despite individuals' reducibility to subsystems like the frontal lobe (156). Pragmatism, in this case, may dictate setting aside thorny ontological questions in favor of a more tractable debate about which social and political entities are worth positing as useful methodological constructs in the interest of knowledge production. Taylor's uncritically reified collective forces may not make the cut, but surely other supra-individual constructs would.

Friedman agrees that we should treat certain supra-individual entities as potentially useful placeholder "metaphors" or "methodological constructs" for reasons of emphasis (149). Yet, Friedman's methodological individualism may raise a second potential set of epistemological issues relating to the emergent properties of social groups. These emergent properties may create forms of knowledge that are poorly captured by treating collectivities as mere metaphors for collections of individuals' beliefs and actions. Just as brains can integrate billions of firing neurons to produce thoughts and qualia over and above the scope of any discrete neuronal firing patterns, socio-political groups can integrate individuals' webs of belief to create logics and knowledge that cannot necessarily be reduced to individuals and their communication.

The clearest recent example of epistemologically irreducible emergent knowledge comes from Christian List and Philip Pettit's work on group agency, which outlines how organized groups of individuals can become agents, developing distinct beliefs and desires from those of their individual members (List and Pettit 2006, 2010, and 2011). Deborah Tollefsen (2015, 60–62; see also Fleming 2017) illustrates this thinking with the simplified example of a three-person admissions committee considering new potential Ph.D. candidates on four grounds: test scores, grades, reference letters, and writing samples. To gain admission, each applicant must pass muster on all four. For a single candidate A, the committee members vote as follows:

Table 1. Admissions Committee Members' votes for candidate A

	Test scores	Grades	Reference Letters	Writing Samples	Accept
Committee Member 1	Yes	No	Yes	No	No
Committee Member 2	No	Yes	Yes	Yes	No
Committee Member 3	Yes	Yes	No	Yes	No
Committee Majority	Yes	Yes	Yes	Yes	Yes

(*Source:* Tollefson 2015, 61.)

This scenario presents a dilemma for the committee. Individually, each member believes that candidate A should not be accepted, as each committee member believes that at least one aspect of the application is lacking. Yet if the committee were to vote on each of the four aspects of the application, a majority would support the application by concluding that the candidate has sufficient test scores, grades, letters, and writing samples. Thus, if voting were to take place on each aspect, rather than on the candidate's entire application, he or she would gain admission.

In order for the committee as a whole to become a rational, consistent actor, ensuring that its decisions form a coherent whole over time, List and Pettit (2011) demonstrate that it must often adopt the premise-based approach that admits the candidate. Otherwise, the group's actions will be inconsistent with its stated intention—in this case, admitting candidates with what are widely accepted to be sufficient grades, test scores, reference letters, and writing samples (see Tollefsen 2015, 62–63). What this means in practice is that the committee members have an incentive to establish the admissions committee as a group agent—one with properties that supervene on those of members, making them irreducible to individuals. This is even more the case in complex groups such as political institutions and states, where decision-making is far more complex than simple voting and individuals may not be privy to complex decision-making structures. Further, in many cases group procedures will remain the same even as membership changes, leading to scenarios in which individual members do not understand the group's formation or the basis for its collectivized methods of rationalization, but accept its procedures for making decisions *as a group*. Whatever the ontological status of the group as a social agent, in such scenarios it produces desires and intentions (knowledge) that cannot be fully explained by reduction to individuals. No member of the group may desire candidate A's admittance, even as the group as a whole does. Without reference to the group, knowledge of the committee's decisions will suffer.

The examples employed here are stylized and simplistic, leaving them open to the counterargument that individuals within groups may construct a metaphorical group agent to regulate their social behavior. But reducing the group to a metaphor neglects the fact that knowledge about its intentions and desires is plainly not reducible to the knowledge of individuals. This conundrum becomes more apparent as groups and the decisions they face become more complex, and their ability to produce intentions and desires even more distant from those of group members increases. This distance is further magnified when group membership changes, but procedures remain in place for collectivizing rationality, as is so often the case in political institutions. For this reason, states are efficient mechanisms for organizing group-level emotions and consciousness, irreducible to the individuals within them, much in the way that brains are efficient organizational hubs for creating similar properties out of neurological subsystems (Lerner 2020c). To be sure, this does not imply endowing groups with any particular ontological status. Rather, it simply demonstrates that continual reduction to individuals and their communication threatens to dissolve the group-level logics and knowledges that are so vital to macro-level political analysis.

Acknowledging the possibility of epistemically irreducible knowledge creates issues for the methodological individualism Friedman favors. It highlights that continual emphasis on reduction will not only make social science needlessly complicated, but will also neglect very real logics, knowledge, and properties that emerge at the group level. My solution here is thus simple and pragmatic. Rather than engaging in intractable debates about social ontology and its potential for reduction to individual ontology, scholarship should embrace a pragmatic pluralism regarding levels of analysis. To a degree, this implies treating all social entities as methodological constructs that may indeed, potentially, be ontologically reducible—from societies down to individuals, neurons, molecules, atoms, and quarks. Yet it also entails accepting that these constructs exist, because at dense levels of organization they can produce emergent properties irreducible to their component parts. Thus, scholarship should select which agents and forces to include in analysis based on their utility in explaining phenomena in question. This approach would recognize multiple possible levels of organization as loci of knowing and not-knowing, not just the level of dense neuronal organization within the individual's brain.

* * *

In spite of my critiques of Friedman's treatment of ideas, as well as my disagreement with his individualism, *Power Without Knowledge* is an immense achievement—one that is worthy of significant debate. Friedman has identified significant pathologies across the social sciences that should worry researchers in virtually all disciplines. His arguments should rightfully bring scrutiny to the self-proclaimed scientific status of many social-science research programs and also fundamentally reshape social scientists' place in the policy-making process. While I have little hope that this book will stymie disciplinary trends (especially present in political science) towards fetishizing methods, and away from more substantive concerns about methodology and epistemology, Friedman has written a potent call for intellectual humility among social scientists and, thus, epistocrats, as well as citizen-technocrats.

In an era dominated by populist movements and fake news that relativize knowledge at every level, Friedman has accurately diagnosed a crisis facing academic knowledge production. Although his prescription is not an easy pill to swallow, it does help reframe the way academics see their potential role in policy debates, as well as the limitations of their expertise.

NOTES

1. Despite my sympathy for the general public's distrust of policymaking elites' confidence, I am still unable to fathom how this loss of faith could possibly lead so many to support the candidacy of Donald Trump. See Friedman 2020.
2. For my own efforts at precisely this type of localized intellectual history, see Lerner 2018 and 2019a.
3. This division, though often invoked in different terms, appears regularly in important theorizations across the social sciences. For example, in his seminal typology of memory, psychologist Endel Tulving (1972) made a distinction between what he referred to as the objective, factual realm of semantic memory and the subjective, experiential realm of episodic memory.

ORCID

Adam B. Lerner http://orcid.org/0000-0002-6715-3197

REFERENCES

Bennett, Karen. 2005. "Why I Am Not a Dualist." http://www.nyu.edu/gsas/dept/philo/courses/consciousness05/BennettDualist.pdf

Bousquet, Antoine, and Simon Curtis. 2011. "Beyond Models and Metaphors: Complexity Theory, Systems Thinking and International Relations." *Cambridge Review of International Affairs* 24(1): 43–62.

Chalmers, David J. 1995. "Facing Up to the Problem of Consciousness." *Journal of Consciousness Studies* 2(3): 200–219.

Chalmers, David John. 1997. *The Conscious Mind: In Search of a Fundamental Theory*. New York: Oxford University Press.

Da, Nan Z. 2019. "The Digital Humanities Debacle." *Chronicle of Higher Education*, 27 March.

Fleming, Sean. 2017. "Artificial Persons and Attributed Actions: How to Interpret Action-Sentences about States." *European Journal of International Relations* 23 (4): 930–50.

Frankish, Keith. 2017. *Illusionism: As a Theory of Consciousness*. Luton, Bedfordshire: Andrews UK.

Friedman, Jeffrey. 2012. "*System Effects* and the Problem of Prediction." *Critical Review* 24(3): 291–312.

Friedman, Jeffrey. 2019. *Power without Knowledge: A Critique of Technocracy*. New York: Oxford University Press.

Friedman, Jeffrey. 2020. "Populists as Technocrats." *Critical Review* 31(3-4): 315-76.

Hoffmann, Matthew J., and John Riley. 2002. "The Science of Political Science: Linearity or Complexity in Designing Social Inquiry." *New Political Science* 24(2): 303–20.

Jackson, Patrick Thaddeus. 2011. *The Conduct of Inquiry in International Relations: Philosophy of Science and Its Implications for the Study of World Politics*. London: Routledge.

Jervis, Robert. 1998. *System Effects: Complexity in Political and Social Life*. Princeton: Princeton University Press.

Kavalski, Emilian. 2007. "The Fifth Debate and the Emergence of Complex International Relations Theory: Notes on the Application of Complexity Theory to the Study of International Life." *Cambridge Review of International Affairs* 20(3): 435–54.

Kuhn, Thomas S. 2009. *The Structure of Scientific Revolutions*, 3rd ed. Chicago: University of Chicago Press.

Lerner, Adam B. 2018. "Political Neo-Malthusianism and the Progression of India's Green Revolution." *Journal of Contemporary Asia* 48(3): 485–507.

Lerner, Adam B. 2019a. "Collective Trauma and the Evolution of Nehru's Worldview: Uncovering the Roots of Nehruvian Non-Alignment." *The International History Review* 41(6): 1276–1300.

Lerner, Adam B. 2019b. "Theorizing Collective Trauma in International Political Economy." *International Studies Review* 21: 549–71.

Lerner, Adam B. 2020a. "Blurring the Boundaries of War: PTSD in American Foreign Policy Discourse." *Perspectives on Politics*, forthcoming.

Lerner, Adam B. 2020b. "Theorizing Unpredictability in International Politics: A Postfoundational Approach to Trump and His Doctrine." *Cambridge Review of International Affairs* (forthcoming).

Lerner, Adam B. 2020c. "What's It like to Be a State? An Argument for State Consciousness." *International Theory*: 1–27.

List, Christian, and Philip Pettit. 2006. "Group Agency and Supervenience." *Southern Journal of Philosophy* 44(S1): 85–105.

List, Christian, and Philip Pettit. 2011. *Group Agency: The Possibility, Design, and Status of Corporate Agents*. New York: Oxford University Press.

Manne, Kate. 2015. "Why I Use Trigger Warnings." *The New York Times*.

Manski, Charles F. 2013. *Public Policy in an Uncertain World: Analysis and Decisions*. Cambridge, Mass.: Harvard University Press.

Nagel, Thomas. 1974. "What Is It Like to Be a Bat?" *The Philosophical Review* 83(4): 435.

Nixon, Ron. 2017. "By Land, Sea or Catapult: How Smugglers Get Drugs Across the Border." *New York Times*, 25 July.

Pettit, Philip. 2010. "Groups with Minds of Their Own." In *Social Epistemology: Essential Readings*, ed. Alvin Goldman and Dennis Whitcomb. Oxford: Oxford University Press.

Robbins, Susan P. 2016. "From the Editor—Sticks and Stones: Trigger Warnings, Microaggressions, and Political Correctness." *Journal of Social Work Education* 52(1): 1–5.

Tollefsen, Deborah. 2015. *Groups as Agents*. Malden, Mass.: Polity.

Tulving, Endel. 1972. "Episodic and Semantic Memory." In *Organization of Memory*, ed. Endel Tulving and Wayne Donaldson. Academic Press.

Tye, Michael. 2018. "Qualia." In *The Stanford Encyclopedia of Philosophy*, ed. Edward N. Zalta. Metaphysics Research Lab, Stanford University.

Wendt, Alexander. 2015. *Quantum Mind and Social Science: Unifying Physical and Social Ontology*. New York: Cambridge University Press.

Eric MacGilvray

THE SPIRAL OF RESPONSIBILITY AND THE PRESSURE TO CONFLICT

ABSTRACT: *This essay calls attention to two blind spots in* Power Without Knowledge. *First, the book has little to say about the role that political institutions can play in promoting effective democratic governance. Drawing on the "mixed government" tradition, I argue that properly designed institutions can correct for the epistemic deficits that Friedman describes by creating what I call the "pressure to conflict." Second and more importantly, the book has nothing to say about the role of responsible leadership in a democratic technocracy. Drawing on Max Weber's analysis of the ethics of responsibility and the ethics of conviction, I argue that responsible leadership can promote judicious technocracy in a dynamic that I call the "spiral of responsibility." The responsible leader recognizes that to recuse oneself from the exercise of technocratic power is to empower the unscrupulous and irresponsible. According to Weber, any theory of politics that fails to embrace the ethics of responsibility will therefore occupy an uneasy middle ground between quietism and enthusiasm. This, I fear, is where* Power Without Knowledge *may leave us.*

Jeffrey Friedman's *Power Without Knowledge* (New York: Oxford University Press, 2019) is an intellectual and scholarly *tour de force*: impressively wide-ranging, refreshingly iconoclastic, and consistently interesting. It provides a penetrating analysis of the pretensions of the prevailing mode of democratic governance, of the psychological and sociological pathologies that give rise to those pretensions, and of the harm that those pretensions and pathologies do to democracy itself. Friedman bridges the divide between empirical social science and normative political theory in an unusually informed and thoughtful way, and the book is sure to provoke debate within—and, one hopes, between—those two camps. I expect Friedmanite catchphrases like the "spiral of conviction" and the "pressure to predict" to enter the canon alongside familiar chestnuts like Walter Lippmann's "pseudo-environment" and "manufacture of consent."

Reading the book was something of a return to roots for me, since I cut my scholarly teeth on the Lippmann-Dewey debate, which makes up the backbone of the critique of "democratic technocracy" that's laid out in Chapters 2 and 3. I was, and am, basically on Lippmann's side in that debate, as I take Friedman to be, and the thrust of my early work in this area was to distinguish Dewey's pragmatic theory of inquiry and justification, which is genuinely original and which I wholeheartedly embrace, from his left-Hegelian theory of democracy, which I find to be largely derivative and unpromising (MacGilvray 1999; MacGilvray 2004 chs. 4-5; MacGilvray 2010). In arguing that those two sets of commitments can be detached from one another, I saw myself as being engaged in a kind of rescue operation on behalf of what I take to be a genuinely pragmatic approach to political inquiry, and I'll engage in a similar kind of rescue operation here. Rather than offer a direct defense of "democratic technocracy," I would instead like to call attention to two important blind spots in Friedman's analysis, and show how a pragmatist who's also committed to democracy might respond to them.

I. TECHNOCRACY AND ITS EPISTEMIC PROBLEMS

As its title suggests, *Power Without Knowledge* offers a fundamental critique of the role that knowledge claims play in the exercise of political power. This may seem at first glance to amount to a rejection of the very possibility of social-scientific knowledge, but the argument is more subtle than that. Instead, the book offers a shrewd analysis of the social and institutional context within which technocratic knowledge claims are developed and deployed, and thus of the incentives that political leaders and would-be technocrats face.

The most immediately striking feature of the argument is that Friedman defines technocracy in such a way that it's associated not only with "epistocrats,"[1] who claim to have special knowledge about how to solve social problems, but also with ordinary citizens—"citizen-technocrats," as he calls them—insofar as they exercise political power in accordance with their own (non-expert) views about how those problems should be solved (13-15). By broadening the definition of technocracy in this way, Friedman is able distinguish the familiar "external" critique of technocracy—the claim that it undermines democracy by giving too much power to experts—from the more far-reaching "internal" critique that he advances, which treats technocracy as a potentially egalitarian orientation toward public life that's nevertheless destructive of democratic rule. "What distinguishes this type of regime from others," according to his definition, "is not the number of its personnel in proportion to the population being governed—'the few' versus 'the many'—but the nature of the regime's mission: to solve, mitigate, and prevent social problems" (21). This mission, Friedman suggests, puts knowledge claims front and center in modern politics, since in order to pursue it we have to know how widespread the problems are, what causes them, and what the effects of trying to solve, mitigate, or prevent them would be. Those who are usually counted as technocrats—that is, epistocrats—claim to have this kind of knowledge, which is what supposedly justifies their political influence. But in some cases ordinary citizens claim to have this kind of knowledge as well, meaning that they, too, should be included in a critique of technocracy.

Friedman's "internal" critique of technocracy, presented in Part I of the book, is grounded in the observation that the people whose behavior technocrats are trying to influence have ideas about how to interpret and respond to their circumstances that are to some extent inaccessible to those very technocrats. This "ideational heterogeneity" will of course make their behavior hard to predict to that extent, and so a "judicious" technocracy necessarily has to assume that this type of heterogeneity can safely be discounted, either because it's counteracted by homogenizing factors such as shared norms (169-73), or because ideational differences are more or less randomly distributed and therefore "cancel out," statistically speaking. In Part II, Friedman assesses how well real-world technocrats manage to take account of ideational heterogeneity (not very well, in his view) and considers what the prospects for improvement might be.

Friedman's dour assessment of the technocratic status quo rests on four key empirical claims. The first two claims have to do with the behavior of epistocratic technocrats. On the one hand (Chapter 5), Friedman argues that as people become better informed—as they acquire the expertise that qualifies them as epistocrats—they also tend to become less receptive to information that contradicts their existing beliefs, making them (ironically) more likely to misapply the knowledge that they already have. He refers to this phenomenon as the "spiral of conviction."[2] On the other hand (Chapter 4), because policymakers have a pressing need to identify and recruit technocratic advisors who can successfully model the future behavior of unknown people, those who express diffidence about the possibility of doing this will thereby "select themselves out" of the technocratic pool, leaving behind the overconfident, the inflexible, and the ambitious. Friedman refers to this phenomenon as the "pressure to predict." Taken together, the spiral of conviction and the pressure to predict are, he concludes, "likely to call forth pathological responses in any real-world epistocracy" (261).

The second two empirical claims on which Friedman rests his internal critique of contemporary technocracy have to do with the behavior of "citizen-technocrats" (Chapter 6). Here he argues on the one hand that ordinary citizens tend to vote "sociotropically" rather than self-interestedly; that is, they exercise political power on behalf of what they take to be the public interest, and not just on behalf of what they think will benefit them personally (although those two motivations may of course overlap). On the other hand, he argues that citizen-technocrats take sociotropic intentions as a proxy for outcomes when deciding how best to pursue the public interest; that is, they decide which candidates to vote for and which policies to support based on what politicians say they want to accomplish, not on the particular mechanisms (plausible or not) by which they propose to do so. This orientation toward public life, which Friedman calls "technocratic voluntarism," emphasizes good intentions and the strength of will necessary to carry them out—and, in contrast, the "evil" influence of anti-sociotropic "special interests"—over fixed ideologies or policy programs. Despite its obvious shortcomings, this kind of credulity is in some ways preferable to the narrow-mindedness and inflexibility that Friedman associates with epistocracy. "And so," he concludes, "we seem to face a dilemma: Would we rather be ruled by epistocrats who are relatively well-informed but doctrinaire, or by citizen-technocrats who are relatively open-minded but ignorant?" (316).

Each of the four empirical claims that I've just described might of course be contested—they are, after all, empirical claims[3]—but taken as a whole Friedman's internal critique of technocracy offers a fresh and compelling take on the problem of knowledge in politics, and opens new and promising paths of inquiry for political theorists and political scientists alike. Rather than call the substance of the critique directly into question, something that many of my colleagues in this forum are better equipped to do than I am, I'd like to raise two broader concerns about the theory of democracy that Friedman builds upon it—each of which arises, as I've already suggested, from what I take to be an important blind spot in his analysis.

The first blind spot, discussed in section II below, is that *Power Without Knowledge* has very little to say about the role that political institutions can play in correcting for the cognitive and moral deficiencies that political leaders, epistocrats, and citizen-technocrats would otherwise display; in particular by creating what I will call, with apologies to Friedman, the "pressure to conflict." Here Lippmann's analysis of modern democracy provides a useful point of reference, since he calls attention to the importance of constructing public debate in a way that encourages or forces a consideration of multiple perspectives.

However, the mere presence of multiple perspectives in the decision-making arena won't suffice to correct the technocratic pathologies that Friedman identifies. This brings me to the second, and I think more serious, blind spot in his analysis (section III): the fact that he has nothing to say about the role that responsible leadership has to play in democratic governance, or indeed in any form of political rule. In particular, he overlooks the fact that responsible leadership can itself create the conditions for responsible (or, as he says, "judicious") technocracy, in a dynamic that I call, again with apologies, the "spiral of responsibility." In developing this line of argument I draw on another famous set piece from the early decades of the twentieth century: the confrontation between adherents of what Max Weber, in his famous lecture on "Politics as a Vocation," called the ethics of conviction and the ethics of responsibility. Weber emphasizes that responsible leaders are able to take prudent but decisive action in pursuit of their political ends, despite the indispensability of unsavory means and the ubiquity of unintended consequences: exactly the features of public life that Friedman argues that democratic technocracy is ill-suited to confront. According to Weber, any theory of politics, democratic or otherwise, that fails to embrace the ethics of responsibility will occupy an uneasy middle ground between quietism and enthusiasm. This, I fear, is the uneasy middle ground on which *Power Without Knowledge*, for all the force of the critique that it offers, leaves us.

Hilary Putnam once defined pragmatism as fallibilism without skepticism,[4] and if I had to put my doubts about *Power Without Knowledge* in a nutshell it would be to say that it tilts in the end from a healthy fallibilism into an unhealthy skepticism, not just about technocracy but also about democratic governance itself. My worry is that this kind of skepticism leads in practice either to an embrace of a crudely emotional politics, or to a desire to flee from politics altogether. Roughly speaking this is, I take it, where Friedman thinks we are on the one hand, and where he thinks we should go, on the other: thus his defense of (or retreat to) what he calls "exitocracy" in the final chapter of the book. I sketch a different path forward in what follows.

II. THE PRESSURE TO CONFLICT

One of the keys to effective governance is to be aware of the moral and cognitive deficiencies that human beings tend to display and to design institutions that correct for them. The importance of correcting for our *moral* deficiencies is of course familiar, since politics is ultimately about the use of power backed by coercive force, and since human beings have a well-known and nearly ubiquitous tendency to seek power and to abuse it when given the chance. This is why it's a fundamental tenet of political wisdom that unchecked power poses a standing threat to the well-being of those who are subject to it, and why (to make a very long story short) the word *democracy* doesn't mean for us, as it did for the Greeks, the rule of a particular class of people—"the many" (*hoi polloi*)—but rather a system of government characterized by competitive elections, accountable parties, an independent judiciary and adversarial legal system, and an effective right on the part of citizens to freely express their political views and criticize their political leaders. It is widely (though not, alas, universally) understood that unless political institutions are designed in such a way that leaders are obliged to take competing beliefs and interests into account—and, of course, unless both leaders and ordinary citizens abide by the constraints that these institutions impose—political rule will amount, as it has for most of human history, to little more than predation. I will refer to this structured form of competition as the "pressure to conflict."

It is less widely recognized, but nevertheless true, that the pressure to conflict can help to correct for the ubiquitous cognitive deficiencies that human beings display, and that Friedman anatomizes so brilliantly. Here again the key is to ensure not only that people are free to express and act upon their political views, but that different views are represented when decisions are being made: that the distribution of political power tracks, at least to some extent, the distribution of cognitive diversity.[5]

Conflict as an Epistemic Corrective

That idea has a long and distinguished pedigree in the history of Western political thought. An early example is Aristotle's analysis of *politeia* or "constitutional government"—the "mixture of oligarchy and democracy" that he considers to be the "constitution which is best suited to cities in general"—in the middle books of the *Politics*. Aristotle emphasizes that democrats and oligarchs are each susceptible to a kind of epistemic blindness: "Many of the measures which are reckoned democratic," he points out, "really undermine democracies," and "many which are reckoned oligarchical actually undermine oligarchies. Those who think that theirs is the only form of goodness [*aretē*; virtue or excellence – EM] push matters to an extreme"; they "begin by making it a worse constitution, and … end by turning it into something which is not a constitution at all." He concludes that "[t]he greatest … of all the means we have … for preserving constitutions is the education of citizens in the spirit of their constitution," and emphasizes that this "does not consist in … doing the actions in which the partisans of oligarchy, or the adherents of democracy, delight," but rather in "doing the actions which make it possible to have an oligarchy, or a democracy."[6] Aristotle doesn't otherwise describe what an education for *politeia* would consist in, but it is reasonable to suppose that it would require that the members of each class be exposed to, and obliged to take into account, the distinct experiences and perspectives of the other.

Aristotle's appeal to the advantages of constructive class conflict was influentially adapted by the Greek historian Polybius, whose analysis of the Roman republic in book 6 of his *Histories* formed the basis for what became known as the "mixed constitution" or "mixed government" tradition. According to Polybius, Rome's strength and resilience can be attributed to the fact that it combined elements of aristocratic, democratic, and monarchical rule in such a way that "it is impossible even for the Romans themselves to declare with certainty whether the whole system [is] an aristocracy, a democracy, or a monarchy." Like Aristotle, he attributes both moral and epistemic benefits to this mixing of political forms. On the one hand, it allowed Rome to reap the benefits of cognitive diversity: "whenever some common external threat compels the three [elements] to unite and work together," he observes, "the strength which the state then develops becomes quite extraordinary ... because all parties vie with one another to find ways of meeting the needs of the hour." On the other hand, the mixed constitution also helped to prevent the abuse of power: "[w]henever one of the three elements swells in importance, becomes overambitious and tends to encroach upon the others," he observes, it "can be blocked or impeded by the rest, with the result that none will unduly dominate the others or treat them with contempt. Thus the whole situation remains in equilibrium since any aggressive impulse is checked, and each estate is apprehensive from the outset of censure from the others."[7]

Polybius's praise of mixed government exercised enormous influence in ancient, medieval, and Renaissance political thought, winning the endorsement of figures as diverse as Cicero, Thomas Aquinas, and Machiavelli.[8] In the early modern period Montesquieu's famous declaration that "power must check power by the arrangement of things" called not just for the separation of executive, legislative, and judicial powers, but for the placing of those powers in the hands of distinct classes or "estates": "All would be lost," he argued, "if the same man or the same body of principal men, either of nobles, or of the people, exercised these three powers."[9] Montesquieu's analysis was of course the leading inspiration for the design of the U.S. Constitution, and much of the novelty of the American system arises from its effort to induce conflict between the different branches of government—and thus between the different interests in society—under conditions in which all power is derived from a single "estate": the people as a whole. Even John Stuart Mill, who was more of a democrat than any of the thinkers named so far, held that a well-designed system of representative government should ensure that "laborers and their affinities on one side, employers of labor and their affinities on the other, [are] in the arrangement of the representative system, equally balanced"; and (in a more epistocratic vein) that "education as such" is given "the degree of superior influence due to it, and sufficient as a counterpoise to the numerical weight of the least educated class."[10]

Lippmann, Dewey, and Conflict

The mixed-government tradition, with its emphasis on the importance of the pressure to conflict, offers a fresh perspective on the Lippmann-Dewey debate, and on the problem of "democratic technocracy" more generally. Although Lippmann (like Dewey) wasn't much of an institutional thinker, his analysis of the challenges facing modern democracy shows a healthy appreciation of the importance of pluralism and constructive conflict, both for experts (epistocrats) and for ordinary citizens. Indeed, Lippmann considers it a distinguishing mark of expertise that one is willing and able to consider problems from several points of view and to remain tentative about one's conclusions. "Expertness in any subject," he argues, "is, in fact, a multiplication of the number of aspects we are prepared to discover, plus the habit of discounting our expectations." More importantly, Lippmann identifies the pressure to conflict as the only remedy for the epistemic limitations of citizen-technocrats, whether they be leaders or ordinary citizens: "on all but a very few matters for short stretches in our lives," he points out, "the utmost independence that we can exercise is to multiply the authorities to whom we give a friendly hearing. As congenital amateurs our quest for truth consists in stirring up the experts, and forcing them to answer any heresy that has the accent of conviction" (Lippmann [1922] 1997, 76, 143).

Lippmann's emphasis on the importance of "multiplying authorities" places his discussion of newspaper-reading habits in chapter 4 of *Public Opinion* in a rather different light. Friedman suggests that Lippmann, because he focuses on the number of newspapers that people regularly read, gives the misleading impression that he thinks that the public simply needs to be supplied with more information, thereby distracting from his broader insight that the fundamental problem with public opinion is that information is overabundant, and therefore in need of interpretation (97-99). However, although Lippmann isn't explicit about this, it's reasonable to suppose that he considered the practice of reading multiple newspapers to be valuable not just because it *adds* to the information that the reader has access to, but also and more importantly because it *multiplies* the perspectives that he or she is obliged to consider (recall that journalism in the early twentieth century was more overtly partisan than it is today). In contemporary terms, people who watch both Fox News and CNN News, who follow both *The New York Times* and *The Wall Street Journal*, or who read both *The Nation* and *National Review*, are likely to have a better appreciation of their ideological blind spots, and are therefore likely to have a more sophisticated ability to interpret public affairs, than people who have a more homogeneous media diet. Needless to say, such people are, as Lippmann and Friedman both emphasize, exceedingly rare. Nevertheless, here as elsewhere the "pressure to conflict"—especially insofar as it is reliably embodied in institutions—offers a tried and true strategy for improving the performance of democratic technocracy.

Even though Dewey is typically seen, and presumably saw himself, as the genuinely democratic party to the Lippmann-Dewey debate, his position is more receptive than Lippmann's is to what Friedman (25) calls "naive technocratic realism": the view that "technocratic questions have self-evident answers."[11] Dewey begins *The Public and Its Problems* by pointing out that all social behavior has consequences not only for the people who are directly involved, but also for various third parties, and that these third parties, once the indirect consequences become serious enough, will try to exercise "control over the actions which produce them ... by some indirect means." Any such group is called a "public" in Dewey's terminology, and any such mechanism of control is called a "state." Dewey's theory of democracy is built on the assumption that "those indirectly and seriously affected for good or for evil form *a* group distinctive enough to require recognition and a name"—a group that he calls "*The* Public" (Dewey 1927, 257-58, emphasis added). In other words, Dewey holds that every society contains an identifiable group whose interests represent those of the whole, and that the proper aim of politics is to ensure that the interests of that group—The Public—are pursued. He therefore takes a clear position on what is perhaps the oldest and most contentious political question: whether there is such a thing as a "common good" that the citizens of a given polity can be expected to recognize and pursue together, or whether politics is, as the mixed-government tradition assumes, fundamentally a matter of accommodating competing beliefs and interests.

Dewey's appeal to The Public helps to explain why he spends so little time in *The Public and Its Problems*, or indeed in any of his political writings, on the question of what form political institutions should take or what ends they should pursue. The real question, from his point of view, is why The Public hasn't mobilized to answer those questions for itself, and the answer, in a nutshell, is that it hasn't yet recognized itself *as* the public, and that when it does the question of ends and means will answer itself. In the meantime "the prime difficulty ... is that of discovering the means by which a scattered, mobile, and manifold public may so recognize itself as to define and express its interests." "When these conditions are brought into being," he suggests, "they will make their own forms," and "[u]ntil they have come about, it is somewhat futile to consider what political machinery will suit them." The problem of democracy is, in short, "primarily and essentially an intellectual problem" (ibid., 314, 317, 327) It's hard to imagine a clearer statement of the premises of naive technocratic realism: a theory of democracy that's built on the assumption that all social problems have a correct answer, at least in principle, and that any failure to identify and pursue that answer must be due to cognitive ("intellectual") rather than moral shortcomings. Notice, however, that the naïveté doesn't follow from the commitment to technocracy—from the belief that the state should make an effort to solve social problems—but rather from the commitment to a holistic social ontology: from Dewey's failure to appreciate the irreducible importance of the "pressure to conflict."[12]

III. THE SPIRAL OF RESPONSIBILITY

Of course, to say that the pressure to conflict *can* mitigate the pathologies of democratic technocracy isn't very helpful if the necessary pressures don't exist, or if political leaders routinely ignore them. As we've seen, this is exactly what Friedman maintains: that the pressure to *pre*dict leads ineluctably to a "pressure to dogmatism," because would-be technocrats who make unclear or ambivalent predictions will be "selected out" of the pool of technocrats that leaders actually listen to. "Policies," he argues, "have to be advocated with confidence if they are to be adopted," because "political decision makers, in attempting to identify which epistocrats can be trusted, can be expected to select those who are more dogmatic than most, even from among a group that is dogmatic on the whole, because those who are less dogmatic than most will tend to be less persuasive in advocating their points of view" (248, 262). The psychological mechanism that Friedman appeals to here is intuitively plausible, and it's easy to think of cases in which the pressure to predict has had exactly the perverse consequences that he identifies; the run-up to the 2003 Iraq War (342-43) is perhaps the clearest recent example. However, in contrast to his discussion of the "spiral of conviction," "sociotropic voting," and "technocratic voluntarism," he doesn't cite any empirical evidence in support of the claim that the effects of the pressure to predict are widespread or ubiquitous enough to make democratic technocracy untenable.

Indeed, however accurate it may be as a description of how some leaders actually behave, Friedman's description of the pressure to predict seems to me to get the *nature* of leadership exactly wrong. Responsible leaders—that is, leaders who are concerned to make decisions that advance their policy goals—encourage their advisors to be candid and to think outside the box, force them to state and question their assumptions (Lippmann's "stirring up the experts"), seek out and listen to dissenting voices (thus the importance of the "pressure to conflict"), try to ensure that worst-case scenarios are considered and off-ramps identified, and so on. Responsible leaders are alert, in other words, to their own epistemic and ideological blind spots, to the potential biases of the information that they consider, to the personal agendas of the people who they rely upon for advice, and to the uncertainty involved in any effort to predict or control human behavior.[13] Moreover, responsible leadership tends to give rise to responsible advising, and thus to responsible technocracy: when those who hope to influence public policy know that a given leader processes information and conducts deliberation in a responsible way, they have an incentive to "play it straight" and avoid exaggerating the certainty of their own beliefs or advice. Under these conditions, it's the dogmatic and overconfident who are "selected out" of the epistocratic pool. I will refer to this dialectical relationship between responsible leadership and responsible technocracy as the "spiral of responsibility."

Needless to say, it isn't easy to be a responsible leader in this sense; it takes intelligence, good judgment, and above all self-confidence: the self-confidence to admit that one doesn't know everything (or indeed most things), to ask for advice (and then ask again), and finally to act decisively in the face of uncertainty. In traditional language, responsible leadership requires a great deal of virtue.[14] And, needless to say, even on-the-whole responsible leaders—like on-the-whole virtuous people—will often fall short. It may therefore seem that any disagreement about the feasibility of democratic technocracy must rest on a deeper disagreement about how likely it is that responsible leaders can reliably be identified, or that the leaders that we have will become or remain responsible. Moreover, it may seem that Friedman's is the counsel of prudence on this point; that we can't afford to sit back and hope that democratic technocracy will find responsible leaders, and should therefore prefer "exitocracy" even to judicious technocracy: "instead of attempting, case by case, to produce solutions to any and all social problems that might arise," he suggests, we should instead "provide a framework within which individuals could attempt to solve—or, better, escape—the problems that afflict them as individuals" and thus "allow exit to trump technocratic voice" (322).[15]

The Ethics of Responsibility in a Technocracy

I think that this (qualified) retreat to exitocracy is misguided, and to show why I'll turn to one of the most profound and influential modern discussions of the nature of political leadership: Weber's remarks on the ethics of responsibility [*Verantwortungsethik*] and the ethics of conviction [*Gesinnungsethik*] in his lecture "Politics as a Vocation," delivered in the immediate aftermath of the First World War. Weber comes in for some good press in *Power Without Knowledge* as a founder and leading advocate of *Verstehende* sociology, and as a skeptic about the scientific pretensions of economists (234, 181). However, he was also a technocrat of sorts; an heir to the "Cameralist" tradition that Friedman discusses in the Afterword, and a pioneering analyst and defender of rational bureaucracy as a necessary tool of modern governance. Moreover, like Lippmann and Dewey, Weber emphasizes that we can only see the world through interpretive frames, that those frames are always limited and biased in various ways, and that we aren't necessarily bound by them; that we can become conscious of their limitations and learn to treat them flexibly and experimentally. For Weber, as for Lippmann and Dewey (though he likely took the point from Nietzsche), objectivity doesn't consist in escaping from interpretation, but rather in multiplying the interpretive standpoints that one is able to inhabit.[16] In short, for Weber, as for the American pragmatists, we can be fallibilists without being skeptics.

Although it appears in the bibliography, "Politics as a Vocation" isn't cited or discussed in *Power Without Knowledge*.[17] This is somewhat surprising, because the lecture is centrally concerned—albeit from an ethical rather than an epistemic angle—with the same problem that preoccupies Friedman: the question of what it means to exercise political power responsibly under modern conditions, and of what kind of people are suited, temperamentally speaking, to do so. It's in response to the latter question that Weber develops his famous contrast between the ethics of responsibility and the ethics of conviction. Roughly speaking, the ethics of responsibility holds that we should act in such a way that the foreseeable consequences of our actions will advance the political cause that we serve, while the ethics of conviction holds that our actions should conform to certain fixed principles, whatever the consequences. Those who adhere to the ethics of conviction blame God, the world, or other people for the fact that their principled actions often lead to disaster, and therefore implicitly wish (impotently) for a better world or for better human beings. Those who adhere to the ethics of responsibility, by contrast, anticipate and try to take into account the moral and cognitive limitations that human beings predictably display, even when this obliges them to do unpleasant or unsavory—"unethical"—things.[18]

A paradigmatic statement of the ethics of conviction is found in Leo Tolstoy's "Letter on Non-Resistance." There, in defense of the Christian doctrine of non-resistance to evil (e.g., Matthew 5:39), Tolstoy ([1896] 2009, 79, 81) considers the hypothetical case of man who sees a robber about to kill an innocent child. Should he kill the robber to save the child? We might of course expect an adherent of the ethics of responsibility—or any ordinary citizen-technocrat—to say yes, and even to consider it an easy case. Tolstoy, however, says no: "By killing the robber," he points out, "he certainly kills, whereas he cannot know positively whether the robber would have killed the child or not. But letting that pass, who shall say whether the child's life was more needed, was better, than the robber's life? … the only rule for his actions must be a reckoning … of what is more profitable for him and for all men: a continuation of the robber's life or of the child's. To decide that, he needs to know what would become of the child whom he saves, and what—had he not killed him—would have been the future of the robber he kills" (talk about the pressure to predict!). Tolstoy concludes that "as he cannot know this, [he] has no sufficient rational ground for killing a robber to save a child," and that when faced with the question of whether to use violence for instrumental purposes we should simply refuse to play: "do what's right, come what may," he argues, "is an expression of profound wisdom."

There's a clear parallel between Tolstoy's radical skepticism about cost-benefit analysis and the radical skepticism about technocracy that animates *Power Without Knowledge*.[19] The difference, of course, is that Tolstoy thought that he knew—and that we all know, in our hearts—what the right thing to do actually is: that violence is always and everywhere wrong. If we weaken that assumption, as I think we must, then the radical critique of consequentialism, and thus of technocracy, has a more perverse implication: that we should listen to our guts and not let the "facts" or the "experts" get in the way. Friedman (344) seems to me to come perilously close to endorsing this position. "People," he argues, "do what their webs of belief demand," and "praising or blaming them for what they do presupposes a match between their webs of belief and ours." "Arguing," he concludes, "is in most cases, no more efficacious than voting," because "if one's interlocutors are worth arguing with, in principle—because they disagree with one's opinions—it probably means that their webs of belief cannot be changed by one's arguments; while one's arguments will only reinforce the prejudices of those ready to accept them into their webs." He takes this to be a counsel of humility: "if one fully recognizes one's ignorance in a given case," he suggests, "one literally has no choice but to select oneself out of the pool of opinion holders" and enter "the intellectual space ... of agnosticism rather than agonism" (ibid.). However it might also be taken as a counsel of obstinacy: if my actions are determined by my web of belief, and if my fellow citizens therefore aren't worth arguing with—and if I have reason to think that they feel the same way about me—then it would be natural for me to conclude that it might as well be my beliefs (or prejudices) that prevail, and turn from the tedious (and, on this account, specious) politics of discussion and compromise to the more exhilarating and toxic politics of the agon.

Weber, like Tolstoy, had a healthy appreciation of the uncertainty that attends all human action: "No ethic in the world," he insists, "can ignore the fact that in many cases the achievement of 'good' ends is inseparable from the use of morally dubious or at least dangerous means and that we cannot escape the possibility or even probability of evil side effects. And no ethic in the world can say when, and to what extent, the ethically good end can 'justify' the ethically dangerous means and its side effects" (Weber [1919] 2004, 84). Weber also understood, however, that only the truly saintly can be expected to abstain consistently from the instrumental use of power, and that (true saints being exceptionally rare) to unilaterally recuse oneself from the exercise of power is simply to empower the unscrupulous and the irresponsible.[20] The responsible leader—and the responsible citizen—recognizes that we must act even in the face of moral and epistemic uncertainty, and do what we can to ensure that the foreseeable consequences of our actions are as beneficial (by our own lights) as possible. "Politics," Weber famously concludes, "means a slow, powerful drilling through hard boards," and "[t]he only man who has a 'vocation' for politics is one who is certain that his spirit will not be broken if the world, when looked at from his point of view, proves too stupid or base to accept what he wishes to offer it, and who, when faced with all that obduracy, can still say 'Nevertheless!' despite everything" (ibid., 93-94).

I don't mean to sound optimistic about the possibility that well-designed institutions and responsible leadership will succeed in mitigating the pathologies of democratic technocracy; I'm not that optimistic. The hubris of technocrats has caused no end of trouble, and *Power Without Knowledge* provides a devastating brief against that kind of hubris. But we get the leaders that we deserve, and we shouldn't lightly abandon the institutions that we've inherited. I therefore think, or would like to think, that the choice that Friedman (361) sets before us—between being "ruled by epistocrats who are relatively well-informed but doctrinaire, or by citizen-technocrats who are relatively open-minded but ignorant"—sells us short. Things only look that way if we flatten democratic politics into a dialogue between politicians who just want answers and citizens who just want results; that is, if we overlook the importance of the spiral of responsibility and the pressure to conflict, and thus underestimate the indispensable role that judicious technocracy has to play in a well-functioning democracy. If we turn away from politics, as Tolstoy did, and as Friedman suggests we should do—if we become skeptics instead of fallibilists—then we simply clear the field for know-nothing populism. That field seems to me to be clear enough already.

NOTES

1. Friedman borrows the terms "epistocrat" and "epistocracy" from Estlund 2008.
2. Friedman (237) argues that the "spiral of conviction" shouldn't be seen as a sign of irrationality: "As one gains confidence in one's beliefs from the accumulating

mass of evidence in favor of them, one *should* tend to become doctrinaire about one's conclusions, not because one is deliberately closing one's mind, but because one's conclusions are based on a growing sample of information that seems reliable—but that, one may fail to recognize, is biased" (original emphasis).

3. Friedman cites influential social-scientific studies in support of three of these claims: for the "spiral of conviction," Taber and Lodge 2006; for "sociotropic voting," Kinder and Kiewiet 1981, among others; for "technocratic voluntarism" (more indirectly) Hibbing and Theiss-Morse 2002. The "pressure to predict" hypothesis, by contrast, is based on a conjecture about the likely behavior of technocrats and public officials. I raise some doubts about this conjecture in section III below.
4. "That one can be both fallibilistic *and* anti-skeptical is perhaps *the* basic insight of American Pragmatism" (Putnam 1995, 21, original emphasis).
5. The epistemic benefits of cognitive diversity have recently attracted a great deal of attention in the form of what the economist Scott Page calls the "diversity trumps ability" theorem: see for example Page 2007 and Landemore 2013.
6. Aristotle [1946] 1995, 134 (book 4, chapter 1/1288b34-5), 151 (book 4, chapter 8/1293b35), 207-8 (book 5, chapter 9/1309b20-5, 33-4; 1310a13-14, 17-23).
7. Polybius 1979, 312, 317-8 (book 6, chs. 11 and 18).
8. Cicero, *De re publica*, book 1 §§41-55, 65-9, book 2 §§57, 65; Aquinas, *Summa Theologiae* 1a2ae q 95 art 4 resp and q 105 art 1 *passim*; Machiavelli, *Discourses on Livy*, book 1, chs. 2-6.
9. Montesquieu [1748] 1989, 155, 157 (book 11, chs. 4 and 6).
10. Mill 1861, 447, 477 (chs. 6 and 8). The latter aim is expressed, of course, in Mill's notorious proposal to grant multiple votes to more highly educated voters, and to exclude those who fall below a certain epistemic threshold from the suffrage altogether: ibid., ch. 8.
11. Friedman (118-23) and I agree on this point.
12. I disagree to this extent with Friedman's suggestion (113-14) that Dewey's simultaneous commitment to technocracy, epistocracy, and democracy in *The Public and Its Problems* is inconsistent or incoherent, although I agree with him in finding the belief that they can be harmonized in the way that Dewey suggests to be naive.
13. The literature on leadership is of course vast, and mostly beyond my ken, but among many possible examples we might look to the most notorious political *advisor* in the history of political thought: "a prudent prince," Machiavelli ([1985] 1998, 94-5) argues, "should behave in such a mode that everyone knows that the more freely he speaks, the more he will be accepted"; "he should be a very broad questioner, and then, in regard to the things he asked about, a patient listener to the truth; indeed, he should become upset when he learns that anyone has any hesitation to speak it to him."
14. To quote Machiavelli again (ibid., 95), "a prince who is not wise will never have united counsel," because "each one of his counselors will think of his own interest; [and] he will not know how to correct them or understand them." It follows that "good counsel, from wherever it comes, must arise from the prudence of the prince, and not the prudence of the prince from good counsel."
15. Friedman's use of the terms "exit" and "voice" is modeled after Hirschman 1970, although he's critical of much of Hirschman's analysis.
16. As Weber ([1904] 1949, 72) puts it, in a passage that might have been written by Lippmann: "There is no absolutely 'objective' scientific analysis of culture

or ... of 'social phenomena' independent of special and 'one-sided' viewpoints according to which—expressly or tacitly, consciously or unconsciously—they are selected, analyzed and organized for expository purposes." Cf. Nietzsche, *On the Genealogy of Morals*, third essay, section 12.

17. Its companion, "Science as a Vocation," is quoted briefly on p. 164, although the passage is misattributed to the "Politics" lecture.
18. As Weber ([1919] 2004, 83, 84, original emphasis) puts it, "an absolutist ethic simply refuses to *inquire* about 'consequences'. ... Such a man believes that if an action performed out of pure conviction has evil consequences, then the responsibility must lie not with the agent but with the world, the stupidity of men—or the will of God who created them thus. With the ethics of responsibility, on the other hand, a man reckons with exactly those average human failings."
19. Friedman writes, for example, that "the magnitudes on both sides of the ledger—the magnitude of the costs and benefits of judicious technocracy and the magnitude of the costs and benefits of injudicious technocracy—appear to be imponderables" (318).
20. As Weber ([1919] 2004, 82, original emphasis) puts it, referring to the ethic of non-violence, "you must be a saint in *all* respects or at least want to be one ... and *then* this ethic will make sense and be the expression of true dignity." However, "the politician must abide by the opposite commandment: 'You *shall* use force to resist evil, for otherwise you will be *responsible* for its running amok.'" It seems to me that we can replace "evil" with "ignorance" or "epistemic hubris" without loss of meaning.

REFERENCES

Aristotle. [1946] 1995. *The Politics*. Trans. Ernest Barker, rev. R. F. Stalley. New York: Oxford University Press.

Dewey, John. 1927. *The Public and Its Problems*. In *The Later Works of John Dewey*, ed. Jo Ann Boydston. Carbondale: Southern Illinois University Press, 1981-1991, vol. 2.

Estlund, David. 2008. *Democratic Authority: A Philosophical Framework*. Princeton: Princeton University Press.

Friedman, Jeffrey. 2019. *Power Without Knowledge*. New York: Oxford University Press.

Hibbing, John R., and Elizabeth Theiss-Morse. 2002. *Stealth Democracy: Americans' Beliefs about How Government Should Work*. Cambridge: Cambridge University Press.

Hirschman, Albert O. 1970. *Exit, Voice, and Loyalty: Responses to Decline in Firms, Organizations, and States*. Cambridge, Mass.: Harvard University Press.

Kinder, Donald R., and D. Roderick Kiewiet. 1981. "Sociotropic Politics: The American Case." *British Journal of Political Science* 11: 129–61.

Landemore, Hélène. 2013. *Democratic Reason: Politics, Collective Intelligence, and the Rule of the Many*. Princeton: Princeton University Press.

MacGilvray, Eric. 1999. "Experiment as Experiment: Some Consequences of Pragmatism for Democratic Theory." *American Journal of Political Science* 43: 542–65.

MacGilvray, Eric. 2004. *Reconstructing Public Reason*. Cambridge, Mass.: Harvard University Press.

MacGilvray, Eric. 2010. "Dewey's Public." *Contemporary Pragmatism* 7: 31–47.

Machiavelli, Niccolò. [1985] 1998. *The Prince*. Ed. and trans. Harvey C. Mansfield. 2nd ed. Chicago: University of Chicago Press.

Mill, John Stuart. 1861. *Considerations on Representative Government*. In idem, *Collected Works*, ed. J. M. Robson. Toronto: University of Toronto Press, 1963–91, vol. 19.

Montesquieu, Charles de. [1748] 1989. *The Spirit of the Laws*. Ed. and trans. Anne Cohler, Basia Miller, and Harold Stone. New York: Cambridge University Press.

Page, Scott E. 2007. *The Difference: How the Power of Diversity Creates Better Groups, Firms, Schools, and Societies*. Princeton: Princeton University Press.

Polybius. 1979. *The Histories*. In idem, *The Rise of the Roman Empire*, ed. F. W. Walbank, trans. Ian Scott-Kilvert. New York: Penguin Press.

Putnam, Hilary. 1995. *Pragmatism: An Open Question*. Oxford: Blackwell.

Taber, Charles S., and Milton Lodge. 2006. "Motivated Skepticism in the Evaluation of Political Beliefs." *American Journal of Political Science* 50: 755–69.

Tolstoy, Leo. [1896] 2009. "Letter on Non-Resistance to Ernest Howard Crosby of New York." Trans. R. F. Christian. In *Last Steps: The Late Writings of Leo Tolstoy*. New York: Penguin.

Weber, Max. [1904] 1949. "'Objectivity' in Social Science and Social Policy." In idem, *Methodology of Social Sciences*. Trans. and ed. Edward Shils and Henry A. Finch. Glencoe, Ill.: Free Press.

Weber, Max. [1919] 2004. "Politics as a Vocation." Trans. Rodney Livingstone. In Max Weber, *The Vocation Lectures*, ed. Tracy Strong. Indianapolis: Hackett.

Alfred Moore

ARCHITECTS AND ENGINEERS: TWO TYPES OF TECHNOCRAT AND THEIR RELATION TO DEMOCRACY

ABSTRACT: *Technocracy is a contested concept, but it is typically associated with the exercise of political power justified by claims to expertise, and is often contrasted with populist forms of politics. In* Power Without Knowledge, *Jeffrey Friedman reframes the concept of technocracy as a form of politics oriented to solving social and economic problems, and thereby extends it to cover not only epistemic elites but ordinary people. This move usefully challenges the simplistic framing of populism and technocracy as opposites, but at the expense of effacing other dimensions of democratic politics. Friedman also suggests that maximizing individuals' exit opportunities will allow them to take advantage of their relatively reliable personal knowledge. The architecture of "exitocracy" would itself, however, be designed by experts who, as such, might be tempted to insulate the institutional architecture they design against democratic interference.*

In recent years there has been a lively debate—much of it carried on in the pages of this journal—about the state of public ignorance and its implications for democratic politics. Some treat public ignorance as grounds for promoting the role of experts in politics (Blinder 1997), or narrowing the scope of democratic decision in favor of markets (Somin 2008). Others have questioned the evidence for the claims of ignorance and defended the qualities of collective public judgment (Chambers 2018). In *Power Without Knowledge: A Critique of Technocracy* (Oxford University Press, 2019), Jeffrey Friedman takes a radically different approach to this debate, focusing on the way in which experts, too, may lack the knowledge needed to effectively solve public problems. In a bracing critique, he gives supposedly expert political scientists and economists in particular the kind of critical treatment they usually dish out to "ordinary" citizens, challenging their knowledge of public opinion and of economic behavior. In the latter case, he mounts a frontal assault on the accuracy of predicting behavior on the basis of incentives alone, an approach that ignores the heterogeneity of economic actors' webs of belief about how to respond to a given incentive, as well as ignoring heterogeneity between economists' own ideas about how to respond to an incentive and the ideas of the agents in question. Moreover, Friedman argues, economic theorists, like more positivistic social scientists who attempt to predict people's behavior on the basis of quantitative data, are typically not even aware that they need—and lack—knowledge of agents' webs of belief. They consequently misunderstand the character of their predictions and cultivate a pathological degree of overconfidence in them.

Friedman says in the preface that *Power Without Knowledge* is "untimely." This hardly seems the moment, he suggests, to claim that our politics is *too* technocratic. But if we take (for instance) the failures of economic governance leading to the 2008 financial crisis to bear some causal responsibility for the rise of populists such as Donald Trump, then Friedman's argument is extremely timely. Significant aspects of our politics have been underpinned by the assumption that it is possible to predict human behavior sufficiently well to craft effective solutions to policy problems. This assumption is reflected in widespread intellectual trends emphasizing, on the positivist side, the adequacy of behavioral "data" for making behavioral predictions, and, on the neoclassical theory side, the rationality of optimizing agents—which, according to Friedman, means, among other things, their "effective omniscience" about how to respond to their incentives—and thus the efficiency of markets (Chapter 4). These assumptions, as Friedman notes, are very much present in the more sophisticated accounts provided by behavioral economists, who recognize limits to agents' ability to optimize their preferences, but treat those limits as themselves being predictable and thus capable of being tamed and controlled (196-200). By stressing the fundamental unpredictability of human behavior, Friedman's argument recalls early twentieth century economic thought, in which the assumption of radical uncertainty was a red thread linking the work of Knight, Keynes, and Hayek. And his book suggests that we take much more seriously the limitations that human unpredictability sets on what we can demand and expect from politics.

His critique is both deep and broad, suggesting that as democratic subjects, we have been habituated into technocratic styles of thinking about politics that are pathological because they transgress those epistemic limitations (Chapter 6). This critique encompasses much of the practice of modern democratic politics as well as the "epistocratic" politics of economists and positivists, insofar as democratic politics is framed around finding policy solutions to social and economic problems. Not only does this Progressive Era view of politics place an "immense epistemic burden on the people" (19), it also—in an almost Foucauldian echo—shapes the democratic citizen in the image of the policy-making problem solver. This is the kind of subjecthood demanded and cultivated by the practices of modern democracy. We are positioned as problem-solvers when surveys and polls from political scientists and parties alike ask us about policy issues, and this way of framing democratic subjects is reinforced in the press, as in a recent *New York Times* "explainer" titled: "How the Democratic Candidates Would Tackle the Housing Crisis" (Astor 2020)—a type of headline that, I hope, is so familiar that it suggests the ubiquity of the phenomena Friedman addresses.

It is this deeper story that I want to discuss in this comment. In particular, I want to focus on the way Friedman conceptualizes "technocracy" and criticizes it, with a view to highlighting the way in which, on the one hand, he expands the scope of technocracy far beyond its usual association with rule by experts, yet on the other hand frames it in such a way as to downplay what I call "architectural" models of technocracy. I will suggest that he thereby misses the extent to which "exitocracy" (ch. 7)—as a form of architectural technocracy—raises a parallel set of questions about the role of experts in designing exitocratic systems, and the crucial question of the relation of exitocracy to democratic politics.

Technocracy Without Knowledge

Technocracy is often associated with the idea of expert rule. The term was coined in 1919 by an American inventor, William H. Smyth, and meant rule by scientists and engineers (echoing Thorstein Veblen's essays of the same year, later published as *Engineers and the Price System* [Veblen 1921]). The early advocates of technocracy thought that the political and economic order was no longer suited to the current stage of industrial and technological development, and that resources could be more efficiently managed by engineers than businessmen or politicians. At least part of the impetus for the movement came from the successful experience of national economic planning boards during World War I. After the onset of the Great Depression, the "technocrat" movement enjoyed a brief moment of public interest before disappearing more or less without trace (Akin 1977). By that point, however, the term itself, as opposed to the movement, had gone beyond the very specific ideas of the movement's leaders (such as using energy surveys to replace the price system), coming to be associated with the more general idea of scientists, engineers, and technical experts of various kinds exercising political power (in the sense of who gets what, when, and how) in virtue of their specialist knowledge. Although the term remains pretty nebulous—in recent years, it has been used variously to refer not only to rule by experts (Caramani 2017; Fischer 1990), bureaucrats (Bickerton and Invernizzi Acetti 2015), and elites in general (Offe 2013), but also to norms of impartiality (Bickerton and Invernizzi Acetti 2015; Urbinati 2014) and even to the conviction that there must be an "evidence base" for public policy (Easterly 2016) —it has tended to retain something of the following structure: the exercise of power by means of, or justified by, specialist knowledge (Putnam 1977, 384).

Friedman, by contrast, describes technocracy as a vision that reduces politics to a set of problems to be solved by legislative and regulatory interventions. The defining mark of the technocrat is the belief that politics consists in addressing social and economic problems—such as how to reduce poverty or control the spread of infectious disease—and that there are better or worse solutions to those problems. For Friedman, then, technocracy is not identical with rule by experts. You can be a technocrat, in the sense of thinking of politics as primarily a matter of problem solving, without actually possessing any specialist knowledge or exercising any special decision-making power in virtue of it. Friedman is not denying that there is an important class of people who *do* claim expertise with respect to some of these problems, whom he calls "epistocrats." The more common manifestation of the technocratic view of politics, however, is found among "citizen-technocrats," who form their own accounts of the causes and cures for social problems and then seek to promote their favored solutions through available political channels. Between them, the "epistocrats" and "citizen-technocrats" encompass most of what contemporary politics and government do. Politicians, Friedman says, often present themselves as having solutions to social and economic problems; voters select candidates on the basis of their resolve to push through popular solutions; and administrators draw on specialist knowledge, predominantly from the discipline of economics, to implement or perhaps constrain the choices made by voters and elected leaders.

One trait that tends to be shared by citizen-technocrats and epistocrats alike is "radical ignorance": ignorance of what they don't know, which, in a technocratic context, means the difficult-to-discern beliefs of those whose behavior technocracy attempts to control. The problem of radical ignorance is, for Friedman, intimately connected to the view of politics as problem solving, for it is the framing of politics as a process of finding solutions to social problems that generates demands for a possibly unfeasible degree of knowledge. The would-be technocrat, he suggests, needs to know (1) which social problems are real and significant (in terms of how broadly and intensely they affect people), (2) what causes those problems, (3) which actions can "solve, mitigate, or prevent" them, and (4) what those solutions would cost, including unintended and thus unanticipated costs (46). It is clear enough that when defined in those terms, the acquisition of technocratic knowledge is a daunting task, not only for citizen-technocrats but also for expert epistocrats. The epistemic problem grows worse once we recognize that the last three requirements, in particular, entail retrodictive and predictive knowledge of the springs of human behavior. Any legislative or regulatory solution to a problem, Friedman points out, can be effective only by controlling people's behavior in order to get them to take desirable actions. Thus, the central epistemic need of technocracy is reliable knowledge of how to predict people's behavior after a policy initiative is implemented (covering the third and fourth types of technocratic knowledge), which also requires an understanding of *why* they acted, in the past, in a manner that leads us to predict certain behavior in the future (the second type).

This epistemic need for retrospective and prospective behavioral knowledge, however, appears to be much more easily met if one is unaware of the fact that those whose behavior is being retrodicted and predicted may have beliefs that would incline them to react idiosyncratically (in the opinion of the epistocrat or citizen-technocrat) to a technocratic initiative. Technocrats' radical ignorance of these idiosyncratic beliefs, then, transforms them from what Friedman calls "judicious" technocrats, who would be "ideationally sensitive," into epistemically arrogant political actors who are blind to the limits of their knowledge, unaware of "their need for, and ... their lack of, the four types of technocratic knowledge" (301).

Focusing on epistocrats (who are experts by definition), their knowledge of this or that aspect of human behavior and public policy, perhaps in great depth and detail, is nonetheless consistent with radical ignorance of what they would really need to know in order to solve social problems, and how far their knowledge falls below this bar. Friedman shows us how an economics Ph.D. and a lifetime of experience in public policy is entirely consistent with, and indeed can even select for,[1] radical ignorance. When economists make predictions based on the effects of incentives, to mention one of his key arguments, they are radically ignorant of the radical ignorance of ordinary people, who do not know all that they would need to know in order to act in the way the theory supposes, introducing a major blind spot into economic knowledge (193).

Democracy as Technocratic

It is worth pausing to consider how far this conception of "technocracy"—as a problem-solving mentality that is in tension with radical ignorance—takes us from the common usage of the term. Friedman's technocrats include ordinary citizens with nominal power and no special knowledge: they, too, seem, at least according to research about U.S. public opinion (in Friedman's interpretation of it), to be radically ignorant of what they would need to know if their policy preferences and political choices were to be reliably accurate (Chapter 6).

On his account, then, technocratic politics is not the dry and bloodless "policy without politics" (Schmidt 2006) with which it is often associated. Rather, what you get when politics is conceived as problem solving, but people fail to see that their own solutions are partial renderings of a complex reality, is not a calm, technical politics, but an especially bloody, bitter, and Manichean politics. Because problems are assumed to have simple and obvious solutions, the key question is identifying those with the will to carry them out, and opposing the bad guys who want to get in the way. Thus, "technocratic politics takes on the appearance of a moral battle over ends, not a debate over difficult-to-parse means" (301). What Friedman calls "technocratic naïveté" or "naïve technocratic realism" leads to a politics in which people do not advance their solutions to problems in the spirit of provisionality and fallibility, but as statements of the obvious. We then ascribe the fact of disagreement not to irreducible differences in judgment in a context of moral and social complexity, but to the ill will of our opponents. The naïve realist fails to see that "obvious" solutions are actually "fallible interpretations of ambiguous realities"—and, further, that "what seems to be a self-disclosing reality is actually a generalization from a partial vision of reality" (37).

The politics of naïve realism was described by Walter Lippmann (one of the heroes of this book) thus:

> The opponent presents himself as the man who says, evil be thou my good. He is an annoyance who does not fit into the scheme of things. Nevertheless he interferes. And since that scheme is based in our minds on incontrovertible fact fortified by irresistible logic, some place has to be found for him in the scheme. Rarely in politics or industrial disputes is a place made for him by the simple admission that he has looked upon the same reality and seen another aspect of it. That would shake the whole scheme. Thus ... out of the opposition we make villains and conspiracies. (Lippmann [1922] 1997, 82–83)

Again—and this is one of the great strengths of the book—this critique is not directed only at the ordinary citizen. Friedman contends that many political scientists and economists who have commented on "public ignorance" are themselves naive realists with respect to their own claims to knowledge. Thus, someone like Bryan Caplan, whose *Myth of the Rational Voter: Why Democracies Choose Bad Policies* (2008) benchmarks political ignorance against the knowledge claimed by economists, does not recognize that economists are making knowledge *claims* rather than simply "knowing." Moreover, Caplan attributes this very "knowledge"—that is, the knowledge claims of economists—to voters, such that when they act as if they disagree with economists, it really means that they are irrationally but deliberately *choosing* to behave ignorantly or "ideologically" while knowing that this is what they are doing (61-64). Friedman finds such epistemological naïveté, too, in the very different figure of Theodor Adorno, who, in his interpretation of the interviews on which he based the "authoritarian personality" thesis, consistently attributes to anti-Semites the knowledge that Jews do not really possess the terrible traits the anti-Semites attribute to them (210-219). Like Caplan, Adorno treats his own knowledge as so self-evident that those he is interpreting cannot possibly be ignorant of it. At the most general level, Friedman is targeting any unreflexive claim to knowledge of social reality, one that is unaware of its nature as a partial and fallible interpretation with which others may (rightly or wrongly) disagree.

This analysis leads Friedman to a provocative claim: that populism and technocracy are not opposites, but are two sides of the same coin. The apogee of the technocratic mentality, on his account, is not a figure like Mario Monti, the Italian economist appointed to the Italian Senate and then made Prime Minister without ever having been elected, but rather Donald Trump, who Friedman describes as the "technocrat-in-chief" (291). Trump was, of course, deeply opposed to professional bureaucrats, scientists, and policy experts. But he nonetheless presented himself as a problem solver, grounding his claim to know better than the experts in his experience as a businessman (in this he was, of course, tapping a long tradition in American politics). Furthermore, he presented his solutions as simple and obvious, and focused on the need for resolute execution in the face of opposition, both the overt opposition of protestors and the secret opposition of the "deep state."

While the idea of Trump as a technocrat is provocative, I don't find it entirely persuasive. Or rather, I think Friedman's account flattens out the complexities in the relations between populist and (what is usually called) technocratic political styles. One thing that populists and technocrats seem to share is a commitment to uncontested executive power. Both promise to get things done at a time when we seem unable to forge agreement on political action through public debate and parliamentary procedure. Yet, as recent commentators have suggested, populism and technocracy are best thought of not as two manifestations of the same tendency, nor as simple opposites, but as "complements" (Bickerton and Invernizzi-Accetti 2015). They interact and feed off one another in a mutually reinforcing dynamic, where each responds to the perceived excesses of the other, and thereby confirms the other's worst fears

(Urbinati 2014). What they have in common is a hostility to democratic pluralism and to the dispersal of power implied by party competition (Caramani 2017), but they remain distinct, and their relationship to one another is a more complex dynamic that narrows the space for democratic pluralism. This sort of dynamic disappears in Friedman's view, which rather suggests that the space of pluralist politics itself has been thoroughly colonized by the technocratic mentality. On his view, parties compete to offer solutions to social problems, epistocrats claim to be able to solve social problems without input from voters, and populists claim to know how to solve social problems if only they could win the acclaim of the majority and execute their program without obstruction or compromise. Yet this may be stretching the concept too far. If technocracy is everywhere, then the critique of technocracy becomes an undifferentiated critique of more or less the whole of modern democratic politics.

Architects and Engineers

Although Friedman's critique has an unusually wide scope, it is at the same time restricted to what we might call an "engineering" conception of technocracy. Friedman, as we saw above, rejects the identification of technocracy with rule by experts, and thus would not sign on to the even more specific idea of rule by engineers invoked by the early twentieth-century "technocrat" movement. However, I think it's fair to describe his target in terms of the "assimilation of politics to engineering" invoked by Michael Oakeshott (1962, 4) in his account of rationalism in politics:

> The conduct of affairs, for the Rationalist, is a matter of solving problems. … In this activity the character which the Rationalist claims for himself is the character of the engineer, whose mind (it is supposed) is controlled throughout by the appropriate technique and whose first step is to dismiss from his attention everything not directly related to his specific intentions. This assimilation of politics to engineering is, indeed, what may be called the myth of rationalist politics.[2]

The engineering model of technocracy views politics as a set of problems to be solved, advocates continuous interventions in complex social and economic systems, and presupposes the possibility of a degree of prediction and control centered on administrative power and underpinned by social science. It treats social problems, such as reducing poverty or providing abundant low-cost housing, as technically difficult but conceptually straightforward. The engineering model is thus characterized by what Friedman calls the "simple-society ontology," which treats society as, in principle, not only knowable, but also transparent (that is, *easily* knowable).

Modern society, of course, is not simple. It is "epistemically complex" (27). The epistemic complexity of society, brought about (at least in part) by the "ideational heterogeneity" of its human constituents, undermines assumptions of uniformity in human behavior, and makes prediction and control difficult at best. Indeed, absent "homogenizing counterforces" (169), the prediction of people's behavior would require a "complete history of [their] relevant ideational exposures" and of the interaction of those exposures in their webs of belief, a task "more difficult than mind reading" (144) (although that probably won't stop Google trying). Friedman holds that epistemic complexity sets a limit on the sorts of things we can credibly attempt to do to each other with any hope of success. However, since there *may* be homogenizing counterforces in any given case, such as shared norms across individuals' webs of belief, we cannot say in advance where these limits are or how insurmountable they might be.

Thus, Part I of *Power Without Knowledge,* through an exploration of the Lippmann-Dewey debate of the 1920s (Chapter 2) and an elaboration of the epistemology implicit in Lippmann's position (Chapter 3), makes a presumptive case in favor of unpredictable ideational heterogeneity, which would lead to some degree of technocratic failure (171, 317-19). Epistemic complexity can, however, be recognized and acknowledged, and we can try to work within its limits. It is in this spirit that Part II explores the practices and ideas of contemporary epistocrats and citizen-technocrats. Here Friedman criticizes the "injudicious" neglect, by both groups, of the ideational character of the human beings whose behavior they are trying to predict and control. A judicious or "ideationally sensitive" technocrat would try to determine "where the areas of predictability are located, how wide they are against a backdrop of presumptively unpredictable ideas, and the behavior they are likely to cause" (169), but neither citizen-technocrats nor epistocrats tend to do this at present. Instead, they implicitly treat people as non-ideational and thus fully transparent and predictable. Part III introduces "exitocracy" as a conceptual "alternative to really existing technocracy" (318), with the aim of establishing a *comparative* "hierarchy of technocratic legitimacy," according to which judicious technocracy can be expected to do better (to some unknown extent) than injudicious technocracy, but exitocracy can be expected to do better than either (341).

An exitocracy is a state whose "cardinal goal would be to provide a framework within which individuals could attempt to solve—or, better, escape—the problems that afflict them as individuals." Exitocracy would "forego, wherever possible, the frontal analytic assault on social problems, society-wide, that typifies 'ordinary' technocracy, whether judicious or injudicious" (322). Instead it would rely on competition among a range of private providers and employers, and citizens empowered to exit from any one of them in search of better solutions. Friedman takes the exit mechanism to have "inherently beneficial epistemic properties" (318), rooted in the situated judgment of customers and workers. Those running the firms and businesses are no better placed, epistemically, to predict behavior and craft solutions to problems than are ordinary technocrats: both businesspeople and technocrats are trying to predict human behavior. But if (i) there are several competing providers; (ii) they are diverse (thanks to ideational heterogeneity) and thus produce a variety of solutions; and (iii) they are in competition with one another for customers, more effective solutions are likely to emerge. The customers and workers choosing between these providers are the same people who are called upon, as citizens, to make technocratic judgments in a democratic technocracy, but when they use the exit mechanism they need not predict the behavior and thus the ideas of millions of "anonymous others," as they must in their capacity as citizen-technocrats (331). Rather, they are called on to make situated judgments about how to handle immediate and personal problems. Friedman thus opens the chapter with an approving citation of Schumpeter's distinction between a citizen's knowledge of distant affairs mediated through the testimony and interpretation of others and direct knowledge of "things which are familiar to him independently of what his newspaper tells him" (cited at 321). Our attempts to judge matters close to our experience, while still fallible, are at least epistemically superior to our attempts to make sense of and articulate society-wide claims about the causes and cures of social problems or—I might add—about the system of rules under which we live.

Although Friedman describes exitocracy as a (conceptual) alternative to technocracy (318) and speaks of the "choice between exitocracy and technocracy" (347), he also describes exitocracy as itself "an unusual or "extraordinary" version of technocracy" (322). By this he principally means that exitocracy would inevitably be nested within technocracy. That is to say, no state can rely wholly on exit-based empowerments for the simple reason that the state has to "provide a framework" within which competition among providers can be fostered and choice by consumers and workers enabled (ibid.). An exitocracy needs to supply the "primary" public goods of "redistribution and a legal system" to ensure that people have the capacity to make use of exit (341); then there are "secondary" public goods, that is, "nonprimary public goods that are justified on exitocratic grounds by virtue of exitocrats' ability to build exit-like devices into the provision of the goods," such as a carbon tax (ibid.). Finally, there are "tertiary" public goods, such as "territorial military defense, foreign policy, and many, many others" (342). Exitocracy thus depends on and is embedded within "ordinary" technocracy. Therefore, exitocracy is not merely a conceptual alternative to ordinary technocracy but an institutional or policy alternative only in those domains in which consumer choice and competition among providers is judged to be the most effective way for individuals to solve—or escape—their problems; and in non-market domains where personal, experiential knowledge is relevant; as well as in cases that arise in the private sphere where voice is more effective (again, in personal settings) than it is in the public sphere of technocracy (331–33). What makes exitocracy, for Friedman, an unusual form of technocracy is simply that it is a technocracy that limits its frontal analytic assault on social and economic problems to those domains where the epistemically superior exit mechanism is not available, and to putting in place conditions for the effective use of the exit mechanism.

However, the affinity between exitocracy and ordinary technocracy goes deeper than just the nesting of the former within the latter, because I think we can usefully describe exitocracy as an "architectural" model of technocracy. This is a sort of second-order model that attempts to avoid prediction and control, but holds that laws and institutions can be designed to promote the emergence and competitive selection of effective solutions to the problems faced by individuals. As in an ordinary technocracy, this involves designing and building laws, regulations, and institutions, and it depends on a theory of the implications of social complexity.[3] It reminds me of what Hayek recommended in *The Road to Serfdom* as "liberal" (as opposed to "socialist") planning, which involves "an intelligently designed and continually adjusted legal framework" (Hayek [1944] 2001, 40), one "designed both to preserve competition and to make it operate as beneficially as possible." That this echoed the rationalist politics to which he was so strongly opposed was picked up on by Oakeshott. The significance of Hayek's *Road to Serfdom*, he wrote, is "not the cogency of his doctrine, but the fact that it is a doctrine. A plan to resist all planning may be better than its opposite, but it belongs to the same style of politics. And only in a society already deeply infected with Rationalism will the conversion of the traditional resources of resistance to the tyranny of Rationalism into a self-conscious ideology be considered a strengthening of those resources" (Oakeshott 1962, 21-22). The architectural metaphor is not perfect, but I think it works in one respect: rather than constant intervention, the architect makes some sort of claim about the future performance of the building, the behavior it will encourage, how people will live in it, and so on. But once it is built there is to be no ongoing monitoring of, and intervention in, the behavior of the inhabitants.

Thinking of exitocracy as a form of architectural technocracy draws attention to the "exitocrats" who would be charged with designing, building, and maintaining such effective frameworks for competitive interaction (340ff). We might then ask questions about the character of the exitocrat that resemble those that Friedman asks about the character of the epistocrat. Friedman associates technocracy (in both epistocratic and citizen versions) with a kind of arrogance, which in turn is rooted in a simple-society ontology. He associates the recognition of complexity, by contrast, with intellectual humility. He cites a psychology study by Philip M. Fernbach et al. (2013) suggesting that asking people about the mechanisms by which policies would have their intended effects, rather than simply eliciting their reasons for supporting a policy (i.e., asking how it would achieve their objectives—prompts the recognition of complexity and reduces epistemic confidence in policy opinions, which we can see as signaling a kind of humility (295). Yet while there might indeed be a sort of epistemological humility implied by the complex-society ontology, it might also ground its own kind of arrogance: "We don't know much, but at least we know what we don't know, and that's a lot more than those people who don't know what they don't know!" Indeed, the history of architectural technocracy suggests that the "complex-society" ontology can come with its own glib certainties and a belief in the ability of judicious exitocrats to beneficially structure laws and policies to promote exit and competition.

At the end of the chapter on public ignorance, Friedman notes that critics seeking to deflate the "intentions heuristic" by showing the complexity of modern society can themselves be embedded within their own ideology (313), but he does not consider the exitocratic variant of this problem. For real-world examples, consider the role of Western economists in the restructuring of economic, legal, and political institutions of post-Soviet Eastern Europe (Johnson 2016) and South America (Dargent 2015), as well as the more general power of economists in limiting the scope of democratic politics (Levy and Peart 2016). The selective pressures that favor arrogance and overconfidence among experts involved in first-order problem-solving should also apply to experts designing second-order exitocratic structures. Experts who firmly believe in the basic complexity of society and the limits to human knowledge should believe, as well, that this justifies the insulation of exitocratic policy design from the misguided interventions of the purveyors of the simple-society ontology. It would be logical for them to seek to escape or limit a democratic politics which seemed unable to recognize that complexity.

Moreover, we still have to confront the question of how the scope and boundaries of exitocracy are to be determined. Who decides which issues or problems are best approached directly through frontal analytic assault and which problems are best handled indirectly in the private sphere, as through the mechanism of exit? Consider a problem like flooding. The protection of one's property from flooding could be viewed as an individual problem. I could then build a watertight wall around my property (and a range of private providers might compete to provide the best individualized flood-protection system). However, in the event of a flood, the water I keep off my property will be distributed to my neighbors' property. This might seem an open-and-shut argument for collective flood management (it certainly seems that way to the Dutch), and indeed for the use of the coercive power of the state to prevent free riding on collective solutions. But it is disputable—and it is disputed—in places like Miami, where there are buildings with private sea walls (Kuper 2020). We then find ourselves faced with a conflict over whether to regard something as a (possibly tertiary?) public good or as a matter better left to exitocratic mechanisms. This conflict raises normative and empirical questions about how to evaluate two very different strategies, one framed around individual problem solving, another around collective problem solving. And it raises the question of how we are then to decide between them.

One option at this point would be to invoke democracy as some part of the answer. Jack Knight and James Johnson (2011, 19), for instance, describe democracy as the presumptively best way of "negotiat[ing] unavoidable social disagreement over institutional arrangements." Their argument is that "democracy enjoys a priority precisely because it is uniquely useful in approaching the crucial, complex, and conflictual tasks involved in the ongoing process of selecting, implementing, and maintaining effective institutional arrangements" (ibid., 12). In so far as democracy introduces diverse ideas and agents into collective decision processes, and involves "an institutionalised process of experimentation, inquiry and testing" (ibid., 159), it manifests competition at the second-order level of "selecting, implementing and maintaining *effective* institutional arrangements" (ibid., 19). Yet this option is not really open to Friedman, not least because (to stick with the flooding example) those sorts of judgments move far away from our direct experience. We might say, of course, that we directly experience a flood. But we do not directly experience a *risk* of flooding. And when a flood happens, whether we experience it as an act of God, or a manageable risk, or an effect of climate change, or something else entirely, is a matter of interpretation. And then we are back with Friedman's basic problem—that we don't know enough to make these judgments, or at least that these judgments would seem to be as much of a problem for exitocracy as they are for democratic technocracy. That is, it is hard to see on this account how the politics of deciding the boundaries of exitocracy would not just reproduce the sort of pathological politics produced by disputes over first-order problem-solving.

The boundary problem raises a further question. I take it that Friedman conceives exitocracy as a sort of self-limiting technocracy, one which foregoes a direct approach to social problems when those problems are better left to individuals and competing private providers. But how exactly is it supposed to limit itself? On Friedman's account, it's hard to see how this limitation could be internal to democratic politics itself. His central argument for the beneficial epistemic effects of exitocracy is that exit is epistemically superior to voice. Indeed, he regards the "habituat[ion] ... to advocacy, to debate, to arguing and otherwise attempting to persuade" as a pathological feature of technocratic culture (344). He describes the addiction to argument about matters beyond one's comprehension as itself a product of a political culture that makes people think they should have opinions about policies. Democratic technocracy habituates citizens into "hot hatreds." The "mental habits fostered by regular use of the exit mechanism," by contrast, generate a "cold rationality" (345). Even if we accept this view of the consequences of citizen-technocratic subjecthood, it does not explain how we might get from there to exitocracy, or how the self-limitation involved in exitocracy can arise within a citizen-technocratic political culture. It seems to me that Friedman's claims for a self-limiting form of politics characterized by cold rationality don't make sense unless we understand those limits as coming from somewhere other than democratic politics itself.

* * *

By framing Friedman's argument in terms of a distinction between engineering and architectural models of technocracy, I mean both to emphasize the continuities between them and to raise questions about their relation to democratic politics. Exitocracy implies policies, laws, and regulations designed by various experts and voted on by citizen-technocrats. Even though neither citizens nor experts in this scenario are supposed to be engaging in "engineering"-style first-order problem solving, they are nonetheless called to make judgments about how to organize and adjust legal and regulatory systems to promote competition, how to "build exit-like devices" (341), and to judge what counts as a public good and what counts as a domain best given over to private competition and exit. There are thus potential continuities between engineering and architectural models of technocracy both at the level of the role and character of experts—epistocrats and exitocrats alike—and at the level of ordinary citizens—citizen-technocrats and citizen-exitocrats. Why, then, would an exitocracy not exhibit a similar sort of expert arrogance and heated popular politics that we (arguably) find in the politics of a mixed democratic/epistocratic technocracy such as our own? (The political conflicts in the United States over the question of whether health care, for instance, is best thought of as a problem to be dealt with through a frontal analytic assault by a centralized administration or better left to competition and exit seems shot through with hot hatreds, even though it turns on something like a question of the boundaries of exitocracy.) Friedman suggests that our politics generates too much heat by requiring both citizens and experts to address problems at a collective level that would be better handled by individuals and competing private providers. Exitocracy would take the heat out of politics by imposing a self-limitation on the sorts of demands it makes on citizens and experts alike. Yet where is the self-limitation that is characteristic of the cooler politics of exitocracy supposed to come from? It is hard to see, on Friedman's account, how such self-limitation can arise from within democratic politics (that is, from within democratic technocracy or epistocracy). It is for this reason that architectural technocracy—at least to me—implies the dethroning of politics by limiting the scope for *democratic* technocracy.

NOTES

1. Real-world epistocracy, Friedman suggests, generates a pressure to predict, which selects for positivism or naive realism; and a pressure to overstate one's confidence, which leads to what he calls the "spiral of conviction."
2. While Oakeshott is associated with political conservatism, a similar critique of technocracy as a sort of rationalism is well rooted on the left, and in particular among participatory democrats (see Fischer 1990).
3. Hayek, for instance, developed a theory of complex systems which purported to show the impossibility of knowledge sufficient for prediction and control of the system, but claimed the possibility of knowledge of behavioral "patterns." Economics, he thought, can tell us "under which general conditions a pattern of this sort will form itself," which in turn "enable[s] us to create such conditions and to observe whether a pattern of the kind predicted will appear" (Hayek [1964] 1967, 36). Thus, while Hayek powerfully rejected the aspiration to prediction and control of complex social systems that he thought underpinned any attempt at economic planning, he regarded his own approach as one grounded firmly in the science of complex systems.

REFERENCES

Akin, William E. 1977. *Technocracy and the American Dream: The Technocrat Movement, 1900-1941*. Berkeley: University of California Press.

Astor, Maggie. 2020. "How the Democratic Candidates Would Tackle the Housing Crisis." *New York Times*, 3 March.

Bickerton, Christopher, and Carlo Invernizzi Accetti. 2015. "Populism and Technocracy: Opposites or Complements?" *Critical Review of International Social and Political Philosophy* 20(2): 186-206.

Blinder, Alan. 1997. "Is Government Too Political?" *Foreign Affairs* 76: 115-126.

Caramani, Daniele. 2017. "Will vs. Reason: The Populist and Technocratic Forms of Political Representation and Their Critique of Party Government." *American Political Science Review* 111(1): 54-67.

Chambers, Simone. 2018. "Human Life Is Group Life: Deliberative Democracy for Realists." *Critical Review* 30(1-2): 36-48.

Dargent, Eduardo. 2015. *Technocracy and Democracy in Latin America: The Experts Running Government.* Cambridge: Cambridge University Press.

Easterly, William. 2016. "Democracy is Dying as Technocrats Watch." *Foreign Policy*, December 23.

Fernbach, Philip M., Todd Rogers, Craig R. Fox, and Steven A. Sloman. 2013. "Political Extremism Is Supported by an Illusion of Understanding." *Psychological Science* 24(6): 939–46.

Fischer, Frank. 1990. *Technocracy and the Politics of Expertise.* London: SAGE Publications.

Friedman, Jeffrey. 2019. *Power Without Knowledge: A Critique of Technocracy.* New York: Oxford University Press.

Hayek, F. A. [1944] 2001. *The Road to Serfdom.* London: Routledge.

Hayek, F. A. [1964] 1967. "The Theory of Complex Phenomena." In idem, *Studies in Philosophy, Politics and Economics.* London: Routledge and Kegan Paul.

Johnson, Juliet. 2016. *Priests of Prosperity: How Central Bankers Transformed the Postcommunist World.* Ithaca: Cornell University Press.

Knight, Jack, and James Johnson. 2011. *The Priority of Democracy: Political Consequences of Pragmatism.* Princeton: Princeton University Press.

Kuper, Simon. 2020. "Can the Dutch Save the World from the Danger of Rising Sea Levels?" *Financial Times*, January 20.

Levy, David M., and Sandra J. Peart. 2016. *Escape from Democracy: The Role of Experts and the Public in Economic Policy.* Cambridge: Cambridge University Press.

Moore, Alfred. 2016. "Hayek, Conspiracy, and Democracy." *Critical Review* 28(1): 44-62.

Oakeshott, Michael. 1962. *Rationalism in Politics and Other Essays.* London: Methuen.

Offe, Claus. 2013. "Europe Entrapped." *Modern Law Review* 19(5): 595–611.

Putnam, Robert. 1977. "Elite Transformation in Advanced Industrial Societies: An Empirical Assessment of the Theory of Technocracy." *Comparative Political Studies*, 10(3): 383-412.

Schmidt, Vivien. 2006. *Democracy in Europe: The EU and National Polities.* Oxford: Oxford University Press.

Somin, Ilya. 2008. "Voter Ignorance and the Democratic Ideal." *Critical Review* 12(4): 413-58.

Smyth, William H. 1919. "Technocracy: National Industrial Management." *Industrial Management* 57 (March): 208-212.

Urbinati, Nadia. 2014. *Democracy Disfigured: Opinion, Truth, and the People.* Cambridge, Mass.: Harvard University Press.

Veblen, Thorstein. 1921. *Engineers and the Price System.* New York: B. W. Huebsch.

Zeynep Pamuk

WHAT FOLLOWS FROM THE PROBLEM OF IGNORANCE?

ABSTRACT: *In* Power Without Knowledge, *Jeffrey Friedman develops a critique of social science to argue that current technocratic practices are prone to predictive failures and unintended consequences. However, he does not provide evidence that the cause he singles out—"ideational heterogeneity"—is in fact a non-negligible source of technocratic limitations, more than or alongside better-known problems such as missing data, measurement issues, interpretive difficulties, and researcher bias. Even if we grant ideational heterogeneity, Friedman's preferred institutional solution of exitocracy does not necessarily follow. His critical epistemology would also be compatible with radical forms of collective action.*

"I foresee all sorts of unforeseen problems," remarks Sir Humphrey Appleby, the prime minister from the 1980s British television series *Yes, Prime Minister*, to his cabinet secretary. The line expresses one of the fundamental facts of political life: there will always be unintended and unwanted consequences. Jeffrey Friedman's excellent new book, *Power Without Knowledge: A Critique of Technocracy* (Oxford University Press, 2019), takes this fact seriously and argues that it poses a challenge to the justification of current political institutions, which he believes are overwhelmingly technocratic.

The book starts from the observation that modern states are oriented towards solving social and economic problems through policies designed for specific ends: reducing crime, increasing economic growth, controlling inflation, improving air quality, ensuring product safety and so on. This orientation toward problem solving assumes the ready availability of knowledge that can connect proposed policies to the desired ends, but Friedman argues that the knowledge that would make such means-ends reasoning possible is extremely difficult to obtain, given the profound obstacles facing predictive social science.

Friedman believes that this problem of ignorance should be of central concern to both political theory and political practice. He traces the implications of this epistemic problem for existing political institutions and develops a proposal for the institutions that should supplement them. Two points about the project are worth clarifying from the start. The first is that Friedman uses the word *technocracy* in a very broad sense. Any government or person who attempts to use state power to solve, mitigate or prevent social and economic problems qualifies as a technocrat. This is much broader than the standard usage of the word, which typically denotes rule by technical experts. Friedman challenges not just expert rule, but also more democratic variants of state-led problem solving, such as ordinary government regulation or democratic socialism. Citizens, too, count as technocrats if they support the mission of solving social problems through government action.

The second thing to clarify is that Friedman has a distinct, and in my view more interesting, conceptualization of the problem of ignorance than most scholars writing on this increasingly popular topic. The literature on the so-called problem of ignorance has mostly been concerned with the issues that arise from the well-documented fact that the citizenry is deplorably ignorant of basic facts about politics, which arguably prevents them from making informed political choices. This is the focus of recent books by Jason Brennan (2016), Ilya Somin (2013), and Bryan Caplan (2007), which attack democracy on epistemic grounds. Debates in this area usually involve arguments about whether the kind of knowledge citizens lack is relevant for the decisions they need to make, whether citizens can reliably use heuristics and shortcuts to compensate for their lack of knowledge (e.g., Popkin 1991, Lupia and McCubbins 1998), and whether any of this is relevant for justifications of democracy.

Friedman cuts through this tangle by pointing out that scholars on both sides of the debate are implicitly assuming the availability and accessibility of knowledge—usually to themselves or to fellow social scientists—in order to assess how citizens fare with respect to it. In doing so, they often overstate what is known, for instance because they take agreement among a number of experts to stand in for truth. Both optimists and pessimists about citizen competence are thus too assured of the self-evidence of the relevant facts. By contrast, Friedman wonders if *anyone* possesses sufficient knowledge to design policies that can reliably be foreseen to bring about more good than harm. This is because social science faces severe obstacles in producing the kind of knowledge that would make this possible. Friedman's critique of technocracy may at times sound similar to Hayek's claim that states cannot have access to the knowledge required for effective control of the economy, but it is important to note that Hayek readily admitted that specialized scientific knowledge could be centralized in the hands of experts. His concern was that experts wouldn't be able to access the dispersed information held by individuals. Friedman, on the other hand, argues that both experts and ordinary citizens may lack the necessary knowledge.

Despite this difference, there is a crucial structural similarity between Friedman's project and Hayek's in that they both start from epistemological claims and derive implications for political theory. This effective structure can also be found in others thinkers, including Plato, Hobbes, and Dewey. Arguments with this structure can be opposed in one of two ways: one can either challenge the epistemology and thereby undermine the political theory or challenge the link between the epistemology and the political theory. My goal in this essay is to develop one argument of the first kind and another of the second. The first section raises some doubts about Friedman's diagnosis of the source of the predictive problems of social science and examines their implications. The second section grants his epistemology and considers what else might follow from it politically besides what Friedman recommends.

The Predictive Problems of Social Science

The observation that the social sciences are not good at prediction is not particularly controversial. There are many explanations for why this is the case: the difficulty of randomized controlled experiments, the unavailability of data, measurement problems, the inherent subjectivity of concept definitions, design and modeling choices, the ethics of manipulating human subjects ... among many others. Friedman is not interested in most of these well-known and well-examined problems that exercise social scientists. Instead, he singles out a different problem: that of "ideational heterogeneity." Predictive social science is based on the assumption that humans will respond in uniform and predictable ways to changes in external conditions, much like plants or physical objects. However, unlike plants or physical objects, the behavior of humans is determined by their beliefs and ideas, and each individual's web of beliefs and ideas is idiosyncratic. This is what Friedman (27) calls ideational heterogeneity. Since the social sciences assume uniformity rather than heterogeneity, they are essentially built on a false premise. Technocratic policies may go awry because of their failure to acknowledge and respond to ideational heterogeneity, which results in unintended and unforeseen consequences.

However, there is no evidence in the book that ideational heterogeneity is in fact a major source of the predictive failures of social science. It is not clear, for instance, how it compares in importance to some of the other serious challenges faced by social science mentioned above. Friedman does not undertake a comparative evaluation of different explanations or even attempt to argue that ideational heterogeneity is a major issue rather than a minor or even negligible one. The book's main argument is framed simply as a possibility: *if* ideational heterogeneity is widespread and is not counteracted, then technocracy *may* be prone to bad predictions. Friedman's argumentative strategy consists in persuading the reader that humans are ideationally heterogeneous and that social science systematically ignores this fact. Both of these seem clearly true, but do not establish the real-world significance of ideational heterogeneity. In the absence of empirical evidence for the magnitude of the problem, it remains plausible that the effects of ideational heterogeneity are in fact negligible, and that technocrats would benefit more from keeping the focus on all the other, better-known limitations of social science. Let me sketch the argument for why this might be the case.

We could think of social science as operating with a background model of human behavior, which is based on the assumption of law-like regularities in human responses to changes in external conditions or stimuli. This assumption is obviously false, and it is hard to imagine anyone disputing this. But all models make some false assumptions for the sake of simplicity and usability. It is still possible to get pretty good predictions from a model that makes false assumptions. Newton's theory of gravity is false, strictly speaking, but it is good enough for the predictive purposes of engineering. The important question is whether the assumption of uniformity is useful—or useful enough. As Friedman himself points out (169), it is reasonable to believe that on some issues people do behave very predictably, responding to financial incentives and following widely accepted social and behavioral norms. Other areas may be entirely unpredictable. We cannot tell ex ante how much this assumption will skew the predictions of the model.

Of course, social science often fails to produce good predictions. The difficulty is that even when a model does not produce good predictions, it is hard to establish whether one of the false assumptions of the model is causing the problem or something else, such as measurement errors or researcher bias. It is possible, for instance, that individual heterogeneity is far less significant than cultural heterogeneity or that both are less significant than the inherent causal complexity or randomness of certain events or that all of these would pale into insignificance if we could acquire massive amounts of data on the social world. If our model involves several different false assumptions, it will be impossible to determine which one is causing the problem. Demonstrating the falsehood of an assumption does not get us very far in establishing it as the main reason why the predictions are no good.

To give an example, Friedman (205-7) briefly discusses the problems of external validity facing randomized control trials and suggests that these too are due to ideational heterogeneity. However, he does not discuss other reasons why external validity may be difficult, such as the myriad differences in culture, geography, demographics, political institutions, legal regimes, history and social norms between different contexts. If experimental results from a village in Kenya don't hold in a village in India, this could be due to innumerable different factors; ideational heterogeneity does not strike me as the most persuasive one. If Friedman wanted to establish that ideational heterogeneity truly is important, he would need evidence that shows, for instance, that different samples of randomly selected people from the same village (or the same university lab) respond very differently to the same policy intervention at around the same time and under similar experimental conditions. This would be a surprising finding that would support Friedman's hypothesis that idiosyncrasies at the individual level are the crucial obstacles to prediction and that behavioral regularity is a truly misguided assumption.

My aim here is not to argue against the importance of ideational heterogeneity, but rather to invite Friedman to give more evidence to establish that ideational heterogeneity really is the source of some problems with technocracy more than, or at least alongside, other plausible explanations, which have received more attention from social scientists and philosophers of science (e.g., Cartwright and Hardie 2012). His reluctance to do so may protect him from the charge of over-claiming, but it comes at the cost of reducing the force of his argument. It is disappointing, for instance, that Friedman cannot even rule out the possibility that ideational heterogeneity may have no effects at all in practice.

Why does it matter whether the limitations of technocratic knowledge are due to ideational heterogeneity or something else? Friedman could have listed a range of factors that threaten the reliability of social science and asked what follows from all these issues. This too would have been an interesting line of inquiry. The source of the problem matters because it determines which responses to technocracy would be appropriate: tweak it a little, change it dramatically (if so, in what direction) or abandon it altogether. Many of the widely acknowledged problems of social science could be improved through better social science: bigger data sets, machine learning algorithms for prediction, improved randomized experiments, more sophisticated methodologies, careful assessment of background assumptions, critical scrutiny of subjective judgments and researcher bias, increased norms of transparency and replication. … These could improve social science without attention to ideational heterogeneity. This, I take it, is what well-meaning social scientists are currently striving to do.

Ideational heterogeneity, on the other hand, stands in more fundamental tension with the generalizing aspirations of predictive social science and therefore of the technocratic project. If each individual is truly idiosyncratic, the task of seeking regularities and making general interventions is undermined from the start. Friedman may be right that a perfect technocracy would be fully individualized and would need to be able to predict each individual's behavior by understanding and interpreting her web of beliefs. The problem is that this is extremely difficult; a "judicious technocracy" that pays attention to the ideas and beliefs of individuals may well be out of reach.

Friedman himself offers technocrats a way out, and it is a plausible one. He points out that despite ideational heterogeneity, there are probably some homogenizing behavioral forces, such as social norms and culture. (I would also add the basic biological and psychological makeup of the human species as well as education and upbringing.) These counteract the effects of heterogeneity and may ensure that humans do in fact behave in predictable ways after all (169). What technocrats need to do is to better understand these forces and improve their knowledge of the conditions under which humans behave predictably and those in which they behave less predictably. In other words, they need to refine and improve their behavioral assumptions so that their model becomes more sophisticated and complex, if still based on strictly false assumptions. Instead of a blanket assumption of behavioral uniformity, they could make the uniformity assumption conditional and contextual. Once technocrats have a better sense of the strength and limitations of their knowledge and their background behavioral model, they could develop policy approaches and decision procedures that are better suited to different degrees of ignorance. They could recognize that they should not attempt prediction in certain areas, while becoming more confident of success in others. In fact, I think establishing the theoretical limits to the possibility of predictive accuracy for an event or system is one of the most valuable things technocrats could do, alongside working to establish the external validity of their findings. All of this is eminently reasonable and does not depend on accepting ideational heterogeneity.

Friedman is deeply pessimistic about current technocrats' ability to make these improvements, but seems paradoxically optimistic about the possibility of revolutionizing technocracy wholesale. Optimism and pessimism, however, may be largely beside the point. The crucial question is what other alternatives exist. Friedman's preferred alternative is exitocracy, which consists in allowing people as much freedom as possible to exit social arrangements that they are not satisfied with. He defends this on epistemic grounds, rather than on the basis of the value of individual liberty or choice. He argues that because people possess better knowledge about their own discontentment, allowing them to exit situations that they are not happy with would be on firmer epistemic grounds than making policies based on dubious social scientific claims.

However, this line of argument cannot determine whether ordinary technocracy or exitocracy would bring about better consequences because it is silent on the question of the magnitude of the overall costs of the former and the expected benefits of the latter. More generally, philosophical argumentation cannot ground the claim that exit "can, overall, be expected to better address people's discomforts than can the use of voice" (31) without some evidence comparing the overall states of affairs we could expect from following these two approaches. Exitocracy might exacerbate existing social problems even more than any possible course of policy action and it might also create new and unforeseen problems. Or it might not; we just cannot know. To make his proposal more credible, Friedman could have at least discussed the likely systemic consequences of exit in more detail and explained why allowing discontented individuals to exit would not make outcomes even worse. The claim that individuals know their discontent best is too weak a basis for a proposal that is likely to have systemic ramifications. If we use Friedman's expansive definition of technocracy as a dedication to solving, mitigating or preventing social and economic problems through policy action, it seems preferable to me to try to improve technocracy as much as possible before we consider alternatives based on exit, simply because facilitating the avoidance of social problems seems worse than collectively seeking better ways to solve them.

Ignorance and Democracy

I now want to turn to the relationship between the epistemological critique of social science and the possibility and desirability of democracy. Early on in the book, Friedman divides defenders of democracy into two. On one side is a robust tradition that values democracy on purely non-epistemic grounds—as a check against the tyranny of elites or to realize equality, freedom, or dignity. This tradition does not claim that democracy has any special wisdom, nor does it take wisdom to be necessary to the justification of political authority. Friedman puts Locke, Rousseau, Schumpeter and Popper in this category, among others. On the other side are utilitarians and Progressives of various stripes, who believe that good outcomes are crucial for the justification of authority, and who defend democracy on the grounds that it can effectively solve social problems and advance the common good. These "democratic technocrats" are in the awkward position of either showing that democracy does indeed have this superior epistemic capacity or biting the bullet on the preferability of epistocracy or another wiser form of government.

Friedman's argument does not fall into either category, but shares the democratic technocrats' focus on epistemic criteria. His argument is an internal critique of technocracy, which maintains that it is not possible to demonstrate such epistemic superiority in government—for democracy, epistocracy or any other regime.

Friedman thus believes that democracy can be defended either on non-epistemic grounds or from a position of naive optimism about its epistemic advantages. This misses an important third possibility, which is that a critical epistemology of the sort Friedman favors may be one of the strongest foundations upon which democracy can be justified. Those who believe that political or scientific truths are attainable will be tempted to conclude that political authority should be entrusted to those who have access to these truths. This was Plato's view. But if we start from the belief that it is impossible for anyone to attain such truths and that such truths will always be subject to deep disagreement, it makes sense to distribute power equally among citizens—not because citizens are wise, but because no one is. Democracy can then be justified as a fair and peaceful way of resolving deep epistemic disagreement in the absence of an external mechanism that can provide the correct answer. What legitimates it is not that the outcome will be good, but that everyone has assented to it.

Hobbes's moral and political theory was built on the foundation of a deep skepticism of this sort. Hobbes believed in the impossibility of establishing truths on both moral and factual matters, such as: "what is to be called right, what good, what virtue, what much, what little, what meum and tuum, what a pound, what a quart" (*The Elements of Law*, II.10.8). His solution to this epistemic quandary was to settle factual matters through acts of the sovereign—through politics. It was not the sovereign's superior knowledge that justified this, but the need to reach an agreement in the absence of the truth, to avoid conflict and paralysis. Assuming the difficulty of attaining reliable knowledge thus frees politics from the pressure for legitimation through claims to truth, which in turn makes democratic sovereignty truly possible. Note that this is not an intrinsic-value argument for democracy, but one that derives a political theory from an epistemological foundation.

It is curious that Friedman does not consider the possibility that the natural political upshot of his epistemology would be a radical form of democracy along these lines. He may want to object on the grounds that this would lead to irrational and dangerous outcomes, but this common objection requires asserting knowledge about which arrangements are likely to bring about better outcomes. Those who doubt our ability to make such knowledge claims do not have the grounds for making an argument of this sort.

One of the most significant contributions of Friedman's provocative book is to draw attention to the significance of the limits of social scientific knowledge for political theory. This is a productive starting point that can lead to many interesting places. In this essay, my goal has been to imagine a broader range of political conclusions that might be drawn from it. While Friedman ends on a pessimistic and apolitical note, with a defense of the individual's ability to escape from social problems by literally exiting the system, it is equally plausible to conclude that different forms of collective action could be justified on the basis of the same epistemology, including more radically democratic forms of action. Friedman may be right that neither social science nor philosophy can protect us from the unforeseen consequences of action, but I hope to have shown that both disciplines can have interesting insights to contribute to the debate on what follows from this fact.

REFERENCES

Brennan, Jason. 2016. *Against Democracy*. Princeton: Princeton University Press.

Caplan, Bryan. 2007. *The Myth of the Rational Voter*. Princeton: Princeton University Press.

Cartwright, Nancy, and Jeremy Hardie. 2012. *Evidence-Based Policy: A Practical Guide to Doing It Better*. Oxford: Oxford Unviersity Press.

Friedman, Jeffrey. 2019. *Power Without Knowledge: A Critique of Technocracy*. New York: Oxford University Press.

Lupia, Arthur, and Mathew D. McCubbins. 1998. *The Democratic Dilemma: Can Citizens Learn What They Need to Know?* New York: Cambridge University Press.

Popkin, Samuel L. 1991. *The Reasoning Voter: Communication and Persuasion in Presidential Campaigns*. Chicago: University of Chicago Press.

Somin, Ilya. 2013. *Democracy and Political Ignorance*. Stanford: Stanford University Press.

Robert Reamer

POWER, KNOWLEDGE, AND ANARCHISM

ABSTRACT: *While Jeffrey Friedman's* Power Without Knowledge *offers a welcome corrective to the technocratic statism that dominates modern politics, Wittgenstein's view of language suggests that the problem of ideational heterogeneity is less worrisome than Friedman maintains. In addition, Friedman's "exitocracy" is as epistemically demanding as ordinary technocracy and thus cannot provide an alternative to it. Anarchism, however, might provide a more consistent alternative to technocracy.*

Power Without Knowledge: A Critique of Technocracy (Oxford University Press 2019) is a remarkable and timely book. It presents a powerful argument relevant to issues at the heart of contemporary politics, while simultaneously participating in and extending debates that are as old as political philosophy. It is truly an accomplishment to address questions that are both perennial and immediate in a manner that is so original and so challenging.

Like Plato, Friedman reflects on the nature of knowledge and its relation to political rule. Like Aristotle, he considers the type of knowledge appropriate and possible in the realm of political things. And like Hobbes, he highlights the unreliability of people's knowledge, the intractability of their disagreements, and the need to overcome the chaos generated by this predicament. Friedman addresses themes that are timeless with considerations that are striking and new.

The book is also refreshingly iconoclastic. Challenging conventional wisdom, Friedman takes aim at the assumption at the heart of much modern politics: that the knowledge required for policy expertise, and thus for effective technocratic intervention, exists. Friedman pulls no punches, writing a book that will upset almost everyone. Leftist "statists" and neoclassical economists alike are described as sharing epistemic delusions. Like Socrates, Friedman confronts all interlocutors with the reality of their unacknowledged ignorance. *Power Without Knowledge* places questions of knowledge and rule at the center of contemporary political debate, right where (in my opinion) they deserve to be. The book's argument provides a salutary corrective to the tendency toward technocratic statism that has become the default mode of politics in recent years.

Friedman's book attacks the problem of technocracy at an admirably high level of generality. Abstracting from the details of concrete policy debates, it asks what justifies us in believing that we have the knowledge required reliably to identify and solve social problems at all. Through an insightful reading of technocratic literature, as well as a detailed reconstruction of Walter Lippmann's treatment of the problem of interpretation in political life, Friedman offers a powerful argument against the very possibility of technocratic knowledge. This does not mean that technocracy can never obtain its goals, but rather that it cannot, in general, be justified by appeal to the cost-benefit calculations that are the coin of the technocratic realm, because the knowledge required for such calculations may be lacking.

Furthermore, the target of Friedman's critique is much broader than what we commonly take technocracy to be. It is not uncommon to hear technocracy criticized from the standpoint of democracy: it is "the people," not elite epistocrats, who should rule. On Friedman's account, however, matters are not so simple. Insofar as it is premised on people's ability to identify relevant social problems and to decide on effective means of addressing them, contemporary democracy itself should be regarded as technocratic. Friedman thus radicalizes the debate by conceptualizing modern democracy not as an alternative to technocracy, but as a form of it. This widening of the problem of technocracy makes the book's argument original and challenging.

To put my cards on the table from the beginning, I think that much of Friedman's critique of technocratic knowledge is right. I share his skepticism of "expert," bureaucratic prescriptions and believe that epistemic humility is far more warranted than technocracy tends to acknowledge. I am persuaded that the general complexity of the social world and the difficulty of reliably obtaining technocratic knowledge give us good reasons to be skeptical of technocratic rule. Like Friedman, I am sympathetic to alternative political arrangements that seek to give people the resources to solve their own problems as they understand them.

What I think Friedman's book gets importantly and centrally right, then, is the degree to which untenable epistemological assumptions are at the heart of the technocratic worldview. The early part of Friedman's book, in which he emphasizes the interpretive nature of our relation to social reality and the existence of interminable disagreement among policy experts, is wholly persuasive. His critique undermines the plausibility of what he calls "naive technocratic realism," showing that the interpretive complexities involved in the evaluation of the results of policy interventions make meaningful judgment regarding the efficacy of technocratic policies incredibly difficult.

While I think that this aspect of Friedman's argument is persuasive, however, I have some reservations about his specific elaboration of it in the book's central chapters. While the early sections of the book rest on broad considerations of social-scientific analysis (such as the challenges posed by the absence of counterfactual knowledge and the difficulty of meaningfully measuring "costs" and "benefits"), the subsequent argument focuses on the difficulties involved in behavioral prediction. The book's distinctive theory of technocracy (as opposed to its broad critique of naive technocratic realism) is rooted in claims (to be elaborated below) about ideational heterogeneity and the challenge it poses for behavioral prediction. While this theory is certainly insightful, I found it less satisfying than the earlier sections of the book.

This is, in part, because I am less skeptical than Friedman about our ability to predict behavior. As I argue below, I believe that we have good reasons to think that ideational homogeneities are often identifiable and that this makes at least minimal forms of behavioral prediction possible. This does not entail a blanket justification of technocracy, on my view, both because such predictions remain *uncertain* (as Friedman persuasively argues) and because the ability to predict behavior in this minimal way still does not enable us to make reliable calculations of the overall costs and benefits of our interventions. So considered, however, democratic (or suitably consensual) forms of technocracy seem less objectionable than elite, "epistocratic" forms. The fact that we can't know all the costs and benefits of our interventions seems less important when we are choosing for ourselves than when we are choosing for others. If our ignorance cannot be eliminated, but no forms of political life can do without technocratic judgment (including, as Friedman admits, his "exitocratic" alternative), then questions of legitimacy and accountability become at least as important as questions of knowledge. It thus seems to me that, rather than ruling out all applications of means-end thinking in politics, Friedman's critique points toward the need for more consensual and participatory approaches to political decision making and more experimental and responsive forms of policy implementation that take this ineliminable uncertainty into account.[1]

I will develop my analysis in three sections. The first section outlines my concerns with Friedman's "ideational heterogeneity" thesis. I argue that we have good reason to expect that identifiable ideational homogeneities should make certain forms of technocratic behavioral prediction tractable. In the second section, I evaluate the persuasiveness of Friedman's comparative justification of exitocracy. In the third, I suggest an alternative political possibility, individualist anarchism, that might be more responsive than exitocracy to Friedman's epistemological concerns.

Ideational Heterogeneity and the Problem of Convergence

Friedman's argument is sophisticated and subtle. Starting out from the reality of technocratic disagreement, he exposes the flaws of what he terms "naive technocratic realism," the idea that "the truth about social problems is self-evident" (24). Using disagreements among "experts" to show that this is not the case, Friedman creates a skeptical conundrum for advocates of technocracy. He does not deny that social scientific knowledge *might* exist. But given the nature of technocratic disagreement, how can the true technocrats—those with real access to the truth—be identified? This problem of "epistocratic identification" (69-70) is severe, as is the conclusion Friedman ultimately draws from it.

After reflecting on attempts by political epistemologists to address this problem, Friedman concludes that there is no non-question-begging way to resolve disagreements about specific technocratic initiatives. He thus proposes to leave aside "first-order" questions of the truth of various technocratic predictions and to employ an alternative strategy. He recommends the use of a "second-order" approach to political epistemology: one which turns not on the rightness or wrongness of *specific* technocratic claims (72–73) or on the overall evaluation of the track record of actually existing technocracy (76, 318), but rather on general considerations of "the reliability or unreliability of the types of information available to various political actors" (73). He then seeks to adduce such second-order reasons, suggesting that "there are specific reasons to think that we are unlikely to know the consequences of technocratic actions" (79).

This is the work that the thesis of "ideational heterogeneity" is meant to do. It provides the key to his claim that technocratic knowledge might be unreliable. The argument goes, roughly, that because people are subjected to idiosyncratic "ideational inputs," their webs of belief should be expected to vary in idiosyncratic and unpredictable ways. Because people's actions are determined by their beliefs, these actions should likewise be considered unpredictable and thus not, under normal circumstances, amenable to successful technocratic manipulation. This is a claim as broad as it is powerful.

As initially stated, the heterogeneity thesis is also quite plausible. Surely none of us would (on reflection) deny that others remain at least somewhat opaque, mysterious, and unpredictable to us. But Friedman draws much more significant conclusions from this observation. Bracketing the question of the "magnitude" of the behavioral consequences of ideational variation, which is admitted to be unknowable (146), Friedman turns to the "frequency" of ideational variation. Having identified a mechanism for generating unpredictable ideational heterogeneity, Friedman argues that there should be a "presumption" in its favor. "Given diverse ideational inputs," he states, "we have no reason to posit uniformity as the default assumption about the outputs" (147). Since there is no "unitary human idea generator," we cannot expect people's ideas to be uniform (ibid.). This, too, is persuasive. Friedman's reflections, alongside consideration of the surprising behavior of the people we know or encounter, should convince us that no two people have *identical* beliefs. Ideational heterogeneity, so understood, is a reality with which we must contend.

The conclusion Friedman draws from these observations, however, goes much farther. The "presumption" of heterogeneity, he goes on to say, should be our default assumption absent the discovery of counteracting homogenizing factors. The claim that no two people should be expected to think *exactly* alike thus expands into the far broader claim that, unless and until countervailing "homogenizing" forces can be identified, the expectation of potential disagreement about anything and everything should be our default position. The argument, in other words, places the burden of proof squarely on the shoulders of those supposing any kind of ideational uniformity or homogeneity. Ideas, on this view, are innocent of homogeneity until proven guilty.

This poses a clear challenge for technocracy, although not one that Friedman thinks is necessarily insurmountable. His discussion of ideational heterogeneity takes place in the third of three chapters in the book's first part; the second part is devoted to seeing if technocrats in the real world attempt to investigate whether, case by first-order case, homogenizing factors—such as shared social norms and mass-mediated beliefs and assumptions—offset the presumption of ideational heterogeneity. Friedman argues that, at present, technocrats fail to do this, for the most part, but that a radical change in their ideas, such that they recognized the possibility of ideational heterogeneity, could create a "judicious" technocracy that would be up to the challenge. Thus, Friedman's argument against extant technocracy is dependent on his successfully shifting the burden of proof onto those claiming homogeneities and then showing that the practices of actually existing technocrats are not responsive to the problem of heterogeneity that he has identified. I didn't find this crucial aspect of the argument totally satisfying.

When Friedman introduces the notion of "ideational heterogeneity" (in the initial sense of "no two people think exactly alike"), he offers two central pieces of evidence for its existence. One is the hypothesized causal mechanism through which beliefs arise. Since belief formation is idiosyncratic in the sense that every individual is subject to unique "ideational inputs," it stands to reason that the resultant webs of belief will be idiosyncratic as well. Thus we all, on this model, are likely to have unique (and potentially quite bizarre) beliefs that make our behavior unpredictable from the standpoint of a technocrat.[2] The second piece of evidence is Friedman's personal experience. He asserts that he is continually taken aback by the surprising ideas expressed by those he encounters, finding that he "often" disagrees with them about "nearly everything" (147). While Friedman likely does not mean this literally (he presumably means "nearly everything we discuss"), the locution is still telling. What does our ordinary experience of communication with others indicate about ideational heterogeneity?

A brief digression on Wittgenstein is in order here. In his investigations regarding communication, skepticism, and doubt, one of Wittgenstein's central insights is that we are inducted into a form of life by means of the acquisition of language. This language is not, as we sometimes imagine, communicated to us piece by piece through atomized bits of information (e.g., "this is called a rock"). Wittgenstein holds that this "primitive" view of language acquisition neglects the various ways in which language is *used*. When we imagine language being acquired this way, we are analogizing from the experience of learning a *new* language after we already know how to use at least one (Wittgenstein 2009, §32).

When we first learn to speak, we don't simply internalize labels for objects. Rather, we learn how to *do things* with language: how to inform, argue, inquire, etc. This involves learning "language games," a locution Wittgenstein chooses in order to "emphasize the fact that the *speaking* of language is part of an activity, or of a form of life" (ibid., §23). Included in this way of acquiring language, Wittgenstein argues, is the gradual internalization of a "*Weltbild*"—a picture of the world on which our linguistic practices depend (see Wittgenstein 1972, §94-95). In a memorable formulation, Wittgenstein suggests that, in language acquisition, "light dawns gradually on the whole" (ibid., §141). We acquire a set of interconnected meanings and practices. Many aspects of our worldviews are never directly or explicitly taught. Rather, they are absorbed as part of the larger image of reality in which our language games have sense.

What this means, practically, is that I share a staggeringly large number of "beliefs" with anyone with whom I am capable of communicating. This is not initially obvious because we seldom imagine the many bizarre things that someone could *in principle* disagree with us about. It takes speculative philosophy or science fiction to bring this realization home. Imagine meeting someone with whom you disagreed about "nearly everything." How could you even communicate? Imagine someone who didn't "believe in" time, personal identity, physical reality, cause and effect, or basic laws of logic (such as non-contradiction). At the limit, the speech of someone with whom you disagreed about "nearly everything" would be completely unintelligible to you—perhaps not even recognizable as speech (see Rorty 1972).

Friedman argues, persuasively, that there is "no reason" to expect *complete* uniformity in our beliefs absent a "unitary idea generator." But if Wittgenstein's reflections are persuasive, the mere fact that we have a common language gives us a good reason to expect broad and identifiable uniformities. The fact that we share "forms of life," broadly construed, means that we have innumerable things in common. The assumptions embedded in our linguistic forms of life provide a truly significant degree of uniformity in belief that we have good reason to anticipate discovering among our fellow language-users. Language itself, on this view, is a significant "homogenizing force."

In disputing Charles Taylor's "methodological holism," Friedman distinguishes sharply between our linguistic "meanings" (i.e., the definitions of our words), which may exhibit significant commonalities, and our "ideas." Words and concepts are understood as discrete "building blocks," out of which we construct "ideational structures" (154). This implies that we learn "words" in isolation and then independently build "ideas" and "beliefs" out of them. Yet, on the basis of Wittgenstein's analysis, I find this implausible. The nature of language use is such that "beliefs" and "words" are acquired simultaneously. In fact, it can plausibly be argued that there is ultimately no clear-cut way to distinguish between changes in the meanings of my words and changes in my beliefs about the world; they shade into one another (see Rorty 1982, 28).[3] Language use does not exhaustively *determine* beliefs, of course—people still have idiosyncratic thoughts—but the common "world-picture" is the "inherited background" within which such thoughts have meaning.

It is hard to prove this, of course. But it seems to me an accurate and persuasive account of what language use entails. This view does not involve positing any additional "ontological" realities separate from individual subjects; it is fully consistent (I believe) with Friedman's understanding of "epistemological individualism," which he defines as combining "methodological individualism, the fallibility and potential ignorance of individuals, communication among individuals, and the possibility that their ideas will be heterogeneous" (150). Yet the Wittgenstein view gives us reason to think that the process of language acquisition can plausibly be expected to lead to a good deal of convergence in people's beliefs. There is not, admittedly, a "unitary idea generator." But the realities of language use and the common assumptions embedded in our language games and forms of life suggest that we have good reason to expect a significant degree of uniformity among language users.

Crucially, moreover, Wittgenstein's reflections suggest that not all "beliefs" are on a par. Some are negotiable, some not. Some (such as "the external world exists") have such a centrality that one could not readily give them up without one's entire worldview dissolving. These commitments are foundational because of the role they play in our linguistic practices (Wittgenstein 1972, §152). They are simply non-negotiable, from our present point of view, because our sense of the world would lose its coherence without them. They "hold fast" for us not because they are inherently more obvious than other propositions, but because so much else is connected to them (ibid., §112, §144).[4] What is central and what is peripheral can change over time (Wittgenstein uses the metaphor of the "river" and the "river-bed" to make these distinctions), but at a given moment it is, over a wide range of issues, relatively fixed (ibid., §96-9). We would not be mildly surprised, but simply dumbfounded, if we actually encountered people who didn't share these foundational beliefs.

Given this realization, one might wonder what kind of challenge the thesis of ideational heterogeneity really poses. It is true that people often express beliefs that I find surprising—sometimes incomprehensible. But these beliefs are so striking precisely because they proceed from people who in general and on the whole seem to live in the same world as I do. I find these aberrations shocking because over a vast range of beliefs and meanings these people seem to share my linguistic universe with most of its presuppositions and commitments. The occasional pronounced deviation is the exception that proves the rule.

This is not a radical thesis, of course. It is the basic presupposition of all communication and social reflection. Thus Friedman himself acknowledges significant ideational uniformity when discussing modern society. The claim that we live in a "technocratic society" at all is premised on the notion that there is broad (and identifiable) convergence in the beliefs of people in modern society—beliefs which Friedman thinks he can reliably identify and which allow a kind of behavioral prediction. The book's argument depends on the possibility of reliably identifying ideational uniformities in one's own society, through some combination of reflection and data collection. Friedman (182-83) avoids contradiction in this regard by claiming that he is not attempting prediction but simply using observed regularities to suggest possibilities, engage in retrodiction, and "speculate." This is fair enough. But if these uniformities are reliable enough to be worth talking about and building persuasive arguments upon, it still seems to suggest that ideational heterogeneity may not be as concerning as Friedman suggests—and, crucially, that the book's second-order reflections regarding heterogeneity need not give rise to deep worries about their potential behavioral consequences.

Friedman is surely correct both that speakers of the same language can sometimes discover that they use a given word differently and that the existence of linguistic conventions does not rule out the possibility of individual innovations in linguistic use (how else would language change over time?). But one can grant all this while holding onto the central insight developed above. The point is not to *deny* idiosyncratic variation in language or belief, but to suggest that it occurs against the background of broadly shared beliefs and meanings in a way that renders the general problem of ideational heterogeneity less worrying. Innovations do, of course, take place. Wittgenstein's point is simply that these innovations, when they happen, are communicable precisely because so much remains "held in place" around them. Idiosyncrasy, if intelligible, presupposes broad uniformity and stability.

The relevant question, then, is not whether ideas vary idiosyncratically (they do), but whether there are identifiable commonalities sufficiently deep and broad as to render behavior at least somewhat amenable to prediction despite this idiosyncratic variation. If so, one might think that technocratic interventions that attempt to build upon beliefs that are likely to vary idiosyncratically will risk misfire, whereas technocratic interventions that target widely shared "bedrock" beliefs will be more likely to succeed. This is essentially a reformulation of Friedman's notion of "judicious technocracy." But if we are persuaded by these second-order reasons for believing that ideational homogeneities might be broad and identifiable, such a judicious technocracy no longer seems as distant from extant practices as Friedman's critique suggests.

This raises some questions about the book's argumentative strategy. Friedman offers the heterogeneity thesis as a second-order argument for the possible unreliability of technocratic knowledge. But if there are other second-order considerations that blunt the force of the heterogeneity thesis, where does that leave us? Friedman offers persuasive considerations in favor of a presumption of (some) heterogeneity. Yet there are also persuasive considerations, of the kind I have offered above, that point in the opposite direction. Which of them is more important would depend, ultimately, on what turns out to be empirically true. But adjudicating this would require the kind of first-order knowledge (of whether we can in fact engage in reliable technocratic intervention on the basis of identifiable, widely shared beliefs) which Friedman means to rule out by shifting to second-order considerations.[5] What this disagreement suggests, then, is that resolution of the problem at the level of second-order considerations might be just as problematic as resolution at the first-order level. There may be room for interpretive dispute and reasonable disagreement all the way down (or up).

On Friedman's account, there is no way to know, at the second order, whether ideational heterogeneity will in fact be frequent or consequential. His argument, however, is that this uncertainty itself places the "burden of proof" on those claiming knowledge of homogeneities. Friedman acknowledges that one might conceivably provide a second-order account of why heterogeneity "will rarely obtain" (147), though it is not clear what the standard would be for demonstrating this. Having shown that at least some heterogeneity will exist (since no two people think exactly alike), however, Friedman proceeds on the assumption that heterogeneity will be "presumptively frequent" (171) and inquires as to whether technocrats have the resources to identify when and where "homogenizing counterweights" might counteract the "heterogenizing force of ideas." He holds that judicious technocracy might be feasible if technocrats had the capacity to "determine, fairly precisely" (ibid.), the areas in which homogeneity adequate to prediction might exist. Part II of the book is dedicated to adjudicating whether technocrats are up to this challenge. There it is claimed that contemporary technocratic practice does not appear to be addressing this problem and is thus failing to meet the challenge posed by presumptively frequent ideational heterogeneity. From the viewpoint developed above, however, this evaluation seems dependent on the (contestable) belief that there are no straightforward mechanisms (such as language use) that might make the identification of homogeneity a tractable and fairly straightforward undertaking.

The importance of this problem comes to the fore in Friedman's critique of the "positivist" approach to technocracy represented by the new experimentalism in social science. On the face of it, such experimental approaches might seem conducive to combating the kind of dogmatism by which Friedman claims that social science is plagued. Experimentalists take whatever provisional knowledge of human behavior they believe they have acquired and use it to formulate hypotheses that they then test experimentally. Experimental approaches that formulate such hypotheses, test them in randomized trials, and revise the hypotheses based on the results, might seem like an ideal instance of judicious technocratic theorizing. Yet Friedman rejects such approaches on the grounds that they evince an ignorance of the problem of ideational heterogeneity. Critiquing experimental social science, he insists that "heterogeneity should be the assumed default, and the burden of argument should rest with those who claim knowledge of homogeneities, not those who challenge these claims" (206). We "have reason," he claims, "to think that behavioral heterogeneity is the rule, not the exception" (ibid.).[6]

Thus, Friedman asserts that the burden of proof is always on those claiming that any particular experimental finding will generalize. "Those who make homogeneity claims should have to explain why we should generalize from their local data to universalistic conclusions, even if the universe is 'the West' rather than 'everyone,' or 'unemployment in America' rather than 'everywhere,' or 'unemployment among teenagers working at fast-food restaurants' rather than 'among teenagers at large'— or rather than 'unemployment among teenagers at this restaurant on this particular day,' or rather than 'the unemployment of this particular teenager'" (206). Every population—every individual—is to be presumed *sui generis*, and we need an argument in every instance justifying our belief that a uniformity we have identified in one place will be present in another. But for someone persuaded by the Wittgensteinian view of language, linguistic reflection itself might count as such an explanation, providing a provisional reason for thinking that observed homogeneities are not completely particular. If a hypothesis was formulated on the basis of ideational homogeneities supposed to be widely distributed throughout a population, and the hypothesis was confirmed experimentally on a subset of this population, this seems to provide a good reason for thinking that the finding might be general with respect to the population under consideration. From this perspective, Friedman's insistence that experimentalists need to provide a *reason* for believing that their results will generalize seems to overlook the reasons that they might actually have.

In critiquing experimentalists, Friedman claims that the "only way to 'know' [that homogeneities exist] while knowing nothing about the agents' subjective ideas, is to impute homogeneity to human behavior by ignoring the role of subjective ideas" (205). If the Wittgensteinian view of language is correct, however, reflecting on whether a belief is likely to be widespread in the relevant linguistic community might be enough to give us a provisional reason to hypothesize something about the behavior of its members. Again, this supposition would be provisional and would need to be subjected to empirical testing. It might turn out to be wrong. But it would not involve ignoring the importance of ideas. Thus our judgment regarding whether experimentalists are "ignoring the role of subjective ideas" or justifiably advancing hypotheses about a population's expected behavior might depend on what we are already inclined to think about the nature of language and heterogeneity.

If the Wittgensteinian view is correct, it gives us reason to expect significant and broadly identifiable homogeneity along a range of beliefs among those who share a linguistic form of life. Additionally, it gives us reason to suspect that identifying beliefs that are likely to be dependably uniform throughout a given population may not be an especially demanding task. From this perspective, Friedman's critique seems to confuse the question of whether we can *know* that homogeneities exist without testing them empirically (we can't) with the question of whether we have reason to *hypothesize* that homogeneities exist merely on the basis of linguistic reflection or shared "forms of life" (we do, or so I have suggested). From the Wittgensteinian point of view, the process of hypothesis generation regarding human behavior would, under normal circumstances, include reflection on the ideas that others are likely to have about their circumstances. When Friedman accuses experimentalists of "ignoring" the problem of heterogeneity, this seems to assume either that those formulating hypotheses to be tested experimentally do not consider the ideas likely to govern people's behavior when carrying out this task or that they have "no reason" for supposing these homogeneities to exist unless they have offered an explicit account of how they are contending with the problem of "presumptively frequent" heterogeneity.[7]

Thus I worry that Friedman faults experimentalists for failing to do something that they might in fact be doing. What he describes as "ignorance" of the causal role of ideas might just as well be the belief that contending with this causal role is not as demanding as Friedman implies. Friedman's account of heterogeneity suggests that additional, explicit work would have to be done to render experimentalism "judicious" and ideationally sensitive. But on the account developed above, we might reasonably suppose that experimentalists appear to ignore the problem Friedman raises because they do not find it especially problematic. It's not clear how to tell, from an external standpoint, whether people are "ignoring" the issue of heterogeneity or proceeding according to the conviction that their current practices are already addressing it. In other words, the stark distinction between judicious and injudicious experimentalism seems to collapse if we think that consideration of people's ideas is included in normal reflection on human behavior and that being a human language user often puts one in a good position to hypothesize about the "bedrock" beliefs of others.

Exitocracy as Technocracy

Regardless of whether this is right, however, Friedman's fundamental concern about technocracy still remains. In Part III of the book, he concludes that we cannot know, on the basis of second-order reflection, whether judicious *or* injudicious technocracy would cause more good than harm (318). Even judicious technocracy, then, might not be capable of meeting that "preliminary standard" of technocratic legitimacy. Yet, he wisely reminds us, theorists are equally unable to know the consequences of technocratic "inactions" (ibid.). As a result, no choice can be justified. We seem to have reached a dead end, with no way to choose among the courses of action (or inaction) available to us. Friedman's way out of this conundrum is to turn to a comparative method of justification that will allow a more definitive resolution of this problem. He suggests an alternative political arrangement, "exitocracy," which seeks to avoid the problems with technocratic prediction. We can rest content in our ignorance of the consequences of technocratic interventions if we can find a form of social order that eschews reliance on such judgments in favor of an epistemically superior mechanism of problem solving.

Friedman puts forth exitocracy as precisely such an alternative. Exitocracy is unique in that "instead of attempting, case by case, to produce solutions to any and all social problems that might arise, its cardinal goal would be to provide a framework within which individuals could attempt to solve—or, better, escape— the problems that afflict them as individuals, whatever their origin (society-wide or not)" (322). Friedman suggests that "exit" is "epistemically superior" to "voice," as it provides a means of addressing perceived problems that is epistemically undemanding. People need not understand the sources of a problem (or the means of solving it collectively) in order to deal with it. They can simply exit from what they take to be problematic (by no longer consuming a service, for instance, or by moving geographically).

Given the shortcomings of technocracy, this is an appealing vision. If exit could truly provide a substitute for voice, there would be a strong case for pursuing it. Friedman acknowledges, however, that exitocracy does not truly escape the need for technocracy; it is, rather, an "extraordinary version" of it (ibid.). This is because exitocracy can only be constructed via various forms of intervention that are themselves technocratic. This means that exit is always to some degree dependent on prior utilizations of voice. The dependence of exitocracy on technocratic judgment, however, raises serious questions regarding whether its comparative justification can succeed. I will suggest in what follows that, if we accept Friedman's first-order skepticism, it can't.

As Friedman describes it, "exitocracy" relies on two central mechanisms: private property and redistribution. The construction of each of these, however, involves endlessly complex technocratic judgments. In the case of redistribution, we must deal with questions of the type of property to be subject to redistribution, its measurement, taxation rates, the mechanisms of collection, the manner of redistribution, and who is eligible to receive it. The need for complex technocratic judgments is pervasive. Friedman certainly acknowledges this reality, but I'm not sure he fully reckons with its consequences.

As Friedman admits, there is no reason to think that the issues of technocratic prediction involved in such schemes are at all minor. How uncertain all this is can be seen in the recent debates over proposals to implement a wealth tax in America. While many Americans favor the idea of taxing the very wealthy to blunt the effects of economic inequality, it is far from obvious how to implement such a tax or what its overall effects would be. Elizabeth Warren and Bernie Sanders each proposed a version of such a policy. Yet many have questioned the feasibility of these proposals, citing the ease with which the very wealthy can move their wealth offshore to avoid paying. This incentive to tax avoidance (together with the large administrative costs), it is argued, means that a wealth tax might fail to increase revenue while also discouraging investment in the United States, ultimately contracting its economy and making most U.S. residents worse off (thus making the wealth tax self-defeating).[8] This is just the kind of possible policy backfire that Friedman considers in the opening sections of the book.

I am not attempting to adjudicate the plausibility of this claim. But it seems clear that redistribution as a political program is just as subject to technocratic debate and disagreement as other policy proposals. It is not obvious why exitocracy should be judged superior to technocracy if establishing and maintaining it is dependent upon complex and uncertain technocratic judgments of the kind Friedman has so ably critiqued. If we avoid first-order judgments of technocratic feasibility, yet the possibility of exitocracy is dependent on the successful implementation of at least one such technocratic policy, it's not clear how exitocracy can be justified.

Friedman addresses this problem in a general way by arguing that the effects of technocratic error would be "offset, to some (putatively significant) extent" by the epistemic benefits of exit (341). But this seems to risk begging the question. The mere fact that technocracy is deployed with the *intention* of facilitating exit does not guarantee that the unintended consequences of the proposed mechanisms will not be severe and, perhaps, catastrophic. The question of whether adequate redistribution can be enacted without backfiring is essential to the question of whether exitocracy really provides an epistemically superior alternative to traditional technocracy.

On the same page, Friedman acknowledges that we can't know whether the costs of exitocracy's technocratic interventions will be larger than the benefits that result. He then claims, however, that "we are entitled to say that the mix of benefits and costs should be more favorable in an exitocracy" than in other technocratic regimes (ibid.). I had trouble following the logic of this claim. It would seem to rely on the idea that the costs of technocratic interventions should be held constant across regimes (as unknowable) and that since secured exit provides *some* benefits (however minimal they may turn out to be), it must be judged superior. But this only holds if we have ruled out the possibility that the interventions required to create an exitocracy could not possibly have *far worse* consequences than the interventions likely under ordinary (or judicious) technocracy and, once again, could not possibly backfire in a way that renders exitocracy self-undermining. I find it hard to see how, consistent with Friedman's position, we could possibly have this knowledge.

Similarly, it is hard to see how Friedman's division of technocratic functions into the provision of primary, secondary, and tertiary exitocratic goods does not create problems just as epistemically demanding as those of ordinary technocratic prediction. This division corresponds, roughly, to the division between (1) arenas in which exit can be used,(2) arenas in which exit-like mechanisms can be designed, and

(3) arenas in which neither of these is true and ordinary technocracy must be deployed. Yet the text contains no explicit discussion of how we might determine which issues fall into which category. It may be true, as Hayek claimed, that competition is preferable as a mechanism of problem-solving "where it can be made to function" (Hayek 2007, 87).[9] But the question of where it *can* be made to function, and where externalities and collective action problems necessitate other forms of legal intervention, is itself a complex and technocratic one. Given the complexity of this problem, "exitocracy" seems just as epistemically burdensome as the ordinary technocracy that it is meant to supplant.

A similar problem arises when considering Friedman's example of a carbon tax as an exit-like mechanism for dealing with climate change (and thus a way of providing a secondary exitocratic good). He claims that this would be superior to something like a Green New Deal because "the discovery of how to [reduce carbon emissions] would be left to individual agents seeking to reduce the tax they pay" (341). I have no personal opposition to this statement. It may well be true. But I'm not sure that Friedman can (consistently) think it's true, as it seems to involve the kind of behavioral prediction that he has criticized as being epistemically unjustified in his earlier analysis of technocracy. A carbon tax would be an effective means of dealing with climate change granted that technocratic issues of measurement and pricing can be resolved and, crucially, that people can be known to respond reliably to incentives in roughly the way economists predict (i.e., they consume less of easily substitutable goods when their prices rise). It seems reasonable to think that a carbon tax (coupled with a redistributed "dividend" to render it progressive) could be an effective (and comparatively non-paternalistic) means of dealing with the issue of climate change (though it might need to be extended to include other "greenhouse gases" such as methane—another thorny technocratic judgment). But this belief hinges on acceptance of the kind of behavioral prediction whose reliability Friedman has called into question. Additionally, as just noted, the policy's successful implementation would be dependent upon a whole host of correct technocratic judgments regarding pricing and enforcement, without which the "exit-like" mechanism would surely fail to achieve its stated goals. Thus, it seems to me, providing such a "secondary" exitocratic good is just as epistemically demanding as any other technocratic intervention.

These problems seem to militate against the persuasiveness of Friedman's comparative method of justification. Even if exitocracies allow people to solve their own problems in the "private" sphere, the possibility of undealt-with collective action problems, catastrophic externalities, and severe policy backfires suggests that the choice between technocracy and exitocracy on negative-utilitarian grounds would itself depend on contestable technocratic judgments, making the comparison impossible on Friedman's terms. The uncertainty surrounding technocratic prediction would seem to deprive us of the kind of knowledge we would need to make meaningful comparisons across regimes. At some point, the unknowns become so large that meaningful comparison becomes impossible and we have no reason to prefer anything to anything else. We can only shrug our shoulders in ignorance.

The Anarchist Alternative?

Exitocracy as Friedman describes it is appealing in many ways. I am personally persuaded, by Friedman's considerations as well as arguments articulated by Robert Taylor (2017), that "exit-based" mechanisms have much to be said for them. But, as argued above, it seems that exitocracy's reliance on technocratic judgment militates against its ability to serve as an alternative to technocracy. If all of our interventions (including "exitocratic" ones) require technocratic judgments of the sort that Friedman has called into question, then we may be incapable of justifying any political intervention whatsoever (even comparatively). Absent independent normative criteria for political legitimacy, no political activity seems justified. In short, it seems to me that, were we convinced by the bulk of Friedman's arguments against technocracy, the logical political conclusion would be some form of anarchism.

I find this possibility intriguing and wish Friedman had given it some consideration. Anarchism seems especially worthy of discussion in light of his method of comparative justification, in which judicious technocracy is better than injudicious technocracy and exitocracy is better than both. If all we have is the comparative method, why not at least consider the possibility that the most justifiable form of society is that in which no imposed authority exists at all and thus, by definition, technocratic rule is abolished? Given the problems of technocratic judgment that (by Friedman's own admission) beset even the creation of an "exitocratic" regime, why not explore the possibility of a world in which people are thrown onto their own judgments regarding every aspect of life and are permitted to devise solutions to their problems in a voluntary and consensual manner as seems best to them?

One way to understand the political problem Friedman poses is to recognize that human action is, in general, uncertain. All of our actions have, at least potentially, unintended consequences that are difficult or impossible to foresee. Virtually no human action is without such risks. The problem with technocracy, whether elite or democratic, is that it allows some actors to decide for others which risks are worth taking. This seems, on the face of it, objectionable—especially when the decision-makers lack reliable knowledge of the consequences of their interventions. If all human action is uncertain, then taking such risks might be unavoidable. Yet it seems intuitively plausible that where uncertainty and risk are at play, people ought to be able to make their own decisions.

These are some of the considerations grounding the anarchist commitment to consensus. If no one has the knowledge required to judge such matters reliably, the best we can do is maximize people's ability to decide for themselves. (Democracy, of course, can be advocated on the basis of a similar intuition, but it simply allows the majority to impose their preferred solution on the rest of society.) People will, undoubtedly, continue to make mistakes in such matters. Yet now, just as in their personal lives, these mistakes will at least be their own.

I would be interested to know Friedman's thoughts about this possibility. His exitocracy is meant to address this general problem, but still (as he acknowledges) relies on a significant degree of technocratic knowledge as a means of guaranteeing exit. A more direct way to guarantee "exit," however, might be to abolish political authority altogether.[10] A maximally consensual society would be a society in which people take their own risks upon themselves. The uncertainties of human action are not eliminated here (they cannot be, as Friedman demonstrates), but the burden of technocratic judgment (insofar as it involves making such decisions for others) is. I would have liked to see some consideration of this possibility in the concluding sections of the book.

In particular, it seems to me that Friedman's endorsement of exit and competition as responses to ignorance might point in the direction of "individualist" anarchism. According to Benjamin Tucker, an early proponent of this view, such anarchists "are simply unterrified Jeffersonian Democrats. They believe that 'the best government is that which governs least,' and that that which governs least is no government at all. Even the simple police function of protecting person and property they deny to governments supported by compulsory taxation" (Tucker 1888). He summarizes this outlook with the motto "Competition everywhere and always" (ibid.). On this view, monopoly (the suppression of exit) is the universal problem and competition the universal solution (it would thus be reasonable to call this position "competitive anarchism").

Unlike communist or collectivist forms of anarchism associated with names like Kropotkin or Bakunin, individualist anarchism explicitly repudiates any form of imposed social organization. As Voltairine de Cleyre put the case, individualists "have no scheme for regulating distribution" and "make no plans," simply "trust[ing] to the unfailing balance of supply and demand" (de Cleyre and Slobodinsky 1891). In fact, de Cleyre grounded her opposition to anarchist communism explicitly on the conviction that anarchism must, by definition, allow competition and exit: "Now, you must admit, either that there will be under freedom, different social arrangements in different societies, some Communistic, others quite the reverse, and that competition will necessarily rise between them, leaving to results to determine which is the best, or you must crush competition, institute Communism, deny freedom, and fly in the face of progress" (ibid.).

This perspective is taken up by such contemporary anarchists as Michael Huemer (2013), who argues that everything that the state might legitimately try to achieve (such as personal protection or defense of property) can be better (i.e., more efficiently and less coercively) realized through competitive provision in an open market (or voluntary cooperation). The epistemic (and moral) virtues of exit, on this view, make it preferable to monopolistic state provision. Such an anarchist world would seem to be the ultimate exitocracy; everything would be decided by voluntary collaboration or market competition, including the legal regimes that codified property relations, the security services that provided protection, and the courts that provided arbitration and awarded damages.

Applied to Friedman's exitocratic aspirations, this seems to provide an elegant solution. The problem with technocracy is that it imposes policies that may be epistemically unjustified (insofar as technocrats lack access to the individual beliefs and preferences of those subjected to their rules) on people who cannot escape them. Exitocracy, which Friedman crafts technocratically, is meant to facilitate such escape. Competitive anarchism, however, would apply exitocratic thinking to the establishment of exitocracy itself. Why shouldn't the provision of the appropriate laws and property arrangements also be subjected to the testing of the exit mechanism? Given the uncertainty that attends all the technocratic judgments required to make exitocracy workable, might it not make sense to seek to implement exitocracy in an exitocratic manner?

I am not at all certain whether such a regime would be preferable to the exitocratic arrangements that Friedman describes (which resemble contemporary capitalism but with massive redistribution of wealth). But this is irrelevant to the point I'm hoping to raise. If exitocracy is meant to be the solution to technocratic ignorance of people's ideas, then it seems reasonable to consider whether exitocratic reasoning might be applied to the provision of basic exitocratic goods. Given Friedman's approach, the epistemic superiority of exit would seem to dictate that the exit mechanism be applied to the creation of legal regimes themselves as the most effective means of avoiding technocratic error and coping with the inherent difficulties of technocratic judgment. The fact that one can't be sure what would result from these arrangements is beside the point, as it is precisely under such conditions of uncertainty regarding consequences that exit is said to be necessary.

An obvious objection to this suggestion would be that, for Friedman, an exitocratic regime requires massive state redistribution of wealth. This is so because "exit opportunities will often require economic resources" (334). This is certainly a sensible view. To repeat, however, the trouble from an epistemological point of view is that technocratic judgments are required to craft such redistributive arrangements. As Friedman ably shows, there is significant uncertainty attending these complex technocratic interventions. Thus, determining the exact details of the legal regime meant to secure exit is a process that is highly prone to error (as well as, under current circumstances, capture).

The alternative I have sketched above involves the creation of competitive legal regimes, so that the provision of legal rules (including those governing property) would itself be subject to the kind of feedback mechanism provided by market competition. Of course, there is no guarantee that, under such competitive conditions, legal regimes providing large-scale redistribution would arise. Without compulsion, it is hard to imagine that a significant number of mega-wealthy people would voluntarily opt for legal regimes with steep rates of taxation. This leads to the understandable worry that, absent significant redistribution, the most vulnerable in society would effectively lack exit options and would thus be subject to objectionable levels of domination.

There are a few possible rejoinders worthy of consideration, however. The first is simply (to repeat) that this empirical worry ignores the central insight of Friedman's epistemology. Since crafting a redistributive legal regime requires technocratic judgments that are subject to error, we simply have no reason (on my reading of Friedman's view) to expect that technocratically crafted exitocracies will cause more good than harm. Such decisions should thus be left to the actors themselves, who are best able to judge the outcomes they experience. Given second-order skepticism about technocratic interventions, there is no way to rule out the possibility that attempts to craft an exitocratic order technocratically might result in unintended consequences that render the order self-undermining. This is the kind of worry that motivates the turn to exitocracy in the first place. If technocratic interventions could be known to secure the goods at which they aimed, exitocracy would lack the epistemological justification that Friedman develops. In the absence of such knowledge, the arrangement that makes maximal use of the exit mechanism should be judged most desirable from an epistemological perspective.

Another consideration in favor of this approach, however, is the possibility that, under competitive anarchism, property regimes might emerge that simply did not allow for massive resource concentrations to persist. A common anarchist objection to current concentrations of wealth is that they are the consequence of the state deploying its monopoly on violence to enforce property titles that are fraudulent and unjust (and that would never be tolerated in a consensual society). Under conditions of legal competition, it is argued, rules regulating property would emerge that would defend only property that was justly acquired.[11] Thus individualist anarchists hold that in a stateless world many extant property titles would be invalidated, allowing for a rectification of past injustice: a bottom-up form of reparations that would result in considerably more equality of resources than currently prevails (see, e.g., Chartier 2013, 328-51). Creating competing legal regimes thus might be expected to have a redistributive *effect*, despite the absence of a redistributing state. This would be an outcome functionally equivalent to Friedman's redistributive scheme, but without the uncertainties that attend its technocratic implementation.

There is no way to guarantee that this would occur, of course. I am not here evaluating the plausibility of the predictions that some scholars make regarding the types of legal regimes that might emerge under anarchy (for detailed discussion see Stringham 2007 and Chartier 2013). I am merely suggesting the possibility that someone committed to Friedman's views regarding technocracy might have reason to consider anarchism and the competitive provision of legal order as an alternative to the technocratic provision of primary exitocratic goods.

Given Friedman's own premises, it's not clear why we shouldn't expect anarchy to do better than exitocracy. If the goal is to give people the ability experimentally to solve their own problems, utilizing the epistemic benefits of the exit mechanism, then a world without centralized state authority might plausibly be thought to be the most appealing imaginable solution. Certainly some people throughout history have believed that such anarchist arrangements would be the ones most compatible with negative utilitarianism (a point that is rendered more plausible by consideration of the significant human suffering arising from state warfare and incarceration, as well as the plausibly expected increases in human well-being that would follow the abolition of state borders and the resultant opportunity for free migration—perhaps the most consequential conceivable application of the exit mechanism). Regardless of the validity of these predictions, however, the central point still stands. If technocratic rule is unjustified and even exitocracy relies upon it, doesn't anarchism follow by default? On internal grounds, shouldn't we prefer the regime that makes maximal use of the exit mechanism? If not, I suspect that this would have to be based on considerations that are not merely epistemological, in which case we have left the realm of Friedman's analysis.

* * *

Power Without Knowledge is important and timely. By advancing a critique so broad and challenging, it puts putative technocrats (elite or popular) on the defensive—which is surely to the good. The book's fundamental critique of technocratic knowledge is powerful and compelling. The book is highly effective in challenging a central assumption of the modern technocratic worldview and exposing its vacuity. Through its critical epistemology, the book certainly succeeds in unsettling our complacent acceptance of technocratic statism. The book's insightful argument challenges settled dogmas and places the burden of proof precisely where it should be: on the shoulders of those who claim to possess the knowledge necessary to impose their judgments on others.

I have offered some reasons to think that ideational heterogeneity may not be as worrying as Friedman suggests and that experimental social science might play a useful role in addressing social problems. But even if this is right, it would not serve as a justification for actually existing technocracy. The kinds of fallibilism and experimentalism that this perspective commends are not in evidence in current approaches to policymaking. Anyone wishing to defend the political relevance of contemporary social science in light of this book's argument has their work cut out for them.

Thus Friedman's book, my concerns notwithstanding, must be judged a success. It demands scrutiny of cherished ideas and greater specificity regarding how claims to political knowledge might be subjected to ongoing testing and refinement. Whatever one comes to conclude about ideational heterogeneity or exitocracy, Friedman's contribution here must be contended with. By challenging the assumptions underlying the usual justifications for technocracy, Friedman forces a reconsideration of the legitimacy of our basic approach to policymaking. Whether the best way forward turns out to be exitocracy, anarchism, or something else altogether, taking Friedman's epistemological critique seriously makes it difficult to imagine that anything short of a fairly radical reconstruction of current political arrangements would succeed in rendering most of our policies either intelligent or just.

NOTES

1. This amounts to saying that, in Friedman's terms, we might have good reasons (not reducible to the question of technocratic knowledge) to grasp the "second horn of the [technocratic] dilemma" (316) and embrace people's right to govern their own affairs despite their potential ignorance. We might, that is, decide that they are entitled to "power without knowledge." This conviction is consistent, however, with the idea that we should seek forms of political decision making that are maximally responsive to the reality of pervasive ignorance and uncertainty.
2. Though I will not explore this further here, a puzzling aspect of Friedman's position on ideational heterogeneity is his claim that, because belief formation is deterministic, idiosyncratic ideas are "not random" and thus can't be dealt with through "probability theory" (144). I found this assertion confusing. Calling variation "random" for purposes of statistical analysis implies only that the variation in question is not systematically correlated with the variable(s) of interest, not that the variation is uncaused. The fact that ideational variation has deterministic causes, then, does not entail that it cannot be dealt with through statistical methods. I would have liked to see this point elaborated in the text, as it seems important to Friedman's argument. If idiosyncratic variation

can be dealt with through statistical methods (as I suspect it often can), this would offer an additional reason for optimism about behavioral prediction.

3. Rorty here associates this view with Quinean holism. Given that the "web of belief" idea on which Friedman draws is also of Quinean origin, Friedman might have reason to be committed to a similar view.
4. This is the kind of thing that philosophers of science have explored through the notion of a "paradigm" (Kuhn), "thought collective" (Fleck), or "sociologic" (Latour). Friedman himself explores similar ideas in his discussion of "spirals of conviction," but does not consider whether such dynamics might apply to ordinary linguistic communities as well. Latour (1987, ch. 5) explicitly discusses scientific paradigms as paralleling ordinary linguistic paradigms.
5. Friedman holds that while first-order knowledge can be drawn on to determine, "case by case," whether particular homogeneities exist, it cannot provide evidence that heterogeneity *in general* is not worryingly pervasive. Thus, on Friedman's view, no amount of successful behavioral prediction can alleviate the worry posed by the heterogeneity thesis (which is a purely second-order consideration).
6. This seems to be an important (and perhaps unjustified) shift in Friedman's argument. While earlier he claimed not to know whether ideational heterogeneity would be consequential for behavior, at this point in the argument he seems to be claiming such knowledge. It's not clear how the fact that no two webs of belief are identical establishes *behavioral* heterogeneity as a "rule." It's hard to see how Friedman's modest heterogeneity thesis—i.e., that no two webs of belief are identical—could give rise to such a conclusion. Whether such ideational heterogeneity actually leads to behavioral heterogeneity would seem to be unknowable at the second order.
7. A problem here might be that in these passages Friedman only considers experimental inquiry in a rigidly positivist vein (i.e., as focused exclusively on detecting correlations, with no theoretical underpinnings whatsoever). It is hard to imagine that real experiments are ever carried out in this way. What could possibly motivate one to carry out a field or policy experiment absent a theory guiding the specific choices of treatment administered and outcomes measured? Friedman (48, 208) himself makes similar observations. While his criticisms of a purely "positivist" experimentalism are certainly persuasive, I find it hard to imagine that this extreme positivist position is pervasive among social scientists using experimental methods. The text he cites in defense of this characterization (Green et al. 2010) considers reasons why definite causal identification is difficult in experimental social science. It claims that dealing with complex questions of "causal mediation" through experimentation is often very challenging and that strong causal claims should be scaled back. Admitting that experimental evidence cannot directly prove a specific causal theory, however, is not equivalent to saying that no theory should be guiding the generation of hypotheses (nor that consideration of people's ideas should not be part of the process of hypothesis formation). Friedman's criticism seems to conflate these positions.
8. For a general analysis of wealth taxes that highlights some of these issues, see OECD 2018.
9. Though Friedman's endorsement of competition is not explicitly Hayekian and he is in fact quite critical of Hayek's epistemology, Hayek's observations about the role of technocratic knowledge in determining where competition can be "made to function" still seem germane.

10. This seems especially appealing in light of Friedman's admission that even what we consider to be "natural" arenas of exit, "such as consumer goods and labor markets," are in fact dependent on technocratic judgment (342). Many anarchists have held that the specific understandings of property and law dominant in the modern world are skewed towards the interests of the wealthy (which the state tends to privilege). Given the reality of disagreement concerning even these basic components of "exitocracy," it seems that maximally consensual arrangements regarding these institutions would be preferable to their technocratic imposition.
11. Some anarchists also believe that consensual property regimes would restrict the amount (or type) of property that one could justifiably accumulate, but there is no consensus on this issue.

REFERENCES

Chartier, Gary. 2013. *Anarchy and Legal Order: Law and Politics for a Stateless Society*. Cambridge: Cambridge University Press.

De Cleyre, Voltairine, and Rosa Slobodinsky. 1891. "The Individualist and the Communist." https://www.panarchy.org/voltairine/dialogue.html

Friedman, Jeffrey. 2019. *Power Without Knowledge: A Critique of Technocracy*. New York: Oxford University Press

Green, Donald P., Shang E. Ha, and John G. Bullock. 2010. "Enough Already about 'Black Box' Experiments: Studying Mediation Is More Difficult Than Most Scholars Suppose." *Annals of the American Academy of Political and Social Science* 628(1): 200–208.

Hayek, Friedrich A. 2007. *The Road to Serfdom*. Chicago: University of Chicago Press.

Huemer, Michael. 2013. *The Problem of Political Authority: An Examination of the Right to Coerce and the Duty to Obey*. Basingstoke: Palgrave Macmillan.

Latour, Bruno. 1987. *Science in Action: How to Follow Scientists and Engineers through Society*. Cambridge, Mass.: Harvard University Press.

OECD. 2018. "The Role and Design of Net Wealth Taxes in the OECD." *OECD Tax Policy Studies*, no. 26.

Rorty, Richard. 1972. "The World Well Lost." *The Journal of Philosophy* 69(19): 649–65.

Rorty, Richard. 1982. "Keeping Philosophy Pure: An Essay on Wittgenstein." In idem, *Consequences of Pragmatism*. Minneapolis: University of Minnesota Press.

Stringham, Edward. 2007. *Anarchy and Law: The Political Economy of Choice*. New Brunswick, N.J.: Transaction Publishers.

Taylor, Robert S. 2017. *Exit Left: Markets and Mobility in Republican Thought*. Oxford: Oxford University Press.

Tucker, Benjamin. 1888. "State Socialism and Anarchism: How Far They Agree, and Wherein They Differ." http://praxeology.net/BT-SSA.htm.

Wittgenstein, Ludwig. 1972. *On Certainty*. New York: Harper & Row.

Wittgenstein, Ludwig. 2009. *Philosophical investigations*, rev. 4th ed. Chichester, West Sussex, U.K.: Wiley-Blackwell.

Julian Reiss

WHY DO EXPERTS DISAGREE?

ABSTRACT: *Jeffrey Friedman's* Power Without Knowledge *argues forcefully that there are inherent limitations to the predictability of human action, due to a circumstance he calls "ideational heterogeneity." However, our resources for predicting human action somewhat reliably in the light of ideational heterogeneity have not been exhausted yet, and there are no in-principle barriers to progress in tackling the problem. There are, however, other strong reasons to think that disagreement among epistocrats is bound to persist, such that it will be difficult to decide who has "the right answer" to a given technocratic problem. These reasons have to do with competing visions of the good society, fact/value entanglement, and the fragility of the facts of the social sciences.*

The Corona crisis has made plain that the role of scientific experts in democracies is among the most significant and urgent problems we face, and should be a core concern in contemporary political theory and adjacent fields such as economics, economic methodology, the philosophy of science, and science and technology studies. On the one hand, democracies face fundamental challenges that call for a close collaboration between science and politics; the pandemic is the most current and

---

obvious but by no means unique example. On the other hand, there are boatloads of reasons to think that expert judgment is not always reliable and trustworthy. Again, most currently and obviously: experts recommended against the wearing of face masks early in the crisis only to reverse their judgments a few months later, without any new evidence to support this change of mind. Why should we think that they have got it right this time around? Contributions to the recent debate about experts in democracies aim to resolve this dilemma in one way or another.

We can distinguish two camps in this literature. Those we may refer to as *apologists* acknowledge (to varying degrees) the limitations of expert judgment but argue that the role of experts in democracies should nevertheless be strengthened because the alternative is worse. Examples include Jason Brennan's *Against Democracy* (2016; see also Collins and Evans 2017 and Nichols 2017). Those opposing the apologists are the *critics*. They propose to introduce institutions that aim to keep experts in check or to motivate them right so that failure and overreach are relatively unlikely. Examples of this latter group include William Easterly's *The Tyranny of Experts* (2013; see also Levy and Peart 2017 and Koppl 2018). *Power Without Knowledge* (Oxford University Press, 2019) belongs squarely in this camp.

According to Stephen Turner (2001), there is a "problem with experts" in a democracy. The problem, in short, is this: heeding expert advice contravenes one of the most deeply held democratic principles, viz. the fundamental equality of all citizens. Three solutions offer themselves. Populist approaches address the problem by ignoring expertise and making political decisions a matter of mob psychology. Technocratic and epistocratic approaches subject citizens to rule by experts (on the distinction, see Van Bouwel 2009, 3). Deliberative democratic approaches maintain that the process of democratic deliberation can balance the two demands more fairly (Habermas 1971; Kitcher 2011).

Friedman's book is highly original in that it challenges the premise from which all these approaches start: that there is anything special about expert knowledge to begin with. Focusing on predicting the likely effects of interventions aiming to solve social problems such as unemployment, inflation, failing schools, a dysfunctional health care system, or drug addiction (5), Friedman argues that there are inherent limitations to such predictions. Worse than that, given the way social science is currently practiced, social scientists are unlikely to make reliable predictions to the extent that this is possible, and there are good reasons to believe that this won't change anytime soon.

In what follows I will first discuss Friedman's skeptical arguments concerning social scientists' ability to predict the effects of policy interventions. To anticipate my main response, I am somewhat more optimistic than he is about reliable predictions. I do think that human action is generally very hard to predict, but there are predictable aspects, and there are methodological strategies to discover what these aspects are. I will then outline my own reasons for thinking that social science is an unlikely source of the knowledge necessary for making epistocracy feasible, and will come to a conclusion that is, if anything, even more anti-technocratic than Friedman's.

I should emphasize at the beginning that I am in broad agreement with many of Friedman's core claims. Like Friedman, I am critical of any existing form of technocracy, and I agree that the reasons for rejecting technocracy are in large part epistemic. I do think exitocracy is an interesting alternative, and although a society organized according to Rawls's Difference Principle isn't my preferred vision of the good society, I agree that an exitocracy would require that each citizen dispose of an amount of resources sufficient to be capable of making use of the freedom to exit, should he or she want to do so. One difference between us is that I believe that the epistemic limitations of successful technocracy are of a more fundamental and less practical nature than Friedman supposes.

Technocracy, Epistocracy, and the Problem of Prediction

Friedman uses a broad definition of technocracy, according to which ordinary citizens who attempt to solve social problems politically count as "citizen-technocrats," alongside the "epistocrats"—expert social scientists—who are usually defined as the only technocrats there are. Friedman's rationale for this definition begins with the question of what it is that distinguishes "technocrats," in ordinary usage, from everybody else. The answer is that technocrats—in Friedman's usage, epistocrats—claim to know how best to design public policies that will solve the social and economic problems of the populace. Friedman wants to scrutinize this knowledge claim, but that means that he cannot take for granted, as the ordinary definition does, that "technocrats" (epistocrats) actually possess problem-solving knowledge that is superior to that possessed by ordinary citizens. That is, epistocrats cannot be treated as true experts rather than *putative* experts if we are to investigate whether their claimed expertise is real. We need to investigate the possibility that it is not because, after all, if epistocrats were no more epistemically qualified than average citizens to shape public policy, there would be no reason not to decide policies by more direct democratic means. If epistocrats know no better than ordinary citizens, why should they be given more power than ordinary citizens have?

On the other hand, though, Friedman interprets U.S. public-opinion research to show that ordinary citizens often seem to think that they, too, know how to solve social and economic problems. If we no longer simply assume that, on the whole, such "non-experts'" knowledge claims must be disregarded, then ordinary citizens' knowledge claims about how to solve social and economic problems must, prior to the investigation, be put into the same category as "experts'" knowledge claims: both groups claim to know how to solve social and economic problems, and it would beg the question to assert, by definitional fiat, that one group is right and the other wrong. Thus, both groups must be defined as technocratic, in that both groups consist of fallible human beings who think they know how to solve the problems a technocracy tries to solve (13-21).

If this seems to be an overly broad definition, it allows Friedman to specify rather precisely just what type of knowledge *any* technocrat needs. Insofar as the technocratic agenda is to solve (or alleviate, or prevent) social and economic problems, a technocracy, to be viable and legitimate, needs to predict reliably the effects of policy interventions on the social and economic problems toward which they are directed. This, in turn, amounts to predicting how targeted groups of social actors will react to the incentives created by the interventions. Therefore, Friedman's scrutiny of technocratic knowledge claims begins with a general inquiry into the determinants of human behavior, which he takes to be ideational (Part I). People's beliefs determine their actions, and their beliefs are the products of streams of incoming information and interpretation that will, to some extent, vary from person to person (Chapter 3). The task of the "judicious," ideationally sensitive technocrat, then, will be to discover homogeneities across people's webs of belief that enable reliable predictions to be made about the behavior that is likely to occur in response to a technocratic intervention.

This task, Friedman argues in Part II, is not even attempted by most "expert" social scientists nowadays, who instead assume away the possibly confounding role of heterogeneous beliefs (Chapter 4), and who tend to be caught up in self-confirmatory "spirals of conviction" that persuade them of the accuracy of their non-ideational theories by screening out or misinterpreting conflicting evidence (Chapter 5). Citizen-technocrats, however, fare no better: while they tend to be more open minded than epistocrats, due to their lack of self-confirming information, they tend to assume that policy intentions translate unproblematically into policy results, effacing the complexities of human behavior that might be caused by factors such as ideational heterogeneity (Chapter 6). In the concluding Chapter 7, Friedman outlines the limited promise of a regime that minimizes technocratic prediction in favor of affording individuals the "exit option," which enables them to draw on their personal, experiential knowledge in navigating modern society rather than requiring them to predict the behavior of faceless masses of other people—as they must do when they assume the role of technocrat.

Are There Inherent Limits to Predictability?

I am skeptical about highly generic arguments concerning the inherent limitations to the predictability of human action (Reiss 2008, 155ff.). Perhaps my thinking has been influenced by Otto Neurath ([1932] 1987, 13), who wrote that

> In some cases a physicist is a worse prophet than a behaviouristician, as when he is supposed to specify where in St. Stephen's Square a thousand dollar bill swept away by the wind will land, whereas a behaviouristician can specify the result of a conditioning experiment rather accurately. If someone complains about the difficulties of making behaviouristic experiments, let him seek consolation in geology and astronomy where experiments are virtually unknown, except for ones involving small-scale models under radically different conditions.

Neurath's point was: when assessing the predictability of human action in the wild, we shouldn't take laboratory physics as the standard. Uncontrolled physics phenomena are often hard to predict, whereas there are many cases of human action that are predictable under the right circumstances.

Friedman's argument to the effect that technocrats cannot predict the effects of policy interventions to the degree required by technocracy is built on a set of theses Friedman dubs "Lippmannesque" to honor their pedigree in Walter Lippmann's *Public Opinion* (Lippmann [1922] 1997). It is worth quoting them in full (Friedman 2019, 140-41, 143):

> *Thesis 1 (interpretive determinism).* At least insofar as an agent is acting deliberately, her interpretation of which action is advisable under her perceived circumstances will determine which action she takes.
>
> *Thesis 2 (ideational determinism).* An agent's interpretation of which action is advisable under her perceived circumstances will be determined by the web of those of her ideas that seem (to her) relevant to (a) the circumstances themselves, (b) the purpose of actions that (for her) count as normatively advisable in those circumstances, and (c) the effects ... that seem (to her) likely be produced by such actions in those circumstances. Also playing a part will be the implicit assumptions and other tacit ideas that stand behind ideas about (a), (b), and (c).
>
> *Thesis 3 (ideational heterogeneity).* The ideas, and thus the interpretations, that determine agents' deliberate actions, as well as the ideas of the technocrats attempting to predict and control agents' actions, vary from person to person to some extent, making each person's actions somewhat unpredictable to the others.

Friedman is right, of course, to assume that different interpretations often lead to different actions. A good example is Joseph Henrich et al.'s study of ultimatum games in 15 small-scale societies. One of their conclusions is that "there is considerably more behavioral variability across groups than had been found in previous cross-cultural research, and the canonical model fails in a wider variety of ways than in previous experiments" (Henrich et al. 2001, 73). Yet there appear to be aspects of human action that are reliably predictable. To use a drab example, I rely every day on the prediction that the market vendor won't poison me. Friedman appeals to such examples to argue that ideational homogeneities (such as the norm that one should not poison people), stemming from cultural sources, may counteract the "presumption of ideational heterogeneity" and should therefore be a prime object of judicious technocratic inquiry (169, 147).

Let me give some examples from an area of research that focuses on behavioral *modification*: marketing, or, more broadly, the science of persuasion. Marketing researchers and psychologists now understand pretty well how to affect people's behavior (on average). Robert Cialdini, Regents' Professor Emeritus of Psychology and Marketing at Arizona

State University, for instance, has condensed the research evidence into six rules of influence (Cialdini 2001; Cialdini 2016): reciprocation, liking, social proof, authority, scarcity, and consistency. For instance, people are more likely to buy a good or donate to a cause after having received a free gift, when the seller is (or pretends to be) "much like them," or when the good is (or is claimed to be) "the last available item" for sale. A principle more directly relevant to policy is that of social proof, which states that people tend to regard as correct that which they think others think is correct. A study of India's Green Rating Project (GRP), a public disclosure program that collects and disseminates information about firms' environmental performance, found that GRP achieved significant reductions in pollution loadings among dirty plants (Powers et al. 2011). This example is particularly instructive because (a) it concerns pollution, which is arguably a social problem technocrats would like to address, and (b) the study was conducted in a non-WEIRD (Western, educated, industrialized, rich, and democratic) context, which shows that the principle applies widely (206).

I agree with Friedman that ideational heterogeneity creates obstacles to reliably predicting the consequences of policy interventions. I also agree that pernicious heterogeneity, i.e., heterogeneity that affects actual behavior in unpredictable fashion, must be the default assumption. But instead of a principal obstacle to the predictability of behavioral responses to policy interventions, it could be treated as a methodological problem that needs to be addressed, but which may on occasion either show up only in an attenuated fashion or be solvable.

Friedman himself gives an example of a problem of interpretation in economic experiments that appears to have been solved satisfactorily: Linda the feminist bank teller, adduced by Amos Tversky and Daniel Kahneman in what has become a world-famous experiment (198). It appeared to Tversky and Kahneman (1983, 297), that their experimental subjects violated the laws of the probability calculus because they thought that it was more likely that Linda, who as a college student had been a philosophy major who was "deeply concerned with issues of discrimination and social justice, and also participated in anti-nuclear demonstration," would become a feminist bank teller than that she would become a bank teller without qualification—even though the set of bank tellers must be larger than the subset of feminist bank tellers. However, when the question was later asked in terms of frequencies rather than probabilities, the violation largely disappeared (Fiedler

1988). Friedman accepts that experiments that frame the question in terms of frequencies are less subject to the interpretive missteps he attributes to Tversky and Kahneman, such that we can say that such experiments represent progress toward accurate predictive knowledge. Similarly, policy makers could try to frame policies in such a way that the desired behavioral modifications are likely to obtain (results from the science of persuasion will help them achieve that), and such that interpretive problems are unlikely to interfere. Thus, while there is certainly a methodological issue to be addressed, I am not yet convinced that ideational heterogeneity poses an overriding obstacle to successful policy.

Let me explain what I mean by the "methodological issue to be addressed" in more detail. Section 4.4 of *Power Without Knowledge* criticizes a recent movement in empirical economics, which is commonly known as "design-based econometrics" (e.g., Reiss 2013, ch. 9), and which Friedman includes under the heading of "positivist social science." Design-based econometrics starts from the observation that social scientists don't have theories that are both strong enough to determine crucial aspects of the empirical specification such as covariates, functional form, and distribution of the error terms; and empirically supported enough to be regarded as credible by a majority of researchers (e.g., Freedman 1991). The randomized experiment is the methodological "gold standard" for overcoming these problems of causal inference, and if randomized experimentation is impossible, according to this type of positivist, designs should be sought that mimic randomized experiments as closely as possible. Instrumental variables, difference-in-differences, regression discontinuity, and similar techniques work by exploiting situations that occur naturally (in that the central variation to be analyzed is found rather than created by the analyst) but they resemble experiments nonetheless (Angrist and Pischke 2010).

There are two fundamental problems of causal inference. The first is to ascertain that the identified causal relationship does in fact hold for the population at hand. The other is to determine whether and to what extent the relationship holds also for other populations, i.e., populations that are not described by the data set at hand. It is sometimes postulated that when choosing a research method, researchers face a tradeoff between the two fundamental problems (Just and Roe 2009). Some methods are really good at solving the first problem because their protocol makes sure that the method applies only under conditions that make virtually certain that no explanation other than the targeted causal explanation can account for the data. Randomized experiments are an example of this type. The problem, however, is that because of the strict protocol, results tend not to travel far beyond the test population, for example because experiments create certain artefacts that make people behave differently than normally. As W. Allen Wallis and Milton Friedman (1942) put it a long time ago, "It is questionable whether a subject in so artificial an experimental situation could know what choices he would make in an economic situation; not knowing, it is almost inevitable that he would, in entire good faith, systematize his answers in such a way as to produce plausible but spurious results."

Other methods, such as ordinary least squares, apply more widely and do not create artefacts. But they are not very good at ruling out all salient competing hypotheses. Using these methods, researchers are free to choose data sets they think are highly representative, but they cannot be terribly certain of the results.

Econometricians affiliated with the design-based school tend to resolve the tradeoff by focusing almost exclusively on the first problem of causal inference. To the extent that they do so, Friedman correctly criticizes the school for ignoring the second problem of inference. Thus, design-based econometrics "treats [agents] as if they act homogeneously in response to whatever objective variables the economist deems worthy of investigating experimentally" (205). In light of Friedman's argument for the presumption of ideational heterogeneity in Chapter 3, he maintains in Chapter 4 that judicious social scientists would treat homogeneity as the exception rather than the rule, not the other way around.

The inference rule Friedman is criticizing—"assume homogeneity unless there is some specific reason to think otherwise"— has been called "simple induction." It is indeed highly fallible. As Daniel Steel (2008, 82) argues, "simple induction is limited, and ... it is highly desirable that it be supplemented with some more sophisticated inferential strategy." In the past 15 years or so, methodologists have spent a lot of effort on developing such more sophisticated inferential strategies. Steel's own approach builds on knowledge of mechanisms, Nancy Cartwright's on knowledge of causal capacities (Cartwright and Munro 2010), Judea Pearl's on knowledge of causal structure (Bareinboim and Pearl 2014), Francesco Guala's on certain kinds of analogies (Guala 2010), and in joint work with a former student I have defended an approach that combines Guala's analogical reasoning with the construction of latent classes (van Eersel et al. 2019). None of these approaches assumes homogeneity, but instead each tries to distinguish between predictable and unpredictable aspects of behavior in order to make inferences from experimental populations to other populations more reliable.

All these approaches are highly abstract in that they do not specify the source of heterogeneity any more concretely than with respect to underlying "mechanisms" or "structures" or simply "causes." But to the extent that ideas or "webs of belief" cause behavior, ideational heterogeneity is one specific reason among others why predictions may fail. And to the extent that behavior is not entirely random but varies systematically with aspects of the settings within which it occurs, these approaches can pick up on the systematic variation. Information about "homogenizing factors" such as social norms can help a great deal in this process.

Importantly, predicting the effects of policy interventions is a special case of solving the second fundamental problem of causal inference. Here, the new context to which a result is applied is not an existing context but one created by the policy. Much of the recent methodological work on the second problem of inference is concerned exactly with these kinds of predictions (e.g., Reiss 2008, chs. 9-10; Cartwright and Hardie 2012). However, this does not show that social science, as it is actually practiced, takes the possibility of ideational heterogeneity (or in fact any other kind of heterogeneity) into account when making predictions. In that sense, the criticism Friedman makes of standard neoclassical economics, the new econometrics, and behavioral economics (along with social psychology) in Chapter 4 is well taken. Economists and other social scientists do rely on *a priori* theory and simple induction too often (a point I have also made in *Error in Economics*, 2008). However, I agree with Friedman, too, that a more judicious social science is possible. Indeed, recent discussions in methodology suggest strategies for making social science more judicious.

So the question is whether there aren't any in-principle obstacles to judicious social science. Chapter 5 argues there is at least one: the spiral of conviction (although Friedman does not state that the barrier is insurmountable).

The Spiral of Conviction

The spiral of conviction starts with Lippmann's idea that everyone uses interpretive stereotypes in order to make sense of the "great blooming, buzzing confusion" that is reality. Every conscious agent receives far more information than he could make sense of. Stereotypes help one to navigate by screening out information that is inconsistent with one's stereotypes. The more one knows about a subject, the more one's stereotype will get reinforced. Children and, more generally, newcomers to a subject thus tend to be relatively open minded when confronted with new ideas, as they have not had time to develop and reinforce stereotypes, while those who have acquired a great deal of knowledge about it—such as experts—lean on the stereotype to make sense of the knowledge, while leaning on the knowledge to reinforce the stereotype. In short, they tend to become dogmatic about the stereotype.

I think that there is a great deal of truth to this theory. It does explain observations such as this one from Max Planck (1950, 33): "A new scientific truth does not triumph by convincing its opponents and making them see the light, but rather because its opponents eventually die, and a new generation grows up that is familiar with it" (which has come to be known as "Planck's Principle"; see Hull et al. 1978). Similarly, there is the fact that many scientific innovations are made by outsiders to the field (in biology, for instance, see Harman and Dietrich 2013).

However, the spiral of conviction is at best a tendency. That is, it is a mechanism that operates in some individuals but not all, and even where it operates, there are countervailing mechanisms that prevent it from complete dominance. As Friedman puts it, "as people gain knowledge of a topic, their opinions about it *tend* to rigidify," there exists "a *pressure* for dogmatism" or a "*propensity* to dogmatism' (29, 232, 246, emphases added). We can imagine, then, that some researchers might become aware of this tendency (as they become aware of other cognitive biases, such as confirmation bias) and take active steps to combat it. Here is one recipe. Identify the "crowning postures" in your belief system, to use terminology Friedman (234) borrows from Philip E. Converse to denote beliefs that are crucial to your interpretive schema. Treat them not, in a realist manner, as representations of reality but rather, in instrumentalist fashion, as tools for prediction. Identify one or a small set of *alternative* crowning postures. Derive predictions from the alternative belief constellations. (By "predictions," here, I do not mean statements about the future effects of interventions, but answers to the question: What observations would we expect to make if the crowning posture were true? Chapter 5 uses this method in the context of discussing alternatives to the spiral-of-conviction model. Take the score of failed and successful predictions for each alternative constellation of beliefs. If an alternative outperforms one's crowning postures to some pre-determined degree, switch to the alternative.

Of course, such countervailing mechanisms won't be perfect. I just use this to illustrate the idea that the spiral of conviction is a tendency rather than an inescapable trap. What is more important is that even if every scientist were dogmatic individually, this would not mean that science as a whole could not make progress. Gebhard Kirchgässner (2003, 269–70) makes this point in discussing dogmatism and ideology among economists, borrowing a Popperian idea. It is worthwhile quoting him in full:

> One might argue that this is not a problem of individual attitudes of scientists but a "systemic request": objectivity of individual scientists might be seen as a necessary condition for scientific progress. However, Popper ([Popper 1976], p. 95) begs to differ: "It is a mistake to assume that the objectivity of a science depends on the objectivity of the scientist. And it is a mistake to believe that the attitude of the natural scientist is more objective than that of the social scientist. … The objectivity of science is not a matter of the individual scientists but rather the social result of their mutual criticisms, of the friendly-hostile division of labour among scientists, of their co-operation and also of their competition."…
>
> To get a satisfactory answer to this question, it is necessary to take into account, as K. Popper emphasises, that science is not the business of separate individuals but that it is a social process, in which some scientists make conjectures and others criticise these. Some of these conjectures will (at least temporarily) survive criticism and be taken as approved hypotheses, while others will be refuted because of logical deficiencies or incompatibility with the available empirical data. What is decisive is not whether the individual scientist is objective or not, but that the scientific discourse takes place in a climate where criticisms are not only allowed but even desired. Only criticisms of our conjectures enable us to detect their weaknesses and to proceed to better conjectures. … If we had to rely on the objectivity of the individual scientist to reach scientific progress, then the chance for progress would be rather limited, because scientists—like all other human beings—are generally biased in favour of their own ideas. Whether scientific progress is possible or not in a society depends much more on the (rational) organisation of the scientific process than on the intentions of the individual scientists.

So even if *every* individual scientist is subject to the spiral of conviction, it does not mean that science as a whole cannot use mechanisms that control the influence of individual biases and thus enable progress. This I take to be the lesson of Planck's Principle: science does advance after all, even if one funeral at a time. Thus, I think we have to identify a different kind of obstacle to a well-functioning technocracy.

Why Epistocrats Disagree

My reservations about epistocratic knowledge start earlier than at the point of extrapolating from existing results to policy predictions. Essentially, it is highly unlikely that experts will agree even on what the relevant (social scientific) facts are. (Cf. also Friedman's discussion of the "Fact of Technocratic Disagreement," 38ff). But expert agreement is essential to the feasibility of technocracy and epistocracy. Without expert agreement, policy makers would have to choose among the disagreeing experts. How could they do that in a way that doesn't bias selection along political lines and in the absence of social science expertise on their part? Or, as Friedman suggests, they could do it in a way that is biased toward the confidence shown by some experts, which would institutionalize the closed-mindedness he derives from the theory of the spiral of conviction—not because they take an expert's confidence as a sign of having gotten hold of truth, but because less-confident experts will tend not to want to enter into political debate with more-dogmatic experts, having less confidence that their position should be defended at all costs (262).

Very abstract principles such as those proposed by Alvin Goldman (2001) would not seem to help in this case. Nor will we usually have the time to force agreement in a consensus conference, or by means of Habermas's "unforced force of the better argument" applied to epistocrats—the epistemic reasonableness of which is dubious anyway (Solomon 2007).

Beyond the problem of epistocrats' disagreement about facts is the problem of *all* technocrats' (potential) disagreement about values. This problem, however, will aggravate the fact of *expert* disagreement, making it difficult for citizen-technocrats or their political agents to choose among experts in mixed epistocratic-democratic technocracies such as ours. Let me break this problem down into the following four issues:

- Experts disagree about values.
- Disagreement about values feeds through to factual opinions because of fact/value entanglement.
- The fragility of social science facts raises a different kind of interpretive problem.

- There are currently no evidential standards that are widely shared among social scientists, nor are they likely to emerge in the near future.

In what follows, I will address each point in turn.

Alternative Visions of the Good Society

Early on in *Power Without Knowledge*, Friedman uses survey data from twentieth-century America to contend that there seems to have been a broad public consensus in favor of technocracy-friendly policy objectives, such as low inflation and low unemployment (8-9). Further examples are "a high standard of living, freedom, peace and a better life for one's children" (8, quoting public-opinion scholar Bernard Berelson). I certainly do not deny that these are all valuable objectives, and I suspect that most social science experts agree. Nonetheless, I do not think that there is a value consensus among experts in the relevant sense. Disagreement about which of a number of policy options is best therefore stems not only from possible disagreement about which policy is best to achieve a given end, which is Friedman's focus, but also from disagreement about the ends themselves.

My starting point is value pluralism of the kind articulated by Isaiah Berlin (e.g., Berlin 1958). Genuine values are many, and different values may stand in conflict with each other, necessitating a choice between them. The first source of disagreement given plural values is what to put on the list. What is conspicuously absent from Berelson's/Friedman's list is equality, which is likely to be very high on many policy experts' lists. Does a society in which everyone has "enough" according to some accepted standard, while the most advantaged members nevertheless command far more resources than the least advantaged, suffer from a "social or economic problem"? There is no consensus on this question.

Disagreements about what to put on the list of valuable things could be resolved in two ways. The conjunctive approach would include only items we can find on every expert's list. Apart from the risk of ending up with an empty list, the approach would be skewed against some visions of the good society. A society in which inflation is zero, no one is unemployed, and everyone lives freely and enjoys a high standard of living is not a good society, according to some experts, if (say) material inequality is rampant, and according to others if (say) everyone pursues their own hedonistic pleasures without regard for transcendent goals. The disjunctive approach would put every item on the list that is valued by at least one expert. Here the opposite considerations apply. Progressives might, for instance, deny that sanctity or tradition are values to begin with.

The second source of disagreement stems from the fact that values are not merely plural, but stand in conflict with each other. When they do, choices have to be made about which of two or more conflicting values are more important in the situation at hand. This is a point Friedman takes up, but he discusses it in the context of expert knowledge, not value judgments. Thus, he argues that experts often lack "knowledge of which social problems are not only real but *significant*, in the sense that they affect large numbers of people — or small numbers intensely" (46). But whether or not a social problem is significant or not is a value judgment, not something that can be decided on the basis of evidence alone. Is widespread drug abuse or inflation the more pressing social problem (or a problem at all)? That will depend, among other things, on whether freedom or well-being is regarded as the more important value. Even in the counterfactual situation in which all experts agree on what is on the list, there will be disagreements about which of two or more conflicting values has priority, and therefore which social problems are the most significant.

The third source of disagreement concerns the interpretation and application of any given value to a given situation. "Freedom," "an adequate standard of living," "equality," and so on all mean different things to different people. Can I be truly free if I don't have resources? Do we enjoy an adequate standard of living if others have vastly more? Can society be truly equal if it grants mere formal equality in the sense of equal rights and ignores outcomes? Even the more technical-sounding aims, such as "low inflation," are open to multiple interpretations that are influenced by further value judgments. Is a 2 percent inflation target adequate or not? Arguably, no one's well-being is greatly affected by 2 percent inflation. However, over time resources are redistributed from creditor to debtor, which at least some would regard as unfair. Thus, whether 2 percent counts as "low" inflation depends on value judgments.

In 1953, Milton Friedman (no relation to the author of *Power Without Knowledge*) famously argued that differences in opinion about policy stem primarily from differences in opinion about which of a number of policies is most likely to get us closer to an agreed-upon goal:

> I venture the judgment, however, that currently in the Western world, and especially in the United States, differences about economic policy

> among disinterested citizens derive predominantly from different predictions about the economic consequences of taking action—differences that in principle can be eliminated by the progress of positive economics—rather than from fundamental differences in basic values, differences about which men can ultimately only fight. An obvious and not unimportant example is minimum-wage legislation. Underneath the welter of arguments offered for and against such legislation there is an underlying consensus on the objective of achieving a "living wage" for all, to use the ambiguous phrase so common in such discussions. The difference of opinion is largely grounded on an implicit or explicit difference in predictions about the efficacy of this particular means in furthering the agreed-on end. (Friedman 1953, 2-3)

But this mistaken. Even if everyone concerned agreed that "achieving a living wage for all" is a worthwhile goal, judgments about minimum-wage policies will be affected by value judgments concerning what other goals economic policy should pursue, the *relative* importance of achieving a living wage vis-à-vis these other goals, and what the phrase "living wage for all" amounts to in the situation at hand. We cannot therefore neatly separate "positive" questions about the efficacy of means from "normative" questions about the desirability of ends.

Fact/Value Entanglement

The second reason why experts disagree is that their disagreement about values feeds through to their opinions about what the facts are and what predictions follow from them.

Value judgments affect scientific results in a number of ways, and attempts to eliminate the influence of values will ultimately be frustrated, to the detriment of the quality of scientific output. In previous work I have argued this at length in the context of positive economics (Reiss 2017) and evidence-based policy (Khosrowi and Reiss 2019), so let me illustrate it by returning to Milton Friedman's example, that of minimum-wage legislation. Are differences in predictions about the effects of the minimum wage value free, such that these differences can "in principle can be eliminated by the progress of positive economics"? It would not appear to be so, at least if we grant that positive economics has made progress in the almost 70 years since Friedman wrote these words. There is still disagreement among economists about the effects of increases in minimum wages on the employment rate, despite vastly better data, vastly improved computing power, and vastly more studies having been conducted since 1953.

Ironically, it was also in 1953 that philosopher of social science Richard Rudner published a paper attacking the neat separability of "positive" claims and "normative" claims about the desirability of outcomes (Rudner 1953). He argued, very generally, that hypothesis tests are always subject to uncertainty: no matter how long and hard scientists try, their judgments concerning the truth or falsehood of a hypothesis may be wrong. But since there are two types of error (accepting a false hypothesis vs. rejecting a true hypothesis), and there is a tradeoff between the two, scientists must consider, when deciding how to resolve the tradeoff, which of the two errors has graver consequences. This cannot be done without value judgments. Applied to the effect of increases in the minimum wage on the employment rate, an economist might wrongly accept the null hypothesis of no effect or might wrongly reject it, judging that there is a (negative) effect. In the first case (assuming that the scientific judgment would be implemented as a technocratic policy), the error would throw some people out of their jobs, decreasing employment. In the second case, low-wage employees would miss wage increases they could have had, had the policy been implemented. Which error is worse? This depends on whether one regards unemployment or forgone wage rises as the more significant social ill.

Apart from obvious reasoning flaws such as confirmation bias, one reason why economists disagree about the effects of raising minimum wages is thus because they disagree about whether unemployment or wage stagnation is a worse possible consequence, which in turn will be affected by differences about more fundamental values such as freedom, equality, and well-being. This is why advances in positive economics —better data, better methods, more computing power, more events that have happened and are therefore amenable to scientific analysis— will not eliminate disagreements about the effectiveness of policies.

There is another source of fact/value entanglement that is relevant here: we cannot measure social phenomena without making value judgments. Many choices required in the construction of a socio-economic indicator such as the consumer-price index (CPI) cannot be justified on the basis of "the facts" alone. A price index is fully accurate only when nothing changes in the economy except the prices of goods. However, many things do change. People substitute away from goods the price of which has increased relatively; their tastes change; the quality of goods changes; new goods appear and old goods are discontinued; new distribution outlets such as discounters and online platforms are introduced; the environment changes; and so on (Reiss 2008). None of these changes can be put into the CPI or left out of it without making value judgments. Consider quality changes. When a product the price of which was included when CPI was last measured has disappeared, but a similar product has become available, a statistician must make a judgment about whether the two goods are comparable. If they are not comparable, one of a number of adjustment methods can be used. But comparable according to what standard? The CPI aims to measure the cost of living. If the price of a good goes up but its quality improves at the same time, has the cost of living gone up? This question is hard to decide, especially if the former version of the good becomes unavailable so that consumers are forced to buy the new version (or something else altogether). Ultimately, at any rate, a judgment has to be made whether (and to what extent) a consumer *benefits* from the alteration. And that is certainly a value judgment.

This is relevant to the discussion, in *Power Without Knowledge,* of Lippman's proposal to eschew problems of interpretation by collecting and publishing objective statistics that the public and government decision-makers could use directly (100-101). In addition to the problems that (Jeffrey) Friedman mentions with using statistics in this manner (the fact that statistics treat unlike as like, the inability of statistics to demonstrate causality, the unrepresentativeness of the sample from which a given statistic is drawn), the problem with using statistics is that values are not eschewed but at best buried under a lather of procedures and instructions that either implement earlier value judgments or call for new ones in their application (as the example of quality changes was meant to show).

Fragile Facts

Moving now away from values, a third source of disagreement among experts about the effectiveness of policies is related to the sensitivity of answers to the precise formulation of policy questions. There will rarely be a unique answer to a question as general as "Do increases in minimum wages lower employment opportunities?" Note that I am talking here about the facts themselves, not our inferences about them.

It is the facts that are fragile, not (merely) our knowledge of them. There may be one fact about what's true in the short run, a different one about what's true in the middle or long run, and so on. I call them fragile because what is true in one fully specified context often does not tell us very much about what is true in an only slightly altered context. Correct answers to policy questions will often depend on the following dimensions: horizon, the time and place of application, contrast, and the choice of outcome variable.

Horizon. The effects of policies unfold over time, and short-run and long-run effects may differ markedly. That is, policies can have a desirable effect in the short run but an adverse effect in the long run and vice versa. It has been argued, for example, that even if it were true that minimum-wage increases have no negative effects on the employment rate (Card and Krueger 1995), this observation holds true only of the short run. In the long run, relatively labor-intensive businesses will shut down and get replaced by relatively capital-intensive alternatives, thus decreasing employment opportunities in a manner that may be invisible when looking for employment effects by means of natural experimentation (Sorkin 2015). This variability of effectiveness with respect to the examined horizon is widespread in economic policy. For example, Keynesian countercyclical policies may well help in the short run but damage economies in the long run (Sinn 2014); "nudges" may help individuals achieve their goals in the short but undermine their decision-making capacity in the long run (Bovens 2009).

When experts disagree about a question such as whether increases in minimum wages lower employment opportunities, then, they may simply be interpreting the question differently. Or they may know that the effects differ over time but attribute a different degree of significance to the short or the long run.

Time and Place of Application. Causal relations in the social world depend on complex arrangements of individuals and the social structures within which they operate. These arrangements differ from place to place, and in a given place over time. The effects of minimum-wage increases will differ, for instance, depending on the starting point (i.e., whether the existing minimum wages are already quite high or rather low), on employment laws and business regulation, on social norms, industry practices, and a host of other factors. What is true in the United States may not be true in Mexico, and what was true in the United States in 1960 may no longer be true now. Thus, when two economists disagree about the effects of policy, they may simply be talking about different applications. (Friedman makes similar points in Sections 3.4.3, "The Problem of Novel Circumstances," and 3.4.4, "The Problem of Heterogeneous Agents.")

Contrast. One way to think about causal factors is that they are "differences that make a difference" (Holland 1986). Thus, an intervention is judged to be effective if its implementation makes a difference to some outcome variable of interest. The difference in the cause is between the intervention and a situation without the intervention; the difference in the effect is between the outcome variable with and without the intervention. In many experiments, it is clear what this means. In a clinical trial, for instance, there will be a treatment group and a control group, and one measures the outcome variable in both groups. However, in a policy context, it is not always clear which two situations we should compare. When we ask, say, whether free trade is beneficial for a nation, do we mean "relative to a thoroughly protectionist regime" or rather "relative to an intelligent mix of protectionist and market elements"? The answer is likely to differ from expert to expert. Thus, when two economists disagree about the effectiveness of policies, they might in fact disagree about which of a number of alternatives is the most relevant one.

Outcome variable. In the minimum-wage case, the employment rate is usually the chosen outcome variable. It is questionable, however, whether this is the best choice. The employment rate does not reflect the number of hours worked, for instance. Thus, the employment rate may respond in one way to an increase in the minimum wage, the full-time equivalent (FTE) employment rate in another. The FTE rate, however, is insensitive to the number of people employed. And neither rate reflects the type of employment contract being used. Especially in the long run, more permanent contracts may be replaced by temporary arrangements, changing the nature of the employment relationship. Nor do the two rates reflect other aspects of work, such as job satisfaction or stress related to particular jobs.

The choice of outcome variable may also reflect hidden value judgments. For some people, a job is merely a means of making ends meet, while for others it is a source of satisfaction and for others, a way to get ahead in life, or retire early, or impress others. We may therefore ask if some measure of well-being would not be the more appropriate outcome variable than the sheer fact of employment. But the measurement of well-being is, of course, fraught with conceptual and practical difficulties (see for instance Alexandrova 2017). Do we mean by "well-being" preference satisfaction, as most neoclassical economists do, or shall we use an alternative conception such as happiness (Layard 2005) or capabilities (Sen 1999; Nussbaum 2000)? If we stick with preference satisfaction, shall we assume that people's actual choices reflect their preferences or shall we allow for mistakes? If we allow for mistakes, how can we avoid the paternalistic imputation of preferences by the economist? The point of this is: there is no unique outcome variable; the effect a policy has on one variable may differ on its effect on an alternative variable; and the choice of variable may be irreducibly normative.

Fragile facts are those that are sensitive to the choice of horizon, time and place of application, contrast, and outcome variable (Reiss 2019). Many if not most social facts are fragile in this sense. When two experts disagree about a policy question, it may be due to a different interpretation of the question they are being asked, or it may be due to a different judgment of which facts are most relevant for making a prediction about a future intervention.

The Absence of Evidentiary Standards

There is a further source of potential disagreement among social science experts about what the facts are. Methodological battles have plagued the social sciences almost since the birth of economics, which was the first social science to be separated from moral philosophy. Many of these battles have revolved around the proper place of social theory in learning about the principles that describe and explain social phenomena (Reiss unpublished). One side maintains that all inference starts from theory, leaving relatively little room for inductive reasoning from facts (no room at all, in the case of the Austrian school of economics). The other side maintains that social science does not yet have credible theory and must therefore rely on inductive reasoning from facts, leaving relatively little room for theory (no room at all, in the case of some members of the German historical school of economics).

The recent debate in economics about the role of randomized trials and natural experiments is an installment in the ongoing methodological battles. Proponents of randomized and natural experiments are the descendants of the older inductivists. Their critics tend to argue that inductive inference without guiding theory is likely to be unreliable, making them the descendants of the older deductivists. I do not think that there is a straightforward solution to these debates. Deductivists rightly say that induction without theory is blind; but inductivists rightly respond that deduction from poor theory is empty.

Given this meta-disagreement, it seems unlikely that there will be widespread agreement on evidentiary standards soon. But agreement on evidentiary standards is needed for an agreement on what the facts are.

* * *

The "fact of technocratic disagreement" is, in my view, the main reason why epistocracy is a bad idea. If expert disagreement is likely to persist, as I have argued here, a major prerequisite of an epistocracy that does its job will not be met. If anything, I am thus more skeptical of at least the epistocratic version of technocracy, and mixed versions, than Friedman is, but for slightly different, albeit also epistemic, reasons.

REFERENCES

Alexandrova, Anna. 2017. *A Philosophy for the Science of Well-Being*. Oxford: Oxford University Press.

Angrist, Joshua, and Jörn-Steffen Pischke. 2010. "The Credibility Revolution in Empirical Economics: How Better Research Design Is Taking the Con Out of Econometrics." *Journal of Economic Perspectives* 24(2): 3–30.

Bareinboim, Elias, and Judea Pearl. 2014. "A General Algorithm for Deciding Transportability of Experimental Results." *Journal of Causal Inference* 1(1): 107–134.

Berlin, Isaiah. 1958. *Two Concepts of Liberty*. Oxford: Clarendon Press.

Bovens, Luc. 2009. "The Ethics of Nudge." In *Preference Change: Approaches from Philosophy, Economics, and Psychology*, ed. Till Grüne-Yanoff and Sven Ove Hansson. Dordrecht: Springer.

Brennan, Jason 2016. *Against Democracy*. Princeton: Princeton University Press.

Card, David, and Alan Krueger. 1995. *Myth and Measurement: The New Economics of the Minimum Wage*. Princeton: Princeton University Press.

Cartwright, Nancy, and Jeremy Hardie. 2012. *Evidence-Based Policy: A Practical Guide to Doing It Better*. Oxford: Oxford University Press.

Cartwright, Nancy, and Eileen Munro. 2010. "The Limitations of Randomized Controlled Trials in Predicting Effectiveness." *Journal of Evaluation in Clinical Practice* 16(2): 260–266.

Cialdini, Robert. 2001. *Influence: Science and Practice*, 4th ed. Boston: Allyn & Bacon.

Cialdini, Robert. 2016. *Pre-suasion*. New York: Simon & Schuster.

Collins, Harry, and Robert Evans. 2017. *Why Democracies Need Science*. Cambridge: Polity.

Easterly, William. 2013. *The Tyranny of Experts: Economists, Dictators, and the Forgotton Rights of the Poor.* New York: Basic Books.

Fiedler, Klaus. 1988. "The Dependence of the Conjunction Fallacy on Subtle Linguistic Factors." *Psychological Research* 50: 123-129.

Freedman, David. 1991. "Statistical Models and Shoe Leather." *Statistical Methodology* 21: 291-313.

Friedman, Jeffrey. 2019. *Power Without Knowledge: A Critique of Technocracy.* New York: Oxford University Press.

Friedman, Milton. 1953. "The Methodology of Positive Economics." In idem, *Essays in Positive Economics.* Chicago: University of Chicago Press.

Goldman, Alvin. 2001. "Experts: Which Ones Should You Trust?" *Philosophy and Phenomenological Research* 63(1): 85-110.

Guala, Francesco. 2010. "Extrapolation, Analogy, and Comparative Process Tracing." *Philosophy of Science* 77(5): 1070-1082.

Habermas, Jürgen. 1971. *Toward a Rational Society: Student Protest, Science, and Politics.* Boston: Beacon Press.

Harman, Oren, and Michael Dietrich. 2013. *Outsider Scientists: Routes to Innovation in Biology.* Chicago: University of Chicago Press.

Henrich, Joseph, Robert Boyd, Samuel Bowles, Colin Camerer, Ernst Fehr, Herbert Gintis, and Richard McElreath. 2001. "In Search of Homo Economicus: Behavioral Experiments in 15 Small-Scale Societies." *American Economic Review* 91(2): 73-78.

Holland, Paul. 1986. "Statistics and Causal Inference." *Journal of the American Statistical Association* 81(396): 945-960.

Hull, David, Peter Tessner, and Arthur Diamond. 1978. "Planck's Principle." *Science* 202(4369): 717-723.

Just, David, and Brian Roe. 2009. "Internal and External Validity in Economics Research: Tradeoffs Between Experiments, Field Experiments, Natural Experiments, and Field Data." *American Journal of Agricultural Economics* 91(5): 1266-1271.

Khosrowi, Donal, and Julian Reiss. 2019. "Evidence-Based Policy: The Tension Between the Epistemic and the Normative." *Critical Review* 31(2): 179-197.

Kirchgässner, Gebhard. 2003. "Empirical Economic Research and Economic Policy Advice: Some Remarks." In *Economic Policy Issues for the Next Decade*, ed. Karl Aiginger and Gernot Hutschenreiter. New York: Springer.

Kitcher, Philip. 2011. *Science in a Democratic Society.* Amherst, N.Y.: Prometheus.

Koppl, Roger. 2018. *Expert Failure.* Cambridge: Cambridge University Press.

Layard, Richard. 2005. *Happiness: Lessons from a New Science.* New York: Penguin.

Levy, David, and Sandra Peart. 2017. *Escape from Democracy: The Role of Experts and the Public in Economic Policy.* Cambridge: Cambridge University Press.

Lippmann, Walter. [1922] 1997. *Public Opinion.* New York: Free Press.

Neurath, Otto [1932] 1987. "Unified Science and Psychology." In *Unified Science*, ed. Brian McGuinness. Dordrecht: Reidel.

Nichols, Thomas. 2017. *The Death of Expertise: The Campaign Against Knowledge and Why It Matters.* Oxford: Oxford University Press.

Nussbaum, Martha. 2000. *Women and Human Development: The Capabilities Approach.* Cambridge: Cambridge University Press.

Planck, Max. 1950. *Scientific Autobiography and Other Papers*. New York: Philosophical Library.
Popper, Karl. 1976. "On the Logic of the Social Sciences." In Theodor Adorno, et al., *The Positivist Dispute in German Sociology*, trans. Glyn Adey and David Frisby. London: Heinemann.
Powers, Nicholas, Allen Blackman, Thomas Lyon, and Urvashi Narain. 2011. "Does Disclosure Reduce Pollution? Evidence from India's Green Rating Project." *Environmental and Resource Economics* 50: 131-155.
Reiss, Julian. 2008. *Error in Economics: Towards a More Evidence-Based Methodology*. London: Routledge.
Reiss, Julian. 2013. *Philosophy of Economics: A Contemporary Introduction*. New York: Routledge.
Reiss, Julian. 2017. "Fact-Value Entanglement in Positive Economics." *Journal of Economic Methodology* 24(2): 134-149.
Reiss, Julian. 2019. "Expertise, Agreement, and the Nature of Social Scientific Facts or: Against Epistocracy." *Social Epistemology* 33(2): 183-192.
Reiss, Julian. Unpublished. "The Perennial Methodenstreit: Observation, First Principles, and the Ricardian Vice." Department of Philosophy, Durham University.
Rudner, Richard. 1953. "The Scientist Qua Scientist Makes Value Judgments." *Philosophy of Science* 20(1): 1-6.
Sen, Amartya 1999. *Development as Freedom*. Oxford: Oxford University Press.
Sinn, Hans-Werner. 2014. *The Euro Trap: On Bursting Bubbles, Budgets, and Beliefs*. Oxford: Oxford University Press.
Solomon, Miriam. 2007. "The Social Epistemology of NIH Consensus Conferences." In *Establishing Medical Reality*, ed. Harold Kincaid and Jennifer McKitrick. New York: Springer.
Sorkin, Isaac. 2015. "Are There Long-Run Effects of the Minimum Wage?" *Review of Economic Dynamics* 18(2): 306-333.
Steel, Daniel. 2008. "Across the Boundaries: Extrapolation in Biology and Social Science." Oxford: Oxford University Press.
Turner, Stephen 2001. "What Is the Problem with Experts?" *Social Studies of Science* 31(1): 123-149.
Tversky, Amos, and Daniel Kahneman. 1983. "Extensional versus Intuitive Reasoning: The Conjunction Fallacy in Probability Judgment." *Psychological Review* 90(4): 293–315.
Van Bouwel, Jeroen, ed. 2009. *The Social Sciences and Democracy*. Houndmills: Palgrave Macmillan.
van Eersel, Gerdien, Gabriela Koppenol-Gonzales, and Julian Reiss. 2019. "Extrapolation of Experimental Results through Analogical Reasoning from Latent Classes." *Philosophy of Science* 86(2): 219-235.
Wallis, W. Allen, and Milton Friedman. 1942. "The Empirical Derivation of Indifference Functions." *Studies in Mathematical Economics and Econometrics in Memory of Henry Schultz*, ed. O. Lange, F. McIntyre and T. O. Yntema. Chicago: University of Chicago Press.

Jeffrey Friedman

POLITICAL EPISTEMOLOGY, TECHNOCRACY, AND POLITICAL ANTHROPOLOGY: REPLY TO A SYMPOSIUM ON *POWER WITHOUT KNOWLEDGE*

ABSTRACT: *A political epistemology that enables us to determine if political actors are likely to know what they need to know must be rooted in an ontology of the actors and of the human objects of their knowledge; that is, a political anthropology. The political anthropology developed in* Power Without Knowledge *envisions human beings as creatures whose conscious actions are determined by their interpretations of what seem to them to be relevant circumstances; and whose interpretations are, in turn, determined by webs of belief built from somewhat heterogeneous streams of incoming ideas. This anthropology, then, has two components. Ideational* heterogeneity *undermines the aspiration of technocracy to predict human behavior and the aspiration of social science to arrive at lawlike generalizations about it. Ideational* determinism, *however, which is less important than ideational heterogeneity to the critique of technocracy, may be more important to generating epistemological approaches to other forms of politics, all of which involve the actions of human beings who, as such, are largely at the mercy of the fallible ideas to which they have been exposed.*

It is a pleasure to be able to reply to such a diverse and probing set of responses to my *Power Without Knowledge: A Critique of Technocracy* (Oxford University Press, 2019). The book tries to establish, above all, that human beings are ideationally heterogeneous, as suggested by how surprising and interesting we are to each other. This symposium bears out the book's thesis, as my interlocutors' responses are consistently surprising and interesting, at least to me.

Perhaps the greatest surprise is that none of them disputes the book's core argument: that human actions are ideationally determined; that the ideas that determine people's actions are (to various degrees) heterogeneous; and that, for practical purposes, this means that people's actions are (to some extent) unpredictable, or surprising. One implication of this argument is that virtually all contemporary social science and social theory is unsound, so I expected it to receive at least a little pushback. However, the radical implications of the argument do not seem to have been fully registered by most of my interlocutors, who grant the argument in general terms but minimize its ramifications by recourse to the very social science and social theory that it calls into question. Thus, a clear majority of my critics tries to subject the argument to the positivist standards of proof that are one of its primary targets. (By positivism, I mean "the widespread assumption that by probing behavioral 'data' we can discover reliable behavioral homogeneities—without reference to, and even in defiance of, agents' ideas"; 201). The other participants in the symposium accept the argument's radical implications but, in the main, wonder if there is any escape from the technocratic paralysis to which they think the argument leads.

I will engage with both types of interlocutor in section III, after a brief outline of the book in section II. In section IV, I discuss two responses that challenge technocracy on democratic grounds. These responses are orthogonal to the argument of the book, as they ask whether this argument is applicable to non-technocratic democratic politics. I think it is, but perhaps only by shifting the anthropological emphasis from ideational heterogeneity, which is essential to my critique of technocracy, to ideational determinism, which raises questions (to which I have no answers) about the determination of democratic action by the streams of information emanating, inter alia, from the mass media. The article closes with a list of errata in *Power Without Knowledge*.

Before getting underway, I would like to address something else about which I received little pushback from my interlocutors: the broad definition of technocracy upon which everything in *Power Without Knowledge* depends. Because of the positivistic assumptions of so many of my critics, section III will be devoted in large part to questions in the philosophy of social science that implicate *any* political anthropology. In section I, therefore, I want to suggest how the broad definition of technocracy leads, in particular, to the political anthropology of ideational determination and heterogeneity.

I. TECHNOCRACY, POLITICAL ANTHROPOLOGY, AND THE PHILOSOPHY OF SOCIAL (HUMAN) SCIENCE

Power Without Knowledge defines technocracy as rule by *anyone* who claims knowledge of how to solve social and economic problems: not just "cognitive elites" who make this claim, but ordinary citizens, too.

In my view, the chief merit of this very broad definition, ironically, is that it requires the political epistemologist to be quite specific about the type of knowledge being theorized. Typically, political epistemologists have pursued the question of the knowledge available to "the many" rather than "the few" or vice versa, with the limited specificity of these two categories displacing any specificity at all about the types of knowledge that the few or the many need. By instead treating the rulers as indefinite in number but distinctive in the types of knowledge they need, we can assess how *realistic* our epistemology is by asking how likely it is that under specified conditions, claims for those specific types of knowledge will be reliable. Answering this question about technocracy, in turn, will require us to articulate a political anthropology: a statement of the conditions under which human perceivers will be able to anticipate the actions of those whose behavior might be altered so as to alleviate social and economic problems.

The political anthropology in *Power Without Knowledge* consists of two claims. First, humanity is ideationally determined. Thus, our conscious behavior is motivated by our ideas—contrary (as I will argue, at length, in section III) to the characteristic assumptions of positivist social science, economic theory, social psychology, and grand social theory. Second, ideas are, to some presumptively significant degree, heterogeneous across individuals. (I call this "the presumption of ideational heterogeneity"; 147-48.) These two claims ground an internal critique of technocracy that is unlike what we would get from a social-scientific or social-theoretic approach, in contrast to an anthropological approach. The problem posed for technocracy by ideational determination and heterogeneity is not, for example, that "modern society" is too "complex" (in the sense of containing too many interacting agents or independent variables) for its problems to be solved by central planners, as maintained by grand social theorists such as Hayek, systems theorists such as Luhmann, and complexity theorists such as those in the Santa Fe school. Rather, the problem is that virtually all solutions to social and economic problems require manipulations of the behavior of *anonymous others* so they will act in ways that will rectify the poverty, poor education, drug abuse, or other tangible "social and economic problems" caused by these anonymous others' actions. This entails being able to predict anonymous others' behavior reliably. Thus, we need to know what reliable prediction would presuppose about the human beings being predicted and, too, about the human beings predicting them—respectively, the objects and the subjects of technocratic action. The epistemic problem here is not that we may lack sufficient knowledge of the mysteries of society, but sufficient knowledge of the mysteries of individuals. Thus, we need a political anthropology, not a social theory, and that is what *Power Without Knowledge* provides.

The standard definition of technocracy, as rule by epistemic elites ("the few"), effaces both anthropological issues and issues in the philosophy of social science, and thus it elides the question of whether—despite their claims to expertise—epistemic elites might be unable to get a handle on the epistemic problem of behavioral prediction. This is because the standard definition does not specify the types of knowledge required of technocrats. This leads to complacency about whether epistemic elites can realistically be expected to possess the requisite knowledge, even if they are credentialed specialists in social science. The standard definition excludes by fiat the possibility that social scientists' knowledge of human behavior is unreliable, as it treats their knowledge *claims* as reliable "knowledge," conflating their opinions about the truth with truth itself. Another defect of the standard definition is that by equating technocracy and epistocracy, it obscures the fact that the negative-utilitarian goal of epistocratic policy making—to relieve human distress by solving, preventing, or at least mitigating social and economic problems—also animates a great deal of contemporary mass politics.

To avoid these defects and others (15-21), I redefine technocracy as a fundamentally epistemic project rather than a fundamentally elitist one. A technocracy, in this view, is a polity that attempts to solve, mitigate, or prevent social and economic conditions that cause suffering or discomfort—regardless of whether the polity does this by empowering elites or masses or (as in most modern polities) both. What matters, for a technocracy, is not the number of those governing but whether they have reliable (not perfect) knowledge of: [1] the extent and seriousness of social problems, [2] their causes, [3] the efficacy of proposed solutions, and [4] the solutions' costs, both anticipated and unintended (46). With this epistemic catalogue in hand, we can realistically assess whether the knowledge claims of any particular group of ordinary citizens ("citizen-technocrats") or elites ("epistocrats") are likely to be reliable. In particular, item [4] may be problematic if people's actions are determined by unpredictably heterogeneous ideas. Thus, the redefinition of technocracy, by specifying the types of knowledge needed by technocrats, points to the need for a philosophy of social science oriented toward the question of whether, and under what conditions, human behavior is predictable—that is, a philosophy of *human* science.

Although I will refer to "social science" and "the social sciences" when discussing positivism, neoclassical economics, and other ideationally insensitive approaches to behavioral prediction, "social" distracts us from the fact that these "sciences" are trying to predict *people.* People are not iron filings arranged by the magnetism of hypostasized social forces or pushed around by hypostasized social structures. So I will call the anthropological alternative to social hypostasization "human science," although not in the positivistic sense of "science": an enterprise grounded in and seeking for laws or lawlike tendencies. It is scientific in a different sense: it is grounded in empirical realities that are ignored by social "science" and social theory; and it seeks to understand people, and perhaps even predict their behavior, on the basis of those realities—"anthropological" realities.

II. *POWER WITHOUT KNOWLEDGE* IN BRIEF

The book's Introduction fully explains the rationale for my redefinition of technocracy, and suggests the need for an internal critique of technocracy that, by stipulating the negative-utilitarian ends of a technocracy, can focus on its epistemic capacity for achieving those ends.

Chapter 1 then makes a preemptive strike against *naïve technocratic realism*. This is the view that technocratic knowledge is self-evident—which, if true, would obviate the need for an epistemological examination of technocratic efficacy. If technocratic knowledge is self-evident, then the epistemic reliability of technocracy cannot be questioned. If the four types of technocratic knowledge are matters of veridical intuition or "common sense," then we need engage in no critical theorizing about whether we are likely to have access to reliable technocratic knowledge: such knowledge is immediately apparent. Thus, if we fail to solve social and economic problems, it can be due only to failures of intention, not failures of knowledge: we know what to do but fail to do it—defeated by the bad intentions of special interests, self-interested social classes, or corrupt politicians. This, of course, is how we often think of politics: as a contest of good against evil, where both sides *know* who is good and who is evil because this is self-evident. This view of politics allows for little genuine confusion or unwitting, innocent ignorance. The only epistemic problem, in this view of politics, is posed by the liar or propagandist who throws sand in people's eyes, blinding them to what would otherwise be obvious.

However, this naïvely realistic view of *politics* cannot account for the fact of political disagreement. And naïve political realism applied to *technocratic* issues yields naïve technocratic politics, which cannot account for the fact of technocratic disagreement, i.e., the legitimate contestability of all four types of knowledge, particularly the fourth (38-46). *Unintended* technocratic costs, as such, cannot possibly be self-evident, so if unintended costs are possible, technocratic disagreement is justifiable, in principle. The political anthropology presented in Chapters 2 and 3 will explore some of the conditions of this possibility.

However, the critique of naïve technocratic realism in Chapter 1 is not, in itself, a critique of technocratic knowledge. The former critique suggests the need for the latter, but the latter would have to show not only that technocratic knowledge claims are not self-evidently true, but that they are, or tend to be, false or unreliable. In order to show this, one would either have to contend that specific first-order technocratic claims are false or that there is some second-order reason for suspecting that all such claims are problematic, as opposed to false. The first-order critical strategy, however, would beg the epistemic question by unwarrantedly treating the critic's own first-order technocratic knowledge claims as stemming from a position of epistemic adequacy that is not defended as adequate on second-order grounds. Too often, political epistemologists have begged the question in just this manner—judging mass democracy, for example, to be epistemically unreliable if it endorses policies with which a given theorist disagrees or reliable if it endorses policies with which a theorist agrees, but failing to explain why we should treat the theorist's policy opinions as touchstones of the truth (61–71). If we are interested in testing the epistemic warrant of certain types of knowledge claim, we cannot exempt our own claims of that type from the same tests by treating others' knowledge claims skeptically but our own as if they are self-evidently reliable. A rigorous political epistemology, therefore, would bracket the epistemologist's first-order technocratic opinions and concentrate on identifying second-order reasons for confidence in or skepticism about *categories* of such opinions (71–75).

That is what Chapters 2 and 3 attempt to do. They do not contend that reliable technocratic knowledge is impossible (as some of my interlocutors think) or that technocratic knowledge is unreliable merely because it is not self-evident (as others think). Very little human knowledge is self-evidently true, but this does not make all human knowledge claims (other than the *cogito*) false, nor even unreliable. Chapter 1's challenge to naïve technocratic realism, then, does not cast doubt on the reliability of technocratic knowledge claims or knowledge claimants; it merely points out that the latter, being human, are fallible. Fallibilism entails a healthy skepticism about all knowledge claims, but not an argument against any of them or against the reliability of all of them: the fallibility of knowledge does not entail its inaccuracy. Therefore, the book's critique of the reliability of certain types of technocratic knowledge claim does not amount to a Pyrrhonean skepticism about them—because it does *not* rest on the first chapter's critique of naïve technocratic realism.

That said, Chapter 1 does have implications for the chapters that follow. The main implication is the need, in a rational technocracy, for some kind of technocratic "science"—in the minimal sense of an attempt to get beyond our untested intuitions about the four types of technocratic knowledge. Thus, we will need a philosophy of science that will allow normative political epistemologists to assess the reliability (or, more accurately, the conditions of reliability) of the four types of knowledge claim. Such a philosophy of science, in turn, will presuppose a description of the epistemic position of human beings in mass societies, because both technocrats and the agents who are the objects of their policy making are human beings situated in mass societies. The science in question, then, is what is typically designated social science; the better term would be human science.

Chapters 2 and 3 develop a conception of modern humanity that is appropriate to evaluating the reliability of various categories of technocratic knowledge claim. It is worth emphasizing that this political anthropology does not contradict Marx's most important insight: that what we take to be natural and necessary may simply be historical and contingent.[1] The term *anthropology* is justified by the fact that it is fair to identify human beings as naturally (i.e., evolutionarily) "ideational" creatures. But the particular problems facing a technocracy are contingent upon two post-Paleolithic historical conditions of humanity: (1) the fact that in mass societies, we tend to be anonymous to one another; and (2) the fact that we are all exposed to streams of ideas and experiences that are to some extent variable, affecting each of us somewhat differently. The second condition grounds the thesis of presumptive, but defeasible, ideational heterogeneity.

Both of the conditions are empirical tendencies that make people's ideas somewhat difficult to discern. This difficulty can, to some extent, be expected to cause problems for technocratic behavioral prediction given the thesis of our necessary ideational determination (139-43): the dependence of each human being's conscious actions on webs of belief (which, in turn, are presumptively heterogeneous). The deterministic element, accessible to introspection and plausibly enabled by the size and structure of the human brain, is the element of the book's political anthropology that qualifies as truly anthropological, as it extends back into the Paleolithic and beyond and seems, therefore, to better capture the "human essence" than historically contingent notions such as *Homo politicus* (a vision that may have been peculiarly relevant only in classical Athens), *Homo economicus* (a product of eighteenth-century Scotland), *Homo socius* (a nineteenth-century reaction against *Homo economicus*), or *Homo faber* (an anthropologization of features that became highly visible during the Industrial Revolution). While it might seem that one could say of ideational heterogeneity that it overinflates mass mediation and anonymity into permanent and essential human characteristics, my intention is to distinguish these clearly historical and therefore (potentially) transient features of modern life from ideational determination, which truly is permanent.

This is not to say, however, that the *idea* of ideational determination does not have historical origins. One distant historical source, but by no means the only one (one might also mention Aquinas and Spinoza), is Leibniz's notion of "moral" (as opposed to mechanical and metaphysical) determination; a more proximate but implicit source, elaborated upon in Chapter 2, is the political epistemology expressed by Walter Lippmann and challenged by John Dewey in the 1920s.

Lippmann, reflecting on the overabundance of information about politics and policy in his era (vividly embodied in a plethora of newspapers), recognized the need to *interpret* information, not merely register it as "data." Only by interpreting what it all means can we select some information as relevant, plausible, and indeed intelligible, screening out all the rest as irrelevant, implausible, or nonsensical. This is how we decide which newspapers to read, which articles to read, and which of the claims related in the articles, as well as which of the interpretations there related, to believe.

By calling our interpretations of information "stereotypes," Lippmann departed from the hermeneutical tradition by emphasizing the partiality and fallibility of our interpretations. We need to interpret the world in order to distinguish between plausible and implausible information about it. But the interpretations are produced by fallible and ignorant creatures, and thus *may* be incorrect. They may not get at the real meaning of it all at all. Standing behind Lippmann's interpretivism seems to be a roughly Kantian application to politics of Leibniz's derivation, from the principle of sufficient reason, of the conclusion that God's decisions must be determined by something: if not heteronomous "mechanical" causation or necessitarian "metaphysical" causation, then "moral" causation (*la cause morale*), or the determination of God's actions by His antecedent ideas (Leibniz [1709] 1951, 124). Extended to human beings, this analysis suggests that our actions may not be for "the best" (as in "the best of all possible worlds") because human ideas, unlike divine ones, are fallible.

In Chapter 3, I move beyond ideational determinism to ideational heterogeneity. Lippmann was discussing the fallible interpretations of political subjects, such as citizens, journalists, and politicians, but the objects of technocratic policy, too, are fundamentally interpretive creatures. Their interpretations, too, and thus their actions, are determined by fallible ideas that enter their webs of belief through fallible processes of cognition and communication. Under modern conditions, these processes produce presumptively ubiquitous ideational heterogeneity, which is likely to render technocratic prediction unreliable if this tendency is not counteracted.

The ubiquity of the tendency, or the defeasible presumption of ideational heterogeneity (147), is established through reflection on the differences in the streams of experience and information we each receive, which seems to explain the surprisingness of people's ideas and the frequency with which we disagree with one another. Fortunately (for technocracy), the same reflections suggest that ideational heterogeneity is counteracted, to some extent, by the homogenizing effect of mass communication and other factors, which can be expected to introduce a degree of ideational sameness alongside ideational difference. Thus, a human science that reflects modern conditions sufficiently well as to contribute reliable technocratic knowledge would need to attempt, case by case, to determine where the balance lies between, on the one hand, homogeneous ideas that might be imposed upon masses of people by such means as uniform education or mass culture, and, on the other, the heterogeneity presumptively created by variations in the streams of ideas reaching each individual member of a mass society. I label this empirical balance-seeking "judicious" technocratic policy making (171–77).

Chapters 1–3 constitute Part I of *Power Without Knowledge*. In Part II (Chapters 4–6), I contend that contemporary technocracy is far from judicious. Chapter 4 argues that the sets of ideas that currently exert the greatest (homogeneous) influence on technocratic policy making—

positivism, neoclassical economics, and behavioral economics—are pathologically hostile to a judicious recognition of ideational heterogeneity. Chapter 5 contends that, in addition, epistocrats are likely to be dogmatic about any theory or ideology that enables them to see human behavior as predictable—such as positivism, neoclassical economics, or behavioral economics. Dogmatism, I contend, is natural to experts of all kinds because of how interpretive beings rationally learn: by selecting for information that is rendered legible and plausible by an interpretation that appears to be sound, while screening out interpretation-incongruent information. This process of selective information acquisition should produce a growing quantity of knowledge that biases one's web of belief in favor of the interpretation that makes the selection possible. In addition to pathologically anti-ideational ideas, then, contemporary epistocracy faces the challenge of epistocrats caught up in dogmatic "spirals of conviction." Finally, Chapter 6 suggests that the popular culture of *democratic* technocracy is so naïvely realistic, at present, that questions of unintended consequences and heterogeneity are rarely even considered. We therefore face a Hobson's choice, for now, between rule by doctrinaire but knowledgeable epistocrats—whose knowledge, however, does not encompass agents' ideas—and citizen-technocrats who are ignorant of the possibility of heterogeneity or any other source of unintended consequences; but who are, by virtue of their ignorance, less likely than epistocrats to be dogmatic.

The Hobson's choice of technocracy expresses uncertainty about whether epistocracy or citizen-technocracy is preferable. Similarly, however, it is uncertain whether technocracy of any kind—even a judicious technocracy—can be considered legitimate, according to the absolute standard of doing more good than harm in its attempts to solve, mitigate, or prevent social and economic problems. Even if one accepts my argument for presumptive ideational heterogeneity, I cannot establish the *magnitude* of the problems this may cause for technocracy. That quantity (if it even makes sense to think of it as a quantity) will depend not only on the presence, from case to case, of identifiable ideational homogeneities that render behavioral prediction possible, but on the ability of *particular* technocrats to identify these *particular* homogeneities competently and generate accurate behavioral predictions based on them. Sometimes they will succeed, sometimes they will fail. But there is no way to know, theoretically or empirically, how often success or failure will occur, the size of the improvement in the human condition that will stem from the successes, or whether diminutions in it, stemming from the failures, will be negligible or disastrous. Therefore, as I suggest in the preface to Part III (317-19), normative theorists need to replace the internal technocratic standard of doing more good than harm with a comparative standard that allows a ranking of different types of technocracy based on the likelihood that any one of them will do *less* harm and *more* good than the others. This way, we may be able to make educated guesses about *relative* magnitudes even though we cannot estimate their absolute value.

Thus, it is logical to guess that judicious technocracies are preferable to injudicious ones, because the knowledge of technocrats who try to take account of agents' diverse ideas is likely to be more reliable than the knowledge of technocrats who do not. Similarly, an "exitocracy" might be preferable to both judicious and injudicious technocracy (Chapter 7). An exitocracy is a technocracy that enables people to exit from what they perceive as problems that they personally face. Exit allows them to make use of their relatively reliable knowledge of whether they are personally helped by trading one situation for another —in contrast to their relatively unreliable knowledge of the extent and causes of the social and economic problems of masses of anonymous others, and the effects of society-wide attempts to solve, mitigate, or prevent these problems (324-32). Yet exitocracy is not a cure-all for the problem of ideational heterogeneity. The exit mechanism cannot be used to supply most public goods (342-43), the exit mechanism itself must be technocratically designed to achieve its desired effect (340-41), and people's "knowledge" of their own personal dissatisfaction, and their correlations of this condition with the personal circumstances from which they might then want to exit, is far from perfect (332-34).

Therefore, the epistemic critique of technocracy does not culminate in Chapter 7's institutional proposal for including exit mechanisms in a judicious technocracy. The more important goal is a cultural critique of the pathological modes of thought that are grounded in non-ideational anthropologies, such as those of contemporary social scientists: a critique of the inhumanity of the culture out of which these approaches grow, and which they help to perpetuate (343-45).

III. RESPONSES TO CRITICS

Before responding to each of the symposiasts—Jonathan Benson, Étienne Brown, Kevin Elliott, Oscar Larsson, Adam Lerner, Eric MacGilvray, Alfred Moore, Zeynep Pamuk, Robert Reamer, Julian Reiss, and Zoe Phillips Williams—I would like to thank them for their stimulating contributions and express special gratitude to Paul Gunn, who invited the contributors and guest edited the symposium. It is my rare pleasure to be able to devote the space necessary to consider, in depth, each of the symposiasts' main concerns.

Proceeding thematically, I will first discuss three contributions (from Brown and Williams, Elliott, and Moore) that draw out the implications of the broad definition of technocracy for our understanding of populism. Then I turn to six interlocutors who, in various ways, criticize the book from implicitly positivistic directions ranging from methodological collectivism (Lerner) to methodological individualism (Pamuk, Reamer, Reiss, MacGilvray) and even post-structuralism (Larsson). Finally, I discuss contributors who express qualms about exitocracy and propose alternatives to it (Benson, Brown and Williams again, and Reamer again). In part IV I will conclude by addressing questions raised by Brown and Williams, and by Moore, about the relationship between technocracy and democracy.

Populism as Technocratic (Brown and Williams, Elliott, Moore)

In line with the standard, epistocratic definition of technocracy, criticism of technocracy has tended to target its elitism and its depoliticization of the masses—with the perverse implication that egalitarianism and politicization are pitted against technocratic knowledge, which the standard definition treats as being monopolized by technocratic elites. But why should we assume that "the many" lack reliable technocratic knowledge, and how is it that the epistocratic "few" are supposed to have it?

We surely do not want merely to stipulate epistocrats' possession of this knowledge by defining them as *adequately* knowledgeable "experts," rubber-stamping their epistemic pretensions by definitional fiat. If we are going to inspect these pretensions critically, we need to define epistocratic knowledge as a possibility, not necessarily an actuality. This entails redefining technocracy as rule by those who *claim* to know. But epistocrats are not the only ones who claim to know. Ordinary citizens often claim to know the extent and causes of social and economic problems and how best to solve, mitigate, or prevent them. A definition of technocracy that does not beg the question of whether these claims are justified, or of the circumstances under which they may be justified, should allow that technocracy may be run by epistocrats, "citizen-technocrats," or both: that is, by anyone who makes technocratic knowledge claims (claims about one or more of the four types of technocratic knowledge in the case of a particular social or economic problem).

This redefinition allows Kevin Elliott and Alfred Moore to notice a neglected aspect of contemporary populism: its technocratic aspect. As Moore puts it, the redefinition of technocracy leads to the view that "parties compete to offer solutions to social problems, epistocrats claim to be able to solve social problems without input from voters, and populists claim to know how to solve social problems if only they could win the acclaim of the majority and execute their program without obstruction or compromise." Moore, however, is not sure this view is accurate, as it omits populists' "hostility to democratic pluralism and to the dispersal of power implied by party competition."

Yet Elliott's analysis suggests that populist anti-pluralism is a *function* of its technocratic orientation, at least in the United States. "When a populist leader inveighs against the media or another party," he writes, "it is invariably on the grounds that journalists or opposition politicians are trying to block the leader's agenda, which (at least ostensibly) aims to solve the people's problems. The sin of mediating institutions is thus not interfering with the mystical communion between the leader and the people but instead preventing the leader from smoothly cleaving the Gordian knot of the country's problems." I would add that the notion that populists are against pluralism per se dissolves, in the U.S. case, once we notice that what may look like opposition to plural *interests* is actually opposition to *special* interests that, as such, are antithetical to the technocratic mandate to solve *common* problems (Friedman 2019a). Populists stormed the Capitol not because they opposed pluralism but because they opposed what they saw as the attempt by one party (and the media) to steal an election won by the people's tribune; they did not oppose elections among plural parties, but elections whose rules had, they thought, been twisted and violated. And their devotion to their tribune was based not on his attempt to "unify" the people (an attempt made, in fact, by President Biden), but by President Trump's claim that he was draining the "swamp" that drowned all attempts to solve the people's problems. That this claim may be laughable to us does not reduce its importance to his followers.

The populist preoccupation with special interests is reflected in Étienne Brown and Zoe Phillips Williams's contribution, which adduces the spending of special interests on lobbying, and the efforts of fossil-fuel companies to cover up evidence of global warming, to suggest that sometimes real-world technocratic disagreement is not in good faith, such that "the fact of technocratic disagreement" is sometimes a sham. As they acknowledge, however, I did not deny that. I claimed only that recourse to the argument from special interests is naïvely realistic if it is not buttressed by evidence—that is, if it is treated as an a priori, all-purpose explanation of the failure to solve the people's problems, thereby excluding the possibility of epistemic failures. This is not to suggest that fossil-fuel companies' denial of global warming is a unique or rare case of bad intentions in real-world technocratic policy debate. But the fact of genuine or honest technocratic disagreement is established a priori, by means of reflection on the possibility of unintended consequences, not by cherry picking this or that real-world example. To avoid cherry picking and, more important, to avoid begging the epistemic question, we should not draw general lessons from any specific case or cases unless we have a second-order reason to.[2] Otherwise we will block the possibility of a truly open-minded political epistemology by starting from our own first-order technocratic preoccupations, which we treat as so self-evidently warranted that they can ground "knowledge" of the disingenuousness of technocratic opinions with which we disagree.

Moore's view of populism suffers or may suffer, I think, from a subtler problem than reliance on first-order opinions, but it is a problem that has a similar structure: the projection onto other political actors of the theorist's own preoccupations. A common preoccupation of political theorists in our day is political pluralism, and it is easy to assume that our fellow citizens share our preoccupations, such that when *we* see populists objectively threatening political pluralism through their actions, we assume that this is what they subjectively intend to do. However, at least in the United States (I cannot say anything about populism elsewhere), there is little evidence that populists share this preoccupation—even as there is plenty of evidence that they are, in reality, preoccupied with solving social and economic problems (Friedman 2019a). In this view, populists oppose this or that political group or party not on the grounds that there should be a unified will of the people—a matter that we have no reason to think is pondered by populists, as Elliott points out—but on the grounds that this *particular* group or party, the populists' opponent of the hour, is a pack of liars in hock to special interests who aim to consolidate their own wealth and power at the expense of everyone else.

However, reconceptualizing populism in this way—as a fundamentally simplistic technocratic mindset, not a fundamentally antidemocratic one—does not preclude the existence of other subjective dimensions of the phenomenon, such as the possibility that, as Moore writes, populism and epistocracy "interact and feed off one another in a mutually reinforcing dynamic, where each responds to the perceived excesses of the other, and thereby confirms the other's worst fears." In my view there is such a dynamic, at least in the United States: between experts and populists who believe that the experts' expertise is bogus (ibid.). The dynamic, I propose, got started when the journalists who retail experts' claims to the public lost the trust of significant segments of their audience, who retreated to alternative media sources that aggravated distrust not only of mainstream journalism but of the experts whom mainstream journalists consider legitimate. (I will say more about this in section IV.) In response, however, the journalists, the experts themselves, and the journalistic audiences that accede to their expertise, could not help but see the populists' rejection of (what populists see as) bogus expertise as a rejection of expertise itself, of facts, of science, of reason, and even of truth: hence the fashionable "post-truth" trope (ibid.). Populists themselves, of course, do not see themselves this way, so they interpret the claim that they have rejected facts, science, reason, and truth as suggesting an infuriating conspiracy to insulate expert "elites" from critical scrutiny.

The post-truth trope, then, seems to me to be seriously misleading. Even if it were logically coherent to *believe* that one's own beliefs are "beyond truth" (and I do not see how it could be), if one somehow attained this posture one would hardly be *angry* at people who have different beliefs (those who profess a belief in the truth, the facts, reason, and so on). One might laugh at their foolishness, but one would not be infuriated at them. Any account of populism, I think, needs to understand this fury—as an epistemic (rather than post-epistemic) account enables us to do.

Positivism I: Post-Structuralism, Technocracy, and Grand Theory (Larsson)

A majority of my interlocutors shares, in one degree or another, an unspoken commitment to what *Power Without Knowledge* calls positivism: the assumption that, in principle, any objective variable that can be empirically correlated with a human behavior in a given time and place should be considered a cause of the behavior everywhere and always, or at least within the bounds set by an epoch within which these laws, and not others, operate.[3] This surprises me because all of my interlocutors are political theorists, who I assumed would be as skeptical of positivism as I am.

In different ways and to different degrees, Larsson, Lerner, MacGilvray, Pamuk, Reamer, and Reiss seem to understand *Power Without Knowledge* as a plea to add new independent variables—ideational heterogeneity and dogmatism—to the list of the determinants of human action that have been proposed by positivist social scientists and social theorists. Understandably, then, all of these contributors, in one way or another, worry that I fail to provide "empirical evidence"—that is, positivistic evidence—that would establish the significance of these new variables. To combat this unexpected expansion of technocratic thinking into the precincts of political theory, I will devote a great deal of attention to the positivist dimension of their contributions, at the cost of scanting some of their other concerns. What is at stake, I think, is not just the legitimacy of technocracy but the possibility of social science and social theory, the nature of the human, and the question of whether political theorists should proceed as if human "nature" is indistinguishable from automatic, mindless, "mechanically determined"nature.

Oscar Larsson's contribution is the most surprising of this group. I would not have expected that anyone could produce a post-structuralist defense of technocracy, but that is what Larsson's Foucauldian positivism has allowed him to do. Insofar as we take his contribution as representative of post-structuralist thought (and I allow that perhaps we should not: it certainly flies in the face of Deleuze and Guattari's post-structuralism and is, as we shall see, in an obvious sense antagonistic to Foucault's), his ability to pull this off may suggest that, for all the sophistication of Foucault's theorizing about power, his theorization of knowledge is lacking. Larsson simply takes it for granted that "we possess substantial knowledge" about how to solve people's social and economic problems, begging the question asked by *Power Without Knowledge*. I had not seen, before reading his paper, that such a glaring species of naïve technocratic realism might be justified by Foucault's understanding of the relationship between the individual and the social, or that this understanding maps directly onto a positivist view of what and how "we" know.

At the end of Part I of *Power Without Knowledge* (174-76), I called a certain oracular mode of social analysis "grand theory" and named not only Foucault but Durkheim, Freud, Hayek, Marx, Montesquieu, Rousseau, Smith, and Tocqueville as some of its most prominent exemplars. What makes these theorists oracular is that they offer a synoptic view of something—modern society—that can be "seen" only by homogenizing or ignoring the heterogeneous ideas of the individuals of which it consists. The seer can only convey the vision in the abstract, as a revelation of reality abstracted from the particularity of the ideas of those whose actions create the reality. Any theory of society, social forces, or social structures will have this abstract cast, with the attendant risk of error. As a rough way of putting the issue, no grand social theory is compatible with history, so long as the latter is seen as an account of the (ideationally) contingent actions of concrete, living, particular human beings (regardless of whether they are elites or "ordinary" people). Any given grand theory, then, may be an illusion, not merely because all theories abstract from reality (in the manner of an ideal type), but because grand theories *ignore* the reality of heterogeneous ideas, which is the very stuff of history as the analysis of contingent (yet causally determined) actions.

This is not to deny that it may be possible to gain limited insight into specific belief homogeneities of historically particular segments of humanity; this is what judicious "social" or human scientists would do. In the previous section I tried to do something similar, by describing an array of American populists' actual, contingent beliefs in support of a theory about their peculiar behavior, not the behavior of everyone in all modern societies. Yet this required speculating about millions of people I have not met, based on journalistic and survey research, recounted elsewhere (Friedman 2019a), that is sure to incompletely report the views of those being directly discussed and, perhaps, to be misleading about both them and those to whom my theory of populism extrapolates. A judicious or ideationally sensitive human science would consist of just this type of speculation—which is so obviously tenuous that it would always, clearly, be contestable and would always, one hopes, be contested. Despite its tenuousness, however, the limited, non-synoptic objectives of this type of speculation would not be impossible to achieve, just as the difficulty of doing intellectual history well does not prevent intellectual historians from sometimes doing it well (160-68).

In contrast, both the form of grand theory and its content push the reader of any given grand theory toward uncritical acceptance or uncritical rejection. The power of a given grand theory—the degree to which one considers "the division of labor" or "spontaneous order" or "anomie" or "capital" or "neoliberalism" or "power-knowledge" or "epistemes" or "discourses" to be the key to unlocking the mysteries of the otherwise-unseen society, and thus the degree to which one considers the propagator of this vision a genius or a poseur—stems not from incomplete and possibly misleading evidence but from the verisimilitude, for the consumer of grand theory, of the picture to which the theory contributes. This aesthetic quality is, as a practical matter, uncriticizable. As Simmel put it, "the very image of the *whole*, which seems to imply the fullest and purest objectivity, reflects the peculiarity of its possessor much more than the objective image of any particular thing usually reflects it" (quoted, 174). This may account for the tendency of grand social theories to turn into ideologies, and for the biographies of grand theorists to be either hagiographies or exercises in character assassination.

Another way of putting this is that the adept of any given grand theory will respond favorably to it as if it is a self-evident first-order truth. But in a world of heterogeneous interpretive beings, the beguiling metaphors of grand theory are likely to be, in fact, not revelations but mirages that dissolve when we walk up close and squint hard at the brush strokes portraying the unseen whole. We do this when we inquire about the actual ideas of the real people who actually constitute the whole—in their particularity. But the critique of grand theory stems not from a preference for the particular over the universal, a rejection of theory per se, or radical skepticism, but from a desire for historical accuracy, grounded in attentiveness to one specific factor that is necessarily abstracted from any grand theory: the individually determined contingency of all human beings' ideas. Given this fact, historical accuracy cannot be achieved by explaining behavior through the social forces and structures putatively identified by grand theorists, as this has the effect of effacing the heterogeneous historical sources of specific individuals' actual beliefs and actions.

If, however, we take this fact to be given, are we not merely committing ourselves to a different grand social theory, the anthropology of ideational determinism and heterogeneity, which posits the individually determined contingency of all human beings' ideas? I don't think so, because the object of this anthropology is not a possibly unknowable social whole, but the knowable nature of the human beings within it. We can know our ideational determination a priori and our ideational heterogeneity a posteriori, or so I argue in Chapter 3.

In effect, I think, Larsson confirms the parallel drawn, at the end of that chapter, between injudicious technocrats' and grand theorists' obliviousness to ideational heterogeneity. The heterogeneities noticed from on high by grand theorists—the many behavioral determinants they identify, such as classes, personality types, identities, institutions, social structures, and social forces—are, from the perspective of the individuals below, plural, objective *homogeneities* that are falsely supposed to determine them (us) non-contingently (non-idiosyncratically) and non-ideationally, even when theorists allow that there are *many* objective determinants that, combined, produce grand-theoretic predictions of "probable" individual behavior. Here the grand theorist shades off into the positivist social scientist, who views the individual as an intersection of objective social and psychological forces: non-ideational independent variables. Yet we know from introspection, if we are rigorous about it, that our decisions are not produced by objective determinants, uninterpreted by subjective ideas. We vote for a candidate or party not because of our determination by our objective class position (the same applies to our gender, race, income level, years of formal education, or any other "objective" variable) or the unmediated influence on us of what political scientists claim to have identified as "fundamental" (e.g., economic) factors, but because we have been subjectively persuaded (1) that it is legitimate to vote on the basis of some criterion such as class interest or retrospective economic performance, and (2) that a particular candidate or party is likely to satisfy that criterion. We are subjectively persuaded by the fallible, contingent ideational inputs into our webs of belief, which to some extent vary from person to person—not by the infallible force of uninterpreted reality: this fact is introspectively knowable by us all.

Following Foucault's grand theory, Larsson asserts that his preferred objective homogeneities, "institutions and discourses," manage to "subsume the players. If individuals either act or resist in accordance with what is socially expected of them, at least in respect to their social capacities, desires, and beliefs, then we may analyze society from the top down and produce systemic theories of society." In Larsson's hands this synoptic perspective legitimates technocratic behavior modification that would have been anathema, I assume, to Foucault. Yet Larsson may have identified something more robust about the parallel between Foucault's grand theory and positivist social science than I recognized in merely analogizing them at the end of Chapter 3.

It may be worth noting that the post-structuralist label can be misleading, depending on whether "post" is taken to mean "in continuation of" or "having passed through and left behind." In support of the first reading of Foucault, Sunil Khilnani (2003, 310-11) argues that he extended structuralist analysis from language into history by replacing the history of sequentially causal (and, I would add, individual and ideational) contingencies with the history of "transhistorical structures of thought and society"—knowledge of which would provide "the certainty of scientific truths." Khilnani goes so far as to point out that the rise of structuralism "coincided with the consolidation of Charles de Gaulle's Fifth Republic, itself committed to a technocratic vision." The positivistic mode of Larsson's argument suggests that the unlikely juxtaposition of de Gaulle and (via structuralism) Foucault may be more than coincidental. Foucault ([1984] 1997, 115) once pointed out that he had been classified as not only an anarchist, leftist, liberal, and Marxist, but as a "technocrat in the service of Gaullism." While it would be absurd to take this characterization too seriously, he did not deny that there was an element of truth to it, and affirmed that he "rather like[d]" the fact that all of these characterizations had been made of him.

Larsson takes at face value the scientific status of "nudge theory," and thus the behavioral economics on which it is built. He even construes nudge theory as compatible with my critique of contemporary social science because, in departing from the neoclassical model of rational choice criticized in Chapter 4, it is (professedly) "realistic." But behavioral economics is just as unrealistic as rational-choice theory, as I also point out in Chapter 4 (196-200). Indeed, the similarities are much more telling than the differences. For the neoclassical economist, *Homo economicus* is "rational" in a manner that makes human behavior entirely predictable. Posit the incentives *objectively* facing human agents and you can predict their behavior, everywhere and always. For the behavioral economist, people are rational in predictable fashion except when they are irrational—in predictable fashion. Append, to the rationalistic model of *Homo economicus,* an ever-growing list of "heuristics and biases," and you can predict human behavior, everywhere and always.

Both the "rationalists" and "irrationalists" share a presuppositional faith in the predictability of human behavior, extending what Hume ([1772] 1999, 159) called "uniformity in the operations of nature" to the operations of human beings. The assumption of uniformity is the engine of positivism. It is the means by which not only neoclassical economists but positivist social scientists, including behavioral economists, imagine that inevitably local, time-bound, historically contingent "findings" drawn from this or that data set, laboratory experiment, natural experiment, or randomized controlled trial can be generalized to apply everywhere and always, producing a "science" of human behavior. This assumption is challenged by the presumption of ideational heterogeneity (147-48).

Larsson responds to this challenge by recounting his own subordination to the norm of standing in a queue, and his inability to resist for long the convenience of using a computer system to which he had philosophical objections. To him, these examples suggest that the individual is largely powerless in the face of systemic social pressures that can be identified, from the top down, by both the social theorist (Foucault) and the social scientist (e.g., the nudge theorist). This analysis strikes me as inadequate, because the presumption of ideational heterogeneity, as a presumption, is defeasible. There may be homogenizing counterforces to ideational heterogeneity, such as shared norms and superordinate ideas (169-71), the identification of which would be the mission of a judicious, ideationally sensitive human science (171-73). Larsson is describing his own ideational determination by homogeneous norms and ideas, but this does not undermine the presumption of ideational heterogeneity. It simply indicates that ideational heterogeneity, while presumptively ubiquitous, does not reign absolutely.

What actually does the work of responding to the presumption of heterogeneity is Larsson's positivist assumption that the *subjective*, contingent ideational homogeneities to which he was subjected in these two cases exemplify the grand-theoretic claim that the individual is subsumed by objective "institutions and discourses that subsume the players" everywhere and always, such that the social scientist who identifies an institution or discourse operative in a given historical epoch, or even transhistorically, has established a sound basis for generalizing to all players. Yet subjectively, it seems, Larsson *does* consider jumping long queues and *did* resist the lure of the objectionable computer system, at least for a while. Larsson's universalizing, objectivizing interpretation of his experiences turns a blind eye to his own ideational idiosyncracies, which might be even more pronounced for other individuals. His positivistic extrapolation from his subordination to "institutions and discourses" to uniformity in the operations of society, courtesy of the grand-theoretic perspective afforded by Foucault, effaces the possibility that other human beings will, in particular cases, be even more idiosyncratically rebellious than he was in these particular cases.

Larsson invokes the dichotomy of structure and agency to tie my invocation of heterogeneous, anti-structural individual behavior to the sin of "voluntarism." Voluntarism entails the underdetermination of the agent's will. Yet I posit such a strict determination of human action that the notion of will, let alone free will, loses all sense (142). Ideational determinism entails the strict causation of each of the nodes in a given individual's web of belief by the ideational influences to which the individual has been exposed. Belief heterogeneity, then, does not imply some magical exemption from efficient causation, as would voluntarism—an Epicurean swerve that explains variation against a backdrop of sameness. The backdrop itself is variable, but it strictly determines each of us—each in our own way.

In the modern world, each of us has ideas that distinguish our own webs of belief from those of other human beings, thanks to such historical developments as the rise of cultural elites that generate complicated and abundant streams of ideas; the invention of writing to memorialize these ideas; mass literacy, which makes these ideas widely available; and the diversification of the experiences to be interpreted by means of these ideas (145-46). Mass literacy, mass education, and mass culture often spread the same ideas to many, but sometimes they spread slightly or radically different ideas, and even homogeneous ideas are received in a slightly variable order that may differentially affect how the recipients interpret the incoming ideas (143-44). The world of our ideas, the world that determines our conscious actions, is fully determinate (144)—yet, being a subjective world, it is difficult to access, rendering its heterogeneities difficult to detect, understand, and predict.

That, in a nutshell, is the epistemic problem facing grand theory, social science, and technocracy alike. It is not a problem caused by free will or some other wrinkle in the fabric of Humean uniformity. We can assume that, at bottom, the *processes* of perception, belief formation, interpretation, and communication are basically uniform across our shared psychological architecture (our neural physiology), which we can treat as nomological (137). But in practice, this is not very helpful, because our ignorance of the contingent ideational *inputs* into others' nomological processes of interpretation makes it look, at least initially, *as if* they have free will. This appearance does not stem from randomness, which could be statistically mastered. The beliefs controlling our conscious actions are contingent but not, by virtue of that, arbitrary. They are contingent on fully determined nonrandom historical circumstance, i.e., on the ideas to which each of us happens to have been exposed at any given moment. Any appearance of free will produced by ideational heterogeneity is an illusion created, interpersonally, by variation among determining ideas that is often opaque to observers; and, introspectively, by the clash of competing beliefs when one attempts to make a decision. Without what we take to be good reasons for our actions, however, we would be caught in the indecision of Buridan's Ass and thus unable to act (Friedman 2013). As Leibniz saw, conscious actions are determined by reasons; as Quine saw, our reasons are determined by our webs of belief; and as Lippmann saw, our webs of belief are determined by the history of our ideational exposures, as processed by our cognitive architecture. Nowhere in this process is there an underdetermined, "voluntary" moment.

In contrast, Foucault's preoccupation with power *is* voluntaristic—normatively. Power is, no doubt, omnipresent, as he recognized; this, I think, was his truly great contribution. But one would find the omnipresence of power disturbing, as he did, only in implicit contrast to the ideal of a self-determining subject, free from power's reach. Ideational determinism tells us that this aspiration, the aspiration to freedom, is an impossible dream. The determining power of our ideas over us—indeed, our constitution by them—means that freedom is absolutely unattainable. But this in no way precludes the goodness of our lives: the lives of human, ideationally determined, interpretive beings; the lives that technocrats (effectively or not) seek to enhance. This is not an endorsement of technocracy, but of the humanistic values that an ideal technocracy aims to advance by relieving human distress.

Larsson, however, seems to think that technocracy is legitimate only if it can be squared with freedom: like Foucault, he is a normative voluntarist. Thus, for example, he finds it odd that I do not embrace a "nudging" technocracy, not just because it is "realistic," but because it would not, after all, *force* people to do anything. Yet Foucault himself, in noticing the omnipresence of power, allows us to see that the overt force exercised by non-nudging, obtrusively coercive states is not necessarily the most important kind of power. Nudging exemplifies a practice that is less obtrusive than overt coercion but that is, *for that very reason* (as Foucault would surely have pointed out), a more insidious and potentially more efficacious and important form of coercion.

Larsson is, I think, conflating the epistemic problem facing technocracy—the problem of knowing the specific ideas at work in the determination of particular individuals' actions—with the entirely separate normative question of whether technocratic action can be harnessed to break the grip of determinacy on the subject. This conflation of the epistemic with the kratic may also explain Larsson's assumption that technocracy is legitimate so long as whatever coercion it deploys accords with values that are agreed upon through collective deliberation (and his befuddlement at the idea that socialism can be endorsed on grounds of individual welfare, not collective self-determination). Here he has synthesized Foucault with the grandest of all grand theorists, Habermas, but the effect is, again, to disengage from the epistemic in favor of the kratic—in this case, the democratic.

I began the book by pointing out that the young Habermas's critique of technocracy, on the grounds of its subversion of democratic deliberation about ends, cannot comfortably ground a critical inspection of the means by which technocrats try to make good on their promises (1-2). Indeed, for Habermas it was essential to maintain that technocrats (i.e., for him, epistocrats) somehow manage to achieve whatever they set out to achieve—entailing that they have truly "scientific" knowledge of human behavior—because it is only their success in solving the people's social and economic problems that persuades the people to disengage from democratic deliberation about ends, and it is this disengagement that he wanted to criticize on kratic grounds (3-4). Thus, Habermas baked a form of naïve technocratic realism into his critique of technocracy. My contention was that to avoid this trap, one must adopt (for the sake of argument) an internal technocratic perspective, which allows us to question whether *any* identifiable group of technocrats is likely to have the knowledge needed to solve people's problems. Larsson, however, trades this internal technocratic concern about the instrumental efficacy of public policy for Habermas's external concern about the technocratic dampening of democratic deliberation. "Collaborative governance" arrangements are legitimate, in Larsson's view, because they allow democratic "stakeholders" to "attend to public problems, often with a technocratic outlook, in an effort to resolve social and political problems through the pragmatic utilization of existing knowledge"—begging the question of whether stakeholders' knowledge claims are reliable proxies for actual knowledge. Every type of technocracy, by definition, makes "efforts to resolve problems through the pragmatic utilization of existing knowledge"; but this says nothing about whether "existing knowledge" is reliably accurate and, thus, whether its utilization is, in fact, pragmatic.

Whereas, for Feuerbach, God is a projection of real human attributes onto an imaginary being, for grand theorists in the tradition stretching back to Rousseau, social institutions, forces, discourses, powers, and "society" play the role of *reverse* projections of a single *imaginary* human attribute: freedom. Because these theorists are alienated from the introspectively knowable reality of their own ideational determination, they imagine that in principle we can be free. The normative backdrop to these theorists' hypostasization of the social is that of our agency liberated from the impersonal, inhuman force of social control that their theories of society depict. Our task, then, is to wrest this control back into our own hands so we can at last exert our agency. For Foucault, this task, while desirable, may be unfeasible because social control is so strong and pervasive. But for Larsson, *democratic* technocracy can control the social forces that, being so strong and pervasive, shape our behavior into easily predictable form. Technocracy can thus be used to engineer a form of collective self-determination: a form of agency that is the mirror image of an alienated view of humanity, which itself hypostasizes a realm of power that is then to be tamed through its democratization.

I think, then, that the surprising lessons of Larsson's Foucauldian critique of *Power Without Knowledge* are the compatibility of certain emancipatory imperatives with technocracy; the alienation of not only technocracy, but of these emancipatory imperatives themselves, from the human reality of ideational determination; and the resulting tendency to treat theoretically conjured objective social "structures" or forces as realities, as they are the only forms of reality that can be seen, or imagined, synoptically—at the cost of downplaying or effacing subjective ideational heterogeneity, and the coercive power over each of us exercised by our ideas.

Positivism II: Social Hypostasization in International Relations (Lerner)

Yet social hypostasization need not necessarily be linked to emancipation as its antithesis. Hypostasization can also take a purely descriptive form. This is the form defended in Adam Lerner's fascinating contribution to the symposium.

Lerner argues that it is "useful" for social scientists to treat "certain supra-individual entities," namely "states," *as if* they are real. A similar theme is taken up by Zeynep Pamuk, to whom I respond in the next subsection, who suggests that "all models make some false assumptions for the sake of simplicity and usability." But why would social scientists, or technocrats, want to make this tradeoff—assuming that their overarching interest is in truth, i.e., accuracy?

I can imagine two reasons. First, it might be argued that a false assumption is only *slightly* inaccurate in certain cases. This is what Pamuk seems to mean in referring to our continued reliance, in most contexts, on Newtonian physics, despite its supersession by quantum physics. This, however, begs the question of whether social-scientific predictions are indeed comparable, in their accuracy, to the predictions made possible by Newtonian physics. If we had a body of knowledge of human behavior that enabled that degree of precision, it would be churlish to condemn this knowledge for its slight inaccuracies. But we have no reason to think that human sciences are or can be that reliable.

The second reason for trading off accuracy against simplicity and usability exemplifies the type of technocratic thinking labeled "pathological" in Chapter 4. There, I playfully introduce a figurative hypostasization to capture the fact that contemporary social-scientific assumptions are constructed *as if* to deliberately avoid the possibility of what Julian Reiss (to whom I respond in a subsequent subsection) elegantly calls "pernicious heterogeneity": the type of heterogeneity that would block Newtonian reliability in the human sciences; the type that would occur if Hume's assumption of uniformity (inspired, no doubt, by Newton) did not apply, as a practical matter, to human behavior. It is, I suggest, *as if* technocracy is a real but perverse entity, like Descartes' evil genius, that (somehow) forces social scientists to make unrealistic assumptions merely for the sake of producing an endless stream of simple, usable policy recommendations—heedless of whether they are accurate.

While the usefulness of false assumptions in producing a stream of predictions is undeniable, assumptions must at least be *largely* accurate, although not as accurate as the assumptions of Newtonian physics, if the predictions themselves are to be largely accurate—which is what a non-pathological technocracy requires. The figure of a perverse technocratic entity, then, is intended to illustrate the perversity of contemporary social scientists' *ideas*. The real sources of epistocratic perversity are not demons or social "systems" such as technocracy, but the assumptions of contemporary social scientists, among which positivism figures significantly—and to which the pragmatic argument for unrealistic assumptions, which can also be an argument for unrealistic hypostasizations, contributes mightily.

The most influential pragmatic argument for an inadvertently pathological use of false assumptions was made long ago by Milton Friedman (no relation) in "The Methodology of Positive Economics" (1953). According to Friedman, inaccurate assumptions can nonetheless produce good predictions. Friedman asks us to consider the neoclassical assumption that business firms have "full knowledge of the data needed to succeed in" maximizing their expected returns (ibid., 21). To defend the usefulness of this assumption, Friedman analogizes the business manager to an "expert" billiard player, who acts "*as if* he knew the complicated mathematical formulas that would give the optimum directions of travel, could estimate accurately by eye the angles, etc., describing the location of the balls, could make lightning calculations from the formulas, and could then make the balls travel in the direction indicated by the formulas" (ibid., author's emphasis). Predictions of this billiard player's shots, based on the assumption of full knowledge, would capture her stipulated expertise. Friedman urges us to use similar assumptions about real-world businesspeople on the grounds that, unless their behavior "in some way or another approximated behavior consistent with the maximization of returns, it seems unlikely that they would remain in business for long" (ibid., 22).

However, Friedman's analogy effaces the reality that many businesses do not, in fact, remain in business for long, just as many billiard players are not, in fact, experts. We distort the situation immeasurably if we simply assume that optimal behavior is the norm among billiard players, businesspeople, or any other human beings. Why engage, then, in the distortion? Friedman's Darwinian argument about the long-run unsustainability of inexpertly run businesses does not justify the conclusion that, at any given moment, the population of businesspeople has been weeded down to those who are expert. Moreover, Friedman is using this as a mere example of the usefulness of unrealistic assumptions; his overall point is independent of any particular mechanism (such as "natural" selection), and amounts to saying that the test of an assumption is the accuracy of its predictions, not its realism in some other sense than that. In short, Friedman is arguing that theoretical assumptions are *not* approximations of reality, even though the predictions they yield should approximate it. But in that case we would not need to worry about whether there is a Darwinian mechanism or any other that might explain the predictive success of an assumption; all that would matter is the predictive success itself.

Why, then, does Friedman offer a Darwinian explanation for approximately unerring revenue-maximizing behavior, and why does he analogize the prediction of this behavior to the prediction that expert billiard players act as if they have perfect knowledge of the effects of their actions? None of this is necessary if we take seriously his strictly instrumentalist position. Indeed, no *theory* would be necessary: all one would want are accurate predictions. But if we want to understand what is causing accurate predictions' accuracy, we need a theory that specifies a mechanism. And it would be imprudent not to attempt such an understanding given the imperfection of our knowledge. Without an understanding of the mechanism, we would rightly wonder if our predictions were only adventitiously accurate. Perhaps business people who act adaptively in the times and places for which we happen to have data will act maladaptively in other times and places. To deal with this problem, we cannot be pure instrumentalists; we must test heretofore accurate predictions against the plausibility of a theorized mechanism that would explain them, enabling us to know when and where they might *and might not* be generalizable. This would constitute a step away from instrumentalist positivism toward a "judicious" human science—if we made the additional step of testing proposed mechanisms against our ideational "nature." Friedman goes through the motions of taking the first step by making any mention of mechanisms at all. But by not taking the second step, he leaves us with the patently impractical injunction to treat businesses *as if* they "had full knowledge of the data needed," which can justify future predictions only if it is plausible; yet it is not plausible, because businesses are managed by fallible human beings.

For all its pretensions to pragmatism, then, Friedman's instrumentalist approach to unrealistic assumptions actually solves no practical problems except, perhaps, the sleeplessness of economists who worry that they are engaged in magical thinking whenever they "assume a ladder," as the old joke has it.[4] However, Friedman did, at least, insert ideational entities—individuals—into his functionalist model of the behavior of business firms. The unrealism of the model stems from the magical epistemic capacities attributed to individual business managers, but the fact that those capacities are attributed to individuals enables us to see how unrealistic it is. Because of our introspective familiarity with ourselves and our experiential familiarity with others, we know that actual human individuals have fallible and heterogeneous beliefs, and we can infer that some of these beliefs will be economically functional and others, not so much.

By contrast, had Friedman attributed a functional level of knowledge not to businesspeople but to the "firms" they run—hypostasizing and anthropomorphizing the latter—it would be difficult to spot the flaw in his argument. Since business firms are legal fictions, we have no first-hand knowledge of "their" fallibility and are more likely to fall for attributions of near-omniscience to "them" than to individuals. People have been falling for such fantastic attributions at least since the rise of the organic metaphor of society, which is particularly conducive to *sociological* functionalism. Neoclassical economists such as Friedman transferred this functionalism to the micro level, but in both cases the reality of individuals' heterogeneous and fallible ideas was obscured, just as it is obscured in grand social theory.

At the macro level, I chose to contest social hypostasization (149-60) by criticizing Charles Taylor's canonical paper, "Interpretation and the Sciences of Man" ([1971] 1985). Taylor, I argued, by hypostasizing culture, effaces both the heterogeneity and the fallibility of the individuals who create it. This type of unrealism, I think, may be an unintended consequence of Lerner's pragmatism, even though Lerner carefully brackets ontological claims such as Taylor's.

Taylor attributes a species of functional percipience to cultural wholes that, I argued, is dispelled as illusory once we notice the fallible and humanly ignorant individuals who are the originators, transmitters, and recipients of the ideas that make up any particular culture. For example, in Taylor's discussion of a cultural movement with which he clearly agrees (loosely speaking, "the" counterculture of the Sixties), he attributes effective omniscience to "the children" who propagated the counterculture. According to Taylor, the children simply *knew* (somehow) that "the free, productive, bargaining culture [that had] claimed to be sufficient for man in the 1950s" was not, in fact, sufficient (ibid., 49). Thus, Taylor obviates the need for a genuinely scientific understanding of the counterculture (an intellectual history of it, in the broadest sense) by means of a congratulatory endorsement of it as an unexplained recognition of self-evident truth, just as Friedman obviated the need for research into the actual behavior of fallible business managers by means of a specious attribution of effective omniscience to them.

I, too, sympathize with countercultural ideas (346-47), but I'd certainly benefit from understanding their historical roots in the fallible beliefs of specific people (which is not necessarily to say incorrect beliefs). That cannot happen if we conceive of the counterculture as a supra-individual consciousness—the consciousness possessed by a hypostasized "intersubjective" being—rather than recognizing it as the intersubjective effect of historically contingent ideas developed and believed by, and interpersonally communicated among, fallible individuals.[5] The epistemic purpose of my epistemological individualism, then, is as pragmatic as the purpose attributed by Friedman to unrealistic assumptions. By sticking to the realistic assumption that ideas are originated by, thought about, and communicated among fallible and diverse individuals, we enable ourselves to ask questions about the uniformity and accuracy (for example, the functionality) of homogeneously shared ideas. If we hypostasize collective actors as the subjects holding these ideas, we will be unable to see either disagreement or fallibility among the actual loci of ideas, individuals.

To avoid misunderstanding, I want to point out that I consider collective actors to be hypostasizations not because I adhere to physicalist reductionism, nor because I think it best to reduce phenomena to their smallest components, but because I see no reason to believe that collective entities are, in fact, anything but historically contingent fictions that obscure the real activity of ideas: the activity of perception, comprehension, memory, and logical or more loosely associative (or metaphorical) processing—all of which occurs solely (so far as we know) in what we have come to call the minds of "individuals." The *pragmatic* question, then, is where the burden of proof rests. In the form of our daily experience of our minds, we have plenty of evidence for the reality of ideas and, indeed, the reality of individual minds as comprehension and processing sites for ideas. It stands to reason that keeping these realities front and center will serve us well by steering us away from the homogenizing, defallibilizing tendencies that follow from the practice of hypostasizing the social—a practice that is not backed up by any evidence at all. It is logically possible that there are metaphysically real collective actors, and I offer no *reductivist* reason to deny that they exist. But there is also no reason to affirm their reality, and doing so necessarily obscures the action of what we *can* affirm as real: the action of individual minds that are fallible, and may be heterogeneous.

In the academic study of international relations, the chief object of collective hypostasization, as well as anthropomorphization, is the state. "To say that states are 'actors' or 'persons,'" Alexander Wendt (2004, 289) points out, "is to attribute to them properties we associate first with human beings—rationality, identities, interests, beliefs, and so on. Such attributions are found in the work of realists, liberals, institutionalists,

Marxists, constructivists, behaviouralists, feminists, postmodernists, international lawyers, and almost everyone in between." Wendt concludes that, "in a field in which almost everything is contested," the hypostasization and anthropomorphization of the state "seems to be one thing on which almost all of us agree." John J. Mearsheimer (1994/5, 9), for example, characterizes realism as the view that "states look for opportunities to take advantage of each other, and therefore have little reason to trust each other."

Unfortunately, though, in Wendt's view, while most IR scholars hypostasize and anthropomorphize the state in actual practice, they also acknowledge that the behavior and "beliefs" of anthropomorphized "states" are nothing but the behavior and beliefs of individual human beings. The hypostasized and anthropomorphized state turns out to be a mere metaphor for the actions of individuals that, taken together, look state-like. Wendt wants us to resist this concession to what I am calling epistemological individualism. He asks: "If state personhood is merely a useful fiction, then why does its attribution work so well in helping us to make sense of world politics? Why, in short, is the concept so 'useful'? . . . Given how well theories based on state personhood work, it would be a miracle if it did not refer to something real" (ibid., 290).

Wendt, I think, is confusing miracles with self-fulfilling prophecies. We do not infer that God exists from the fact that people behave *as if* God exists, nor is it miraculous that they behave this way once we recognize that the idea of God, and the attendant behavioral norms, have been taught to them. Nor is it miraculous that countercultural "children" acted *as if* bourgeois norms had revealed themselves as self-evidently inadequate: this is exactly how they would be expected to act had they been taught to believe in this inadequacy—taught not by reality itself, but by fallible bearers of theories of modern society. It is hardly miraculous that "state" personnel act as if the states they serve are real and have rationality, identities, interests, and beliefs if this is, in effect, what they have been taught to think, if only by means of the language of "states"—i.e., the ubiquitous use of the state metaphor. It would be even less miraculous if state personnel acted as if states were real if they had been explicitly trained to think this way by, for example, professors of international relations. The true miracle would be for state personnel to act as if states were real because they actually *are* real—defying everything we know, from introspective experience, about where reason, (perceived) interests, and beliefs are actually located: in the minds of individuals. That, at least, is the core claim of epistemological individualism (148–59).

I should note that the location of ideas in individual minds does not entail the hypostasization of individuals: they are metaphorical too. Individuals, like states, can be disaggregated into component sub-realities; it is only for pragmatic reasons that we call an aggregation of the cells of a human body an "individual." One such reason is the usefulness of a verbal shorthand to describe such a vast array of physical phenomena as those contained in a human "body," but there are also more substantive pragmatic reasons, such as the fact that the human body actually *is* a (nonmetaphorical) functional organism. So while "the individual" is a metaphor, it is a metaphor that is pragmatically justified because it refers to realities for which we have reason to want to refer in the way that the metaphor allows—even as the metaphor does not cause confusion by obscuring reality: states and other collective metaphors, unlike individuals, are *not* realities except insofar as they denote individuals' actions and the ideas that cause them; beyond that, they are *mere* metaphors. As we shall see, we do have a weak pragmatic reason (a reason of mere convenience) to continue using these metaphors, but we should always beware that in using them we run the risk of obscuring the reality that states are nothing but the statelike actions taken by individuals—who are ideationally determined, fallible, and to some extent heterogeneous. These realities are effaced if we take the state metaphor literally.

Both human ideas and human individuals are real, even though the individual body, as such, is a metaphorical description of the biological housing of the mind and of the physical means by which ideas are translated into actions. It is pragmatic to refer to minds as properties of individual bodies because of the reality that we are conscious of ideas only insofar as ideas appear to our individual minds—that is, minds located in the "individual bodies" over which, in turn, these minds exercise a constantly reaffirmed degree of direct, conscious control, even as they receive from them a constant stream of sensory feedback that is often beyond our control. As Lerner puts it, the minds that are located in brains that are located in individual bodies "can integrate billions of firing neurons to produce thoughts and qualia over and above the scope of any discrete neuronal firing patterns." But we know this because of qualial perceptions of mental effects, such as analytical and synthetic operations on ideas, that occur *only*, to our knowledge, in individual minds.

When we anthropomorphize the Internet as a "hive mind," or draw a parallel between internal deliberation and interpersonal deliberation, we are forgetting that no social medium per se or conversation per se has the capacity to consciously integrate the ideas expressed by the individual minds that are interpersonally mediated or expressed. When I make a statement to you, in person or in writing or electronically, and you reply with a statement of your own, the two statements are understood, and mental operations are performed upon them, only (if at all) in our individual minds or those of individual observers. Without integration by individual minds, there would be no integration at all: no deliberation. The statements would remain unacknowledged sound waves, marks on paper, or electrons: unacknowledged because we have no evidence that there is anyone or anything out there but individual minds that might be capable of understanding and thinking about them. (The reason that AIs pose hard questions for theories of consciousness is that they do appear to think, in a seemingly non-qualial way; but this would, at best, simply make them individual minds, not collective minds.)

Lerner's emphasis on qualia underscores a significant lacuna in *Power Without Knowledge:* the fact that the term *ideas,* even in the very broad sense in which I used it (covering perceptions, beliefs, interpretations, hypotheses, theories, strokes of inspiration, and assumptions, implicit and explicit; 140), does not capture subjective *experiences* that—precisely because they are experienced by individuals—may be sources of heterogeneity that frustrate social scientists' and technocrats' attempt to predict the behavior of individuals. Part of the temptation to hypostasize culture may be that otherwise, subjectivity takes on an overly intellectualized cast that is untrue to our qualial experience. Although our ideationality is crucial to our subjectivity, so are less explicitly conscious modes of being that may produce conscious and semi-conscious action, such as habitual action. These modes are important but difficult to theorize, lending themselves to hypostasization as a substitute for realistic analysis.

I did not include an account of experiential qualia because, unlike ideas, the determinants of qualia are plausibly seen as physiological and thus homogeneous across individuals—to take Lerner's example, the capacity to experience pain. For the same reason, I did not identify emotions as a source of heterogeneity. Lerner points out, however, that in cases where behavioral prediction is attempted, the experiential *triggers* of qualia may well differ from individual to individual in ways that are inaccessible to social scientists, leading to unpredictability despite the presumptively homogeneous neurological architecture that makes qualia possible. I agree.

However, this insight seems to be in tension with Lerner's willingness to bracket whether supra-individual "people"—states—are real. One of the most pervasive qualia is the experience of one's mind as the self-contained locus of one's web of belief—except insofar as ideas are communicated into it from others, and out of it by ourselves. Bracketing communication, though, we each (individually) experience thinking within the confines of our own web of beliefs (and there alone), we each experience trying to remember how particular beliefs got there, we each experience our inability to directly access other individuals' webs as we can directly access our own, we each sense our webs' internal limits (where the explicit shades into the implicit and the remembered into the forgotten), and we each experience the conscious ability to temporarily conclude deliberations within the web by taking an action with the one human body that has always been experientially under our (incomplete) individual control—the body we experience as attached to the individual mind. We live our entire lives inside individual minds—that is, in the compass of our ideas and qualia—and the meta-experience of this fact constitutes qualial knowledge of the reality of this individual mind. We have nothing like this experiential confirmation of states, societies, or any other collectivities as real entities, let alone conscious ones.

Historically, moreover, both the concept of the state and the "reality" of individual states were inventions of individual human minds that were deliberately inculcated into other minds by means of nationalist programs of educational indoctrination (e.g., Weber 1976). We know, too, of many other historical examples of inculcated, hypostasized ideas whose only actual contact with reality is that they convinced people to behave *as if* the ideas denoted realities by persuading them that, indeed, the ideas did denote realities (e.g., the idea of God). While the fact that the idea of the state can be historically traced to human invention does not preclude the logical possibility that states are real, the likelier explanation for state-like behavior is that states are *mere* metaphors for a variety of individual actions, metaphors that many people have come to treat as real because they have been taught to do so. The question Lerner raises, then, is why we should want to engage in a Milton Friedmanesque bracketing of the inaccuracy of the state metaphor—which risks, I think, the very same elision of the real fallibility and the real heterogeneity of individuals that is accomplished by both Friedman's bracketing of the fallibility of businesspeople and Taylor's embrace of collective metaphors as real.

It seems to me that in reality, the most pragmatic course—if we are to avoid that mistake—is to couple the use of convenient collective metaphors with an ever-present awareness that that is what they are. This requires taking a firm stand against collectivist ontology, not bracketing it. When a historian tells us that "in January, 2017, the National Archives and Records Administration conferred with the White House to establish rules for record-keeping" (Lepore 2020, 25), we are acutely aware that there was no literal conferral between these two metaphorical entities. We can therefore accept their anthropomorphization as a linguistic shorthand that in no way undermines the fact that it was individuals who actually conferred, even though the historian does not tell us who those individuals were. The metaphorical hypostasization of the National Archives and the White House does not in the least suggest that there is something amiss in the ontology of individual minds as the sole loci of consciously thought ideas—nor does the metaphorical hypostasization of states. To treat collectivist ontology as an open question would only have the effect of obscuring the fact that individuals in the National Archives and the White House conferred with each other, and that their ideas alone determined the agreement. Likewise, we say that "Germany invaded Poland in 1939" not because we have any reason to think, ontically, that something "more" happened than that *armed individuals who identified as "German" crossed an imaginary boundary separating "their country" from Poland*, but because it would be cumbersome to constantly write phrases like that—which, moreover, only scratch the surface of the reality of millions of individuals' invasion-related decisions and the ideas and assumptions, explicit and tacit, upon which they were based, but of which we often know very little.

Lerner draws the inference that epistemological individualism requires "unravelling every thread of every social sweater," but this conclusion, while understandable, is not justified. Epistemological individualism does *invite* us to unravel the threads, but we do not have to accept the invitation if we are not interested in understanding the actual ideas of the real individuals, such as Adolf Hitler, who made the decision to invade Poland: we can, in that case, stick with the metaphor, as in the case of the National Archives and the White House. Nor can we expect that, if we accept the invitation, we will always be able to unravel all the individual ideational threads. Epistemological individualism merely reminds us that the threads are there, and that we risk homogenizing the heterogeneous and deifying the fallible if we ignore them by hypostasizing the metaphor. But when we cannot, in practice, unravel every thread, or when we choose not to, we are free to use shorthand that fuzzes over all the missing threads that we know *must* really be there (ontically): the individuals' beliefs, which *could* be unraveled if we had "perfect hindsight" into their ideational antecedents (153). The starting point of *Power Without Knowledge,* of course, is that we *don't* have perfect hindsight—or foresight. We establish the principle of "epistemological individualism" through introspective knowledge of the location of ideas in individual minds, yet the difficulty of trying to trace each idea in other individual minds compels us, in most cases, merely to gesture toward the ideational origins of a given action, for we have not been able to identify these origins and may never be able to. This does not, however, make them any less real, any less important (causally), or any less likely to render social hypostasizations inaccurate.

Even if all we know is that armed "individuals" who identified as "German" "soldiers" crossed an imaginary boundary, we can infer that an array of ideas (and qualia) must have motivated each of them to take that action; but until we do some research we cannot know what the ideas were. This is the type of research that empirically rigorous IR scholars would undertake, whenever possible. If they did *not* bracket the underlying ontology—if, in line with epistemological individualism, they kept the metaphorical nature of the "state" firmly in mind, just as we do when we read about "the White House" and "the National Archives"—then IR scholars' use of the metaphor would invite them to do this research, because the figurative nature of the metaphor would remind them of what they do not yet know and really must discover if they are to get to the bottom of what happened: which individuals' ideas motivated the invasion, and what were these ideas? However, if they bracket the ontology suggested by the metaphor, they may feel no need to get to the bottom of things, because the metaphor will create the impression that *it* (the state as conscious entity) may itself be the bottom of things.

If IR scholars bracket the ontology they may delude themselves that by theorizing *as if* "Germany" were real, they have revealed what actually happened in 1939. In this way, IR research about empirical reality is displaced by IR theory that is as realistic as speculation about how many angels can dance on the head of a pin—speculation that is quite important and terribly interesting, but only if angels really exist. The project for which it would be pragmatic to bracket the ontology of states—the project of coming up with universalistic generalizations about "their" behavior—would seem almost necessarily to drive IR scholars toward pointless theorizing about non-existent entities rather than the research they would continually be invited to do if they kept in mind that the state metaphor is merely figurative: epistemologically individualistic ideational research into the reasons for people's figuratively state-like actions.

Such research is now left to journalists and historians, precisely because journalism and historical research (properly speaking—research into the beliefs and actions of historical individuals) *cannot* reveal the impersonal forces or structures that positivists construct to stand behind mere individual decisions. Why should positivist IR scholars care whether, say, the invasion of "Iraq" in 2003 stemmed (arguably) from mutual incomprehension between Saddam Hussein and the Western intelligence analysts assigned to decipher his belligerent behavior in the years that followed the first Gulf War (Jervis 2010, ch. 3)? After all, knowing about the mistakes of these mere individuals is not useful for making predictions of the behavior of "states" *in general*. It would seem, then, that the universalistic, technocratic aspirations of IR scholars dovetail with treating the state metaphor *as if* it is not merely a metaphor—even if, unlike Wendt, the scholars do not actually believe that it is more than a metaphor. By bracketing their disbelief, they license their own disregard, in practice, for the truth being bracketed (assuming that epistemological individualism captures that truth). Only in a perverse epistemic system, such as an injudicious technocracy, would it be considered *useful* to bracket the truth just so we can get on with the task of making lawlike generalizations, even when this procedure, by ignoring the fallibility and heterogeneity of state actors, is bound to produce misconstruals of the actual reasons for state actions, defeating the purpose of theorizing, accurate prediction, which requires that we avoid merely adventitiously accurate predictive inferences from extant data that are therefore likely to become inaccurate.

The problem of unraveling the threads that were woven into ideational webs that could produce actions neatly summarizable by phrases such as "Germany invaded Poland in 1939," or "Coalition forces invaded Iraq in 2003," is nothing more than, precisely, a pragmatic problem, but the source of the problem is epistemological, not ontological. It is difficult to know what particular individuals think, thought, or will think, and this difficulty is a product of the fact that other individuals' thoughts are not only opaque (epistemically) but different, to some extent (ontically), from our own. But that ontological fact does not in any way impugn the reality that "individual" minds, and (apparently) only they, think; while epistemically, it becomes impossible, rather than merely difficult, to know what "individuals" think if we stop our analysis after lumping them together under a homogenizing metaphor such as "the state." The pragmatic problem caused by bracketing the individual ideational causes of "collective" action is that instead of deliberately fuzzing over the gaps in our knowledge of the threads in the sweater, which invites us to get out a magnifying glass to take a closer look, ontological bracketing fuzzes over the fact that there are threads at all and that, as human products, they are idiosyncratic, flawed, and thus may lead to unexpected outcomes —in the case of international relations, disastrous ones.

By treating collectives *as if* they think, Lerner suggests, we can recognize that "very real logics, knowledge, and properties . . . emerge at the group level," but the notion of "emergent properties," so familiar from the literature on "complex systems," seems to me to be another counterproductive hypostasization. This, I think, is suggested by Lerner's appeal to a scenario devised by Deborah Tollefson (2015), in which individuals on an admissions committee need to act as if the committee is real and as if its work is irreducible to the individuals' preferences. Only in this way can they can achieve what they set out to do according to established committee rules. Thus, they may end up making a different decision than any of them would have made individually. But *all* collective decisions may deviate from the preferences of the individuals who participate in making them; epistemological individualism does not impede us from recognizing this, although *methodological* individualism might. The latter, in some variants, reduces all human action to direct reflections of individuals' preferences, which would preclude unintended consequences; epistemological individualism does not. Tollefson explains how committee members, as individuals who subordinate their actions to the rules of a figurative collective, can produce a consequence unintended by any of them. Similarly, individuals may subordinate their actions to the rules of a figurative entity that they fail to recognize is figurative, such as God, the state, the proletariat, or society. There is no "emergent" mystery here that requires collectivist ontology to resolve.

Nor does the fact that collective decisions may diverge from individual decisions suggest that the former embody "knowledge" that must somehow be treated as residing outside the minds of individuals, rather than in the minds of individual observers (such as journalists, historians, or human scientists) of the individuals who constitute the group. The knowledge that Joe Biden won the popular vote in 2020 is predicated on the collective actions of 166 million voters and on previously, collectively established rules that had to be followed before the outcome could be known. The rules and actions produced an outcome that was not intended by 48.6 percent of those who followed them (who voted for candidates other than Biden). But this is fully understandable if we, the observers, interpret the outcome as the joint effect of 166 million individual actions and the rules they followed. It would only mystify the situation to attribute it to the conscious actions of a collective entity, which would stymie our interest in the diversity of the electorate and efface "its" fallibility. Having hypostasized the electorate as a collective entity, we would have no interest in discovering why 48.6 percent of "it" voted against what turned out to be "its" collective will. The fact that "the electorate chose" Biden elides the fact that there was a great deal of heterogeneity, and error, among the real decisions made by the real individuals whom we metaphorically call "the electorate." And the pragmatic, epistemic payoff for this elision is nil. Unlike water molecules, which act much differently than do hydrogen and oxygen atoms alone, "the electorate" acts no differently than do its individuals in communication with one another, when electoral rules are among the communicated ideas. I cannot see, then, how social collectivities are emergent phenomena compared to *ideational* individuals (rather than the monadic individuals of methodological individulism), in the way that chemistry is an emergent phenomenon compared to physics.

Similarly, neither the fact that, as Lerner notes, group procedures may "remain the same even as [group] membership changes," nor the fact that individuals may then fail to "understand the group's formation or the basis for its collectivized methods of rationalization," even as they "accept its procedures for making decisions *as a group*," requires hypostasizing the group. Indeed, it is difficult to imagine how we could understand misperceptions about group origins and rules without recourse to epistemological individualism. From this perspective we may notice that individuals are credulous, that they are capable of believing pretty much anything they are taught, and that both they and their teachers, being fallible, may be taught and may teach things that aren't true. People's failure to understand a group's formation or the reasons for its rules does contradict methodological individualism, which (as an offshoot of neoclassical economics) posits that individuals have knowledge adequate to their objective situations. But this is one thing that separates methodological from epistemological individualism.

Thus, I do not see how the notion that groups have emergent properties that are irreducible to the effects produced by communicating individuals, and (thus) by their ideas, contributes anything to our understanding. And I am concerned that it obscures the diversity and mistakenness of many of the ideas that actually motivate all conscious human action, including action in groups and in international relations. It is to oppose obscurantism that I insist on epistemological individualism as a methodology, as opposed to insisting merely on the ontology upon which the methodology is based: the ontology of ideas that are woven into webs that are perceived as qualia of individual minds governing the behavior of biologically "individual" bodies. If we treat ideas as if they are collective, even if only as a method adopted for pragmatic purposes, we are turning a blind eye to disagreement and mistake. Just as Milton Friedman's "pragmatic" insistence on using unrealistic assumptions obscured variability and error in business behavior, IR scholars who treat states as unitary actors will fail to understand how "Iraq" could have been so stupid as to invite its invasion by defying UN resolutions that threatened it with invasion; why "the United States," "the United Kingdom," "Australia," and "Poland" "thought" that "Iraq" was harboring WMD; why "Germany" could have done something so rash as to declare war on the United States in 1941; why "France" could have been so foolish as to invade Russia in 1812, or why "it" put all its chips on the Maginot Line in 1940; etc., ad infinitum. These historical mysteries can only be resolved when we investigate the fallible ideas of the individuals who made these decisions and the individuals who advised them. Restricting ourselves to Iraq, we surely do not need to think of the 2003 invasion as an emergent phenomenon, and thus as incomprehensible unless its outcome is treated as a type of collective knowledge. It is fully comprehensible as a collision of fallible, idiosyncratic individuals, at least one of whom (Saddam Hussein) wrongly calculated that the invasion would not happen because he incorrectly interpreted what was going through the fallible, individual minds of his "Coalition" counterparts.

If we fail to recognize that historical events, being human events, are traceable to the heterogeneous and often mistaken ideas of individuals, we will necessarily end up chasing pseudo-explanations merely for the sake of explaining, or predicting, what would, admittedly, take much more painstaking work to explain if we trained our sights on ideational realities—so as to resolve their fuzziness.

Positivism III: Escaping the "Empirical" Circle (Pamuk)

Lerner, like Larsson, turns to collective hypostasizations in the service of social-scientific prediction. I count this move as positivistic because the pragmatic purpose of bracketing ontology is to generalize about and predict IR behavior across time and place, regardless of the particularity of individual human beings' ideas. Zeynep Pamuk has a similar purpose in mind: the technocratic purpose of "seeking regularities and making general interventions." She is clear-eyed about the fact that ideational heterogeneity undermines this purpose, but she does not reject it out of hand or bracket it, although, as we have seen, she recognizes the potential utility (in Milton Friedman's sense) of doing so. Instead, she prudently seeks an estimate of the magnitude of the effects of ideational heterogeneity so as to judge how pernicious, in Reiss's terminology, it really is. Yet insofar as it is pernicious, it is precisely because it is incompatible with being estimated. Its potential perniciousness lies in its variability across individuals, but any measurements of it that we might make would cover only an adventitious sample of individuals. Thus, what Pamuk calls "empirical evidence for the magnitude of the problem" caused by ideational heterogeneity would suffer from that very problem. Such evidence would be positivistic; positivism rests on the assumption of uniformity; and the assumption of uniformity contradicts the presumption of pernicious heterogeneity.

Thus, the empirical grounding of presumptive *ideational* heterogeneity is provided not by "empirical evidence" in the positivistic sense—statistics or experiments that are taken to be universally applicable across individuals and their webs of belief—but by the putatively universal experience of discovering that others' ideas are different from one's own, to some extent (147-48). Such evidence, regrettably, does not admit of quantification, nor does the phenomenon that would be measured by the evidence, which is pernicious precisely because it can be expected to vary unpredictably—defeating attempts to extrapolate from evidence about its presence among an adventitious sample of individuals. There may well be clever ways to proxy the daily-life experience of ideational heterogeneity statistically or experimentally, but that which is being experienced undermines the assumption of uniformity that would underwrite the external validity of such proxies.

The experience of ubiquitous ideational heterogeneity does not ground a presumption of *complete* heterogeneity, but of some degree of it that varies across individuals. The ideas of everyone we meet are somewhat different from those of everyone else we meet, but the ideas of each person we meet are not *equally* different from our own. Ideational heterogeneity will vary according to the topic, too, not just the person. For these reasons, ideational heterogeneity defies any attempt to produce a universal coefficient of its magnitude, as the validity of this coefficient across instances would have to be sustained by the assumption of its uniformity or invariability. Ideational heterogeneity not only resists quantification, but undermines all social science that is rooted in the assumption of uniformity—except those forms of psychology that concern genetically (rather than ideationally) determined neurological homogeneities. If something as fundamental to human behavior as ideation, hence interpretation, varies in a manner that cannot be uniformly generalized, then we should doubt the validity of every positivist finding that concerns behavior that is plausibly determined by people's ideas rather than their genes.[6]

When seeing other human beings in person on a daily basis, the positivist social scientist notices (one hopes) that they are interesting, and thus worth talking to, precisely because their ideas are somewhat surprising—that is, different from those of the positivist social scientist herself. I take this to be a universal experience in the modern world, an experience that establishes a presumption of ubiquitous ideational heterogeneity. Yet it seems that when positivist social scientists enter their offices, they flip a switch that transforms the interesting, surprising others with whom they have just interacted into homogeneous ciphers, among whom any heterogeneity is a product of invariant objective factors. Their alterity, otherwise a potentially fatal threat to positivism, is transmogrified into a statistical regularity. On the internal terms of my critique of technocracy, I cannot lodge an ethical objection to the positivist's alienation from the other, or from humanity itself; I can only point to the inaccuracies it is bound to produce. However, I cannot possibly establish the magnitude of the inaccuracies, since that would entail using positivist analysis that inaccurately dehumanizes the other: analysis predicated on the assumption of uniformity. Thus, Pamuk is asking me to do the impossible. Nobody could use positivist "evidence" to prove that ideational heterogeneity is significant everywhere and always (which, in any case, I am not trying to do: the presumption of heterogeneity is defeasible in any given case). Nor could they use it to deny the significance of ideational heterogeneity everywhere and always.

Pamuk's request may stem from a misunderstanding of the purpose of *Power Without Knowledge*. She sees the book as attempting to account for "the observation that social science is not good at prediction"—a positivistic observation of a putatively universal tendency. In truth, the book never makes this observation and never attempts to account for it. The book does, however, make claims about ideational heterogeneity as an empirical reality, which to positivist eyes *must* be claims that should be verifiable with "empirical" evidence, i.e., experimental or observational statistical evidence.

Pamuk goes on to suggest that, since the book fails to provide such evidence, the putative explanandum (bad social-scientific predictions) may better be explained by factors that positivists themselves might adduce, such as "the difficulty of randomized controlled experiments, the unavailability of data, measurement problems, the inherent subjectivity of concept definitions, design and modeling choices, and the ethics of manipulating human subjects," to which one might add the file-drawer problem, p-hacking, publication bias, replicability problems, the problem of fraudulent data, and many other problems. Yet we are not faced with a binary choice. I would never deny that social scientists who lack adequate data or who inadequately measure their variables are prone to making bad predictions; I want only to add that so, too, are ideationally insensitive social scientists—including positivist social scientists who have adequately measured non-ideational data, who have not exaggerated their findings' statistical significance, and so on—because, being ideationally insensitive, such scientists ignore a fundamental empirical reality that is established experientially and introspectively, not by means of observationally or experimentally derived statistics. Nor do I claim that the factors on Pamuk's list are *less* significant in magnitude than ideational heterogeneity. I do not claim this because the only way to back up such a claim would be to adduce positivist evidence of the magnitude of the various factors she lists versus the magnitude of ideational heterogeneity, which would ignore the perniciousness of ideational heterogeneity.

Suppose I had produced a study showing that, say, measurement problems caused a low magnitude of bad predictions in comparison to ideational heterogeneity—in some particular sample. How could we know that the sample is representative of the universe that normative theorists of technocracy want to know about: the predictive performance of technocrats in the future? The thesis being tested, the thesis of ideational heterogeneity, gives us no reason to think that either rates of bad measurement or rates of ideational heterogeneity are constant, and it gives us good reason to think they are not. Measurement techniques are, after all, determined by the ideas of individual social scientists, which vary across them at any given time—to some extent—and can change radically over time. And ideational heterogeneity among those studied by social scientists is (according to the thesis) a product of streams of information that were not divinely arranged to be constant from time to time and place to place. Both types of heterogeneity (heterogeneity among social scientists and among those whose behavior they are measuring) would be obscured by averaging them into coefficients that are supposed to hold across individuals past, present, and future. Such coefficients would treat what is (according to the thesis) variable as if it were constant. It would, in short, beg the question raised by the thesis: the question of whether ideas *are* so heterogeneous as to cause prediction problems.

I confess, however, that *Power Without Knowledge* began, circa 2004, in much the way that Pamuk construes it as ending: as an attempt to explain a putative propensity toward technocratic predictive failures. I thought then that the book would open with a long chapter on the failed prediction that Iraq would be shown to be harboring WMD, and in 2009 I began working on a chapter on the failure of financial regulators to anticipate the problems that caused the financial crisis of 2008. Thus, I envisioned a positivist account in which two case studies were going to suggest a dysfunctional technocratic whole. But as I began to write, I came to see that in arguing that human behavior is unpredictable because of ideational heterogeneities that may disrupt behavioral homogeneities—including homogeneities between past and future individuals' behavior—I could not very well appeal to past evidence, as I had intended to do in those two chapters. Such an appeal would amount to the prediction that past technocrats' behavior will be homogeneous with future technocrats' behavior. It would amount to relying on Hume's assumption of uniformity in the operations of nature to prove that this very assumption cannot be relied upon, as a practical matter, when it comes to human behavior.

So I abandoned my initial plan for the book. Instead of inferring future predictive failures from Iraq or the financial crisis or any other past predictive failures, the book argues that failed predictions are, as a matter of logic, likelier to occur under certain conditions than others. Failure is logically more likely to occur if technocrats' beliefs are (a) ideationally insensitive, i.e., "injudicious," than if technocrats (b) attend to the possibility of ideational heterogeneity. And failure is logically more likely to occur when (c) predicting how anonymous others will behave than when (d) predicting how we ourselves will fare, as individuals, if we continue on an experimental path begun by exercising our power to exit from an unsatisfactory situation. These comparisons are not carried out a posteriori, by inference from observational or experimental statistics, but a priori. However, this logical element of the theory is ultimately empirical, as it is grounded in the everyday experience of ideational heterogeneity. This, it seems to me, makes the theory more scientific—more cognizant of knowable empirical reality—than positivistically established theories, which occlude empirical realities accessible to all human beings.

As published, the book does not claim that social scientists, as a general rule, make failed predictions. This claim would contradict the thesis of pernicious heterogeneity by assuming homogeneous behavior across the past and present. Even attempts to estimate the likelihood of social-scientific failure that did *not* attempt to factor in ideational heterogeneity would founder without the mere stipulation that the empirical basis of these estimates is drawn from a universally representative sample. Consider Philip E. Tetlock's marvelous *Expert Political Judgment* (2005), which asks how inaccurate "experts'" predictions are likely to be—all experts everywhere, it would seem. Tetlock may be the most rigorous, creative, and philosophically scrupulous positivist social scientist of our time. And he was investigating the dependent variable that Pamuk thinks I am investigating and, indeed, the one that I initially set out to investigate: bad social-scientific predictions. Tetlock is also courageous, as shown by his conclusion that experts' predictions are about as accurate as those that would be made by dart-throwing chimps (ibid., ch. 2). But what is the empirical evidence for this striking conclusion? Tetlock's sample of experts consisted of 284 "highly trained professionals" hailing from various academic disciplines, government, the private sector, and journalism, of whom 96 percent had postgraduate education of some kind and 52 percent had earned doctoral degrees (ibid., 239-40). Between 1988 and 1995, these experts offered "subjective probability judgments of possible futures of approximately sixty nations" concerning "continuity of domestic political leadership," "domestic policy and economic performance," "national security and defense policy," and miscellaneous other topics (ibid., 242, 246-48).

In one sense, Tetlock's study was orthogonal to technocracy: he did not seek to test experts' predictions of policy effects. Since he asked simply for forecasts of future conditions, the tasks he set for his experts were, at least arguably, much less demanding than the conditional forecasts that technocrats need to make (if we implement policy X, what will be its effects?) (Buturovic 2010; Tetlock 2010). However, one can readily imagine adjustments to Tetlock's data sample and protocols that would have tested a group of expert social scientists' ability to forecast technocratic policy effects. Yet there is no reason to believe that the ability of any group to make (in)accurate predictions about *their* immediate future tells us anything about the ability of forecasters in general, or epistocrats in general, to make such forecasts *sub specie aeternitatus*. Some of the professionals who get postgraduate training in the future will learn valuable lessons from this training, some will learn wrong-headed paradigms (such as positivism itself); some will be competent, within the bounds set by their ideational paradigm, and others less so; some policy effects will be easier than others to predict, but there is no way for even the most creative positivist to produce a valid "difficulty index" that could be applied to future technocratic policies—designed, as they will be, to alleviate social and economic problems of which we have no knowledge at present. We simply cannot know, then, if a given sample drawn from a particular portion of the past is representative of the total universe about which we are making inferences.

Note that the problem, here, is not necessarily that any group of experts must grapple with the second-order issue of *ideational* heterogeneity. The problem is that any given *observer* of experts, such as Tetlock, must bracket the possibility of variation between the empirical sample and the universe of behavior being predicted. Absent such bracketing, the magnitude of the forecasting errors created by any factor, *including* ideational heterogeneity, has to be counted a known unknown: it is not something we can reliably forecast. The magnitude of the causal effect of any objective independent variable on human behavior cannot be known *sub specie aeternitatus*, nor can that of any subjective variable. This, of course, in general terms, is the problem of induction, to which Hume's assumption of the uniformity of nature is the only positivist solution that has yet been proposed. Only this assumption can justify bracketing pernicious variation. But we musn't forget Hume's point: that it is merely an assumption, such that it cannot be sustained "empirically" (positivistically) except circularly.

I concede that we may want to grant Hume's assumption in the natural sciences because we have no reason to doubt its applicability there. The thesis of ideational heterogeneity, however, suggests one reason we may not want to apply it to human beings. (I do not want to close the door to other reasons). If I may be allowed another personal note, I was trained as a historian before becoming a political theorist. Historians, up against the rock face of *contingency,* have a visceral disdain (or they used to) for necessitarian, functionalist, or hypostasized oversimplifications, whether Hegelian-Marxist oversimplifications that purport to be historical, or positivist over-simplifications that are altogether innocent of history. Having turned myself into a political theorist, *Power Without Knowledge* required me to reflect on the sources of historical contingency—that is, to draw up, in the language of social science and social theory, an inventory of sources of "social complexity." My inventory grew very long very quickly, so I asked myself if there is a common denominator among all the sources I had listed. Ideational heterogeneity is the common factor I came up with, but there may be others.

Had I tried to carry out my original plan, I would have been unable demonstrate that the Iraq war and the financial crisis were representative failures of technocracy rather than one-offs or worst-case scenarios —"perfect storms" of contingency. Thus, I came to see that I cannot know, and should not pretend to prove, what Pamuk wants me to prove. This uncertainty, my own uncertainty, consists of my third-order awareness, as a theorist of technocracy, of my ignorance of the magnitude of the first-order behavioral unpredictability that will result from the main second-order factor to which I point as a possible source of unintended first-order technocratic consequences, ideational heterogeneity, or from any other source of "contingency," i.e., pernicious heterogeneity.

This third-order uncertainty is the only reason for the existence of Part III of the book. In the opening pages of Part III (317-19), I offer two basic reasons for the uncertainty. First, while Part II indicates that at present, technocrats tend to be injudicious, we cannot know just how badly injudicious technocrats will do their jobs in the future, even if we could determine how badly they have done their jobs in the past. It is entirely possible, for example, that even the most incompetent positivist technocrats will blunder into accurate behavioral predictions, and we cannot know how often this will happen. Second, political theorists cannot establish (nor could anyone else establish) the magnitude of the relief that a judicious technocracy might offer from the errors committed by an injudicious technocracy. We cannot peer into the future to determine precisely how competent judicious technocrats will be at predicting the behavior they will need to predict, so we cannot possibly know how well they will do their jobs. Just because judicious technocrats *attempt* to take account of anonymous others' ideas does not entail that they will succeed, nor does it tell us how well they might succeed in any given case. All sorts of imponderables, such as the items on Pamuk's list of social-scientific problems—along with future judicious technocrats' good or bad fortune in coming up with good hypotheses, and the match or mismatch between their ideas and those of the particular target populations whose behavior they might attempt to predict—will affect the degree to which even the most brilliant judicious technocrats succeed and, if they fail, the magnitude of the resulting unintended consequences. Therefore, I concluded, if there is a way forward for normative theorists of technocracy, it would have to be by comparing the *relative* magnitudes of predictive failure that are likely, logically speaking, under injudicious technocracy, judicious technocracy, and, if possible, a third type of technocracy, such as exitocracy. By executing a comparison of this type, we can, to some extent, leave behind the demand for third-order knowledge of absolute magnitudes, shielded from contingent vagaries. This, of course, is the demand Pamuk is now making.

Pamuk expresses the position of a truly open-minded positivist political theorist who is not biased against recognizing ideational heterogeneity, but who wants to know how big a problem it is likely to be. Perhaps this type of question represents a worthwhile direction for political epistemology. It is certainly a familiar one, although it is not one that has usually been followed with the methodological care Pamuk is trying to supply. It is the path followed by all of those, for example, who predicate their defenses or critiques of democracy on positivist studies purporting to demonstrate how ignorant voters are (i.e., how ignorant some voters have been in the past); how "irrational" they are; how prone they are to cognitive biases of the sort that have been uncovered, supposedly, by behavioral economists, such as Kahneman and Tversky; or how effective deliberation is likely to be in correcting citizens' errors and improving their knowledge. Much of the field of normative political epistemology might best be seen, c. 2021, as the site of a confrontation between certain idealized theories of democracy and the universal truths that positivist social scientists think they illuminate every time they publish a study. I helped to pioneer this very approach to normative political epistemology; I was among the first political theorists to try to assess the epistemic capacities of democracy by means of positivist studies (Friedman 1996 and 1998). Although I never took these studies at face value—I assumed that it was my role to inspect them with a critical eye—I simply assumed that, at their best, they allow us to test the applicability of normative theory to empirical reality.

I started down the positivist path because I viewed it as a guard against dogmatic thinking. The Marxist critique of positivism as ideological is itself, I thought, ideological, as it is undisciplined by anything but the theorist's unquestioned (Marxist) assumptions (e.g., Adorno [1957] 1976). The dialectical blender always produces the confection you expected to create. Positivism, in contrast, is so open minded as to consider (seemingly) any and all independent variables as possible causes of behavior, not just those that are pre-approved by ideological biases. But I failed to see that positivist social science underwrites this open-mindedness with a dogmatic rejection of any putative variable, such as ideational heterogeneity, that would disrupt the guiding assumption of uniformity. The open positivist mind snaps shut at the thought that contingency cannot be banished to the tail ends of probabilistic bell curves (making it, too, predictable)—the thought that human behavior is (as a practical matter) exempt from Hume's assumption. Positivism is just as dogmatic about the non-existence of pernicious heterogeneities, including ideational heterogeneity, as Marxism is about the invalidity of bourgeois social science.

The question to be asked about my alternative to positivism would appear, then, to be whether it, too, is dogmatic in insisting on the a priori reality of ideational determinism and heterogeneity. However, it seems to me that the way to press home this question would be to challenge the anthropological reasoning provided in Chapters 2 and 3, just as the way to challenge Marxism would be on substantive grounds, and just as I hope to have challenged positivism on substantive grounds. In short, positivists could try to deny the reality of ideational heterogeneity rather than maintaining Pamuk's or Lerner's stance of openness toward it. But this denial could not be grounded in positivist studies of "the" magnitude of ideational heterogeneity, which would beg the question. The positivist political epistemologist's denial or minimization of heterogeneity would thus have to transcend positivism. Only this could assure us that positivist social science is not, itself, an elaborate castle of sand.

Positivism IV: Natural Science, Psychology, and Intellectual Charity (Reiss)

Julian Reiss's contribution adds, to devastating effect, many potentially important items to the list of social-scientific problems mentioned by Pamuk. As with her portion of the list, I don't find any reason to disagree with Reiss's claim that experts (or citizen-technocrats) may have clashing standards of evidence; or that the short-run effects of a policy, which are the only effects that can be measured through laboratory or field experimentation, may differ from long-run effects. There may also be irresolvable disagreements about which outcome variable to target, and so on: Reiss's list is a good one.

I am a bit more reluctant to sign on to his main argument, however, concerning conflicts of value among experts. To be sure, such conflicts may cause practical problems, which I bracketed by stipulating that a technocracy, to count as a technocracy, would direct "its" (collective) action against consensually defined social and economic problems. I bracketed value differences because many contemporary theorists have been trained to reduce all political phenomena to conflicts of either interests or values, and I wanted to get them to think outside this box, to see the world as technocrats see it.

I should emphasize, then, that my discussion of the fact of technocratic disagreement (38-46), in Chapter 1, was intended solely as a rebuttal to the naïve technocratic realist. If epistocrats or citizen-technocrats disagree about technocratic questions, then the answers cannot be self-evident; but this does not entail, or even suggest, that disagreement is a problem in itself. Likewise, Chapter 1's discussion of "the problem of epistocratic identification" (67-71) was an attempt to block the naïve invocation of a division of epistemic labor that somehow manages to identify the true experts, whose views can be relayed by journalists to the masses, who must then submit to the unforced force of the better epistocratic data set. Neither disagreement nor the problem of epistocratic identification has to do with ideational heterogeneity; in Chapter 1, the political anthropology to be constructed in Chapters 2 and 3 has not yet been broached. I don't see technocratic disagreement or the problem of identification, then, as *inherently* problematic for a technocracy.

Thus, the irresolvability of value disputes does not strike me as particularly troubling, from a technocratic point of view. So long as the values of both parties are utilitarian, technocratic legitimacy is not at stake, whichever party wins the debate—even if neither side can be said to deserve to win, in comparison to the other. If the values are *not* utilitarian, we have left the realm of technocracy as I define it. But where utilitarian ends are not disputed but the means of achieving them are, the parties to a disagreement may both be largely correct despite their differences. Thus, for example, while we can expect that even *judicious* technocrats may disagree with one another because of the difficulty of understanding and predicting anonymous others, this dissensus is not inherently problematic, because all the contending parties would be true empiricists in the sense of heeding the reality of ideational heterogeneity. This is all they need to do to elevate themselves above contemporary social scientists, who, Reiss agrees, are averse to considering the very possibility of pernicious heterogeneity. Conversely, I see no reason to worry about dissensus among these (injudicious) "scientists," as the achievement of consensus around profoundly unscientific predictions is not particularly desirable. The notion of dissensus as inherently problematic may stem from the naïve assumption that consensus would reveal the truth.

Thus, I would hate to see the critical study of social science devolve into a reaffirmation of political theorists' well-honed Weberian, Berlinian, and Rawlsian sensitivity to value dissensus. This would keep us too sedately in the mindset from which it is difficult even to understand the technocratic attempt to explore means to the achievement of genuinely shared ends. Nevertheless, Reiss's catalogue of the problems facing social scientists seems to me to spell out additional reasons for political theorists never again to cite a social-scientific study without carefully inspecting the guts of it—not the statistical guts, which are minutely interrogated by social scientists themselves, but the conceptual means by which measurements are taken, and the interpretive means by which findings are turned into conclusions.

However, another reason to hold social-scientific studies at arm's length is that the interpretive tool by which findings are turned into conclusions is, all too often, the assumption of uniformity. So I cannot go along with Reiss's suggestion that we emulate Otto Neurath, a positivist who found inspiration in the predictive successes of astronomy and geology. Planets and tectonic plates do not change course when they perceive or interpret new conditions (rather than colliding with them). Reiss argues that we should not take laboratory physics as the standard for social science, but I did not propose that we should. Rather, I denied that we should we take laboratory physics or any other natural science as the standard.

The type of epistemic complexity foregrounded in *Power Without Knowledge* is not the type that preoccupies positivists: the complexity faced by social scientists confronting "complex societies" that throw forth so many "factors" or "forces" (so many independent variables) that it is difficult to tease out causality among them. That problem is solved (with exceptions of the sort that are carefully noted by Reiss and Pamuk) by multivariate regression analysis, if the social scientist knows all the variables involved; or, if not, by experimentation—but only if the assumption of uniformity allows the extrapolation of the results produced by these techniques. This is why my critique of positivism begins with the late twentieth-century movement from econometrics to natural experiments and then RCTs (201-28)—a critique guided, in part, by Reiss's superb discussion of this movement (Reiss 2008). Each of these positivist solutions to the struggle with "complexity," defined as the problem of many independent variables, depended on the assumption of uniformity. Each of them, in its own way, *succeeded* as a way of mastering the complexity of many variables. But none of them was capable of dealing with pernicious heterogeneity, including ideational heterogeneity.

The same appears to be true of the sophisticated inferential strategies referred to by Reiss, such as those developed by Nancy Cartwright, Judea Pearl, and Reiss himself. Insofar as these techniques depend on the assumption that, as Reiss puts it, human behavior "varies systematically with aspects of the settings within which it occurs," they continue to treat people as intersections of objective variables that affect them uniformly and comprehensibly, notwithstanding the fact that the variables themselves may vary subjectively. Objective settings (for example, the context created by an experimental lab, or by questions posed or stereotypes fed to them there) are the very things that experimental subjects must interpret before they act; why should we assume, then, that it is the setting rather than the interpreter that varies? As I mentioned in my critique of positivism (206), Reiss's book on *Error in Economics*, which proved invaluable in helping me kick the positivist habit, noted that participants in randomized tests of the ultimatum game "made more generous offers in two experiments in Kansas City than in an identical experiment in Vermont," and that "students in a Kansas City community college offered more than workers in a nearby warehouse" (Reiss 2008, 95). Is it really plausible that it was the location of one experiment in Kansas and another in Vermont, or of one in a classroom and another in a warehouse, that caused the variation rather than variations in the ideas of the people involved? Even supposing that these different settings *triggered* diverse behavior, would this not have had to be by means of how the subjects interpreted the settings, which is subjective and thus vulnerable to pernicious heterogeneity? To focus on the variability of the settings rather than the variability of the interpreters is to continue to ignore the empirical reality of our ideational humanity. This seems to me no better, in principle, than neoclassical economists' reduction of economic agents' behavior to the objective incentives they face, but need not subjectively perceive and interpret.

Nor am I confident that the correction of behavioral-economics findings by positivist means exemplifies "progress toward accurate predictive knowledge," as Reiss suggests. He points out that one of the objectionable features of Tversky and Kahneman's interpretation of their "Linda" experiment was challenged by Klaus Fiedler (1988), whose experimental subjects, unlike Tversky and Kahneman's, did not commit the "conjunction fallacy" when they were asked in "frequentist" rather than probabilistic language to think about the likelihood that Linda, who was described to the subjects as a feminist political activist in college, is now a feminist bank teller rather than a bank teller *simpliciter*. I myself noted Fiedler's successful challenge to Tversky and Kahneman (198), but not because his success somehow demonstrates a broader tendency for positivist methods to bring social-scientific truth to light. The latter view could be justified only if we had reason to think that positivist methods are guarantors of scientific progress. But that would presuppose that these methods allow social scientists to identify universal homogeneities, and this presupposition begs the question of pernicious heterogeneity.

I do not deny that positivists can sometimes get it right—not at all. Tetlock's dart-throwing chimps often get it right, too. Fiedler, however, got it right not by chance but because he asked himself, apparently, whether it is *introspectively plausible* that Tversky and Kahneman's subjects were, as Tversky and Kahneman asserted, irrational. He seems to have tried putting himself in the subjects' shoes to see if they might have been able to justify their behavior to themselves rationally. In effect, then, Fiedler was a *Verstehen* psychologist who tried to understand the subjects with intellectual charity—something that, so far as I can tell, Tversky and Kahneman never once tried to do. Unlike Tversky and Kahneman, Fiedler asked himself how the subjects were interpreting the question put to them in the lab. The objective setting, the lab, had nothing to do with it; the subjects' interpretations of what happened there are what mattered.

I use the term *intellectual charity* because the apter term, *interpretive charity*, was long ago turned to a different use by analytic philosophers. Instead of meaning an interpretation that tries to get at what someone else is actually thinking, interpretive charity in the analytic tradition means attributing to the other "the best arguments" for her position—regardless of whether she is actually making those arguments or, indeed, has ever thought of them. This is a fine strategy if one wants to hone one's own arguments, but not if one wants to understand the other. A lack of understanding indicates that the other is ideationally *different* from oneself; projecting *one's own* arguments into her head is a recipe for the very misunderstanding that *intellectual* charity would attempt to clear up. By intellectual charity, then, I mean the attempt to interpret the other as a rational, ideational being, not necessarily one whose ideas match one's own (Friedman 2021).

One is not being intellectually charitable if one is looking for irrationality, as so many psychologists have been doing since Freud. These psychologists would respond, of course, by saying that it is an "empirical" question whether people really are rational and thus deserve intellectual charity, and that it is this very question that their research is designed to answer. This response depends on excluding introspective evidence from the category of the empirical. Introspection *always* shows that one's own beliefs are rationally held at the time that they are held: that is, one always thinks that one has good reasons for one's beliefs, and thus for the interpretations to which they lead and the actions that result. (Or perhaps I should say that this is a matter of logic, not introspection: I won't try, here, to solve the problem of the relationship between the two.) A belief in *p* that is unjustified by one's perception of the truth of *p* would violate what Ward E. Jones (2002) has dubbed the first-person constraint on doxastic explanation, that is, the fact that one cannot recognize one's own beliefs as being caused by epistemically inadequate reasons, lest one abandon those beliefs due to their recognized inadequacy. Even when looking back on what one now considers one's mistaken beliefs, one must acknowledge, I think, that at the time they did not seem mistaken or one would not have held them. Given this logical-introspective evidence of one's own rationality, one applies an intellectually uncharitable double standard if one assumes that others' beliefs are irrationally held. Is it scientific to ignore logical-introspective evidence when one attempts to understand the other, as if one's own rationality is sui generis?[7]

Even social science that is not conducted by psychologists, and does not explicitly announce the "irrationality" of those being investigated, is intellectually uncharitable if it is positivistic. No political scientist could coherently attribute her own vote to her demographic traits rather than, at most, to her *interpretation* of what someone with those traits *should* vote for, based, say, on what she *believes* to be the objective interests of someone with those traits. Yet positivist political scientists routinely attribute *other* people's votes to their demographic traits, or to "fundamental factors" such as changes in economic statistics, because, pragmatically, it is quite difficult to enter the mental worlds of millions of other people, and political scientists conclude that they should not even try. (Or perhaps it does not even occur to them that objective demographic traits and objective economic phenomena cannot possibly cause subjective beliefs.) All non ideational independent variables are in this sense intellectually uncharitable, because we *never* lack rational, ideational, subjective reasons for our own beliefs, or for the conscious actions to which they lead via interpretations

—this is what it means for them to be conscious actions—such that we never have recourse, in explaining our own conscious behavior, at the moment of decision, to non-rational forces, social structures, and so on. All positivist social science, then, is put at risk by intellectual charitability.

By enacting intellectual charitability, Fiedler was placing himself outside of positivist social science. He was trying to attend to people's ideas, not reduce people to victims of *pre-cognitive* "biases." The fact that others were able to replicate his intellectually charitable reinterpretation of the Linda findings, however, does not show that he had made a step forward in the gradual positivistic accumulation of knowledge of the laws of human behavior. It merely indicates that frequentist ways of thinking about probability were common enough, in German culture in the years when the experiment occurred, to have been dominant among Fiedler's experimental subjects, and that he was intellectually charitable enough to notice it. This is just the type of homogeneity that ideationally sensitive social scientists would look for, and that they might be fortunate enough to discover in a given case, but it does not indicate a universal regularity. If people's ideas about probability changed, so would their laboratory behavior. Positivist social scientists think they are in the business of patiently winnowing hypotheses down to universal truths, incrementally building up our stock of usable knowledge, but a different interpretation is that positivist social science usually amounts to the pointless accumulation of details about the ideas of people in particular times and places, such as university psych labs—details that would be of no wider interest if not for the (mere) assumption that they reveal knowable uniformities in the operations of human nature, because such uniformities necessarily explain all human behavior.

Consider, in this light, the universal principles that Reiss cites under the rubric of "the science of persuasion." Are these the hard-won fruits of careful attention to human nature?

Reiss finds particularly important, for technocratic purposes, "the principle of social proof" that has been unearthed by this putative science: the principle "that people tend to regard as correct that which they think others think is correct." To begin operationalizing intellectual charity, it seems to me, the consumers of social science (and eventually its producers) should ask themselves if any posited principle of behavior or thought applies to themselves. This would help eliminate the double standard on which uncharitability thrives. In the case of the principle of social proof, each of us would ask ourselves: "Do I (in effect) act in accordance with this principle in the conduct of my own life?" (If not, then the principle cannot be a universal law, and it might not be a universal tendency, or even a tendency, or even a phenomenon rather than an illusion.) I think if we are rigorously honest with ourselves, the answer would have to be: "No—I would not regard as correct, for example, whatever *imbeciles* think is correct." (In the form of a rhetorical question: Were I transplanted to Alabama, would I tend to regard as correct what my neighbors regarded as correct if I viewed them as racist, homophobic victims of bourgeois ideology?)

The problem with the principle of social proof is that it is, as one would expect of social psychology, irrationalistic. It conjures into existence a psychological propensity for *indiscriminate* trusting that one might ascribe to foolish people "out there," like the dupes of advertising campaigns, but never to oneself in any actual case (rather than abstractly, in general). But it may be possible, sometimes, not only to use introspection to falsify irrationalist "principles," but to formulate alternative hypotheses, as Fiedler did, that are intellectually charitable toward the experimental subjects. One might draw on one's introspection to hypothesize, for example, that the psychologists who established this principle may have studied subjects who trusted the judgments of "others" only because the subjects viewed *those particular* others as trustworthy. If so, a revised principle would be: People tend to regard as correct that which they think that others *whom they find trustworthy* think is correct.

That is a principle that one certainly *could* apply to oneself, because it is rationalistic. It is rational to trust somebody whom one finds to be trustworthy. But the revised, intellectually charitable principle does not produce the simple, usable predictions generated by the principle of social proof—simple enough, and universal enough, to be used as the basis for technocratic interventions that disregard the possibility of ideational heterogeneity. For example, Reiss is impressed that the unrevised principle may have been at work in generating certain behavioral findings in India, "which shows that the principle applies widely" because India, unlike the countries where the psychological studies on which the principle is based were performed, is not a Western, educated, industrialized (WEIRD) country. But this is relevant only if the subjects in India were actually applying the original principle rather than the revised one, and only if the subjects in the Western experiments were doing the same. If they were using the revised principle, it could be turned into a prediction only after a technocrat or social scientist did some research about the beliefs or assumptions of the *particular* people in question, to see how likely it is that they would find *particular* other people to be, in fact, trustworthy. This particularism shows that the applicability of the revised principle beyond the WEIRD area of the world does not establish the universal applicability of the principle, and thus does not produce easy behavioral predictions.

It turns out that the Indian study concerned the effect of a rating of paper mills' effluents on the rate of effluents they produced. When particular paper mills were rated as particularly dirty, the pollutants they emitted began to decline. According to the study's authors, the ratings were produced by "the Centre for Science and Environment (CSE), one of India's best-known and most influential environmental nongovernmental organizations" (Powers et al. 2011, 7). The authors hypothesize "that environmental performance ratings programs may have an effect by mobilizing local communities and/or regulators to exert pressure for reductions in discharges and by improving managers' information about their own pollution and abatement opportunities." Notice that the authors are overgeneralizing, in true positivist fashion, by interpreting the independent variable as objective rather than subjective. In truth, the study did not produce findings about "environmental ratings programs" in general (ibid., 23), nor about the effect of "disclosure" on pollution, as the title of the paper grandly claims ("Does Disclosure Reduce Pollution? Evidence from India's Green Ratings Project"). The claim is that there is an objective phenomenon, "disclosure" or "environmental ratings," that acts as an independent variable affecting pollution everywhere and always. But what the evidence actually suggests is that a *particular* ratings program that enjoyed a *particular, subjective* reputation in India—a reputation for trustworthiness—may have helped environmental activists apply pressure to the operators of particular paper mills. Reiss's attempt to assimilate this finding to a universal "principle of social proof" strikes me as even less justified than the authors' overgeneralization and the exaggerated claim of the paper's title. If we interpret the findings in the light of the revised principle, by contrast, which does seem warranted, we would be left without the ability to make easy, sweeping—but potentially quite inaccurate—behavioral predictions.

The *unrevised* principle, for example, might lead us to predict that anything that any partisan politician says will tend to be trusted by members of the politician's party (Zaller 1992). This might be particularly tempting for *us* to believe right now (February 2021), but an intellectually charitable interpretation would suggest that the "willingness" of Trump supporters to trust whatever he said must have stemmed from their prior grounds for finding him trustworthy, as this is the way our own trust works: we never trust someone in whom trust seems, to us, to be unwarranted. And indeed, Trump was a product of alternative media to which Republicans turned because they were convinced that the mainstream media were so biased that they had become *un*trustworthy. Trump relentlessly attacked the mainstream media on those very grounds—bolstering his own trustworthiness among the *particular* people who found the mainstream media untrustworthy. But never-Trump Republicans, for example, did not believe anything and everything Trump said, even though he was a Republican president, since they found him to be particularly *untrustworthy*. Conversely, in the 2016 primary campaign, Trump trounced Republicans such as Jeb Bush, the former Republican governor of Florida, brother of a recent Republican president, and son of yet another—someone who had far more claim to Republicans' "trust," using the unrevised (and intellectually uncharitable) principle of social trust, than Trump had. The unrevised principle would have led us to predict that Bush would trounce Trump, who had never before been a Republican politician or even a Republican. But the revised principle allows us to recognize that in this particular case, what Republicans considered trustworthy was not calling oneself a Republican but opposing "untrustworthy" sources of information.

Thus, while I hate to disagree with a Regents' Professor Emeritus of Psychology and Marketing at Arizona State University (Reiss's source for the "science of persuasion"), the neglect, by this so-called science, of the need for intellectual charity suggests that it is actually a pseudoscience that is valuable only pathologically—as the source of easy-to-make but unreliable behavioral predictions. This is not to say, however, that there is no science of *psychology*. Introspection reveals that our minds follow rules of logical inference (imperfectly, to be sure), that we remember things, that we perceive light and sound, that we have the ability to learn languages, that we have the capacity to trust others, etc. And our knowledge of the insights of Darwin and Mendel suggests that the minds housed in our brains must be structured in ways that were basically conducive to the survival and reproduction of our bodies in the environments of evolutionary adaptation where our genome was shaped. It stands to reason that these neurological structures should be fairly constant across all members of the species, for we all descend from ancestors who passed down the genes that produced that neurology. The resulting architecture of our minds has been illuminated through centuries of valuable and judicious psychological research: judicious because it attempts to explain introspectively confirmed realities such as optical illusions, the ways of memory, and the structures of language. But what grew up around this still-expanding and vibrant scientific core in the twentieth century was a vast periphery of putatively universalistic but actually historical findings, such as those produced in abundance in social psychology (including the "science of persuasion"), whose scientific value rests entirely on the assumption that the laboratory behavior of ideationally contingent agents *must* exemplify epistemically accessible universal causal principles—even principles that violate introspective realities, principles that are not intellectually charitable, and principles that, therefore, *cannot* hold universally, insofar as we know from introspection that they do not apply to ourselves, but exclusively to the putatively irrational other.

Positivism V: Does Language Homogenize Ideas? (Reamer)

Robert Reamer's paper develops two interesting thoughts, one of which I will discuss in a separate subsection. Here I want to agree, *in principle,* with his view that a shared language can be an ideational homogenizer that *might* justify limited social-scientific extrapolations from local evidence to a wider population that speaks the same language as those in the local sample. But I need to point out that in practice, language doesn't get us very far, because the ideational heterogeneity that we know to be ubiquitous from experience occurs *within* the bounds set by linguistic homogeneity.

Reamer is using linguistic homogeneity to counter a more sweeping argument for ideational heterogeneity than is actually made in *Power*

Without Knowledge. Even a modest amount of linguistically imposed ideational homogeneity would rebut this argument that I do not make. Reamer contends that I argue that every individual (1) "is to be presumed sui generis," and that, therefore, (2) "we need an argument in every instance justifying our belief that a uniformity we have identified in one place will be present in another." The second statement is accurate, but the first is not.

It is true that I think we need an argument for ideational homogeneity whenever it is claimed. This would effect a shift in the burden of argument that would replace Hume's assumption of uniformity with a (defeasible) presumption of ideational heterogeneity (205-9). Positivists take their every finding to represent a uniformity; in their eyes, the burden is on the critic to provide evidence to the contrary. This, in effect, is the burden that, in their very different ways, Larsson, Lerner, Pamuk, and Reiss attempt to assign to me. Unavoidably, these attempts elide our everyday experience of belief heterogeneity. Reflection upon the reasons for this experience should teach us, I think, that human behavior produced in one lab or survey may not replicate elsewhere, and that even if it has replicated thus far, it may stop replicating tomorrow. My position, then, is that we must reject any ascription of lawlike status to social-scientific generalizations. Generalizations are sure to stop replicating if people's ideas change.

To deal (imperfectly) with this problem, a *human* scientist, as opposed to a social scientist, who posits an ideational homogeneity needs to provide evidence that this thought or way of thinking is likely to be present in the minds of a specific population. Thus, Fiedler's work suggests (as I see it) that a certain population in a certain time and place had a frequentist rather than probabilistic understanding of probability, contradicting Tversky and Kahneman's declaration of the universality of the "bias" they sought to prove, but not establishing Fiedler's intellectually charitable alternative as, itself, universal. So I recommend that human scientists proceed as follows. First, reject uncharitable and universalistic interpretations of findings. Second, if, like Fiedler, one produces an intellectually charitable interpretation of a finding, it should be treated as a hypothesis that might be applicable to a *particular* population. It is then the scientist's responsibility to investigate whether this hypothesis is borne out. She cannot simply take it for granted that it will be borne out everywhere and always, as positivists do, obviating population-specific investigation; she has to prove its applicability here and now by providing a reason to think that a specific ideational homogeneity is widespread in a population and likely to persist during the implementation of a technocratic policy keyed to this homogeneity. This would entail adducing evidence that the idea is in fact widespread, identifying a mechanism (such as mass-mediated communication) that would have made it so, and producing a reason to think that this homogeneity is lasting (e.g., because it is reinforced by a network of other widely communicated ideas that contribute to a cohesive worldview). This is what a judicious technocracy would strive to do. By failing to do this, positivist social scientists are injudiciously failing to meet their burden of argument. They are letting Hume do their jobs for them.

While Reamer recognizes that I demand this shift in the burden of argument, he fails to see that it is inconsistent with the view, which he attributes to me, that every individual's ideas are so utterly different from those of every other individual that we are all completely (as opposed to variably) sui generis. If we were as different from one another as that, it would be impossible to discover any ideational homogeneities after the burden of argument is shifted in the way I want to shift it, so a judicious technocracy would be out of the question. Clearly, then, I cannot be proposing the thesis of total heterogeneity that Reamer attributes to me, and that he rebuts by pointing out that most people agree about a great many things that are expressed, homogeneously, in their common language.

While I do think that it is logically possible for any two people to have completely different ideas, with no overlaps (no homogeneities) between their webs of belief, I do not claim that this is ever in fact the case, let alone that it is likely to be the case everywhere and always. Rather, the defeasible presumption of ubiquitous but incomplete ideational heterogeneity is based on our everyday experience of *some* unpredicted ideas among everyone we encounter (147-48).[8] The fact that some of my ideas are different from some of yours does not mean that we have no ideas in common. It means that if I try to predict your behavior, the prediction may not come true, and that if I want to do better, I should get to know your ideas better. This is what I think social scientists should try to do, transforming them into human scientists. This would require a cultural revolution against positivism, inter alia (314, 342), because positivism is grounded in the assumption of universality, which militates against the shift in the burden of argument that I propose.

Reamer resists this antipositivist shift in the burden of argument because he misinterprets it as logically barring *any* ideational homogeneity; this is because he wrongly attributes to me the thesis of complete ideational heterogeneity. Yet it seems to me that his invocation of Wittgenstein functions as a way to *meet* the new burden of argument. Reamer contends that, in principle, linguistic homogeneities that express a "world-picture" grounded in a common way of life may provide all the ideational homogeneity one needs to extrapolate from a sample of a population to the population as a whole, and I agree—in principle. Just as it is logically possible that two people's webs of belief are completely sui generis, it is logically possible, and even likely, that some of the homogeneities among real people's webs of belief are caused by a common form of life expressed in a common language. It appears, though, that Reamer thinks that linguistic homogeneity has this effect even if it does not indicate *directly relevant* homogeneities in the population's ideas, because *any* homogenization of ideas would defeat the thesis of complete heterogeneity—a thesis that he incorrectly thinks that I defend.

Thus, while I agree that language provides *some* ideational homogeneity, which would defeat the thesis that there is *no* homogeneity, I don't advance that thesis, and I don't see how linguistic homogeneity provides much help with the actual problem we face, which is not total heterogeneity but a ubiquitous tendency toward varying degrees of incomplete heterogeneity among the speakers of the same language (although the problem might be worse if they did not speak the same language).[9] I don't doubt, for example, as I suggested in reply to Lerner, that the constant use of linguistic metaphors such as "the state" may induce many people homogeneously to think of states as realities. This source of ideational homogeneity would be lacking in a culture that had no word for the state. Yet language does not, *for the most part*, determine the content of our ideas, as shown by the gigantic areas of ideational heterogeneity and disagreement that occur among speakers of the same language—as well as the fact that we find it exceedingly easy to revise, redefine, or reject words when they do not express our ideas. I find it so easy to reject the hypostasized conception of the state shared by many of my linguistic peers that I'm not entirely sure that my induction into English ever forced me to think of the state as real, but it might have. Language may sometimes unthinkingly attach us to certain beliefs, but these attachments are very weak and easily dissolved by thought. Thus, language is best seen as a tool by which we express thoughts that may, for other reasons, be homogeneous across individuals—or heterogeneous. In any event, human disagreements rarely concern the meaning of words. Far more often, they concern the perceived, interpreted realities that we use words to describe (154)—suggesting that the real heterogeneities and homogeneities are neither linguistic nor conceptual, but are more like scientific hypotheses, or doctrines, concerning features of the objective world, including the common world upon which Wittgenstein erects his theory of language. Language is primarily a means of expressing ideas about what that world looks like. Sometimes these ideas will be homogeneous, sometimes not.

It does seem to be the case that if, as Reamer suggests, one counts belief in "time, personal identity, physical reality, cause and effect, [and] basic laws of logic" as constitutive of a common world-picture, then it is plausible that our language reflects this picture in a manner that gives the picture credibility for us. But it is even more plausible that this world-picture is what human beings, in common with other animals, had to have had burned into their neurology if they were to survive in an environment that, in truth (one may hypothesize), strongly resembles the world pictured by this list of beliefs. In this view, our language reflects roughly the same *metaphysical* world-picture that would be reflected in the language of talking apes, dolphins, or mollusks. Yet even if we accepted the linguistic rather than evolutionary conjecture about the origins of this metaphysical world-picture, it would not justify the conclusion that linguistic homogeneity so greatly inhibits ideational idiosyncracy among native speakers of the same language that technocratic behavioral predictions can be made without reference to any other ideational homogeneity than the fact that the targets of a technocratic initiative speak the same language. There are many topics to disagree about that do not implicate metaphysics, topics about which our neurology dictates nothing but outer metaphysical boundaries—

boundaries of logical possibility. Within those boundaries is an immense expanse in which ideational idiosyncracy can occur. (Let me reiterate that disagreement itself is not the problem; here, the problem is that it indicates the presence of a possibly pernicious belief heterogeneity.)

Thus, while Reamer concedes the possibility of ideational idiosyncracy, I think he underestimates its potential significance, and thus the hurdle that linguistic homogeneity would have to clear if it were to be of much technocratic importance. Whether for linguistic or evolutionary reasons, it is probably safe for judicious technocrats to assume that most of those who will be subjected to their regulations will have homogeneous metaphysical notions of cause and effect, but this won't help very much if they are trying to predict how people may act *given* their acceptance of those notions: the type of prediction that technocrats regulating, say, the banking industry must make. This is the type of idiosyncracy that produces disagreements among human beings who speak the same language, as we discover in our everyday interactions with fellow language speakers. The fact that, as children, we may learn words linked to certain beliefs does not deterministically tie the words to the beliefs—as shown by presumptive, but perniciously variable, ideational idiosyncracy among adult speakers of the same language. By the same token, the intelligibility of one another's idiosyncratic beliefs is quite variable and often nonexistent, *despite* their expression in words that mean the very same thing to speaker and listener. The error made by Wittgenstein, I think, is his assumption that words come first, then ideas, which puts him too close to the discredited Sapir-Whorf hypothesis.[10] This is an assumption falsified every time we find ourselves at a loss for words—that is, searching for a word, and sometimes inventing a word, to express a wordless idea (151-52). And it is falsified by disagreement among speakers of the same language.

While I do not dispute that whatever mutual intelligibility we enjoy occurs, as Reamer says, "against a backdrop of broadly shared beliefs and meanings," it seems to me that these *beliefs* (about reality) should be distinguished from *meanings* (of words or concepts), to allow for the fact that disagreements about the former are expressed, usually, by means of *shared* words and concepts. This should underscore the difference between epistemological individualism and the hermeneutical tradition. The interpretive problem pointed out by the former is not primarily that of communicated *meanings*, which may differ across languages but rarely across individuals. It is rather the problem of conflicting *beliefs and presuppositions* expressed, ordinarily, in terms of shared meanings. Because beliefs are subjective and thus potentially heterogeneous where meanings are (linguistically) intersubjective and thus largely homogeneous, epistemological individualism replaces a focus on largely predictable meanings with a focus on sometimes unpredictable beliefs.

Now I turn to Reamer's speculation that positivist social scientists are secret Wittgensteinians (or, perhaps more precisely, that they are secret adherents of the Sapir-Whorf hypothesis), who treat language as the ideationally homogenizing mechanism that entitles them to generalize their findings. Thirty years of reading positivist social science suggests (to me) that this speculation is fanciful, so in a moment I will say a few words about why. In principle, however, if Reamer were right, it would mean that we already live in a judicious technocracy, because social scientists are already human scientists who rely on Wittgenstein rather than Hume. Reamer and I differ about whether this is the way things are, empirically. (This is an example of ideational heterogeneity among speakers of the same language.) If Reamer is right, then the cultural revolution against positivism already happened and I slept through it. This would not indicate, however, that such a revolution is not, or rather was not, warranted.

Has the revolution occurred? It seems to me that if social scientists generally assumed that language is the operative homogenizing variable, they would occasionally mention it, or test for other such variables. I have never once seen them do so. (Why would they keep it a secret?) My reading of the situation, then, concurs with Reiss's interpretation of it. Contemporary social scientists simply do not take "the possibility of ideational heterogeneity (or in fact any other kind of heterogeneity) into account when making predictions" (although I assume that Reiss means pernicious heterogeneity, since almost all positivist social scientists do acknowledge, and elaborately test for, *multiple* independent variables; the problem is that they treat each of them as operating homogeneously). They do not talk about language as a homogenizer because they do not think they need to establish homogeneity: homogeneity is simply a default assumption baked into their "methods" training. If you are trained in *how* to perform RCTs or multivariate regression analyses, you will, *in effect,* be trained in the presupposition that makes these methods valuable: the presupposition that their results are not merely local. Otherwise the methods would be relatively pointless, and so would one's research.

Consider, then, the research purposes to which the methods are put: the production of papers such as "Does Disclosure Reduce Pollution? Evidence from India's Green Ratings Project," or "Do Lower Minimum Wages for Young Workers Raise Their Employment? Evidence from a Danish Discontinuity" (Kreiner et al. 2020). There would be no reason to use data from India and Denmark to establish principles of general interest (these papers were not published in area-specific journals) if language is what is supposed to ground the general applicability of the interpretations of evidence—which would limit that applicability to people who speak the language spoken among those whose behavior is being observed or experimentally tested.

Here are excerpts from the abstacts of all of the empirical papers published in the February 2021 issue of the *American Political Science Review* (excluding formal theory and political theory), with my comments in brackets:

1. *"Fundraising for Stigmatized Groups: A Text Messaging Experiment."* "To study other-regarding behavior [in general], we fielded an experiment through a text-to-give campaign in Greece" (Linos et al. 2021, 14).
2. *"'The Wane of Command': Evidence on Drone Strikes and Control Within Terrorist Organizations."* "This paper investigates how counterterrorism targeting terrorist leaders affects terrorist attacks [in general]" (Rigterink 2021, 31).
3. *"UN Peacekeeping and the Rule of Law."* "I develop a theory to explain when UN rule-of-law reform [in general] is likely to succeed, then test the theory using original datasets capturing the number of civilian personnel deployed to each UN mission in Africa [in the past]" (Blair 2021, 51).
4. *"Emigrant Inclusion in Home Country Elections: Theory and Evidence from Sub-Saharan Africa."* "Since 1990, nearly 100 countries extended voting rights to citizens living abroad. . . . Whereas others view diaspora enfranchisement as a signal to emigrant and international audiences, I argue that incumbent parties

[everywhere] expand or restrict emigrant voter access depending on party perceptions of political support abroad," drawing on "an original dataset covering multiple dimensions of external voting in every African election where emigrants had voting rights from 1990 to 2015" (Wellman 2021, 82).

5. *"Electoral Accountability and Particularistic Legislation: Evidence from an Election Reform in Mexico."* Using "a quasi-natural experiment posed by the staggered implementation of the 2014 Mexican Electoral Reform . . . the author conducts a difference-in-differences analysis of the hypothesis that reelection [always] encourages legislators to focus more on policies with the highest 'electoral yield'" (Motolinia 2021, 97).
6. *"Local News, Information, and the Nationalization of U.S. Elections."* "I demonstrate that residents of in-state markets have access to vastly more local television news coverage of their governor and U.S. senators, and this increased coverage translates into greater knowledge of these officeholders. Further, access to in-state television news substantially increases split-ticket voting in gubernatorial and senatorial races" (Moskowitz 2021, 114).
7. *"Political Advertising Online and Offline."* "Data from the newly released Facebook Ad Library API and television data from the Wesleyan Media Project . . . allows us to assess whether and how [all] candidates take advantage of three opportunities afforded by social media: to increase advertising quantity thanks to its lower costs of production and placement, to use advertising for other purposes—like fundraising—that are impractical on television, and to strategically adapt their self-presentation to match the preferences of finely segmented audiences" (Fowler et al. 2021, 130-131).
8. *"Hot Politics: Affective Responses to Political Rhetoric."* "In a large lab study ($N = 397$), participants watched video clips with left-wing or right-wing rhetoric on prominent issues. We find that people [in general] with extreme attitudes [of any kind] experience more arousal in response to political rhetoric and that [all] political rhetoric incongruent with prior attitudes evokes negative affect" (Bakker et al. 2021, 150).
9. *"The Non-Democratic Roots of Mass Education: Evidence from 200 Years."* "To examine the [universal] relationship between democratization

and education provision empirically, I leverage new datasets covering 109 countries and 200 years . . ." (Paglayan 2021, 179).

10. *"Overcoming History Through Exit or Integration: Deep-Rooted Sources of Support for the European Union."* "Empirically, the quasi-random division of the French regions Alsace and Lorraine allows estimating differences in support for integration [across all regions and time periods] with a spatial regression discontinuity design. More negative exposure to nation-state actions causes persistently higher support for European integration in three referenda and less Euroscepticism in EU elections" (Gehring 2021, 199).
11. *"Seniority-Based Nominations and Political Careers."* "Using comprehensive electoral and candidate data from Norwegian local and national elections from 1945 to 2019, we find systematic patterns consistent with [the general applicability of] . . . two norms . . ." (Cirone et al. 2021, 231).
12. *"Attributing Policy Influence Under Coalition Governance."* "Using original data from seven surveys in five countries, we show that voters' attributions of parties' policy-making influence [across time and place] are consistent with our proposed inferential strategy . . ." (Fortunato et al. 2021, 252).
13. *"Citizens as Complicits: Distrust in Politicians and Biased Dissemination of Political Information."* ". . . We support these predictions using novel experimental studies, allowing us to observe transmission rates and opinion effects in actual communication chains. The findings have implications for [a general theory of] understanding and accommodating political distrust" (Bøggild et al. 2021, 269).

The most obvious point to make about these articles is, as my insertions indicate, that the authors tend to assume that their data are generalizable across time and place (and thus, implicitly, across individuals' ideas). Even the papers that sound as if they might have limited scope of application usually turn out, upon inspection, to be universalistic. The article on the EU (10), for example, uses data *from* the EU to make generalizations beyond it, concerning "the origins of voter preferences about the vertical distribution of political power in federal systems" in general (Gehring 2021, 199). The one exception is the article on the nationalization of U.S. elections (6), which, however, in appropriately restraining its scope of applicability to the United

States, may be a function less of deviation from positivism than of the peculiarly place-bound nature of the American politics subfield of political science. A less obvious point is that none of the articles posits any form of ideation as an independent variable. Not surprisingly, then, none of the articles limits applicability on the basis of language or any other possible idea homogenizer. For example, the article on fundraising for "stigmatized minorities" (1) does not limit its scope to Greece even though the data are drawn from Greek NGO donations, nor do the other articles exercise such restraint.

Similarly, Abhijit Banerjee and Esther Duflo (2014, 80), winners of the 2019 Nobel Memorial Prize in economics, explain that the type of work they do (RCTs) aims at answering such questions as "does better access to inputs (textbooks, flipcharts in classes, lower student-teacher ratios) matter for school outcomes (attendance, test scores), and if so, by how much?" Note the absence of qualifiers such as "in English-speaking countries." Nor would it make sense to insert such qualifiers: the variables of interest to Banerjee and Duflo are objective factors that, if they did indeed have some predictable effect on children, would plausibly (through physiological uniformities of visual perception, for example) tend to have the same effect on all children, regardless of what language they speak. The purpose of positivist social science is to produce evidence of lawlike generalizations that follows the universalizable physical model, which, as such, cannot be limited by linguistic homogeneity or any other subjective particularity.

Thus, when Joseph Henrich, Steven J. Heine, and Ara Norenzayan showed, in 2010, that many putatively universal psychological findings did not replicate outside of the "WEIRD" world, it caused a sensation among positivists; the paper has been cited more than 8,000 times as of February 2021. (The fact that Reiss is overly impressed by a study from India reflects, I suspect, the deep impression Henrich et al. made upon social scientists in the West.) Yet if, before their paper was published, social scientists had been confining their conclusions to linguistic groups on Wittgensteinian grounds, they would already have reduced the reach of their generalizations to even smaller populations than the population of the WEIRD area of the globe, where a host of different languages is spoken. In that case, the Henrich et al. findings would not have been the least bit shocking. Its explosive impact suggests that in reality, social scientists had not been confining the geographic scope of their extrapolations in any way.

While Reamer thus seems to me far too sanguine about contemporary social scientists, he is justified in suggesting that *if* they could identify a homogenizing ideational mechanism, whether language or something better, it would be fair for them to hypothesize that empirical findings relevant to that mechanism will generalize to those who have been subjected to it. This would meet the burden of argument I want to impose on social scientists, rendering them "judicious." Then it would be the case that if we define a population as the set of those who are subjected to a certain ideational mechanism, and if that mechanism can be shown to convey *a particular idea or mode of thought* to the population, tacitly or explicitly, we might be justified in extrapolating from the presence of that idea among a sample of the population to its presence, somewhat homogeneously, in the population at large.

Given the fact that language does not very often seem to precede rather than follow from thought, however, *Power Without Knowledge* identifies a different potentially homogenizing mechanism: communication (150-53). The possibility of shared norms to which I frequently appeal (e.g., 169-72), for example, need not spring from a shared language or, more plausibly, from a shared form of life; shared norms may be explicitly taught or implicitly inferred from teachings communicated to wide populations.

Consider the generalizations I have been making about "positivist social scientists" as a group. My evidentiary basis for these generalizations is my reading of a large pile of positivist social science over the last three decades. But I cannot know that this data sample is representative of the whole vast domain of "positivist social science." (This is the very problem, the problem of overabundant information, that launched Lippmann's political epistemology.) Therefore, my interpretation of positivist social science, as resting on Hume's assumption of uniformity, could be dismissed, with good reason, if I did not identify a mechanism by means of which this assumption might be propagated across the entire universe of social scientists to which I am referring. The mechanism I have suggested is the teaching of statistical and experimental methods that would have little purpose absent Hume's assumption. Thus, the students taught these methods proceed to operate *as if* they had been explicitly taught that assumption, even if the assumption is never mentioned to them. We can impute to them the tacit assumption that people are equivalent to unconscious intersections of homogeneous impersonal (psychological and social) forces because this is the implication of the statistical and experimental methods taught to them. Thus, Hume's assumption would have become part of social scientists' "common sense" even if (as is often the case) they have never heard of Hume. This is in part an empirical hypothesis: an anecdotal claim that others could contest, or affirm, by inspecting methods syllabi, interviewing social science students and professors, and so on. But it is also deductive, based on this question: *Why else* would social scientists do the work they do if not because they assume that it is generalizable?

Similarly, Elliott's paper deduces homogeneously technocratic populist attitudes by asking, with intellectual charity, what would make sense of certain populist attitudes, such as anti-elitism. He finds such an explanation in certain tacit presuppositions, such as naïve realism, which might lead populists to infer that they themselves, as non-experts, are capable of deciding which policies are desirable—because they tacitly assume that the desirability of certain policies is self-evident. This type of deductive analysis could be buttressed by invoking a communicative mechanism that would get the ball rolling. For example, *American* citizens, at any rate, are taught (for example, as schoolchildren) that their votes are very important and that these votes should be based on candidates' "platforms"—their positions on issues. Logically, someone imbued with these ideas might be expected to infer that the issues must be easy to understand: even children are supposed to be able to understand them. Pedagogy, here, along with the memes reinforced by mass culture ("every vote counts"), is a communicative mechanism that would undergird the claim that certain populist attitudes indicated in survey data and voter behavior are general and non-adventitiously causal in the population from which the behavioral samples are drawn—because we have reason to think that this population has been taught the communicated message.

On the other hand, the homogenizing communicative mechanism may be less tacit than overt. It is fair to say that people who watch Fox News Channel and not MSNBC are likely to share among themselves certain perceptions about current politics, while those who watch MSNBC and not Fox are likely to share a diametrically opposed group of perceptions. The standard, *methodologically* individualistic explanation of these homogeneities is that Fox viewers and MSNBC viewers have prevenient "political preferences," originating in a mysterious black box, that make them gravitate, as consumers in search of preference satisfaction, to the cable outlet that will make them feel good. The *epistemologically* individualistic explanation, in contrast, opens the black box and finds that it—the human mind—does not produce its ideational content de novo: this comes from mental operations performed on communicated materials: ideational inputs such as those provided by cable news itself—and network news, newspapers, movies, television, social media, novels, plays, preaching, and teaching. Each of these sources can communicate both explicit ideas and tacit inferences. One's political preferences can *stem from* these communicated materials, after which one would seek out sources of information that conform to the preferences—not to feel good or (pointlessly) find confirmation for what one already thinks (although confirmation may be found), but because alternative information sources, which go against one's preferences, *must, ipso facto, be communicating untrustworthy ideas.* Does one watch MSNBC to feel good and to find progressivism affirmed, or because one thinks Rachel Maddow a truth teller and Sean Hannity a liar?

Even if one rejects my contention that language is unlikely to be a significant counter to ideational heterogeneity, then, there can be other counters to it, and communication—particularly mass communication—is an obvious possibility, upon which a judicious technocracy might, in some instances, be built.

Positivism VI: Contestation and the Ethic of Responsibility (MacGilvray)

Larsson, Lerner, Pamuk, Reiss, and Reamer concentrate on Chapter 4's critique of positivism. MacGilvray's response targets Chapter 5, where I discuss dogmatism among epistocrats. I maintain that this pathology is likely because of a spiral of conviction that should tend to afflict all experts—regardless of whether they, like the epistocrats discussed in Chapter 4, fail to recognize human beings' ideational determination and heterogeneity.

A spiral of conviction can develop because it is not possible, Reverend Bayes notwithstanding, to process all the information that one encounters: there is simply too much of it. One must necessarily be selective, and one's selections will be governed by judgments that screen out most of the overabundant information as implausible, uninteresting, or even incomprehensible, leaving only information that is registered, comprehended, and trusted. This information is allowed to enter one's web of belief, where it can contribute to future judgments about the suitability of new candidates for admission. The problem is that these judgments necessarily depend on the very interpretation that previously admitted information consistent with it, producing a growing but self-confirming body of knowledge that may construct a world picture wildly at variance with reality. If the initial interpretation is incorrect, the inaccuracy will tend to ramify by screening in congruent information, while the information that might challenge the interpretation will be screened out. Thus, the spiral of conviction can lead to a closed loop of interpretation an intellectual system that is increasingly isolated from reality.

This, I think, is the most important and frightening implication of ideational *determinism*. Ideational *heterogeneity* does not play a role here. We may all be stuck in the same closed loop of interpretation insofar as we have all been exposed to homogeneous ideational inputs, or we may each be stuck in different loops dependent on different inputs. Nor is this a problem that may afflict only credentialed experts, with their large and ever-growing webs of interpretation-enabled belief. A spiral of conviction may afflict anyone who is introduced to, or who formulates, an interpretation, such as a conspiracy theory, that allows information screening to take place, setting that person apart from people who, lacking a relevant interpretation, do not think they really understand "what is going on out there" and therefore screen in random information or none at all. Where some of us will be stuck in spirals of conviction, others will be relatively interpretation-free, therefore information-free, and therefore relatively open minded.

The spiral of conviction, despite being consistent with the cognitive architecture revealed both to introspection and laboratory experimentation (e.g., in the literature on motivated skepticism), is a mere tendency. The human mind seems incapable of maintaining a completely sealed border around itself, insulating it from every shred of "implausible" information—especially in modern circumstances, where we are exposed to so many candidates for admission into our webs. Some incongruous material is bound to get past the mind's interpretive border patrol, creating anomalies in our webs of belief that might undermine them or at least produce deep and creative thought within them. It is also possible for deliberate de-biasing measures to work, such as the reading of "the other side" that MacGilvray recommends. Positivist scientific debate, too, may in some cases work, as he suggests, by introducing incongruent ideas into scientists' webs of belief.

However, I am not confident that this should reassure us very much. Kuhn's *Structure of Scientific Revolutions* suggests that even in the natural sciences, deliberation has the effect of reinforcing rather than undermining dogma. Experimental evidence must always be interpreted, and the interpreters are likely to be paradigm-besotted dogmatists against whom any fundamental intellectual challenge will have to be in the nature of a revolution, not a discussion. As Reiss points out, my position here tracks Planck's Principle: that paradigms shift not through criticism, but when a new generation arises that has not been thoroughly indoctrinated in the old paradigm. In the social sciences, then, it would seem unlikely that deliberation among those already imbued with positivistic and other antihumanist dogmas will deliver the type of cultural revolution that I hope *Power Without Knowledge* might help to effect (by reaching those not yet sucked into antihumanist spirals of conviction). A dogmatic positivist will simply dismiss antipositivist ideas as implausible, uninteresting, unintelligible, or ridiculous.

Similarly, one might hold out the hope that intellectual contestation can demonstrate to naïvely realistic citizens the fact of technocratic disagreement, falsifying their naïve realism by showing that the truth under discussion is not self-evident: if the truth is debated, then at least one party to the debate is unaware of the truth. But the naïve realist seems likely to discount technocratic debate as a ruse to cover up the self-evidentness of the truth (25-46, 307-9). In daring to challenge this truth in debate, the naïve realist may think, the "other side" is merely pretending that obvious problems are opaque enough to warrant deliberation rather than immediate action.

This, I think, serves as a general diagnosis of the state of political debate in the age of Trump. Virtually everything that people on "the other side" (whether Trump's side or that of his opponents) said was seen as a baseless accusation or an outright lie, making genuine debate both unnecessary and impossible, even while what passed for debate appeared—to each side—to be a gigantic exercise in misinformation. Both sides were so scandalized by the other side's alternative perceptions of facts that, in response, the two sides could only trade accusations of mendacity in a rapidly escalating spiral of defamation. This spiral, I think, is what is likely to result from what MacGilvray calls the pressure to conflict—so long as those who participate in and witness the contest are as naïvely realistic as many of our own fellow citizens, circa 2021, seem to be. This is part of the nightmare of injudicious technocracy in the real world, and why it is so important to recognize that technocracy is not the depoliticized, Spock-like affair that advocates of epistocracy make it out to be.

By the same token, naïve realists are unlikely to be open to the *internal* (mental) debate that MacGilvray hopes will follow from exposing people to multiple perspectives in what they read or hear. I share his hope, in principle, but again I think that in practice, naïve realism is likelier than not to frustrate it. The naïve realist is unlikely to want to read multiple perspectives to begin with, as this is pointless if one already knows the self-evident truth—as naïve realists think they do (45-46). Indeed, if the truth is self-evident, alternative perspectives *must* be deliberate distortions of the truth, so they are not just pointless but dangerous to read. It did not take the Internet to put people into hermetically sealed information cocoons, or to make them hostile to those inhabiting other cocoons. The cocooning instinct is simply the attitude toward information that comes naturally, and rationally, to a naïve realist, and hostility to others is rational if those others are deliberately trying to obscure the truth, as naïve realists believe. It seems to me improbable, then, that the pressure to conflict can defuse naïve realism rather than aggravating it.

Even if naïve realism could be entirely abolished, however, this would not resolve the epistemic quandaries pointed out in *Power Without Knowledge*. A recognition that social and economic problems are, in some vague sense, "complex" enough to generate multiple interpretations that are worth hearing does not say anything about the precise nature of the complexity, nor about how it might be unraveled, such that hearers might be able to distinguish relatively accurate perspectives from those that are not. While the removal of naïve realism may be necessary to unraveling epistemic complexity, then, it is not sufficient.

Ideational heterogeneity is what I take to be the epistemic problem that may trip up a technocracy. Deliberation, debate, conflict, and reading the other side cannot solve this problem if the ideas being debated do not include the idea of ideational heterogeneity; this, however, is the state of affairs in contemporary technocratic culture. On the other hand, there is nothing *inherently* wrong with dogmatism in a technocracy, since a spiral of conviction might have the effect of reinforcing belief in a technocratic truth (262). I see dogmatism as a problem for technocracy only if what is endlessly reinforced is an antihumanist doctrine that would tend to impede accurate behavioral prediction. It may thus be the case that MacGilvray is thinking less about technocracy than democracy *tout court,* where dogmatism might (at least in deliberative conceptions) be a problem in its own right.

MacGilvray's Aristotelian faith in intellectual contestation seems to me to treat epistemic quandaries as much easier to resolve than they are *in a technocracy*. Teaching people the spirit of their constitution, for example (in accordance with MacGilvray's gloss on Aristotle), is surely easier than teaching them what has actually (rather than putatively) caused a recession or a financial crisis and how to fix it. And teaching them the spirit of their constitution by exposing them to the experiences and perspectives of members of other classes (which strikes me as being of questionable efficacy even for the purpose Aristotle has in mind, according to MacGilvray's gloss) will help only if the members of each class possess fragments of the truth that can be deliberatively synthesized into an accurate understanding of the whole. But problems of technocratic interpretation are not, as such, problems of aggregating dispersed knowledge or piecing together different perspectives that each contain a kernel of truth. They are problems of predicting other people's behavior. While seeing all or many sides of any given issue is of course desirable, technocracy has a limited goal that requires four specific types of knowledge, and if the many parties to a debate lack this knowledge there will be no point in dialectically synthesizing their antipathetic positions. The problem is incorrect opinions, not incomplete opinions or even dogmatic opinions per se.

Similarly, Polybius's declaration that Rome's mixed government required all parties to "vie with one another to find ways of meeting the needs of the hour" strikes me as irrelevant to situations in which the needs of the hour demand knowledge, not (or not merely) effort. Ignorance of the four types of technocratic knowledge is not brought about by a failure to vie for it, but by the inherent difficulty of getting into anonymous others' heads so as to predict their behavior. The pathologies that stem from neglecting anonymous others' ideas, and from dogmatism, are not caused by technocrats' laziness, so they cannot be cured by using competition to spur them to work harder. This is why I tried to emphasize the *rationality* of dogmatism (237-38). In the spiral-of-conviction model, the dogmatist is already doing the very best she can to reach the truth—given what seems to her to be overwhelming evidence for the implausibility of other points of view (the evidence that has been allowed into her web of belief by the interpretation that makes this evidence intelligible). Contrary to the theory of motivated skepticism, then—a positivist misinterpretation of findings of dogmatism (244-47)—the dogmatist is already "motivated" to reach the truth. The dogmatists amongst us are the partisans and ideologues who are *certain* they already know the truth. Institutional arrangements to incentivize them to seek the truth do not address their rational certitude, which is where the problem lies. Dogmatism is, in this model, a *product* of vying to get the truth. If anything, further incentives to get it would only exacerbate the problem.

Thus, while it is true that *Power Without Knowledge* eschews any discussion of institutional solutions (other than exitocracy), I cannot agree with MacGilvray that this is a blind spot. Institutions tend to affect habits and incentives, but the epistemic problems discussed in the book are not caused by bad habits or inadequate incentives. MacGilvray's discussions of Aristotle, Montesquieu, Madison, and even Mill (who, unlike previous theorists, was highly attuned to the problem of technocratic ignorance) remind us that while political philosophers in the two millennia after Plato tended to focus on achieving the objective interests of those in a polity, or on balancing objective interests so as to preserve the regime, they devoted scant attention to the need for those interests to be subjectively, fallibly interpreted, and thus to the possibility of erroneous interpretations of how those interests should be furthered.

The most important departures from this tradition of epistemic neglect occurred only in the twentieth century, with the arrival of Lippmann's theory of public opinion and Western Marxist theories of false consciousness and ideology. The advance represented by these theories is that they recognize that political actors' opinions can misrepresent objective interests significantly *and involuntarily*. Both Lippmann and Marxist theorists such as Adorno and Althusser describe deeply ingrained sources of error that can only be corrected, if at all, by means of a revolution radical enough to address those sources—not by means of institutional reform.

The difference between Lippmann and the Western Marxists lay in the fact that Lippmann—a lapsed Progressive whose epistemological disillusionment was filtered through a post-Kantian lens—was able to achieve a thoroughgoing subjectivism that potentially dissolved the causal link between interpretations and the objective realities they aim to interpret. Western Marxists retained that link by grounding people's errors in objective social realities—class interests or social domination more generally—at least "in the final analysis." The effect of Lippmann's radical post-Kantianism was to re-establish the subject-object dualism that Marx had attempted to overcome. Unlike Marxist theories of ideology and of false consciousness, Lippmann's view suggests that interpretations might be autonomous from reality and that, therefore, the errors in subjects' perceptions of objects might be corrected, if at all, by ideational countercurrents alone, such as the cultural revolution I hope to encourage—not by a change in objective social circumstances. Like the Marxists, however, Lippmann defiantly avoided appealing to ancient tropes about human weakness as explanations for epistemic problems.

These tropes assume a state of epistemic equilibrium from which we depart if we fall into bad epistemic habits, or if our thoughts are skewed by non-epistemic motives. In Lippmann's view, by contrast, we are *inherently* ignorant of almost the entirety of the vast society into which we are born—except (sometimes) our (actual or virtual) local corner of it. We project our perceptions of this locality onto the whole, in the form of interpretive stereotypes. Ignorance is our default condition, and our efforts to gain knowledge may result in nothing but the production and communication of myths, or even of a worldview that is entirely mythical. The professional disseminators of information and interpretation—filmmakers, teachers, journalists—along with ordinary people in conversation (or, we would now add, on social media) are perfectly capable of filling our heads with illusions, according to Lippmann, perhaps drawing on his experience as a journalist and World War I propagandist (86-87). What gets put into our webs of belief may even less accurately reflect the truth than the shadows on the cave wall, which, in Plato's account, are at least cast by objective realities. In Lippmann's view it is the mind in communication with other minds, not reality in communication with the mind, that shapes the image of reality. Our minds (plural, individual) are controlled by the ideas that filter into them over a lifetime. They are not controlled by habits or choices that could be changed by institutions. Our ideational determination by illusion is the issue, not our errant wills or misguided motives, so one cannot answer Lippmann's challenge by designing institutions that would straighten out our crooked timber.

Similarly, the interpretive problems discussed in *Power Without Knowledge* are not remediable by the types of action MacGilvray associates with responsible leadership: the encouragement of thinking outside the box, as if the problem is a mere lack of imagination; and the encouragement of candor about advisers' biases or one's own ignorance, as if biases and ignorance are recognizable to the biased and ignorant rather than being rational responses to the epistemic situation in which they find themselves.

Attempts by leaders to control or correct for the spiral of conviction are vulnerable to the problem of epistocratic identification (69-71), i.e., the impossible situation in which the auditors of a debate among experts find themselves (whether they know it or not): how can they reliably judge such a debate without, themselves, being more expert than the experts? Since the spiral of conviction is only a tendency, a debate may include relatively non-dogmatic experts who have been less successful than others in policing the borders of their webs of belief, but precisely because they see more of the cons as well as the pros of their position, they will tend to be less able and less willing to advocate it forcefully, leaving the inexpert judges of the debate to try to distinguish between forceful advocates whose confidence is warranted and those whose confidence is mere dogmatism. Gaming this system by trusting the expert who is relatively tentative is unlikely to work, as lack of confidence may be warranted by the poor quality of the position being defended. It makes no sense to place artificial trust in the position that may be the one least supported by the evidence, just to avoid being taken in by those who confidently but wrongly contend that their position is best supported by the evidence (249). Such a strategy would ignore the fact that, again, even dogmatists may, in a particular case, be doctrinaire proponents of the truth.

This makes the normative import of dogmatism ambiguous in a technocracy. There is no reason to think that the spiral of conviction, in its own right, will lead experts to dogmatically defend untruths rather than truths. But if the doctrine being dogmatically defended is itself conducive to untruth, there is reason for alarm. When the spiral buttresses doctrines such as neoclassical economics and positivism, evidence against *injudicious* analyses of specific cases will not penetrate the webs of belief of the doctrinaire technocrats. This is what I hoped to illustrate by adducing the fiasco of epistocrats who analyzed the financial crisis (249-60). They proved to be utterly immune to *acknowledged* facts that undercut their story that bad incentives caused the crisis.

When MacGilvray complains that the book fails to provide "empirical evidence" to support the view that dogmatic epistocrats will tend to win out, he ignores this fiasco, presumably because it is anecdotal, not statistical or experimental. But statistical and experimental evidence merely provides false assurances against the problem of an adventitious sample, and if we demand such assurances we can overlook empirical realities such as the intellectual gymnastics of the highly esteemed epistocrats analyzed in the chapter on the spiral of conviction. These were much-decorated and much-consulted economists whose baldly incoherent interpretation of the financial crisis won out. It is true that the evidence presented in Chapter 5 establishes merely that some well-regarded, politically successful American epistocrats were caught in a spiral of conviction, and that the doctrine they dogmatically defended was false. But there is no conceivable way that I could have produced such a demonstration statistically or experimentally, since the question is the manner in which they reasoned about a specific subject, which can be revealed only by following their written arguments in detail. Moreover, statistical or experimental evidence of the prevalence of the spiral of conviction among epistocrats, as I have suggested in my responses to Pamuk and Reiss, would have only speciously established this prevalence, given the possiblity of pernicious heterogeneities and the fact that we cannot know who will be named to epistocratic positions in the future and how dogmatic they will happen to be (the magnitude of their dogmatism). In the face of these problems, empirical evidence can only be suggestive, and it seems undeniable that the non-statistical, non-experimental evidence presented in the chapter is, if nothing else, suggestive.

Turning, finally, from MacGilvray's brief lapse into positivism to the hope he places in the ethic of responsibility itself (as opposed to the efforts of responsible politicians to vet expert advice), I'm not sure this is any more realistic than institutional reforms or recourse to the wisdom of the ancients.

To be sure, the ethic of responsibility, which is consequentialist, is wholly appropriate to technocracy. But simply *wanting* to be responsible, in the sense of wanting to take only actions that lead to desirable consequences, does not tell responsible leaders anything about the actual consequences of particular actions, so it does not solve the epistemic problem they need to confront. The ethic of responsibility may lead to awareness of the epistemic problem, to be sure. The adept of the ethic of responsibility may recognize that she needs knowledge of consequences. But awareness of the need for knowledge that is difficult to secure does not secure it. As Lippmann ([1937] 2005, 24) once put it, "devotion to an end does not ensure the discovery of the means."[11]

I think MacGilvray misunderstands me, then, in suggesting that, by trying to answer "the question of what it means to exercise political power responsibly under modern conditions," I am also asking "what kind of people are suited, temperamentally speaking, to do so." I don't think that temperament has very much to do with it—especially when the modern conditions being grappled with are the heterogeneous ideas of anonymous others, and the aim is to manipulate or coerce these others so as to solve, mitigate, or prevent social and economic problems. This is not to say that calm and careful technocrats who responsibly attempt to avoid unintended consequences aren't preferable to those who do not, just as well-designed institutions are preferable to poorly designed institutions, and judicious technocrats are preferable to positivists, naïve realists, and neoclassical economists. But I think it is a category mistake to look to temperament to solve the epistemic problems that might threaten the legitimacy of technocratic regimes, because epistemic problems are *cognitive* features of the human condition, at least under modernity as we know it. Thus, I would categorize the ethic of responsibility and a judicious temperament as desirable but insufficient conditions for a judicious technocracy.

Exitocracy and Its Critics (Benson; Brown and Williams; Reamer)

In Chapter 7 I contend that it stands to reason that people's knowledge of their own well-being is likely to be more reliable, on the whole, than their predictive understanding of anonymous others, even when they make judicious efforts to understand those others' ideas. In principle, we should each have more reliable personal knowledge than the impersonal knowledge we would need if, as citizen-technocrats or epistocrats, we were called upon to craft the laws that technocracies ordinarily use to modify people's behavior (324-31). Thus, insofar as we have the power to use the exit mechanism in our personal lives, we might be able to maneuver our way around some of our problems—for example, by quitting a job we dislike or refusing to repurchase goods and services we dislike. An exitocracy, therefore, which maximizes our power to use exit, would seem to be better, on utilitarian grounds, than even a judicious (ideationally sensitive) technocracy, which in turn is better than an injudicious (ideationally insensitive, e.g., positivistic) one. This is what I call the hierarchy of technocratic legitimacy (343). The comparative standard of legitimacy embodied by the hierarchy obviates our third-order uncertainty about whether even a judicious technocracy would meet the absolute standard of doing more good than harm.

An exitocracy would attempt to maximize everyone's powers of exit so as to minimize the need for technocratic knowledge. To that end, it might (for example) create and enforce private property rights but couple them with a strong program of wealth redistribution, so that everyone, not just a few, could maximize their exit opportunities (323). Clearly this would not put an end to technocracy, as the design of property rights and redistributive rules, along with a host of other legal details required by an exitocracy, would depend on predictions of how anonymous others would tend to respond to these laws (340-41). Moreover, there is no exit from most public goods (342). These goods would have to be provided either judiciously or injudiciously, with the former being preferable (343). Thus, exitocracy is not a true alternative to technocracy but a variant of it: an "extraordinary" variant that gives us a point of contrast against "ordinary" technocracy, where the exit mechanism is unavailable and social problems must, for lack of a better alternative, be solved, mitigated, or prevented by means of voice, preferably with judicious attention to ideational heterogeneity (322).

Given the clear superiority of judicious over injudicious technocracy (according to the argument from ideational heterogeneity developed in Part I, and the critique of the ability of injudicious technocrats to deal with ideational heterogeneity in Part II), I thought that it would be *obviously* preferable for an exitocracy to be judicious rather than injudicious. Just as it would be foolish to perform ordinary technocratic tasks injudiciously if we can perform them judiciously, it would be foolish to undertake exitocratic tasks injudiciously rather than judiciously. But I should have said so explicitly. This would have created a hierarchy with four levels, not three: not exitocracy *simpliciter* followed by judicious and then injudicious technocracy, but judicious exitocracy, injudicious exitocracy, judicious ordinary technocracy, and injudicious ordinary technocracy.[12]

Like any hierarchy, the hierarchy of legitimacy has a top and a bottom, so there will be limits to its utility as a comparative device: one can only compare the status of levels below the top and above the bottom. Thus, there may be something preferable to exitocracy that should go above it; Reamer suggests that this might be an individualistic form of anarchism. At the other end of the hierarchy, we cannot judge the legitimacy of providing the many public goods that rely solely on technocratic voice, not exit, *if* these goods are provided injudiciously, as there is nothing below them to contrast them against, and thus nothing that would establish their comparative legitimacy (343). About public goods that are incompatible with exit, then, all we can do is look upward in the hierarchy and say that it is better for them to be provided judiciously than injudiciously. This underscores the importance of effecting a cultural revolution against barriers to a judicious technocracy, such as positivism. Thus, the main thrust of the book, and the true vocation of the critic of technocracy, is to scrutinize not its institutions but its culture: the naïvely realistic, psychologizing (irrationalist), moralistic (intentions oriented), intellectually uncharitable, and positivist culture that, through its determination of our ideas, makes us treat each other as less than human (343-45). Since culture consists, from an epistemologically individualistic perspective, of the explicit and tacit ideas of individual minds in communication with one another, the main thrust of the book, and the true vocation of the critic of technocracy, is to criticize ideas.

Reamer and Benson, however, are interested in exitocratic institutions, not technocratic culture. Therefore, they are concerned that exitocratic institutions are technocratic, impugning the legitimacy of the former insofar as *Power Without Knowledge* impugns the legitimacy of technocracy *tout court*. However, *Power Without Knowledge* does not impugn the legitimacy of technocracy *tout court*; it is not even the case that it impugns the legitimacy of injudicious or pathological technocracy, but it certainly does not impugn the legitimacy of the judicious technocracy that would emerge from a cultural revolution against those pathologies. In effect, Benson and Reamer argue that the foundation of an exitocracy in ordinary technocratic reasoning (to determine how to design institutions of property and redistribution, for example) transfers the problems of an injudicious ordinary technocracy, problems that they accept as real for the sake of argument, from the bottom to the top of the hierarchy. However, neither Benson nor Reamer notices that this move collapses the hierarchy into two levels, injudicious ordinary technocracy and exitocracy, omitting the transformative role of judicious technocracy—which, so far as we (theorists) know, may completely neutralize the problem to which *Power Without Knowledge* is devoted: ideational heterogeneity (although this seems unlikely, and we are in no position to predict it). Because they treat the book as an undifferentiated critique of technocracy, not an uncertain critique of injudicious technocracy, they fail to recognize that theorists have reason to think that a judicious technocracy might remedy the problem of heterogeneity, such that—if an exitocracy were judicious—we would have no reason to treat that problem as negating its legitimacy. That is why I wish I had been clearer about the obvious preferability of a judicious to an injudicious exitocracy.

Another regret is that I did not explicitly couch the prefatory pages (317-19) of Part III as a discussion of "third-order" uncertainty, in contrast to the second-order nature of the problem of heterogeneity. This omission may have allowed Benson and Reamer to collapse the latter into the former, such that the book presents an undifferentiated epistemological lament about the fallibility of *all* human knowledge—the third-order problem that is, in fact, discussed exclusively in Chapter 1's critique of naïve realism and in Part III—rather than being an anthropologically targeted critique of the reliability of one particular type of knowledge: knowledge of human behavior that is not grounded in awareness of the causal force of presumptively heterogeneous human ideas.

Part III (including Chapter 7), unlike Chapters 2-6, is concerned with the effect of *theorists'* ignorance (of how well technocrats will do their jobs) on *theorists'* knowledge of the legitimacy of technocracy. While a judicious technocracy, by my definition of judiciousness, would *aim* to take account of presumptive ideational heterogeneity, and might very well succeed on the whole, political theorists cannot know in advance how well particular judicious technocrats faced with particular problems will deal with them. Therefore, while we have reason to think that they may make some progress (this reason is provided by Chapters 2-6), we cannot know the magnitude of this progress, which we would need to know if we wanted to judge their efforts by the absolute standard of doing more good than harm. However, if they transferred some of their power to individuals, the latter could use their relatively reliable knowledge of their own well-being in place of even judicious technocrats' relatively unreliable knowledge of how to improve the well-being of others. This gives us a reason (provided by Chapter 7) to judge (judicious) exitocracy as superior to judicious ordinary technocracy, just as we have reason to judge judicious ordinary technocracy as superior to injudicious ordinary technocracy.

That does not mean, however, that an exitocracy would be a panacea for fallibility and contingency. Reamer's and particularly Benson's paper catalogue various things that might go wrong in an exitocracy, and I could not possibly disagree: exitocrats are fallible human beings, so all sorts of things may go wrong (indeed, I maintain that it is "inevitable" that things will go wrong; 341), even to the extent that judicious exitocratic decisions may sometimes have the unintended effect of reducing exit opportunities rather than increasing them. But because both Benson and Reamer run together *theorists'* ignorance of the magnitude of the success produced by judicious technocrats' efforts with *injudicious technocrats'* ignorance of the springs of human behavior, neither author is responsive to my contention that the likelihood of things going wrong is lower in an exitocracy, as it shifts power from (judicious) technocrats to exit users, allowing the latter, potentially, to make use of more reliable knowledge than is available to the former. If no such power transfers were even attempted, there would be no possibility of gaining this epistemic advantage, just as there would be no possibility of improving upon the pathologies of our own technocracy if there were to be no "judicious" cultural revolution against the ideas that produce those pathologies.

In short, because Benson and Reamer conflate the second- and third-order knowledge problems, they ascribe to me an indefensibly conservative critique of injudicious technocracy predicated on the mere third-order possibility of unintended consequences, as if this possibility delegitimizes technocracy. They then apply this critique, which they attribute to me, to exitocracy, yielding the conclusion that because—

for all we know—things *might* go wrong in an exitocracy, it is as illegitimate as is (they think I am arguing) technocracy *tout court*.

Thus, Benson and Reamer are both puzzled by the following passage at the end of Chapter 7:

> While technocratic reasoning will have to be deployed in providing exitocratic public goods—this is what makes exitocracy a form of technocracy, even if an "extraordinary" one—the inevitable errors that result will be offset, to some (putatively significant) extent, by the fact that these public goods will enable people to solve social problems in the private sphere. It is true that we cannot know, in an absolute sense, whether the cost of exitocrats' errors in creating and defending the private sphere will outweigh the benefits of the exit opportunities created thereby. Still, we are entitled to say that the mix of benefits and costs should be more favorable in an exitocracy than in an ordinary technocracy, despite the errors that will undoubtedly plague both exitocrats and ordinary technocrats. (341)

Benson's response is that "if technocratic knowledge is required to understand whether the actions of an exitocracy will actually promote or undermine exit, and if we accept Friedman's critique of such knowledge, then we can have no confidence that an exitocracy will provide any of the benefits associated with exit."[13] This conclusion would follow only if I had argued that we can have no confidence that ordinary technocracy will provide any of the benefits associated with technocratic voice, but I did not. First, even injudicious ordinary (non-exitocratic) technocrats may stumble on policies that do more good than harm, like Tetlock's dart-throwing chimps. This was one of the reasons I offered for our third-order uncertainty about the legitimacy of ordinary technocracy (317), so long as it is judged in terms of the absolute magnitude of its benefits weighed against the absolute magnitude of its costs. Second, we have reason to think that a judicious technocracy should improve upon an injudicious one, although again, we cannot estimate the magnitude of the improvement (ibid.). And third, a (judicious) exitocracy should improve upon a judicious ordinary technocracy (Chapter 7). We begin, then, from an uncertain level of confidence—*which is not equivalent to "no confidence"*—in injudicious technocracy, and we gain increasing confidence as we move up the hierarchy of legitimacy. Benson misconstrues any unspecifiable degree of uncertainty as equivalent to no confidence at all, such that he is unable to recognize the gains to confidence as we move up the hierarchy, in that we never can rid ourselves of *all* uncertainty. Another way of putting it is that he is equating reliable knowledge with absolute certainty.

Reamer, similarly, maintains that in the extracted passage I "rely on the idea that the costs of technocratic interventions should be held constant across regimes (as unknowable) and that since secured exit provides *some* benefits (however minimal they may turn out to be), it must be judged superior. But this only holds if we have ruled out the possibility that the interventions required to create an exitocracy could not possibly have *far worse* consequences than the interventions likely under ordinary (or judicious) technocracy and, once again, could not possibly backfire in a way that renders exitocracy self-undermining. I find it hard to see how, consistent with Friedman's position, we could possibly have this knowledge" (Reamer's emphasis). But while it is, of course, *possible*, on third-order grounds, that any given exitocratic action will have "far worse" consequences than any given ordinary technocratic action, judicious or not, it is also possible that it will have far better consequences. Reamer identifies no reason (second-order, third-order, or perhaps fourth-order) to think that disastrous consequences are relatively likely, rather than merely possible, in an exitocracy. Moreover, like Benson, Reamer overlooks the second-order reason for thinking that it is *less* likely for a given *judicious* action to have negative consequences than a given injudicious action—the attention of judicious technocrats to people's ideas—as well as the second-order reason for thinking that a given exitocratic action will be less likely to have negative consequences than an ordinary technocratic action: exitocratic actions may successfully create exit opportunities, shifting power into better-informed hands than technocrats' own.

Then again, Benson and Reamer emphasize, they may not. A recognition of this possibility constitutes, in part, our third-order uncertainty. But if we have a second-order reason to think that, on the grounds of prisoners' well-being, we should liberate all the inmates of a country's prisons by busing them to nearby cities for release, it remains possible that some of the buses will hurtle off a cliff: a far worse outcome, for those inmates, than if they had stayed in prison. Indeed, it is possible that one of the buses may hurtle off a cliff into a petrochemical plant, and that the gases released in the resulting explosion will kill tens of thousands of bystanders along with the prisoners. Indeed, even worse possibilities are imaginable. But these mere possibilities do not imply that overall, it would be better to keep the prisoners in prison—unless we have some third-order reason to think that buses in this particular country are *likely* to crash. Neither Reamer nor Benson provides any reason for thinking that exitocratic actions are likely to backfire. Instead, both of them assume that *I* have provided such a reason, in the form of what they misconstrue as a blanket critique of (injudicious) technocracy in Parts I and II.

In effect, Benson and Reamer have misunderstood the subtitle of the book. Not all "critiques" are undifferentiated and total rejections. I differentiate not just between judicious and injudicious technocracy (criticizing only the latter), but between injudicious technocrats' ignorance of ideational heterogeneity and political theorists' ignorance of how well judicious technocrats will succeed in taking account of ideational heterogeneity. In overlooking these distinctions Benson and Reamer portray the book as much more radically skeptical of technocratic knowledge than it is. If the book really were an absolute and undifferentiated critique of all technocracy, grounded in radical skepticism of the very possibility of reliable technocratic knowledge, one would be justified in thinking that this skepticism would call the legitimacy of exitocracy as well as ordinary technocracy into doubt, inasmuch as exitocracy is a type of technocracy. But the skepticism generated by Parts I and II is toward injudicious ordinary technocracy alone, and the skepticism is not radical.

The uncertainty that prompts Part III, regarding our knowledge of the ability of injudicious and even judicious technocrats to meet the absolute standard of success (doing more good than harm), is no different from our uncertainty about the likely success of any other human undertaking, such as driving a bus. Like other human beings, even judicious exitocracts will start out from a position of ignorance, they will make mistakes, they will be subject to passions and interests, they may cut corners, etc., ad infinitum. But human imperfection *in general*—a problem that may affect all human undertakings—does not condemn all human undertakings as likely to be counterproductive (nor does it render them just as likely to be counterproductive as successful). Nor does general human imperfection ground a critique of technocratic knowledge in particular. We *can*, loosely speaking, say that general human imperfection grounds Chapter 1's critique of naïve technocratic realism and that it grounds the third-order uncertainties that lead to Chapter 7. But general human imperfection is not the source of the second-order problem, ideational heterogeneity, that is anatomized in Chapters 2-6. As Reamer well puts it, "human action is, in general, uncertain. All of our actions have, at least potentially, unintended consequences that are difficult or impossible to foresee. Virtually no human action is without such risks." But precisely because we face risk in everything we do, the issue of risk is not unique to technocracy and cannot form the basis of a critique of it, or of any particular variant of it. If it did, then I could have ended the book in the middle of Chapter 1, because at that point, by rebutting naïve technocratic realism, I had invoked human fallibility—but against naïve technocratic realism, not technocracy itself.

Despite allusions in Benson's and Reamer's papers, and those of some of the other symposiasts, to the supposedly radical skepticism about technocratic knowledge suffusing *Power Without Knowledge,* its skepticism is in fact cautionary, not radical. Nowhere do I argue that technocrats—even injudicious ones—are *unlikely* to know what they need to know, let alone that they *cannot* know it; this would amount to a magnitude claim of just the type that is barred by third-order uncertainty. I do not argue that our webs of belief are so opaque that we are completely unable to predict others' behavior. Our ability to unveil the truth behind the veil is shown by the fact that we are able to understand and predict those who are relatively close to us on the gradient of familiarity (144-48, 165, 331-32). Only in view of this ability does it make sense for me to call, at the end of Part I, for a new type of social science (i.e., a human science) modeled on intellectual history (160-69)—which attempts to close the gap between self and (historical) other. The object of this new, human "science" would be to identify specific ideational homogeneities (169-78)—a task that I could hardly be contending is impossible, as a radical skeptic would contend. If success at this task were impossible, neither Part II nor Part III would have any purpose. But since success is possible, the worries about the second-order effects of ideational heterogeneity in an injudicious technocracy articulated in Part I may be stilled by the prospect, mooted at the end of each chapter in Part II, of a cultural revolution against inhuman technocratic culture. This leaves general human fallibility—a problem for theorists' absolute judgments about technocratic success, which is why, instead, theorists need to use a comparative standard of judgment.

Let me turn now to Brown and Williams's proposal for dealing with third-order uncertainty about the legitimacy of injudicious ordinary technocratic actions aimed at providing public goods that cannot be provided through exit. Such actions lie at the bottom of the hierarchy, where downward comparisons run out. Here we have nothing worse than injudicious ordinary technocracy to compare it to, and thus no way to establish its comparative legitimacy. Third-order uncertainty, therefore, leaves us unable to decide whether the injudicious voice-based provision of any particular public good is legitimate.

As the authors recognize, this uncertainty "is quite a serious problem if *Power Without Knowledge* is viewed as an institutional critique of technocratic knowledge, i.e., one that issues in recommendations for institutional design," because I offer no institutional remedy for this uncertainty: my only institutional proposal is to offer exit opportunities, which cannot be provided in these cases. For this very reason, I contended, *Power Without Knowledge* should not be viewed as an institutional critique, but "as a form of Adornoesque critical theory that cannot necessarily guide political action; or as a form of cultural action, not political action"—an attempt to unmask "the forms of false consciousness that seem to go with technocracy," such as positivism (344). In pressing on to try to defend the legitimacy of injudicious, non-exitocratic technocracy as an institution, Brown and Williams raise (in my mind) the question of why this pressing on is something political theorists would want to do. We are perfectly capable of engaging in a comparative analysis of injudicious technocracy if we simply look "up" the hierarchy to the next level, judicious ordinary technocracy. Why should we want to defend injudicious ordinary technocracy when there is a clearly better alternative?

One obvious answer is that if we restrict ourselves to the type of cultural critique that would follow from looking upward at the judicious alternative to the status quo, we would be unable to engage in technocratic policy debate within the status quo, or perhaps ever, since we now live in the injudicious technocracy that cultural critique would be challenging. The attempt to preserve, as it were, our right, as political theorists, to intervene in contemporary, injudicious policy debate is my only explanation for why one would try to rescue the legitimacy of injudicious ordinary technocracy by spinning thought experiments about the unrealistic circumstances under which it might be legitimate for technocrats to engage in "epistemic gambling": throwing the dice on a given technocratic policy in the absence of reliable knowledge that it will work. This is one of Brown and Williams's contributions.

However, a *true* epistemic gamble would be akin to drawing random policy proposals from a hat, lacking any reason to think they would work. This would violate the rationalist precept of a technocracy, according to which it is not sufficient to enact a policy merely because *it just might work* (78). A technocracy demands some reason for trying policy A rather than {B, C, D . . . n}, because technocrats who are not naïve realists recognize that the costs of any policy might exceed the benefits. It is worth noting that Benson's and Reamer's argument from uncertainty is of the same nature as Brown and Williams's. For the former, exitocratic policy making *just might fail,* so we *cannot* justify it; for the latter, injudicious ordinary policy making *just might succeed*, so we *can* justify it. Yet a true epistemic gamble, being random and rationally unjustified, would be flying blind. It just might work, but it also just might produce "far worse" consequences (quoting Reamer) than the problem it is supposed to solve. For this reason, a rational technocracy would exclude "just might" scenarios from its calculations.

Brown and Williams's "pillagers" example, however, is not a true epistemic gamble. It is stipulated that we *know* that pillagers of another village were satisfied by an offering of luxury goods. Given this knowledge, the act of making such an offering in our own village is not like gambling on a random proposal drawn from a hat. It is an action proposal based on a reason, not blind chance; and it is a reason that is judicious, because it appeals to a theory about the ideas of the pillagers: that they, like those in the other village, are intent on loot. As the authors note, "this thought experiment stipulates that you . . . have evidence that the strategy you are contemplating worked elsewhere, and a clear estimate of this strategy's cost. Thus, you have the four types of technocratic knowledge." But in that case, how is the thought experiment a defense of injudicious ordinary technocracy?

The authors do not notice that they have stipulated *judicious* technocratic reasoning. Relatedly, they emphasize the unreliability of our technocratic knowledge not in the sense that it is unenlightened by awareness of the causal role of ideas in causing the pillagers' behavior, but in the sense that we "cannot investigate the question of whether your pillagers are dissimilar to the previous pillagers. Still, the status quo may have so little value that an epistemic gamble—i.e., an attempt to solve a social problem through technocratic action, despite the lack of reliable knowledge—might be worthwhile." Brown and Williams are confusing the uncertainty that besets, in various degrees, *all* forms of technocratic "evidence" with the specifically problematic, non-ideational evidence that is produced by positivist social scientists, neoclassical economists, and naïvely realistic citizen-technocrats: not evidence of which we can never be *certain* because the evidence is produced by fallible human beings, but evidence that ignores the causal role of ideas in human behavior—the distinctive feature of an injudicious technocracy.

The villagers here are not injudicious, as they are aware of the causal role of ideas and have a plausible theory about the specifically homogeneous ideas that might be in the pillagers' minds. That they don't have a chance to do ethnographic or survey research to check on this theory does not make them injudicious; it just makes them the victims of a tightly constraining thought experiment.

The argument of *Power Without Knowledge* is not that we should "do nothing" until we have perfect knowledge of the ideas of the objects of our technocratic interventions. Doing nothing is not a coherent option (318), and perfect knowledge is not attainable by human beings (75, 342). However, I don't want to deny the authors' main point, which is that as the benefits of "doing nothing" decline, one should tolerate more uncertainty about the benefits of "doing something." This may get us out of the paralysis we face at the bottom of the pyramid—if matters are as easy in the real world as in the pillagers scenario, and if, unlike the scenario, the only action option on the table is an injudicious ordinary technocratic action. But will this be the case in the real world of technocracy? The crucial differences between a true epistemic gamble and the constrained version in the thought experiment are that the latter narrows down the action options from an infinite number to one; and that this option is justified not by random selection but by a reason and, indeed, a judicious one, albeit one about which the evidence is more uncertain than would be desirable. But when Brown and Williams analogize the thought experiment to the real world of technocracy, it turns into a defense not of tightly constrained epistemic "gambling," but of naïve technocratic realism.

"If we have evidence," they write, "that a health-care policy implemented in a neighboring country—e.g., regulating the price of brand-name and generic medications—proved effective at reducing the costs of medicines, then we may judge that it is worth adopting a similar policy even though it may have unintended consequences." In principle, no technocrat, judicious or injudicious, could disagree; but in practice, the question is what counts as "evidence." If the evidence concerns the presence in both countries of an ideational mechanism that would create homogeneous responses to the unnamed regulation on the part, say, of pharmaceutical companies, then we are not at the bottom of the hierarchy but in the middle of it, as we are acting judiciously. And if the authors' point is that our standards of evidence should decline as our desperation increases, who could argue? But if their point is that it is possible to directly observe another country and thereby gain *adequate* evidence that a certain policy produced a certain effect—just as the thought experiment "stipulated that you can evaluate both the significance and the causes of the problem facing the village through direct observation, something that technocrats who attempt to solve complex social problems may be unable to do"—then it would seem that Brown and Williams are saying that a crisis sufficiently dire justifies lowering evidentiary standards so much that we allow ourselves to act as if we *can* directly observe the truth, i.e., that we act *as if* the truth is self-evident.

Thus, as in the authors' discussion of global warming, Brown and Williams offer a qualified defense of naïve realism—when the stakes are high enough—so I recur to my rebuttal of naïve realism: the fact of technocratic disagreement. In the thought experiment, both the endless irrational disagreement justified by the infinite number of policies that "just might work" (for all we know) and rational technocratic disagreement are artificially extinguished by the facts that there is only one action option and that the option of inaction carries an existentially high price. In the case of pharmaceutical costs and any other real-world technocratic problem, however, there are likely to be several rational options and genuine uncertainty about the costs of each of them, justifying genuine disagreement about what to do (45). It appears, then, that the upshot of analogizing the real world to the thought experiment would be to insist that no disagreement is warranted, as naïve realists insist when they a priori dismiss disagreement as an illusion created by special interests.

This pathology, of course, is (I suggest) dominant in our naïvely realistic mass culture (Chapter 6). It seems to me, then, that it would be a dereliction of duty for political theorists to treat epistemic gambling as relevant to the real world of technocratic policy debate. By doing so, we would resurrect the naïve false consciousness that would be dispelled if we do not suppress the fact of technocratic disagreement.

Reamer's anarcho-capitalist alternative to exitocracy seems more promising than the notion of epistemic gambling, but I cannot accept his claim that anarcho-capitalism, or any other form of anarchism, is a system "in which no imposed authority exists at all and thus, by definition, technocratic rule is abolished," as people would be "permitted to devise solutions to their problems in a voluntary and consensual manner."

It does seem unobjectionable that *in an exitocratic technocracy,* people might be given exit options among competing police forces—aka (in anarcho-capitalist lingo) "protection agencies"—among which they could choose to exit (on the basis of criteria such as how well they solve crimes or prevent them, their price, etc.). But this form of competition would be a technocratically designed and regulated means of solving social problems (such as crime), just like the other forms of capitalist competition that might be allowed by a technocracy. Competition among defense agencies, then, would not transcend technocracy or, therefore, government, authority, or coercion.

A coercive exitocratic authority would have to set the rules of the competition to ensure that protection agencies did not extinguish the exit rights of their customers by forcing them to pay what is known, in the world of organized crime, as protection money. Just as it would be necessary for an exitocracy to do what it could to guard against the perverse outcomes that, according to Reamer (and Benson), threaten the internal legitimacy of exitocracy, it would be necessary for an exitocracy to constrain protection agencies from nullifying the exit mechanism. The overarching agent of this constraint, viewed from an institutional angle, would be a "state" indistinguishable from those that would define and enforce property rights, set up wealth redistribution procedures, and provide other public goods. Then there is the need to ensure that protection agencies do not coercively subject people to unjust treatment. Thus, the technocratic argument for this type of "anarchism" would have to be that, properly regulated by an exitocratic state, competing systems of *policing* would tend to allow people to exit from social problems that might stem from a monopoly system of policing. This argument, however, could not justify exit among competing *legal regimes*. The rules governing competition among police forces (defense agencies) would itself constitute a monopoly legal regime that tried to guard against unjust or exit-blocking actions by the agencies.

Let me now restate that fundamental point without the institutionalist hypostasization of the exitocratic "state." To ensure that, as Reamer would have it, anarcho-capitalism would enhance rather than constricting people's exit opportunities, there would have to be some form of overarching constraint on the competing defense agencies. But this constraint, like all constraints other than those imposed by the laws of physics, chemistry, and so on, would be ideational. That is, it would be imposed on the personnel running "defense agencies" through the coercive enforcement, on these people, of exitocratic ideas. This coercion would either be exercised by other people organized into an exitocratic "state," or, alternatively, by the ideas of defense agency personnel themselves, operating as superordinate norms in their webs of belief. ("We are here to make money, yes, but not by restricting anyone's exit opportunities or treating anyone unjustly.") It is important to think of anarcho-capitalism in this way because otherwise we miss the fact that it, like all social orders, is coercive. And otherwise we lend ourselves to the confused analysis of anarcho-capitalist philosophers, who invariably understand themselves to be advocating an institutional arrangement, not simply the cultural triumph of "libertarian" ideas. When they defend competing legal regimes, they are, in effect, thinking of competing *libertarian* defense agencies whose personnel *voluntarily* restrain themselves from extorting their customers; and, by the same token, from warring against each other to secure the ability to extort funds from (i.e., tax) each other's customers. That is, libertarian philosophers are imagining that defense agency personnel would be restrained by the philosophers' own libertarian ideas, obviating the need for an institutional overlord, such as an exitocracy, to restrain them. But they fail to recognize that this is what they are doing.

This is not to say that by imposing *exitocratic* ideational constraints on defense agencies, we would be enacting libertarianism. An exitocracy would need to enact wealth redistribution to equalize exit opportunities, while so-called libertarians arbitrarily equate freedom with private property, blocking redistribution a priori (Friedman 1997). And as a matter of logic, there must, to govern any area of land or other segment of non-human nature, be a single operative set of rules there, just as there must be such a set of rules to govern the physical actions of any given human being vis-à-vis other human beings, considered as individual bodies. In this sense, a single overarching "state" is simply inescapable, and the notion of competing legal regimes covering the same people and land is logically incoherent.

However, while the libertarian content of the libertarian philosophers' anarcho-capitalism is morally objectionable, and while it is incoherent to think that anarcho-capitalism can extend beyond the competitive policing of *given* assignments of rights to their competitive legal definition, the unacknowledged ideational dimension of libertarians' argument for anarcho-capitalism (as the "institutional" embodiment of libertarian ideas) is comparable to the ideational dimension of my argument, in Chapter 7, for exitocracy (as the institutional embodiment of the idea that personal knowledge will tend to be more reliable than synoptic knowledge of the ideas of millions of anonymous others) or, for that matter, the ideational dimension of constitutional government (as the institutional embodiment of liberal ideas) or (contrary to Marx's own understanding) of communism (as institutionally embodying Marxist ideas). It is important to point this out with regard to anarcho-capitalism because otherwise we fall into hopeless confusions about whether it is, indeed, non-coercive, i.e., whether "no imposed authority exists at all and thus, by definition, technocratic rule is abolished," because people "are permitted to devise solutions to their problems in a voluntary and consensual manner." None of this is true of anarcho-capitalism because none of it is true of any social order (that is, any tacit or explicit arrangement of how people live together). No arrangement of, or abolition of, "institutions" can abolish the direct control of human action by ideas, or the physical coercion set in motion by ideas.

Thus, when we ask what would keep defense agencies from violating the libertarian conception of the "rights" that are supposed to justify anarcho-capitalism, we will inevitably find that the answer is, in effect, an ideational homogeneity imposed on the personnel of the agencies by the imagination of anarcho-capitalist philosophers—just as I, in imagining a judicious technocracy, insert an awareness of ideational heterogeneity into technocrats' heads and, in imagining an exitocracy, insert into their heads an awareness of the relatively great reliability of the personal knowledge that the exit mechanism can put to use; just as liberals insert into the heads of the populace adherence to the rule of law and respect for individual rights; and just as communists insert into people's heads class consciousness. However, anarcho-capitalists do not recognize that this is what they are doing, as it amounts to the imposition of an agency of human control standing above anarcho-capitalist institutions —a "state" in everything but name. Instead of stipulating that the libertarian goal is governance by homogeneously libertarian ideas and then asking by what cultural means such ideas might actually get into people's heads, anarcho-capitalists produce putatively non-ideational arguments about the institutional superiority of anarcho-capitalism.

Thus, Michael Huemer (2013), a libertarian philosopher cited by Reamer, assures us that protection agencies, unlike states, "are chosen by their customers," and that they "are in constant [uncoercive] competition with each other" (ibid., 232, 233) But what keeps them from using coercive force against their customers and competitors alike?

Huemer's first in a long series of answers to this foundational question is the claim that "violent conflict tends to be very dangerous for both parties" (ibid., 233). This is not true, however, if one party is significantly stronger than the other, or perceives itself to be—which might explain why so many wars have broken out among "states." If Huemer's claim were accurate, the historical incidence of war would be impossible to explain, but historical awareness is not a libertarian strong suit. Awareness of this history might alert Huemer that he is importing into the "parties'" heads the convenient idea, regrettably missing from historical actors' webs of belief, that they should refrain from warfare. Similarly, he contends that "business leaders," such as those running defense agencies, "tend to be driven by the profit motive," which militates against wasting money on warfare (ibid., 237). But a war may not be a waste of money if one wins it, securing for oneself a monopoly of tax collection among the conquered populace, as can be seen from the history of early modern state building. Huemer is again inserting a convenient idea into the webs of defense agency personnel's webs of belief. His next argument is that "governments," unlike "defense agencies," are shielded against the costs of war—shielded by their ability to tax the populace. "If each American could choose between a government that carried on these wars [such as in Afghanistan and Iraq] and one that did not . . . then even the most ardent hawks might find themselves thinking twice about the price tag" (ibid.). In other words, *if* defense agencies refrained from taxing the populace, they would not be able to afford to fight wars. But on pain of circularity, this conditional cannot itself be what makes the agencies refrain from taxing the populace, which, therefore, would have to be libertarian ideas. Conversely, Americans don't have the opportunity to withhold taxes for wars of which they disapprove because the personnel of the U.S. government lack libertarian ideas in their webs of belief. Thus, they do not refrain from coercively taxing U.S. citizens to pay for wars. Huemer is saying that *if* the U.S. government made taxes voluntary, it would be unable to afford warfare, but this is precisely why a profit-oriented defense agency might be well advised *not* to make taxes voluntary. Once again, he is illicitly inserting convenient ideas—libertarian ideas—into defense-agency personnel's heads, turning a superordinate ideational constraint on their actions into an illusory "institutional" constraint that has somehow gone missing in the real world.

It would be tedious to continue reviewing Huemer's ad hoc attempts to distinguish states from defense agencies, each of which treats actual but (in his view) undesirable features of modern states, such as the power to tax and the power to compel soldiers to fight, as if they can simply be abolished definitionally by stripping these attributes from "states" and calling the conceptual remainder "defense agencies." This procedure misconstrues a critique of the unlibertarian ideas of those who currently run "states" as a critique of institutional features of the collective "entities" they run. By the same token, it misconstrues the libertarianish behavior of certain "business leaders," i.e., those who do not "coerce" their customers to pay fees for their services (using the tendentiously narrow libertarian definition of coercion),[14] as stemming from the profit motive as some kind of force in its own right rather than from these business leaders' ideas: either their bourgeois norms or their cold calculation that the cost of breaking the law (enforced by "the state"), by extorting fees from their customers (as some profit-oriented business leaders do, e.g., Mafiosi), would not be worth the benefits. Huemer's conceptual confusions transform the standard libertarian position, that states should stop coercing people (given the arbitrarily narrow libertarian definition of coercion)—a morally objectionable position, but methodologically defensible in clearly recognizing that a normative ideational claim is being made, not a suggestion for institutional reform per se—into a preference for "defense agencies" rather than for (the adoption of libertarian ideas by the individuals who control) "states." All of Huemer's philosophical work is being done by the hidden premise that "defense agencies" would *impose on themselves* superordinate libertarian moral principles. This is not a function of a new institutional arrangement, anarcho-capitalism. Rather, anarcho-capitalist institutions would follow from the adoption of self-constraining libertarian ideas by state personnel, and the only guarantor of the continued restraint of the defense agencies would be their personnel's continued subjection to these ideational constraints.

Defense agencies, then, are states run by libertarians. They are by no means non-states; nor are they by any means uncoercive. Even "competitive," unwarlike defense agencies would bring coercive enforcement actions against people who violated libertarian private property rights and rules of interpersonal behavior (such as laws against murder). This would be their very purpose. But coercion is not unique to libertarian forms of "anarchism." There is no escape from some form of coercion and, usually if not always, coercive authority. In a right-anarchist community, a "defense agency" that dared to seize control of individuals' "private property" to turn it into common property would have to be suppressed by the armed agents of an overarching (libertarian) "state" in everything but name. And in a left-anarchist community, a subcommunity that set up an exploitative system of wage labor built on private ownership of the means of production would have to be suppressed by the community at large—making the community at large, for all intents and purposes, a (communist) state.

Thus, any argument for the legitimacy of anarchism on internal exitocratic grounds would entail an overarching coercive ideational framework that sets exit-friendly rules of competition among defense agencies. However, Reamer also would like to justify anarcho-capitalism, at least potentially, on grounds of consent and free will as "independent normative criteria for political legitimacy" that transcend internal technocratic normative criteria. This means that he must forego exitocratically inspired "state" controls over the behavior of the competing defense agencies. Thus, one must ask whether anarchism can meet *its* internal normative criteria. Can anarchism create a *truly* consensual, voluntaristic society? I do not see how.

Wherever we have the power to threaten one another, not just physically but also emotionally, and also through the control of resources that limit opportunities for action, and also (decisively, in my view) ideationally—by affecting what each other thinks—there will be relationships of power and coercion. This is to say that such relationships can never be abolished, regardless of institutional arrangements and, more pertinently, regardless of what we call those arrangements. The omnipresence of power is not diminished by withdrawing formal authorization from it or by calling it "community consent" rather than "state coercion," or by calling "the institutions" authorized by "the community" "defense agencies." What actually happens in an anarchist society is that coercive power continues to be exercised, but without (non-"consensual") authorization.

What, however, of *imposed* authorization, which Reamer contrasts against consensual authorization? It seems to me that the rule of consensus is itself the rule of an imposed authority. It is rulership authorized through the "voluntary" subordination of each individual's actions to a consensus decision rather than to the decision that would otherwise have been made by the (possibly heterogeneous) individuals themselves, whose actions would, in the absence of a collective decision, have been determined by their own webs of belief rather than those of most of the others in the community. The enforcement of a collective decision will have to rely on the presence in most of the community members' webs of belief of a constraining norm that requires them to set aside disagreements and submit to the collective decision; or by fear of the threat of disapproval or other sanctions from those in the community who agree with a decision with which any individual might disagree; or by the absence of disagreement, i.e., the rule over each of homogeneous ideas. Now if we have an exaggerated view of the homogenizing ideational force of language or any other factor, we might imagine that consensus is likely to be obtained without trampling on anyone's dissident ideas. This illusion would be reinforced if our own experiences with attempting to reach consensus are confined to groups self-selected for ideological homogeneity, as in contemporary anarchist communities. Ideological homogeneity might make it look, to the naïvely realistic, as if everyone sees the world in basically the same way. Why, then, one might ask oneself, should people coerce one another rather than just talking out their apparent but superficial differences? But consensualist anarchism is naïve about what it means even when there is genuine ideational homogeneity (consensus). Is action based on ideational homogeneity freer or more voluntary than action taken under threat of violence?

Here I think a dose of Foucault may help. His great insight was the ubiquity of power *even when* there is ideational homogeneity: in such cases we have internalized the dominant ideas. While Foucault treated this as an empirical rather than logical claim, and while he attributed the power of ideas to social forces or structures, the fact remains that when one self-subordinates to the rule of a particular consensus because one agrees with it, one is self-subordinating to the most effective conceivable form of power: the determining power of the ideas with which one is *compelled* to agree by what one's web of belief interprets as the unforced force of the better argument.

This power may reach into one's web of beliefs in any number of ways. One might have been raised in an anarchist community where one was socialized into shared ideas; one might have been deliberately indoctrinated with anarchist (or libertarian) ideas as an adult; or more fortuitous, inadvertent ideational exposures might have homogenized a group of adults' webs of belief. Only if we imagine a free will somehow standing apart from such processes of belief formation would it make sense to entertain the idea of a noncoercive society. Insofar as free will is a myth, though, the power of ideas must be recognized as determining individual action coercively, because truly voluntary action is impossible. Our conscious actions are always determined by our ideas—even the idea that one should submit to consensus. If free will is a myth then so, too, must be a truly voluntary society, no matter how "consensual" it might be.

However, while power is omnipresent and coercion inescapable, it does not necessarily follow that there is always a coercive *authority*, consensual or not. The lines of interpersonal coercion may be so subtle and tangled that there is no clearly superior person or group in terms of either power *or* authority.

If one stands back from one's web of beliefs to ask, "Who is controlling me?" I'm not sure an accurate answer is possible: there are far too many ideational influences on each of us, many of them forgotten, to know. In the space of this epistemic blur, Durkheim answered the question with an ontic hypostasization: "society." We should not repeat this mistake by assuming that "the state" is the chief repository of coercion, or that coercion must be placed into authorized hands for it to exist. Even if we use a more conventional, non-ideational definition of coercion than mine, the difference between "states" and "defense agencies" is solely the fact that the latter are not *called* states because they are not authorized by some sort of formal "political" procedure. They would nevertheless have the power to coerce people who violate their rules, including their rules for interpersonal behavior and the control of property. And in the absence of an overarching technocratic (or other) "institution" that sets the rules for their competition, they would have the power to set those rules. Finally, when we impose libertarian rules on defense agencies, we are positing ideational control that is *more* coercive than the threats of physical force that would be wielded by the agencies, and thus is able to restrain this force when the control is internalized in the webs of belief of defense agency personnel or externalized in the webs of belief of the personnel of an overarching supervisory, rule-setting state.

If we think of states as collective objects whose ideational, individual components are fuzzed over, as IR scholars and libertarians both tend to do, then "states'" distinctive features will, by perceptual default, have to be certain institutional trappings, such as bureaucratic administration, a standing army, or a hierarchical decision-making structure. We may then come to think that if we remove the trappings, we have abolished the state. But a state, viewed from an epistemologically individualistic perspective, is people exercising coercion over one another in accord with the coercion exercised over them by their ideas or those of somebody else. Even if the net effect is to give people exit opportunities from other forms of coercion, as in an exitocracy, this effect is brought about coercively, e.g., by the creation of certain type of property right and a certain type of wealth redistribution, enforced by the coercive sanctions brought against "criminals" by a certain type of "legal" (i.e., ideational) order. Insofar as there are any enforced property rights, any enforced rules of behavior, or any enforced redistribution of wealth, then, we have a state, so long as we do not get hung up on names and appearances. And wherever we have a state or any other institutional arrangement, we have, at the very least (but not exclusively), ideational coercion.

Even the hunter-gatherer communities that are usually taken to epitomize statelessness because they lack overt enforcement mechanisms and explicit authorization protocols must, as a matter of logic, have some structure of ideational coercion that constitutes a trappings-free version of a state. *Somebody* (even if it is "the community as a whole") decides rules and adjudicates conflicts or, at least—in fissiparous communities with robust exit opportunities for anyone who prefers not to remain, who can defuse conflicts by leaving—somebody decides upon the tacit or explicit community norms from which dissidents may secede. By the same token, the dissidents themselves, once they leave and constitute a new community of their own, will have tacit or explicit normative and criterial ideas that make the community state-like, so long as we recognize that coercion is not reducible to the "men with guns" who preoccupy libertarians, and so long as we recognize that power is no less present even when it is not explicitly authorized, and even when it is equally distributed.

Even if there are no overt displays of force or authority, there will be *something* that controls people's behavior, and it is difficult—impossible, I think—to draw a non-arbitrary line between behavioral controls that are "coercive" and those that are not. This is why I consider the force of ideas, which is what decides the actions chosen by even the freest of "free" agents, to be a strict determination of those agents' actions, annihilating the illusion of free will. Whatever it is that determines our actions is, for all intents and purposes, coercive. If so, then coercion is unavoidable, and it makes little sense to structure our social aspirations around freedom of action, which is an impossible goal. (I am not speaking of *complete* freedom of action as utopian, but of *any* freedom of action as incoherent.) But freedom, as the absence of coercion, is not only the aspiration of anarchism but its conceptual foundation. Therefore, anarchism seems to me to be logically incoherent—except in its original, leftist variant, where it amounts to an egalitarian and consensual form of coercion. The point of left anarchism, though, is best seen not as abolition of the state so as to achieve a society free of coercion, but abolition of the capitalist state so as to achieve a communist society, which is not incoherent.

IV. DARK AVENUES OF FUTURE RESEARCH

To bring this long reply to a close, I want to address one last concern shared by several of my interlocutors: the question of democratic legitimacy—a question that points beyond the political epistemology of technocracy.

Moore wonders if the architecture of an exitocracy might not have to be protected from popular meddling, and he asks how exitocrats might produce such an architecture to begin with if not by disregarding popular sentiment. (He does not recognize that the architecture might be produced by citizen-technocrats, not epistocrats.) Similarly, Brown and Williams worry about the legitimacy of technocratic policies that are grounded in reliable epistocratic knowledge but happen to be opposed by the demos. Within the compass of the book, of course, my response to these concerns is to point out that they are external to the negative-utilitarian goal of solving, mitigating, or preventing social and economic problems: the internal goal of any technocracy, as I define it. Democratic legitimacy per se is irrelevant to technocracy in the ideal type that I construct around my epistemic definition of it. In the ideal type, the legitimacy of technocracy stems solely from its problem-solving efficacy, not its foundation in the will of the people. Those who have technocratic knowledge are entitled to rule, regardless of whether they are "the many" or "the few" or "the one." *Power*

Without Knowledge is not an exercise in democratic theory, then, and qualms about the democratic legitimacy of exitocracy are no more germane to the internal technocratic perspective I adopt in the book than is Habermas's concern about the democratic legitimacy of epistocracy, which I bracket—for the sake of conducting an epistemological rather than normative critique—as soon as the book begins (1-4).

I think political theorists may have gotten themselves into a box, or a cave, from inside of which the only features of the world that tend to catch their eye are those that have implications for democracy—whether in the institutional sense of elections, sortition, workplace democracy, participatory democracy, social movements, and other forms of, or strivings for, equal political power; or in the conceptual sense of equality, covering both distributive justice and subtle forms of inequality. This exclusively democratic vision of political theory has a narrowing effect empirically as well as normatively. Moore argues that "if technocracy is everywhere, then the critique of technocracy becomes an undifferentiated critique of more or less the whole of modern democratic politics." But while it is true that technocracy, as I define it, has a democratic variant, and that much of modern politics is best understood as constitutive of this variant, there is more to modern politics than technocratic politics. There is, for example, a dying liberal politics of constitutionalism. And there is an emancipatory, revolutionary politics that began to take root after the financial crisis of 2008, and picked up tremendous momentum under Trump.

Both liberal and emancipatory politics are clearly distinct from the technocratic struggle, both democratic and elitist, over public policies designed to solve discrete social and economic problems. The objective of emancipatory politics is not to engage in "piecemeal social engineering" (Popper [1945] 2013, 148), but to overthrow systems of oppression. The objective of liberal politics is to secure and expand individual freedoms. By establishing that a non-democratic form of contemporary politics, epistocracy, operates alongside democratic forms of at least three types—technocratic (citizen-technocratic) politics, liberal politics, and emancipatory politics—*Power Without Knowledge* may (I hope) train theoretical and empirical attention on all four, by underscoring their differences. The most important of these would seem to be the centrality to technocratic politics, both democratic and epistocratic, of disagreement (actual or potential) about the behavioral effects of public policy, and the absence of this type of epistemic conflict in liberal and emancipatory politics. (This is not intended as an exhaustive list of differences, and the four items on it are ideal types only; only rarely is there a purely emancipatory politics, for example, that does not include proposals for policy or institutional reform.)

Political Epistemology in an "Anthropological" Vein

Needless to say, however, *all* types of politics require people to make truth claims. Therefore, all of them demand critical analysis by political epistemologists, empirical and normative. The political anthropology of ideational beings, then, should be as relevant to emancipatory and liberal types of democratic politics as to technocratic politics, and might be relevant to future research that has little or nothing to do with technocracy.

All human beings are governed by fallible beliefs that are interpersonally communicated. This does not mean, of course, that all human beliefs are wrong or likely to be wrong. It simply means that genuine disagreement is always justifiable, in principle, because no political truths—even the moral truths that are central in liberal and emancipatory politics, and the social-theoretic truths that are central in emancipatory politics—are self-evident. Therefore, when it comes to non-technocratic politics, we should, presumably, begin in the territory with which *Power Without Knowledge* begins (35-39): the territory of naïve *political* realism, as opposed to naïve technocratic realism or, separately, the question of technocratic knowledge (Chapters 2-7).

There may be other overlaps between my book and work in non-technocratic areas of political epistemology. For example, Lippmann's troubling observations about the mass media seem to be applicable to democratic technocracy, liberal democracy, *and* emancipatory democracy once the mass mediators' humanity—specifically, their ideational determination—is taken into account. On the one hand, journalists are not experts in anything, whether the consequences of technocratic politics or the demands of individual autonomy or social justice. Yet as Lippmann ([1920] 2008, 28) recognized, almost everything we think we know about politics and society is mediated to us, giving the media "a power unlike any that has been exercised since the Pope lost his hold on the secular mind." This is something of which political theorists and political scientists alike should be cognizant but which, at present, captures attention only when certain media sources broadcast anti-democratic or illiberal messages, or messages that political theorists and political scientists perceive as anti-democratic or illiberal. There is a burgeoning literature on the biases and impact of Fox News and social media, but this focus of attention is too narrow to correct the preoccupation of political scientists and political theorists alike with objective, non-ideational causes of democratic political action, leading to the dearth of media research that Larry Bartels once called "one of the most notable embarrassments of modern social science" (1993, 267).[15]

To a Lippmannite, a true corrective to this embarrassment would be to place the media, including not only journalism and social media but film, television, primary, secondary, and post-secondary education, nonfiction books and essays, fiction, comedy, religious indoctrination, and so on, at the very center of the attention of political scientists and, too, political theorists—whether we are studying and theorizing the behavior of masses or elites, and whether we are interested in technocratic politics, liberal politics, emancipatory politics, or any other kind. The ideas of both masses and elites, as human beings, are determined by fallible, biased ideas and interpretations—usually mediated to them by someone, then processed by them in accordance with the biased interpretations created by their own webs of belief. The most radical implication of these "anthropological" facts is the possibility of a closed loop of interpretation: the ultra-Platonic possibility that whatever one thinks one knows about politics, government, and society is a self-reinforcing fiction. In my experience, a stubborn crust of naïve realism keeps even the most sophisticated political theorists from accepting this possibility, but perhaps they will rethink now that alternative media have apparently persuaded large numbers of people that a worldwide conspiracy of Satan-worshipping pederasts was being valiantly battled by Donald J. Trump. We blind ourselves, I think, to the true import of this development if we insist that the QAnon conspiracy theory is so *self-evidently* false that those who believed it must have been crazy and can therefore be ignored by everyone but the FBI (and our intellectually uncharitable colleagues in political psychology). If they were not crazy but *misled*—as intellectually charitable interpretation demands—then we must concede that human beings can rather easily be led to believe virtually anything, regardless of how far removed it is from reality.

That, of course, is a lesson we should already have learned from the study of world religions, which are perpetuated through mass indoctrination. Yet we must also concede that we who study and theorize such phenomena are also human beings whose interpretations are as fallibly biased and interpersonally mediated as those of any other human beings, and who *may*, therefore, be just as deluded as QAnon adepts or members of the alt-right. I happen to be in correspondence with a young man who was raised in a religious cult whose founder, he was taught, was the Messiah. (No, this cult is not Christianity.) My correspondent is struggling to leave this cult, but he hesitates, writing, "Everything that I learned, all the teachers, are they all wrong?" This is a question that every one of us should ask—political theorists as much as anyone else.

The Nazi party received a plurality of 37 percent of the German vote in July 1932 and another plurality, 33 percent, in November 1932—the last free election before 1949. That the Nazis fell short of a popular majority should not distract us: they used mass media to establish, in a huge swath of the population, a closed loop of interpretation that was completely disconnected from reality. And once they consolidated their control over the mass media after 1932, imposing through it a single bias, the proportion of the population whose ideas fell into line was, by all indications, far above 50 percent. It would be profoundly unrealistic, then, to imagine that prior to Hitler's seizure of absolute power in 1933, something like the Condorcet Jury Theorem explains why the majority voted against Hitler, as if it was *self-evident* to most Germans that he was evil. Majorities in a mediated society have no intrinsically benign (or malign) epistemic properties, such as the ability to sort good from bad interpretations with a greater than .5 chance of success. Nor do "elites" have such properties. Nor do "fundamental factors" or hypostasized social forces, such as the economic devastation wrought by the Great Depression or, in our day, neoliberalism, determine people's ideas: all objective factors must be subjectively interpreted. In modern cultures, at least, interpretation is historically contingent on whatever ideas happen to be in circulation. Donald Trump gained 46 percent of the popular vote in 2016 and 47 percent in 2020 because of what was broadcast by Fox News Channel, talk radio, his own Twitter feed (which had nearly 89 million followers before it was abolished in 2021), and other online media, such as those that disseminated the QAnon theory. The only way that "deindustrialization" or "globalization" or "immigration" could have caused these events is if these putative objective factors had first been subjectively mediated to the voters, because that is the only way objective factors in a mass society can enter human minds.

A further point that might orient future research is that Trump used alternative mass media to say not only that the government had been captured by special interests, and that these interests favored deindustrialization, globalization, and immigration, and that the mainstream media were covering for those interests (thus far, we are in technocratic territory); but, at the same time, that the mainstream media were passing off their own biased perceptions (not just of technocratic questions but all questions) as self-evident truths. Here the technocratic, populist side of Trump's message merged with a wider message about mediation itself.

Bizarrely, Trump and his most uneducated followers were, on this point, more sophisticated than the most highly educated people in America. Journalists *always* have to select which information seems credible and how to interpret it before they communicate it to their audiences. Given the overabundance of information they might report and the infinite ways they might report it, selectivity—bias—is unavoidable. As Lippmann pointed out, selectivity is enabled by interpretations that treat an *inevitably and rationally* biased information sample as representative of the whole. Of course, Trump and his followers saw media bias as a malign conspiracy, not an epistemic necessity. But the a priori existence of *some* media bias can be disputed only if one is a naïve political realist. It is depressing but true that Trump's media opponents were therefore more naïve than the ignoramus they justifiably opposed.

Indeed, the Trump years saw a new flowering of media naïveté, in the form of journalism that "simply tells the truth" by labeling as "misinformation" or "lies" whatever journalists consider false. While Trump does seem to have lied a great deal (and to have conveyed an immense amount of misinformation), it is very difficult to establish a lie in any given case, as this entails that the putative liar *knew* he was telling a falsehood; this is an especially dicey proposition when dealing with someone as abysmally uninformed, and as prone to believing the moronic, as Trump. Across the front page of the February 1, 2021 *New York Times* ran the headline "77 Days: Trump's Campaign to Subvert the Election," followed by the subhead "How a Lie Stoked the Assault on the Capital." The story itself, however, unwittingly contradicts the subhead. It tells us that "as Election Day approached, Mr. Trump and those closest to him *believed* that his lead would be insurmountable, their views swayed by the assurances of pro-Trump pundits and the unscientific measure of the size and excitement of the president's rally crowds." On the morning of the election, one of Trump's sons "wagered that the president would win at least 320 electoral votes," so it is hardly surprising that that night, "Mr. Trump and his entourage fell into enraged *disbelief* as his lead inexorably dissipated"; or that early the next morning, Trump said on television: "We were getting ready to win this election—frankly, we did win this election." Yet the reporters declare, of this statement, that it "furiously laid down his post-election *lie*" (Rutenberg et al. 2021, A13, emphases mine)—collapsing the distinction between a mistaken belief and a deliberate falsehood. This is a textbook case of naïve journalistic realism—albeit one that would itself surely be called by Trump, and his naïvely realistic supporters, a lie.

This new iteration of naïve realism culminates a dynamic that began with conservative complaints about media bias during the New Deal and has continued down to the present day (Friedman 2019a, 20-23). These relentless complaints created an audience for the alternative media sources that began appearing in the late 1980s, which provided the closed, anti-mainstream loops of interpretation that would come to fuel Trump's attacks on the mainstream media for having themselves created closed loops of "fake news." In reaction to these attacks on the mainstream media, and to Trump's own tenuous connection to reality, mainstream journalists laid ever-greater emphasis on their role as unbiased, unproblematic guardians of truth—which was not just unconvincing but a source of fury to those who had turned to talk radio, Fox News, Breitbart, Reddit, and the presidential Twitter feed precisely because they viewed them as trustworthy alternatives to mainstream media *misinformation*. In their eyes, the "lying mainstream media's" invocations of "the truth," "the science," "the data," and "the facts" not only rang hollow but betokened an attempt to stifle criticism of the media's own reality-shaping power.

Consider Adam Newbold, a former Navy SEAL who, in 2015, had to confront a right-wing conspiracy theory about operation Jade Helm 15. This was a military training exercise in Texas with which Newbold was involved, which was portrayed by right-wing conspiratorialist Alex Jones as "a covert plot to have federal troops invade Texas, seize citizens' guns and impose martial law" (Phillips 2021). At the time, Newbold laughed off this conspiracy theory as "fringe ravings." Yet five years later he joined the Capitol Hill mob, having become convinced that "mountains of evidence of election fraud and voter fraud" supported, as a *New York Times* reporter puts it, "the fabricated theory that the election was rigged by a shadowy cabal of liberal power brokers" (ibid.). The reporter goes on to say:

> Mr. Newbold is a longtime registered Republican who said he voted for Mr. Trump. In the past four years, as mainstream media coverage of the president grew harsher, and Mr. Newbold's sometimes strident support on Facebook drew more rebukes, he migrated to news sources and chat rooms that shared his views. (Ibid.)

But the last three words may be misleading. It wasn't that Newbold originated a conspiracy theory and then sought out confirmation of it. Rather, alienated by perceived mainstream media bias, he turned to alternative media that introduced him to a conspiracy theory that was said to be based on mountains of evidence that the mainstream media refused to cover.

Anti-Epistemological Epistemology

For Republicans, media bias has become the central issue of the age, but for journalists, media bias is a myth or, indeed, a lie. This conviction reiterates the epistemic naïveté that started the whole cycle. The cycle itself, however, has escaped the attention of political theorists and political scientists alike—who tend to be as naïvely realistic as journalists. Naïve accounts of the Beer Belly Putsch, then, such as Shoshana Zuboff's "The Knowledge Coup," provide a template for the type of political epistemology we may soon witness: an anti-epistemological form of "epistemology."

Zuboff (2021), writing across two op-ed pages of the *Times,* blames our "epistemic chaos" on social media companies, which "engineered a fundamentally anti-democratic epistemic coup" that "splinter[ed] shared reality," because the "economic imperatives" of these companies made them "incapable of, and uninterested in, distinguishing truth from lies." Thus, the companies gave Trump "the right to lie at scale," and they thereby eroded "common sense," i.e., "the most taken-for-granted social certainties." Zuboff's argument is entirely dependent on the self-evident truth of these social certainties (whatever they might be). A tragic clash of self-confirming loops of interpretation is turned into a morality tale of good versus evil epistemic actors, the latter empowered by greedy corporations. Moreover, according to Zuboff, epistemic chaos was only allowed to emerge because the corporations were not subject to "democratic governance"—a form of control that, presumably, would have imposed "social certainties" on social media by law, ensuring that whatever biases are once hegemonic will always remain so.

This extremely dangerous form of political theorizing, which, if transformed into action, could only prompt further rage among the epistemically marginalized, was picked up days later by the *Times*'s Kevin Roose (2021), who, in an article titled "Reclaiming Reality from Chaos," argued (citing "experts") that our "muddled, chaotic information system" has led to a "national reality crisis" that may demand "something like a reality czar" in response. Roose, however, takes it for granted that, "after all, many people are drawn to extremist groups like the Proud Boys and conspiracy theories like QAnon not because they're convinced by the facts, but because the beliefs give them a sense of community or purpose, or fills [sic] a void in their lives." Intellectually uncharitable psychologizing, then, rescues the reporter from fully endorsing the "reality czar" idea; another path, "most of the experts agreed," toward fixing "our national reality crisis . . . would be to address the underlying [social and economic] problems that drove" people to extremism in the first place. (Well-adjusted, economically secure people could not believe anything as outlandish as QAnon.) Besides, Roose assures us, the reality bureaucracy need not *dictate* what is true; instead, it could merely "help" media companies "tackle their own extremism and misinformation problems" by pointing out to them that someone on their platforms is denying "the facts." One might see Roose's naïve realism as merely epistocratic, a problem that could be addressed in Larsson's manner, and presumably Zuboff's, by putting democratic "stakeholders" in charge of "resolv[ing] the social and political problems" caused by false beliefs by deciding which facts are true. But what if these stakeholders, being drawn from amongst the people, are themselves Q believers, Nazis, populists, or are in other respects simply wrong about "the facts of reality"?

Here is the outline of an alternative account of "epistemic chaos" that tries to avoid Zuboff's and Roose's naïve realism. In any mass democracy, the masses will have been informed by people who, being human, will, of necessity, be biased (i.e., selective, not necessarily wrong). Journalists' opinions, voters' opinions, and politicians' opinions alike are fallible and prone to interpretive biases. But the mass media can fend off epistemic chaos—i.e., disagreement—by homogenizing the errors and biases, to a significant degree, so long as its personnel themselves are ideologically homogeneous, as they were in the United States until the late 1980s. In 1987, the repeal of the Fairness Doctrine allowed Rush Limbaugh and then others, including Fox News Channel, to begin broadcasting news with an anti-mainstream bias. The epistemic chaos unleashed by media diversity was and is nothing but ideational heterogeneity that had previously been suppressed by media uniformity. The chaos consists of an ongoing conflict, usually subtle but, of late, incredibly loud, over what constitutes the truth.

This account does not rely, as Zuboff and Roose do, on our first-order convictions about which "facts" are true and which are "lies"—i.e., which "social certainties" are or are not *warranted,* or which "realities" *deserve* to be "shared." The theorist's use of such first-order convictions would beg the epistemic question: the question of how we theorists ourselves, who have been exposed to mediated truth claims all our lives, can use them to arbitrate the validity of others' mediated truth claims. Zuboff or Roose would say that Limbaugh and his imitators unleashed an *undesirable* form of chaos because they "peddled lies" or "spouted misinformation," in contrast to the mainstream media's reporting of "the facts." If we were to follow Zuboff's and Roose's example, political epistemology would become a barely disguised continuation of partisan combat by theoretical means—a sham "epistemology" that subjects only the first-order claims of one's political opponents to epistemic scrutiny, sparing one's own (61-71).

The one thing that political epistemologists should know enough *not* to say about epistemically "chaotic" (i.e., contentious and naïve) politics, which pits "taken-for-granted social certainties" against each other, is that we, as theorists, can take for granted which of these claims to certainty are warranted—absent a *second-order* reason for privileging some claims over others as more likely to be accurate. Such taking for granted is the mark of an absence of epistemological thinking. At present, it is just this epistemological void, by repudiating doubt, that turns epistemic chaos into political war.

—*February 28, 2021*

NOTES

1. Separately, one might point out that technocracy itself is historically contingent upon the existence of social and economic problems that, arguably, are caused by modern capitalism. *Power Without Knowledge* brackets this claim (3, 337) because it is orthogonal to an internal examination of whether technocracy can solve these problems. A more challenging Marxist critique of the book would point out that mass society, and thus ideational heterogeneity, are products of, or are at least made possible, in large part, by capitalism. Because this seems undeniable, the epistemic critique of technocracy may not apply to communism (insofar as the latter could not sustain, or would abolish, mass society).
2. Brown and Williams's reference to the fact that special interests spend a lot on lobbying might seem to indicate an empirically established "systemic" problem of bad faith, but lobbyists represent nearly every conceivable interest and, in fact, rarely bribe their targets. Anyone familiar with actual lobbying knows that lobbyists' power stems from their ability to provide information about the effects of pending legislation. The information, of course, is very likely to be biased in favor of the interests they serve. But this does not make the information inherently unreliable, let alone false; our interpretive screens, which bias all information acquisition, are fallible but not, therefore, unreliable. In other words, one's bias may coincide with the truth. What is really doing the work in Brown and Williams's critique of lobbying by special interests is the naïve assumption that special interests *must* be wrong because they contradict what Brown and WIlliams take to be the self-evident truth about, say, global warming.
3. In introducing a conception of historically attuned positivism, I am trying to account for figures such as Foucault and Habermas. I say more about Foucault in my reply to Larsson. In Habermas's contribution to the positivism debate in German sociology ([1963] 1976), he concedes to positivist social science the validity of the lawlike regularities it purports to discover *within the compass of the*

capitalist order, questioning only the positivist separation of fact and value and, more to the present point, the positivist neglect of the historical totality within which the lawlike regularities operate. Because Habermas was (at least in the early years) a methodological collectivist, he accepted the existence and knowability of synchronic laws governing a given historical system; he challenged only their permanence. By contrast, because I am an epistemological individualist, I challenge the existence of such systems and thus the notion that they might supply lawlike regularity to a given era.

4. How many economists does it take to change a light bulb? Two: one to assume the existence of a ladder and the other to climb it and change the bulb.
5. Lerner may have overlooked the crucial role of interpersonal communication for epistemological individualism (150-53). In a paper titled "Theorizing Collective Trauma in International Political Economy" (Lerner 2019), he again defends a pragmatic refusal to embrace either ontological collectivism or individualism, this time in thinking about collective trauma. Therefore, he treats "collective trauma" as a valuable metaphor with uncertain philosophical status, which is how his contribution to the symposium treats "the state." However, the reason he is unwilling to reduce collective trauma to individuals' subjective and fallible perceptions of trauma, as an epistemological individualist would do, is not that he doubts the subjectivity or fallibility of these perceptions, or the ontological reality of the individuals who subjectively perceive them. Rather, it is because individualistic approaches to the topic in the IR literature equate individual perceptions of trauma with Freudian explanations of the source of trauma, "downplay[ing] the complexity inherent in the repeated politically mediated *transmissions and reproductions* necessary for individual trauma to become collective" (ibid., 554, my emphasis). In short, the "social construction" of collective trauma is ignored by the Freudian approach, but this lacuna can be filled by treating "society" as if it is a being with a "collective memory" of traumatic events (ibid., 552). It seems to me that this hypostasization of the collective is unnecessary and mystifies the process of social construction as described by Lerner, which begins when individuals' subjective, fallible perceptions of trauma—or anything else—are "transmitted and reproduced," presumably by means of textbooks, news reports, novels, movies, or any other cultural media. All such media reproduce and then transmit individuals' ideas to other individuals. Methodologically collectivist critics of the Freudian approach, Lerner says, condemn it for "mak[ing] the level of culture . . . disappear" (554), but this happens only because traumatized individual psyches of the sort analyzed by the Freudians cannot communicate ideas or memories to one another unaided by conscious attempts to use communications technology. To correct this deficiency in the Freudian approach, we need not hypostasize the use of communications technology as occurring at a separate and non-individualistic ontological "level," culture. This would repeat exactly the mistake Taylor made, and with the same result: effacing the fallibility and potential heterogeneity of the ideas being culturally communicated.

Thus, the intersubjective communication of ideas among individual subjects by cultural media would seem to resolve the riddle that divides methodological individualists and collectivists and prompts Lerner's prudent reluctance to endorse either side. *Epistemological* individualism, unlike the atomistic type of theorizing that goes under the *methodologically* individualist rubric, allows for intersubjective communication—which, as I see it, is the chief source of subjects' ideational homogeneities and ideational heterogeneities alike. (I hope it is clear, then, that I do not mean, by "epistemological individualism," what Steven Lukes [1973, 107] means by it, namely, "a philosophical doctrine about the nature of knowledge, which asserts that the source of knowledge lies within the individual.") Communication should therefore be a central object of political science research. The fact that it is not, even more than the fact that such research tends to be positivistic, may account for the strikingly unrealistic nature of all three of the discipline's empirical subfields.

6. Obviously the "genes/ideas" dichotomy is a bit too stark, as our genes enable our thoughts by way of our brains. However, our genes do not determine the *content* of our thoughts, which is historically contingent, as opposed to the cognitive architecture that processes them. There may be exceptions—ideas that are genetically encoded—but the kaleidoscopic diversity of the ideas developed during the last few centuries in the West suggests that most ideas are not genetically encoded. Positivist psychologists, however, in common with other positivist social scientists, display an appalling lack of historical awareness.
7. I do not mean, however, to deny the real issues raised by my critique of the positivist psychologist's double standard. Among these are, first, the question of whether one's own rationality may be an illusion; second, whether the double standard may sometimes be justified by differential or asymmetric irrationality; third, whether a psychology of intellectual charity is committed to denying the existence of irrationality or mental illness; and fourth, how to deal with cases where irrationality seems to be the only possible diagnosis. I attempt to make some progress on the fourth issue in Friedman 2021, but it is only a start.
8. When I wrote that one may disagree with some acquaintances about "nearly everything" (147), I meant, as Reamer acknowledges, only everything that one discusses—not every single belief in one's web.
9. In answer to Reamer's second end note, this type of variability is not random, as it is determined by non-random processes of belief formation. Therefore, we cannot treat ideational idiosyncracy as predictable noise on the tail ends of a bell curve.
10. On the difference between the later Wittgenstein and Whorf, see Kienpointer 1996.
11. MacGilvray may, however, have meant the ethic of responsibility to provide an alternative to what the book labels "the transformation of means into ends" (301-3). This is the practice of portraying technocratic policies as good in themselves rather than as means to good ends, such that one does not need to consider whether they will actually achieve those ends. In effect, the transformation of means into ends enacts a transition from the ethic of responsibility to the ethic of conviction and, thereby, a transition out of technocracy into a politics of justice or symbolism rather than a politics of consequences. The manuscript of *Power Without Knowledge* said just that until the last minute, when I noticed that it would be misleading to mention the parallel between the transformation of means into ends and Weber's dichotomy—precisely because it might suggest that all we need, to avoid the transformation of means into ends *and thus achieve a responsible consideration of means*, is politicians imbued with the ethic of responsibility. This is untrue, as the epistemic problems facing such decision makers

cannot be solved merely by intending to know the consequences of their actions, which is all that can be accomplished by the ethic in itself. Conversely, a politician who portrays a given technocratic policy stance as a matter of justice, not efficacy, may simply calculate that this will motivate greater support for the policy than couching it as a matter of cost-benefit analysis, even though cost-benefit analysis is her actual reason for supporting the policy. Such a politician would be a responsible one, in Weber's usage, who is doing whatever it takes to achieve good consequences. Finally, Weber's treatment of the ethic of conviction creates the impression that its adepts are aware of the fact that they are ignoring the consequences of their actions. This might be true in some cases but, as a general claim, it is intellectually uncharitable and, I think, false. For these reasons, I removed my discussion of "Politics as a Vocation" from the text of Chapter 6 but neglected to remove it from the bibliography, as MacGilvray notices.

12. There is an ambiguity about the ranking of the middle two levels. While both an injudicious exitocracy and a judicious ordinary technocracy are logically superior to an injudicious technocracy, and while both are inferior to a judicious exitocracy, I can see no way to determine a priori whether or not a judicious ordinary technocracy is superior to an injudicious exitocracy or vice versa.
13. Note that Benson misconstrues Part III as arguing that "*technocratic* knowledge is required to understand whether the actions of an exitocracy will actually promote or undermine exit" (my emphasis). In reality, the preface to Part III (317–19) points to a variety of reasons for thinking that *theorists* cannot know the magnitude of future judicious or injudicious technocrats' successes and failures. This is not a failure of theorists' technocratic knowledge, even though one of these reasons for their third-order ignorance is that if they were to attempt to weigh the costs and benefits of technocracy by appealing to their own estimation of technocrats' first-order successes and failures, they would beg the question of the reliability of their own first-order technocratic understanding. This picks up on Chapter 1's self-denying ordinance against theorists naïvely exempting their own technocratic knowledge claims from scrutiny, but in light of the intervening five chapters, it amounts to saying that political theorists are not judicious technocrats; it does not amount to saying that even judicious technocrats' knowledge claims would be unreliable, and thus it does not impugn the reliability of judicious *exitocrats'* knowledge claims. Benson also overlooks the other reasons for theorists' ignorance—most obviously that we do not know *how well* technocrats will do their job (317), which *does* apply to judicious exitocrats, but, again, does not impugn the reliability of *their* knowledge, as opposed to *our* knowledge of these yet-unborn human beings' trials and tribulations.
14. Again, see Friedman 1997.
15. I should qualify Bartels's 1993 lament about the embarrassing lack of media research by quoting from a footnote from *Power Without Knowledge* (270n24), where I cited the same lament. Since Bartels wrote, I acknowledged, "laboratory experimentation has demonstrated the persuasive capacities of the news media (see Chong and Druckman 2011 for a brief survey). However, this literature underplays media effects because the three main categories of experimentally demonstrated effects—agenda setting, priming, and framing—each presuppose fixed voter predispositions, uninfluenced by the media. Agenda setting makes

one issue rather than others appear to be important at a given moment; priming emphasizes one issue rather than another in the retrospective evaluation of a politician's performance; and framing emphasizes one or another dimension of an issue. All three types of media effect alter 'the weight component of an attitude through changes in [the] availability, accessibility and/or applicability' of media consumers' *pre-existing beliefs* about the issues in question (Chong and Druckman 2011, 310). None of the three takes seriously the possibility that these beliefs themselves are shaped by the media (including non-news media, such as cinema and formal education)." That is, none of the three takes seriously the possibility of closed loops of interpretation, because media scholars do not recognize the interpretive springs of human action.

REFERENCES

Adorno, Theodor. [1957] 1976. "Sociology and Empirical Research." In Theodor Adorno, Hans Albert, Ralf Dahrendorf, Jürgen Habermas, Harald Pilot, and Karl R. Popper, *The Positivist Dispute in German Sociology*, trans. Glyn Adey and David Frisby. London: Heinemann.

Bakker, Bert N., Gijs Schumacher, and Matthias Rooduijn. 2021. "Hot Politics: Affective Responses to Political Rhetoric." *American Political Science Review* 115(1): 150-64.

Banerjee, Abhijit, and Esther Duflo. 2014. "The Experimental Approach to Development Economics." In *Field Experiments and Their Critics: Essays on the Uses and Abuses of Experimentation in the Social Sciences*, ed. Dawn Langan Teele. New Haven: Yale University Press.

Bartels, Larry M. 1993. "Messages Received: The Political Impact of Media Exposure." *American Political Science Review* 87(2): 267–85.

Benson, Jonathan. 2020. "Exit, Voice and Technocracy." *Critical Review* 32(1-3).

Blair, Robert A. 2021. "UN Peacekeeping and the Rule of Law." *American Political Science Review* 115(1): 51-68.

Bøggild, Troels, Lene Aarøe, and Michael Bang Petersen. 2021. "Citizens as Complicits: Distrust in Politicians and Biased Dissemination of Political Information." *American Political Science Review* 115(1): 269-85.

Brown, Étienne, and Zoe Phillips Williams. 2020. "Disagreement, Epistemic Paralysis, and the Legitimacy of Technocracy." *Critical Review* 32(1-3).

Buturovic, Zeljka. 2010. "Putting Political Experts to the Test." *Critical Review* 22(4): 389-96.

Chong, Dennis, and James N. Druckman. 2011. "Identifying Frames in Political News." In *Sourcebook for Political Communication Research*, ed. Erik P. Bucy and R. Lance Holbert. London: Routledge.

Cirone, Alexandra, Gary C. Cox, and Jon H. Fiva. 2021. "Seniority-Based Nominations and Political Careers." *American Political Science Review* 115(1): 231-54.

Downs, Anthony. 1957. *An Economic Theory of Democracy*. New York: Harper & Row.

Elliott, Kevin. 2020. "A Family Affair: Populism, Technocracy, and Political Epistemology." *Critical Review* 32(1-3).

Fiedler, Klaus. 1988. "The Dependence of the Conjunction Fallacy on Subtle Linguistic Factors." *Psychological Research* 50: 123-29.

Fortunato, David, Nick C. N. Lin, Randolph T. Stevenson, and Mathias Wessel Tromborg. 2021. "Attributing Policy Influence Under Coalition Governance." *American Political Science Review* 115(1): 252-68.

Foucault, Mitchel. [1984] 1997. "Polemics, Politics, and Problematizations." In *Essential Works of Foucault 1954–1984*, ed. Paul Rainbow, vol. I, *Ethics: Subjectivity and Truth*, ed. James D. Faubion. New York: New Press.

Fowler, Erika Franklin, Michael M. Franz, Gregory J. Martin, Zachary Peskowitz, and Travis M. Ridout. 2021. "Political Advertising Online and Offline." *American Political Science Review* 115(1): 130-49.

Friedman, Jeffrey. 1996. "Public Opinion and Democracy." *Critical Review* 10(1): i-xii.

Friedman, Jeffrey. 1997. "What's Wrong with Libertarianism." *Critical Review* 11(3): 407-67.

Friedman, Jeffrey. 1998. "Public Ignorance and Democratic Theory." *Critical Review* 12(4): 397-411.

Friedman, Jeffrey. 2013. "Freedom Has No Intrinsic Value: Liberalism and Voluntarism." *Critical Review* 25(1): 38-85.

Friedman, Jeffrey. 2019a. "Populists as Technocrats." *Critical Review* 31(3-4): 315-76.

Friedman, Jeffrey. 2019b. *Power Without Knowledge: A Critique of Technocracy*. Oxford: Oxford University Press.

Friedman, Jeffrey. 2021. "Is Political Irrationality a Myth?" In *The Routledge Handbook of Political Epistemology*, ed. Michael Hannon and Jeroen de Ridder. London: Routledge.

Friedman, Milton. 1953. "The Methodology of Positive Economics." In idem, *Essays in Positive Economics*. Chicago: University of Chicago Press.

Gehring, Kai. 2021. "Overcoming History Through Exit or Integration: Deep-Rooted Sources of Support for the European Union." *American Political Science Review* 115(1): 199-217.

Habermas, Jürgen. [1963] 1976. "The Analytical Theory of Science and Dialectics: A Postscript to the Controversy Between Popper and Adorno." In Theodor Adorno, Hans Albert, Ralf Dahrendorf, Jürgen Habermas, Harald Pilot, and Karl R. Popper, *The Positivist Dispute in German Sociology*, trans. Glyn Adey and David Frisby. London: Heinemann.

Henrich, Joseph, Steven J. Heine, and Ara Norenzayan. 2010. "The WEIRDest People in the World." *Behavioral and Brain Sciences* 33(2): 61-83.

Hirschman, Albert O. 1970. *Exit, Voice, and Loyalty: Responses to Decline in Firms, Organizations, and States*. Cambridge, Mass.: Harvard University Press.

Huemer, Michael. 2013. *The Problem of Political Authority: An Examination of the Right to Coerce and the Duty to Obey*. New York: Palgrave Macmillan.

Hume, David. [1772] 1999. *An Enquiry Concerning Human Understanding*, ed. Tom L. Beauchamp. Oxford: Oxford University Press.

Jervis, Robert. 2010. *Why Intelligence Fails: Lessons from the Iranian Revolution and the Iraq War*. Ithaca: Cornell University Press.
Jones, Ward E. 2002. "Explaining Our Own Beliefs: Non-Epistemic Believing and Doxastic Instability." *Philosophical Studies* 111: 217–249.
Khilnani, Sunil. 2003. "French Marxism—Existentialism to Structuralism." In *The Cambridge History of Twentieth-Century Political Thought*, ed. Terence Ball and Richard Bellamy. Cambridge: Cambridge University Press.
Kienpointer, M. 1996. "Whorf and Wittgenstein: Language, World View and Argumentation." *Argumentation* 10: 475-94.
Kreiner, Claus Thustrup, Daniel Reck, and Peer Ebbeson Skov. 2020. "Do Lower Minimum Wages for Young Workers Raise Their Employment? Evidence from a Danish Discontinuity." *Review of Economics and Statistics* 102(2): 339-54.
Larsson, Oscar L. 2020. "Technocracy, Governmentality, and Post-Structuralism." *Critical Review* 32(1-3).
Leibniz, Gottfried Wilhelm. [1709] 1951. *Theodicy: Essays on the Goodness of God, the Freedom of Man, and the Origin of Evil*, trans. E. M. Huggard. London: Routledge and Kegan Paul.
Lepore, Jill. 2020. "Will Trump Burn the Evidence?" *The New Yorker*, November 23.
Lerner, Adam B. 2019. "Theorizing Collective Trauma in International Political Economy." *International Studies Review* 21: 549-71.
Lerner, Adam B. 2020. "Social Science and the Problem of Interpretation: A Pragmatic Dual(ist) Approach." *Critical Review* 32(1-3).
Linos, Katerina, Laura Jakli, and Melissa Carlson. 2021. "Fundraising for Stigmatized Groups: A Text Messaging Experiment." *American Political Science Review* 115 (1): 14-30.
Lippmann, Walter. [1920] 2008. *Liberty and the News*. Princeton: Princeton University Press.
Lippmann, Walter. [1937] 2005. *The Good Society*. Boston: Little, Brown.
Lukes, Steven 1973. *Individualism*. London: Basil Blackwell.
MacGilvray, Eric. 2020. "The Spiral of Responsibility and the Pressure to Conflict." *Critical Review* 32(1-3).
Mearsheimer, John J. 1994/1995. "The False Promise of International Institutions." *International Security* 19(3): 5-49.
Moore, Alfred. 2020. "Architects and Engineers: Two Types of Technocrat and Their Relation to Democracy." *Critical Review* 32(1-3).
Moskowitz, Daniel J. 2021. "Local News, Information, and the Nationalization of U.S. Elections." *American Political Science Review* 115(1): 114-29.
Motolinia, Lucia. 2021. "Electoral Accountability and Particularistic Legislation: Evidence from an Election Reform in Mexico." *American Political Science Review* 115(1): 97-113.
Paglayan, Agustina. 2021. "The Non-Democratic Roots of Mass Education: Evidence from 200 Years." *American Political Science Review* 115(1): 179-98.
Pamuk, Zeynep. 2020. "What Follows from the Problem of Ignorance?" *Critical Review* 32(1-3).

Phillips, Dave. 2021. "Navy SEAL in Capitol Mob Sank Into Extremist Ideas." *New York Times*, January 27.

Popper, Karl R. [1945] 2013. *The Open Society and Its Enemies*. Princeton: Princeton University Press.

Powers, Nicholas, Allen Blackman, Thomas Lyon, and Urvashi Narain. 2011. "Does Disclosure Reduce Pollution? Evidence from India's Green Rating Project." *Environmental and Resource Economics* 50: 131-55.

Reamer, Robert. 2020. "Power, Knowledge, and Anarchism." *Critical Review* 32(1-3).

Reiss, Julian. 2008. *Error in Economics: Towards a More Evidence-Based Methodology*. London: Routledge.

Reiss, Julian. 2020. "Why Do Experts Disagree?" *Critical Review* 32(1-3).

Rigterink, Anouk S. 2021."'The Wane of Command': Evidence on Drone Strikes and Control Within Terrorist Organizations." *American Political Science Review* 115(1): 31-50.

Roose, Kevin. 2021. "Reclaiming Reality from Chaos." *New York Times*, February 4.

Rutenberg, Jim, Jo Becker, Eric Lipton, Maggie Haberman, Jonathan Martin, Matthew Rosenberg, and Michael S. Schmidt. 2021. "77 Days: Trump's Campaign to Subvert the Election." *New York Times*, February 1.

Taylor, Charles. [1971] 1985. "Interpretation and the Sciences of Man." In idem, *Philosophical Papers*, vol. 2, *Philosophy and the Human Sciences*. Cambridge: Cambridge University Press.

Tetlock, Philip E. 2005. *Expert Political Judgment: How Good Is It? How Can We Know?* Princeton: Princeton University Press.

Tetlock, Philip E. 2010. "Second Thoughts about Expert Political Judgment." *Critical Review* 22(4): 467-88.

Tollefsen, Deborah. 2015. *Groups as Agents*. Malden, Mass.: Polity.

Weber, Eugen. 1976. *Peasants into Frenchmen: The Modernization of Rural France, 1870-1914*. Stanford: Stanford University Press.

Wellman, Elizabeth Iams. 2021. "Emigrant Inclusion in Home Country Elections: Theory and Evidence from Sub-Saharan Africa." *American Political Science Review* 115(1): 82-96.

Wendt, Alexander 2004. "The State as Person in International Theory." *Review of International Studies* 30(2): 289-316.

Zaller, John. 1992. *The Nature and Origins of Mass Opinion*. New York: Cambridge University Press.

Zuboff, Shoshana. 2021. "The Knowledge Coup." *New York Times*, January 31.

APPENDIX

Errata in *Power Without Knowledge: A Critique of Technocracy* (Oxford, 2019).

p. 16, line 8: technocracy *should read* technocrats

p. 21, line 4: (or any other political actors) *should read* or any other political actors

p. 51, line 3: regulatory backfire *should read* policy backfire

p. 53, lines 24-25: cooptation *should read* disproof

p. 55, line 4: studies of *should read* studies about

p. 77, line 16: such a claim *should read* Hirschman's claim

p. 79, line 9: would for *should read* for

p. 137, line 1: ontological *should read* ontic

p. 137, line 5: ontological *should read* ontic

p. 142, line 11: action *should read* actions

p. 209, line 13: to respond to *should read* respond to

p. 300, line 13: thus *should read* so

p. 303, line 27: the ideas of future citizen-technocrats *should read* future citizen-technocrats

p. 309, last line: naïve technocratic realists *should read* naïve political realists

p. 312, line 13: any information *should read* almost any information

p. 314, line 21: heterogenizing factors *should read* homogenizing factors

p. 324, line 10: epistemological *should read* epistemic

p. 337, line 4: epistemological *should read* epistemic

p. 344, line 24: in the technocratic realm *should read* in the ordinary technocratic realm

p. 351, line 26: has *should read* have

front jacket flap, penultimate line: is nothing *should read* may be nothing

Index

Note: Page numbers followed by "n" denote endnotes.

For Product Safety Concerns and Information please contact our EU representative GPSR@taylorandfrancis.com
Taylor & Francis Verlag GmbH, Kaufingerstraße 24, 80331 München, Germany

www.ingramcontent.com/pod-product-compliance
Ingram Content Group UK Ltd.
Pitfield, Milton Keynes, MK11 3LW, UK
UKHW022155190926
475702UK00003B/34

* 9 7 8 1 0 3 2 3 5 7 5 3 9 *